Contents

Introduction to the Datsun 610 and 810 Series

First introduced in 1972 the 610 Series Datsuns covered by this manual are known in the United Kingdom as the Bluebird range. They have the designation 160B for the 1595 cc saloon and 180B for the 1770 cc Saloon, Coupe and Estate car.

In North America the range is known as the 610 Series and has a 1770 cc (108 cu in) engine in early models and a 1952 cc (119 cu in) engine from 1974 onwards.

The 810 Series Datsuns, introduced in the United Kingdom in 1977, are known as the Bluebird Mk II range. They have a completely redesigned body with slightly larger dimensions so giving more interior room. Mechanically they are basically the same as the 610 Series except for a redesigned rear suspension, giving improved ride and handling characteristics. Where minor differences occur the relevant information throughout the manual is annotated (610 series) or (810 series).

Construction of all models is very rugged and the larger engined versions have a very healthy performance with surprising fuel economy. These models have proven very successful in further establishing the manufacturer's already good reputation.

1973 Datsun 180B SSS Coupe (UK market)

1973 Datsun 180B Estate (UK market)

S and Estate; 1770 cc

atic transmissions

Printed in England   *(372-7N2)*

Haynes Publishing Group
Sparkford Nr Yeovil
Somerset BA22 7JJ England

Haynes Publications, Inc
861 Lawrence Drive
Newbury Park
California 91320 USA

British Library Cataloguing in Publication Data

Gilmour, Bruce
   Datsun Bluebird 1972 – 1980 owners workshop manual.
   –2nd. Ed. (Owners Workshop Manual)
   1. Bluebird automobile
  I. Title   II. Haynes, J.H.
   Datsun 160B & 180B owners workshop manual
   629.28'722   TL215.B56
   ISBN 1–85010–094–2

Acknowledgements

Thanks are due to the Nissan Motor Company Limited of Japan for the supply of technical information and certain technical illustrations, to Castrol Limited for the Lubrication data, and to the Champion Spark Plug Company who supplied the illustrations showing the various spark plug conditions.

Lastly, thanks are due to all those people at Sparkford who helped in the production of the manual.

About this manual

Its aim

The aim of this manual is to help you get the best value from your vehicle. It can do so in several ways. It can help you decide what work must be done (even should you choose to get it done by a garage), provide information on routine maintenance and servicing, and give a logical course of action and diagnosis when random faults occur. However, it is hoped that you will use the manual by tackling the work yourself. On simpler jobs it may even be quicker than booking the car into a garage and going there twice, to leave and collect it. Perhaps most important, a lot of money can be saved by avoiding the costs a garage must charge to cover its labour and overheads.

The manual has drawings and descriptions to show the function of the various components so that their layout can be understood. Then the tasks are described and photographed in a step-by-step sequence so that even a novice can do the work.

Its arrangement

The manual is divided into twelve Chapters, each covering a logical sub-division of the vehicle. The Chapters are each divided into Sections, numbered with single figures, eg 5; and the Sections into paragraphs (or sub-sections), with decimal numbers following on from the Section they are in, eg 5.1, 5.2, 5.3 etc.

It is freely illustrated, especially in those parts where there is a detailed sequence of operations to be carried out. There are two forms of illustration: figures and photographs. The figures are numbered in sequence with decimal numbers, according to their position in the Chapter – eg Fig. 6.4 is the fourth drawing/illustration in Chapter 6. Photographs carry the same number (either individually or in related groups) as the Section or sub-section to which they relate.

There is an alphabetical index at the back of the manual as well as a contents list at the front. Each Chapter is also preceded by its own individual contents list.

References to the 'left' or 'right' of the vehicle are in the sense of a person in the driver's seat facing forwards.

Unless otherwise stated, nuts and bolts are removed by turning anti-clockwise, and tightened by turning clockwise.

Vehicle manufacturers continually make changes to specifications and recommendations, and these, when notified, are incorporated into our manuals at the earliest opportunity.

Whilst every care is taken to ensure that the information in this manual is correct, no liability can be accepted by the authors or publishers for loss, damage or injury caused by any errors in, or omissions from, the information given.

1975 Datsun 610 Sedan (USA market)

1977 Datsun 180B Mk II Saloon (UK market)

Buying spare parts
and vehicle identification numbers

Buying spare parts

Spare parts are available from many sources, for example: Datsun garages, other garages and accessory shops, and motor factors. Our advice regarding spare parts is as follows:

Officially appointed Datsun garages – This is the best source of parts which are peculiar to your car and otherwise not generally available (eg complete cylinder heads, internal gearbox components, badges, interior trim etc). It is also the only place at which you should buy parts if your car is still under warranty; non-Datsun components may invalidate the warranty. To be sure of obtaining the correct parts it will always be necessary to give the storeman your car's engine and chassis number, and if possible, to take the old part along for positive identification. Remember that many parts are available on a factory exchange scheme – any parts returned should always be clean! It obviously makes good sense to go straight to the specialists on your car for this type of part for they are best equipped to supply you.

Other garages and accessory shops – These are often very good places to buy material and components needed for the maintenance of your car (eg oil filters, spark plugs, bulbs, fan belts, oils and grease, touch-up paint, filler paste etc). They also sell general accessories,

usually have convenient opening hours, charge lower prices and can often be found not far from home.

Motor factors – Good factors will stock all of the more important components, (eg. pistons, valves, exhaust systems, brake cylinder/ pipes/hoses/seals/shoes and pads etc). Motor factors will often provide new or reconditioned components on a part exchange basis – this can save a considerable amount of money.

Vehicle identification numbers

Modifications are a continuing and unpublished process in vehicle manufacture quite apart from major model changes. Spare parts manuals and lists are compiled upon a numerical basis, the individual vehicle numbers being essential to correct identification of the component required.

The car identification plate is attached to the centre of the top of the bulkhead and is visible when the bonnet is fully open.

The chassis number is stamped at the top of the bulkhead on the right-hand side.

The engine number is stamped on the right-hand side of the cylinder block.

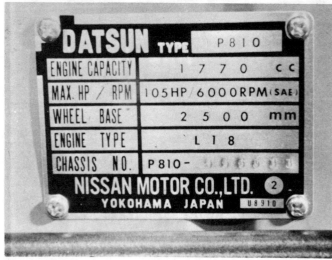

Car identification plate attached to bulkhead

The engine number is stamped on the cylinder block

Tools and working facilities

Introduction

A selection of good tools is a fundamental requirement for anyone contemplating the maintenance and repair of a motor vehicle. For the owner who does not possess any, their purchase will prove a considerable expense, offsetting some of the savings made by doing-it-yourself. However, provided that the tools purchased are of good quality, they will last for many years and prove an extremely worthwhile investment.

To help the average owner to decide which tools are needed to carry out the various tasks detailed in this manual, we have compiled three lists of tools under the following headings: *Maintenance and minor repair, Repair and overhaul,* and *Special.* The newcomer to practical mechanics should start off with the *Maintenance and minor repair* tool kit and confine himself to the simpler jobs around the vehicle. Then, as his confidence and experience grow, he can undertake more difficult tasks, buying extra tools as, and when, they are needed. In this way, a *Maintenance and minor repair* tool kit can be built-up into a *Repair and overhaul* tool kit over a considerable period of time without any major cash outlays. The experienced do-it-yourselfer will have a tool kit good enough for most repair and overhaul procedures and will add tools from the *Special* category when he feels the expense is justified by the amount of use to which these tools will be put.

It is obviously not possible to cover the subject of tools fully here. For those who wish to learn more about tools and their use there is a book entitled *How to Choose and Use Car Tools* available from the publishers of this manual.

Maintenance and minor repair tool kit

The tools given in this list should be considered as a minimum requirement if routine maintenance, servicing and minor repair operations are to be undertaken. We recommend the purchase of combination spanners (ring one end, open-ended the other); although more expensive than open-ended ones, they do give the advantages of both types of spanner.

Combination spanners - 10, 11, 12, 13, 14 & 17 mm
Adjustable spanner - 9 inch
Rear axle drain plug key
Spark plug spanner (with rubber insert)
Spark plug gap adjustment tool
Set of feeler gauges
Brake adjuster spanner
Brake bleed nipple spanner
Screwdriver - 4 in long x $\frac{1}{4}$ in dia (flat blade)
Screwdriver - 4 in long x $\frac{1}{4}$ in dia (cross blade)
Combination pliers - 6 inch
Hacksaw (junior)
Tyre pump
Tyre pressure gauge
Grease gun

Oil can
Fine emery cloth (1 sheet)
Wire brush (small)
Funnel (medium size)

Repair and overhaul tool kit

These tools are virtually essential for anyone undertaking any major repairs to a motor vehicle, and are additional to those given in the *Maintenance and minor repair* list. Included in this list is a comprehensive set of sockets. Although these are expensive they will be found invaluable as they are so versatile - particularly if various drives are included in the set. We recommend the $\frac{1}{2}$ in square-drive type, as this can be used with most proprietary torque wrenches. If you cannot afford a socket set, even bought piecemeal, then inexpensive tubular box spanners are a useful alternative.

The tools in this list will occasionally need to be supplemented by tools from the *Special* list.

Sockets (or box spanners) to cover range in previous list
Reversible ratchet drive (for use with sockets)
Extension piece, 10 inch (for use with sockets)
Universal joint (for use with sockets)
Torque wrench (for use with sockets)
'Mole' wrench - 8 inch
Ball pein hammer
Soft-faced hammer, plastic or rubber
Screwdriver - 6 in long x $\frac{5}{16}$ in dia (flat blade)
Screwdriver - 2 in long x $\frac{5}{16}$ in square (flat blade)
Screwdriver - 1$\frac{1}{2}$ in long x $\frac{1}{4}$ in dia (cross blade)
Screwdriver - 3 in long x $\frac{1}{8}$ in dia (electricians)
Pliers - electricians side cutters
Pliers - needle nosed
Pliers - circlip (internal and external)
Cold chisel - $\frac{1}{2}$ inch
Scriber
Scraper
Centre punch
Pin punch
Hacksaw
Valve grinding tool
Steel rule/straight-edge
Allen keys
Selection of files
Wire brush (large)
Axle-stands
Jack (strong scissor or hydraulic type)

Special tools

The tools in this list are those which are not used regularly, are expensive to buy, or which need to be used in accordance with their manufacturers' instructions. Unless relatively difficult mechanical jobs are undertaken frequently, it will not be economic to buy many of these tools. Where this is the case, you could consider clubbing together with friends (or joining a motorists' club) to make a joint purchase, or borrowing the tools against a deposit from a local garage or tool hire specialist.

The following list contains only those tools and instruments freely available to the public, and not those special tools produced by the vehicle manufacturer specifically for its dealer network. You will find occasional references to these manufacturers' special tools in the text of this manual. Generally, an alternative method of doing the job without the vehicle manufacturers' special tool is given. However, sometimes, there is no alternative to using them. Where this is the case and the relevant tool cannot be bought or borrowed, you will have to entrust the work to a franchised garage.

Valve spring compressor
Piston ring compressor
Balljoint separator
Universal hub/bearing puller
Impact screwdriver
Micrometer and/or vernier gauge
Dial gauge
Stroboscopic timing light
Dwell angle meter/tachometer
Universal electrical multi-meter
Cylinder compression gauge
Lifting tackle
Trolley jack
Light with extension lead

Buying tools

For practically all tools, a tool factor is the best source since he will have a very comprehensive range compared with the average garage or accessory shop. Having said that, accessory shops often offer excellent quality tools at discount prices, so it pays to shop around.

Remember, you don't have to buy the most expensive items on the shelf, but it is always advisable to steer clear of the very cheap tools. There are plenty of good tools around at reasonable prices, so ask the proprietor or manager of the shop for advice before making a purchase.

Care and maintenance of tools

Having purchased a reasonable tool kit, it is necessary to keep the tools in a clean serviceable condition. After use, always wipe off any dirt, grease and metal particles using a clean, dry cloth, before putting the tools away. Never leave them lying around after they have been used. A simple tool rack on the garage or workshop wall, for items such as screwdrivers and pliers is a good idea. Store all normal wrenches and sockets in a metal box. Any measuring instruments, gauges, meters, etc, must be carefully stored where they cannot be damaged or become rusty.

Take a little care when tools are used. Hammer heads inevitably become marked and screwdrivers lose the keen edge on their blades from time to time. A little timely attention with emery cloth or a file will soon restore items like this to a good serviceable finish.

Working facilities

Not to be forgotten when discussing tools, is the workshop itself. If anything more than routine maintenance is to be carried out, some form of suitable working area becomes essential.

It is appreciated that many an owner mechanic is forced by circumstances to remove an engine or similar item, without the benefit of a garage or workshop. Having done this, any repairs should always be done under the cover of a roof.

Wherever possible, any dismantling should be done on a clean, flat workbench or table at a suitable working height.

Any workbench needs a vice: one with a jaw opening of 4 in (100 mm) is suitable for most jobs. As mentioned previously, some clean dry storage space is also required for tools, as well as for lubricants, cleaning fluids, touch-up paints and so on, which become necessary.

Another item which may be required, and which has a much more general usage, is an electric drill with a chuck capacity of at least $\frac{5}{16}$ in (8 mm). This, together with a good range of twist drills, is virtually essential for fitting accessories such as mirrors and reversing lights.

Last, but not least, always keep a supply of old newspapers and clean, lint-free rags available, and try to keep any working area as clean as possible.

Spanner jaw gap comparison table

Jaw gap (in)	Spanner size
0.250	$\frac{1}{4}$ in AF
0.276	7 mm
0.313	$\frac{5}{16}$ in AF
0.315	8 mm
0.344	$\frac{11}{32}$ in AF; $\frac{1}{8}$ in Whitworth
0.354	9 mm
0.375	$\frac{3}{8}$ in AF
0.394	10 mm
0.433	11 mm
0.438	$\frac{7}{16}$ in AF
0.445	$\frac{3}{16}$ in Whitworth; $\frac{1}{4}$ in BSF
0.472	12 mm
0.500	$\frac{1}{2}$ in AF
0.512	13 mm
0.525	$\frac{1}{4}$ in Whitworth; $\frac{5}{16}$ in BSF
0.551	14 mm
0.563	$\frac{9}{16}$ in AF
0.591	15 mm
0.600	$\frac{5}{16}$ in Whitworth; $\frac{3}{8}$ in BSF
0.625	$\frac{5}{8}$ in AF
0.630	16 mm
0.669	17 mm
0.686	$\frac{11}{16}$ in AF
0.709	18 mm
0.710	$\frac{3}{8}$ in Whitworth; $\frac{7}{16}$ in BSF
0.748	19 mm
0.750	$\frac{3}{4}$ in AF
0.813	$\frac{13}{16}$ in AF
0.820	$\frac{7}{16}$ in Whitworth; $\frac{1}{2}$ in BSF
0.866	22 mm
0.875	$\frac{7}{8}$ in AF
0.920	$\frac{1}{2}$ in Whitworth; $\frac{9}{16}$ in BSF
0.938	$\frac{15}{16}$ in AF
0.945	24 mm
1.000	1 in AF
1.010	$\frac{9}{16}$ in Whitworth; $\frac{5}{8}$ in BSF
1.024	26 mm
1.063	$1\frac{1}{16}$ in AF; 27 mm
1.100	$\frac{5}{8}$ in Whitworth; $\frac{11}{16}$ in BSF
1.125	$1\frac{1}{8}$ in AF
1.181	30 mm
1.200	$\frac{11}{16}$ in Whitworth; $\frac{3}{4}$ in BSF
1.250	$1\frac{1}{4}$ in AF
1.260	32 mm
1.300	$\frac{3}{4}$ in Whitworth; $\frac{7}{8}$ in BSF
1.313	$1\frac{5}{16}$ in AF
1.390	$\frac{13}{16}$ in Whitworth; $\frac{15}{16}$ in BSF
1.417	36 mm
1.438	$1\frac{7}{16}$ in AF
1.480	$\frac{7}{8}$ in Whitworth; 1 in BSF
1.500	$1\frac{1}{2}$ in AF
1.575	40 mm; $\frac{15}{16}$ in Whitworth
1.614	41 mm
1.625	$1\frac{5}{8}$ in AF
1.670	1 in Whitworth; $1\frac{1}{8}$ in BSF
1.688	$1\frac{11}{16}$ in AF
1.811	46 mm
1.813	$1\frac{13}{16}$ in AF
1.860	$1\frac{1}{8}$ in Whitworth; $1\frac{1}{4}$ in BSF
1.875	$1\frac{7}{8}$ in AF
1.969	50 mm
2.000	2 in AF
2.050	$1\frac{1}{4}$ in Whitworth; $1\frac{3}{8}$ in BSF
2.165	55 mm
2.362	60 mm

Routine maintenance

Maintenance is essential for ensuring safety and desirable for the purpose of getting the best in terms of performance and economy from the car. Over the years the need for periodic lubrication has been greatly reduced if not totally eliminated. This has, unfortunately, tended to lead some owners to think that because no such action is required, the items either no longer exist or will last for ever. This is certainly not the case and it is essential to carry out regular visual examination as comprehensively as possible in order to spot any possible defects at an early stage before they develop into major and expensive repairs.

The maintenance information given in this Section is not of a detailed nature as the information required to carry out the necessary tasks is to be found in the appropriate Chapters throughout this manual.

Every 250 miles (400 km) or weekly – whichever comes first

Engine
Check the sump oil level; top-up if necessary.
Check the radiator coolant level, top-up if necessary.
Check the level of the electrolyte in the battery, top-up as necessary.

Checking the tyre pressure

TIRE PRESSURE REFERENCE TABLE
kg/cm²(PSI)

CONDITION	NORMAL CONDITION		HIGH SPEED (OVER 100km/H 65MPH)	
TIRE	FRONT	REAR	FRONT	REAR
5.60-13	1.8 (26)	1.8 (26)	2.1 (30)	2.1 (30)
6.45(S)13/14	1.6 (24)	1.6 (24)	1.9 (28)	1.9 (28)
165SR13/14 185/70HR14	2.0 (28)	2.0 (28)	2.0 (28)	2.0 (28)

TOKYO   NISSAN MOTOR CO.,LTD.   JAPAN

The tyre pressure plate is located on the glove compartment door – or consult your dealer

Checking the level of brake fluid in the reservoir

Checking the sump oil level ...

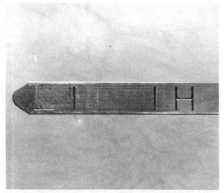
... it should be between the 'H' and 'L' marks

Topping up with engine oil

Checking the coolant level in the radiator

Engine sump drain plug

Checking level of oil in steering box

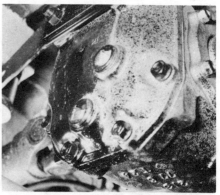
Differential level/filler plug and drain plug

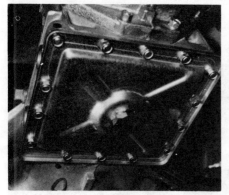
Manual gearbox drain plug

Front towing hook

Rear towing hook (Saloon and Hardtop)

Jacking up the car

Wheel chocks in position

Steering
Check the tyre pressures
Examine the tyres for wear or damage.
Brakes
Check the reservoir fluid level.
Check the efficiency of service brake and handbrake
Lights, wipers and horns
Check that all lights work at the front and rear.
Check the windscreen washer reservoir fluid level.

Every 3000 miles (5000 km)

Engine
Change the engine oil

Every 6000 miles (10 000 km)

Engine
Check drive belts for cracks, fraying and wear. Check for correct tension.
Renew engine oil filter.
Drain and flush cooling system if filled with water.
Clean carburettor air cleaner (dry paper type).
Clean spark plugs and check gap.
Check distributor cap, rotor, contact points and condenser.
Check and adjust dwell angle, ignition timing and idling speed.
Clean battery terminals and check specific gravity of electrolyte.
Check level of oil in carburettor damper.
Check condition of cooling, fuel and vacuum hoses.
Check exhaust system for security and leaks.
Check the air conditioning system hoses and connections for leaks.
Steering
Examine all steering linkage rods, joints and bushes for signs of wear or damage. Check steering wheel play.
Check front wheel hub bearings.
Check tightness of steering box mounting bolts.
Check level of oil in steering box.
Check wheel alignment.
Brakes
Examine disc pads and drum shoes for wear.
Examine all hydraulic pipes, cylinders and unions for signs of chafing, dents or leaks.
Check handbrake lever travel.
Adjust drum type brakes if necessary.
Suspension
Examine all nuts, bolts and balljoints securing the front and rear suspension, and tighten as necessary.
Examine rubber bushes for signs of wear or deterioration.
Check operation of shock absorbers.
Transmission and differential
Check oil level and top up if necessary.
Check for oil leaks.

Check security of propeller shaft and driveshaft bolts.
Clutch
Check fluid reservoir level and top up if necessary.
Check pedal free movement and adjust if necessary.
Check for fluid leakage.
Body
Lubricate all locks and hinges.
Check that water drain holes at bottom of doors are clear.
Check windscreen wiper blades.
Check seat belts, buckles, retractors, anchor points and adjuster.

Every 12 000 miles (20 000 km)

Engine
Check positive crankcase ventilation system.
Check fuel storage evaporation emission control system.
Check cylinder head bolts, manifold nuts and carburettor securing nuts for correct torque.
Check operation of automatic temperature control air cleaner.
Fit new distributor breaker points.
Fit new spark plugs.
Lubricate distributor shaft and cam.
Check exhaust emission control system.
Steering
Check wheel balance.
Brakes
Change brake fluid (with disc brake).

Every 24 000 miles (40 000 km)

Engine
Drain and flush cooling system. Refill with antifreeze mixture.
Renew carburettor air cleaner filter (viscous paper type and dry paper type).
Check ignition wiring and coil.
Renew fuel filter.
Renew positive crankcase ventilation valve and filter.
Renew fuel evaporative system carbon canister filter.
Brakes
Change brake fluid (models with only drum brakes)
Suspension
Repack front wheel bearings with grease.

Every 30 000 miles (50 000 km)

Transmission
Drain manual gearbox and refill with fresh oil.
Drain differential unit and refill with fresh oil.
Grease rear axle driveshaft joints.
Steering
Grease steering linkage and front suspension balljoints.

Jacking and towing

Towing points
If the vehicle has to be towed, any rope or cable should be connected to the hook attached to the front sidemember. On vehicles equipped with automatic transmission, the towing speed should not exceed 20 mph (30 km/h) nor the towing distance 6 miles (10 km) otherwise the transmission may be damaged due to lack of lubrication. If towing distances are excessive, disconnect the propeller shaft from the rear axle pinion flange and tie the shaft up out of the way.
When towing another car, connect the rope to the rear towing hook on saloon and hardtop models, and to the rear leaf spring shackle on estate cars.

Jacking points
The pantograph type jack supplied with the car must only be used at the positions below the body sills. Other types of jack should be located below the front crossmember or rear axle differential casing. If axle stands are to be used, then they must be positioned under the bodyframe sidemembers or rear axle casing. No other positions should be used for jacking or support purposes.
When jacking up the car always chock a wheel on the opposite side, in front and behind.

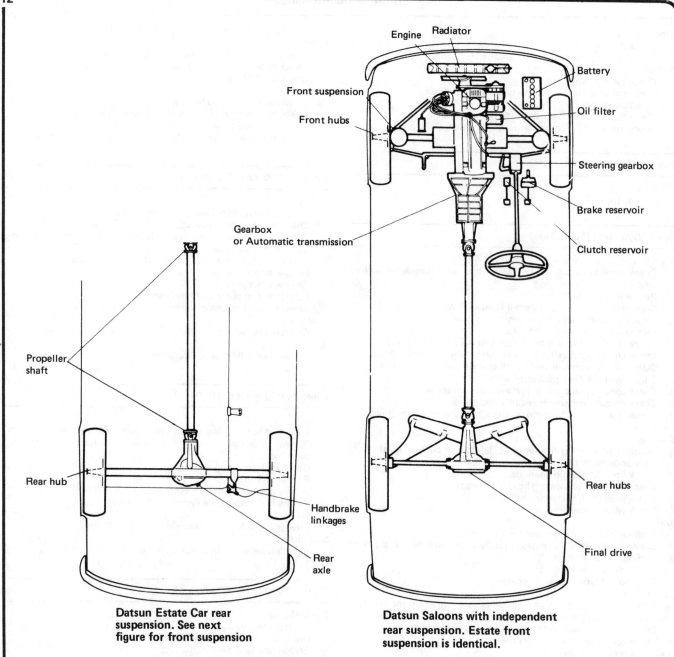

Datsun Estate Car rear suspension. See next figure for front suspension

Datsun Saloons with independent rear suspension. Estate front suspension is identical.

Recommended lubricants and fluids

Component	Lubricant type or specification
Engine	API SE oil or to SAE 20W/40 or 20W/50

Gearbox:
    Manual
    Automatic
	
	API GL-4 oil or to SAE 85W or 85W/90
	Dexron type automatic transmission fluid

Final drive (differential)	API GL-5 oil or to SAE 85W or 85W/90
Steering gearbox	API GL-5 oil or to SAE 85W or 85W/90
Wheel bearings and chassis	Lithium NLG1-2 grease

Note: *The above recommendations are general; lubrication requirements vary from territory-to-territory. Consult the operators handbook supplied with your car.*

Use of English

As this book has been written in England, it uses the appropriate English component names, phrases, and spelling. Some of these differ from those used in America. Normally, these cause no difficulty, but to make sure, a glossary is printed below. In ordering spare parts remember the parts list may use some of these words:

English	American	English	American
Accelerator	Gas pedal	Leading shoe (of brake)	Primary shoe
Aerial	Antenna	Locks	Latches
Anti-roll bar	Stabiliser or sway bar	Methylated spirit	Denatured alcohol
Big-end bearing	Rod bearing	Motorway	Freeway, turnpike etc
Bonnet (engine cover)	Hood	Number plate	License plate
Boot (luggage compartment)	Trunk	Paraffin	Kerosene
Bulkhead	Firewall	Petrol	Gasoline (gas)
Bush	Bushing	Petrol tank	Gas tank
Cam follower or tappet	Valve lifter or tappet	'Pinking'	'Pinging'
Carburettor	Carburetor	Prise (force apart)	Pry
Catch	Latch	Propeller shaft	Driveshaft
Choke/venturi	Barrel	Quarterlight	Quarter window
Circlip	Snap-ring	Retread	Recap
Clearance	Lash	Reverse	Back-up
Crownwheel	Ring gear (of differential)	Rocker cover	Valve cover
Damper	Shock absorber, shock	Saloon	Sedan
Disc (brake)	Rotor/disk	Seized	Frozen
Distance piece	Spacer	Sidelight	Parking light
Drop arm	Pitman arm	Silencer	Muffler
Drop head coupe	Convertible	Sill panel (beneath doors)	Rocker panel
Dynamo	Generator (DC)	Small end, little end	Piston pin or wrist pin
Earth (electrical)	Ground	Spanner	Wrench
Engineer's blue	Prussian blue	Split cotter (for valve spring cap)	Lock (for valve spring retainer)
Estate car	Station wagon	Split pin	Cotter pin
Exhaust manifold	Header	Steering arm	Spindle arm
Fault finding/diagnosis	Troubleshooting	Sump	Oil pan
Float chamber	Float bowl	Swarf	Metal chips or debris
Free-play	Lash	Tab washer	Tang or lock
Freewheel	Coast	Tappet	Valve lifter
Gearbox	Transmission	Thrust bearing	Throw-out bearing
Gearchange	Shift	Top gear	High
Grub screw	Setscrew, Allen screw	Trackrod (of steering)	Tie-rod (or connecting rod)
Gudgeon pin	Piston pin or wrist pin	Trailing shoe (of brake)	Secondary shoe
Halfshaft	Axleshaft	Transmission	Whole drive line
Handbrake	Parking brake	Tyre	Tire
Hood	Soft top	Van	Panel wagon/van
Hot spot	Heat riser	Vice	Vise
Indicator	Turn signal	Wheel nut	Lug nut
Interior light	Dome lamp	Windscreen	Windshield
Layshaft (of gearbox)	Countershaft	Wing/mudguard	Fender

Chapter 1 Engine

Contents

Specifications

General

Engine type	Four cylinder in-line overhead camshaft (ohc)
Engine designation	L16S, L18S, L18T, L20B
Firing order	1 - 3 - 4 - 2

Displacement:
L16S	1595 cc (97.3 cu in)
L18S, L18T	1770 cc (108.0 cu in)
L20B	1952 cc (119.1 cu in)

Bore:
L16S	3.2677 in (83 mm)
L18S, L18T, L20B	3.3465 in (85 mm)

Stroke:
L16S	2.90 in (73.7 mm)
L18S, L18T	3.07 in (78 mm)
L20B	3.39 in (86 mm)

Compression ratio:
L16 and L18, L20B	8.5 : 1

Oil pressure (engine warm at 2000 rpm) .... 49.8 - 56.9 lbf/in^2 (3.5 - 4.0 kgf/cm^2)

Ignition timing:
Refer to Chapter 4 Specifications

Engine idle speed:
Refer to Chapter 3 Specifications

Sump capacity:
(with filter change)	7.5 pints (4.5 US qts/4.3 litre)
(without filter change)	7.0 pints (4 US qts/3.8 litre)

Cylinder head

Type	Aluminium alloy one piece

Valve clearances (hot):
Inlet . . . . 0.010 in (0.25 mm)
Exhaust . . . . 0.012 in (0.30 mm)
Valve head diameter: – L16
Inlet . . . . 1.6535 in (42 mm)
Exhaust . . . . 1.2992 in (33 mm)
                – L18, L20B
Inlet . . . . 1.6535 in (42 mm)
Exhaust . . . . 1.3780 in (35 mm)
Valve stem diameter:
Inlet . . . . 0.3136 – 0.3142 in (7.965 – 7.980 mm)
Exhaust . . . . 0.3128 – 0.3134 in (7.945 – 7.960 mm)
Valve length:
Inlet . . . . 4.524 – 4.535 in (114.9 – 115.2 mm)
Exhaust . . . . 4.555 – 4.567 in (115.7 – 116.0 mm)
Valve lift:
L16S and L18S
Inlet . . . . 0.394 in (10.0 mm)
Exhaust . . . . 0.413 in (10.5 mm)
L18T and L20B
Inlet and exhaust . . . . 0.413 in (10.5 mm)
Valve springs:
Type . . . . Helical coil
Free length (intake and exhaust):
Outer . . . . 1.968 in (49.98 mm)
Inner . . . . 1.766 in (44.85 mm)
Valve guide type . . . . Renewable
Valve guide length:
Inlet . . . . 2.323 in (59.0 mm)
Exhaust . . . . 2.323 in (59.0 mm)
Valve guide protrusion from head surface . . . . 0.417 in (10.6 mm)
Valve guide inner diameter:
Inlet . . . . 0.3150 – 0.3154 in (8.0000 – 8.018 mm)
Exhaust . . . . 0.3150 – 0.3154 in (8.0000 – 8.018 mm)
Valve guide outer diameter:
Inlet . . . . 0.4733 – 0.4738 in (12.023 – 12.034 mm)
Exhaust . . . . 0.4733 – 0.4738 in (12.023 – 12.034 mm)
Valve guide to stem clearance:
Inlet . . . . 0.0008 – 0.0021 in (0.020 – 0.053 mm)
Exhaust . . . . 0.0016 – 0.0029 in (0.040 – 0.073 mm)
Valve seat width:
Inlet . . . . 0.0551 in (1.4 mm)
Exhaust – L16, L18 . . . . 0.0512 in (1.3 mm)
        – L20B . . . . 0.0787 in (2.0 mm)
Valve seat angle . . . . 45° 30'
Valve seat interference fit:
Inlet . . . . 0.0032 – 0.0044 in (0.081 – 0.113 mm)
Exhaust . . . . 0.0025 – 0.0038 in (0.064 – 0.096 mm)
Valve guide interference fit . . . . 0.011 – 0.0019 in (0.027 – 0.049 mm)
Cylinder head temperature for fitting valve seat inserts . . . . 150 – 200°C (302 – 393°F)
Cylinder head face warp limit . . . . 0.004 in (0.10 mm)

Camshaft and timing chain
Camshaft type . . . . Overhead
Number of bearings . . . . 4, steel backed white metal bush
Camshaft journal diameter . . . . 1.8877 – 1.8883 in (47.949 – 47.962 mm)
Camshaft journal wear limit . . . . 0.0039 in (0.10 mm)
Camshaft bearing diameter . . . . 1.8898 – 1.8904 in (48.00 – 48.016 mm)
Camshaft lobe lift: – L16S and L18S
Inlet . . . . 0.2618 in (6.65 mm)
Exhaust . . . . 0.2756 in (7.00 mm)
                – L18T and L20B
Inlet . . . . 0.2756 in (7.00 mm)
Exhaust . . . . 0.2756 in (7.00 mm)
Camshaft journal to bearing clearance . . . . 0.0015 – 0.0026 in (0.038 – 0.067mm)
Bearing clearance limit . . . . 0.0039 in (0.10 mm)
Camshaft end float . . . . 0.0031 – 0.0150 in (0.08 – 0.38 mm)
Camshaft distortion (maximum) . . . . 0.0008 in (0.02 mm)
Camshaft drive type . . . . Sprocket and chain
Camshaft sprocket attachment . . . . Dowel and bolt
Camshaft sprocket attachment . . . . Key
Rocker arm lever ratio . . . . 1.45 : 1

Crankshaft and main bearing
Number of main bearings .... 5, steel shell, white metal lined
Journal diameter .... 2.1631 – 2.1636 (54.942 – 54.955 mm)
Journal taper and out-of-round .... Less than 0.0004 in (0.01 mm)
Endplay .... 0.0020 – 0.007 in (0.05 – 0.18 mm)
Crankpin diameter .... 1.9670 – 1.9675 (49.961 – 49.974 mm)
Crankpin taper and out-of-round .... Less than 0.0004 in (0.01 mm)
Main bearing clearance (max) .... 0.0047 in (0.12 mm)
Undersizes:
    1st .... 0.25 mm
    2nd .... 0.50 mm
    3rd .... 0.75 mm
    4th .... 1.00 mm

Connecting rods and bearings
Length (centre-to-centre)
    L16S .... 5.24 in (133.0 mm)
    L18S, L18T .... 5.132 in (130.35 mm)
    L20B .... 5.748 in (146.0 mm)
Bearing material F770
Bearing thickness (standard) .... 0.0588 – 0.0593 in (1.493 – 1.506 mm)
Big end play .... 0.0079 – 0.0118 in (0.20 – 0.30 mm)
Connecting rod bearing clearance .... 0.0010 – 0.0022 in (0.025 – 0.055 mm)
Undersizes
    1st .... 0.060 mm
    2nd .... 0.120 mm
    3rd .... 0.250 mm
    4th .... 0.500 mm
    5th .... 0.750 mm
    6th .... 1.000 mm

Pistons and rings
Type .... Flat or concave strut, slipper skirt, cast aluminium
Diameter: – standard
    L16 .... 3.2671 – 3.2691 in (82.985 – 83.035 mm)
    L18 and L20B .... 3.3459 – 3.3478 in (84.985 – 85.035 mm)
0.0098 in (0.25 mm) oversize
    L16 .... 3.2762 – 3.2781 in (83.215 – 83.265 mm)
    L18 .... —   —
0.0197 in (0.50 mm) oversize
    L16 .... 3.2860 – 3.2880 in (83.465 – 83.515 mm)
    L18 and L20B .... 3.3648 – 3.3667 in (85.465 – 85.515 mm)
0.0295 in (0.75 mm) oversize
    L16 .... 3.2959 – 3.2978 in (83.715 – 83.765 mm)
    L18 .... —   —
0.0394 in (1.00 mm) oversize
    L16 .... 3.3057 – 3.3077 in (83.965 – 84.015 mm)
    L18 and L20B .... 3.3844 – 3.3864 in (86.965 – 86.015 mm)
0.0492 in (1.25 mm) oversize
    L16 .... 3.3254 – 3.3274 in (84.465 – 84.515 mm)
    L18 .... —   —
Ring groove width
L16, L18
    Top .... 0.0787 in (2.0 mm)
    Second .... 0.0787 in (2.0 mm)
    Oil control .... 0.1575 in (4.0 mm)
L20B
    Top .... 0.0780 – 0.0807 in (2.030 to 2.050 mm)
    Second .... 0.0795 – 0.0803 in (2.020 to 2.040 mm)
    Oil control .... 0.1581 – 0.1591 in (4.015 to 4.040 mm)
    Piston to bore clearance .... 0.0010 – 0.0018 in (0.025 – 0.045 mm)
    Gudgeon pin hole offset .... 0.0374 – 0.0413 in (0.95 – 1.05 mm)
    Gudgeon pin diameter .... 0.8266 – 0.8268 in (20.995 – 21.000 mm)
    Gudgeon pin length .... 2.8445 – 2.8740 in (72.25 – 73.00 mm)
    Gudgeon pin to piston clearance .... 0.00004 – 0.00051 in (0.001 – 0.013 mm)
    Interference fit of piston pin to connecting rod bush .... 0.0006 – 0.0013 in (0.015 – 0.033 mm)
Piston ring side clearance:
    Top – L16 .... 0.0016 – 0.0031 in (0.040 – 0.080 mm)
      – L18 .... 0.0018 – 0.0031 in (0.045 – 0.080 mm)
      – L20B .... 0.0016 – 0.0029 in (0.040 – 0.073 mm)
    Second .... 0.0012 – 0.0028 in (0.030 – 0.070 mm)
Piston ring gap:
    Top – L16 and L20B .... 0.0098 – 0.0157 in (0.25 – 0.40 mm)
      – L18 .... 0.0138 – 0.0217 in (0.35 – 0.55 mm)
    Second – L16 .... 0.0059 – 0.0118 in (0.15 – 0.30 mm)
      – L18 and L20B .... 0.0118 – 0.0197 in (0.30 – 0.50 mm)

Oil control
    L16 . . . . 0.0118 – 0.0354 in (0.30 – 0.90 mm)
    L18 and L20B . . . . 0.0118 – 0.0354 in (0.30 – 0.90 mm)

Cylinder block
Type . . . . 4 cylinder in-line cylinder block, integral with crankcase
Bore diameter (standard):
    L16 . . . . 3.2677 in (83 mm)
    L18 and L20B . . . . 3.3465 in (85 mm)
Bore wear limit . . . . 0.008 in (0.20 mm)
Bore measurement points (from face of block):
    1st . . . . 0.787 in (20 mm)
    2nd . . . . 2.362 in (60 mm)
    3rd . . . . 3.937 in (100 mm)
Cylinder block face warp limit . . . . 0.004 in (0.10 mm)
Oversize pistons
    1st . . . . 0.25 mm
    2nd . . . . 0.50 mm
    3rd . . . . 0.75 mm
    4th . . . . 1.00 mm
    5th . . . . 1.50 mm

Oil pump
Type . . . . Trochoid, inner and outer rotors
Rotor to cover clearance . . . . 0.0012 – 0.0024 in (0.03 – 0.06 mm)
Rotor side clearance . . . . 0.0020 – 0.0047 in (0.05 – 0.12 mm)
Rotor tip clearance . . . . Less than 0.0047 in (0.12 mm)
Outer rotor to body clearance . . . . 0.0059 – 0.0083 in (0.15 – 0.21 mm)
Rotor to bottom cover clearance . . . . 0.0012 – 0.0051 in (0.03 – 0.13 mm)
Oil pressure at idle . . . . 11 – 40 lb/in² (0.8 – 2.8 kg/cm²)
Regulator valve spring:
    Free length . . . . 2.067 in (52.5 mm)
    Pressure length . . . . 1.370 in (34.8 mm)
Regulator valve opening pressure . . . . 50 – 57 lb/in² (3.5 – 5.0 kg/cm²)

Torque wrench settings:
	lbf ft	kgf m
Cylinder head bolts	51 – 61	7.0 – 8.5
Connecting rod big-end nuts	33 – 40	4.5 – 5.5
Flywheel fixing bolts	101 – 116	14 – 16
Main bearing cap bolts	33 – 40	4.5 – 5.5
Camshaft sprocket bolt	87 – 116	12 – 16
Oil sump bolts	4.3 – 6.5	0.6 – 0.9
Oil pump bolts	8.0 – 10.8	1.1 – 1.5
Oil sump drain plug	14 – 22	2 – 3
Rocker pivot lock nuts	36 – 43	5 – 6
Camshaft locating plate bolts	4.3 – 6.5	0.6 – 0.9
Carburettor nuts	3.6 – 7.2	0.5 – 1.0
Manifold nuts	11 – 14	1.5 – 2.0
Fuel pump nuts	8.7 – 13.0	1.2 – 1.8
Crankshaft pulley bolt	87 – 116	12 – 16
Front mounting bracket-to-cylinder block	20 – 27	2.7 – 3.7
Front mounting insulator-to-bracket	12 – 16	1.6 – 2.2
Front insulator-to-suspension crossmember	12 – 16	1.6 – 2.2
Rear mounting insulator-to-transmission	10 – 13	1.4 – 1.8
Rear mounting insulator-to-mounting support	7 – 9	0.9 – 1.2
Mounting support-to-body	20 – 27	2.7 – 3.7
Front cover bolts		
8 mm	7.2 – 9.4	1.0 – 1.3
6 mm	2.9 – 4.3	0.4 – 0.6
Oil pump cover bolt	5.1 – 7.2	0.7 – 1.0
Regulator valve cap nut	29 – 36	4 – 5

1 General description

The engine fitted is of the four cylinder in-line type, with valve operation by means of an overhead camshaft.

The cast iron cylinder block contains the four bores and acts as a rigid support for the five bearing crankshaft. The machined cylinder bores are surrounded by water jackets to dissipate heat and control operating temperature.

A disposable oil filter is located on the right-hand side of the cylinder block and supplies clean oil to the main gallery and various oilways. The main bearings are lubricated from oil holes which run parallel with the cylinder bores. The forged steel crankshaft is suitably drilled for directing lubricating oil so ensuring full bearing lubrication.

To lubricate the connecting rod small end, drillings are located in the big-ends of the rods so that the oil is squirted upwards.

Crankshaft endfloat is controlled by thrust washers located at the centre main bearings.

The pistons are of a special aluminium casting with struts to control thermal expansion. There are two compression and one oil control ring. The gudgeon pin is a hollow steel shaft which is fully floating in the piston and a press fit in the connecting rod little end. The pistons are attached to the crankshaft via forged steel connecting rods.

The cylinder head is of aluminium and incorporates wedge type combustion chambers. A special aluminium bronze valve seat is used for the inlet valve whilst a steel exhaust valve seat is fitted.

Located on the top of the cylinder head is the cast iron camshaft which is supported in four aluminium alloy brackets. The camshaft bearings are lubricated from drillings which lead from the main oil gallery in the cylinder head.

The supply of oil to each cam lobe is through an oil hole drilled in the base circle of each lobe. The actual oil supply is to the front oil gallery from the 2nd camshaft bearing and to the rear oil gallery from the 3rd camshaft bearing. These holes on the base circle of the lobe supply oil to the cam pad surface of the rocker arm and to the valve stem end.

Two valves per cylinder are mounted at a slight angle in the cylinder head and are actuated by a pivot type rocker arm in direct contact with the cam mechanism. Double springs are fitted to each valve.

The camshaft is driven by a double row roller chain from the front of the crankshaft. Chain tension is controlled by a tensioner which is operated by oil and spring pressure. The rubber shoe type tensioner controls vibration and tension of the chain.

The inlet manifold is of a separate aluminium alloy casting with four branches. The carburettor is attached to a flange in the centre of the manifold. The cast iron exhaust manifold has three branches which converge into two for connecting to the exhaust downpipes via a flange and studs. Both are fixed to the right-hand side of the cylinder head.

Any references in the text to the left-hand or right-hand side of the engine are applicable to a person in the drivers seat facing forwards.

2 Operations with engine in place

The following major operations can be carried out to the engine

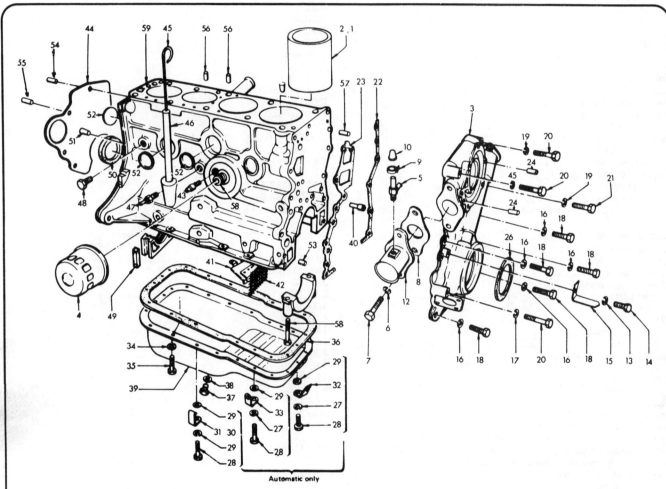

Automatic only

Fig. 1.1 Cylinder block, sump and front cover assemblies (Sec 1)

1 Block cylinder liner	17 Lockwasher spring	31 Tube clamp	46 Oil level gauge guide
2 Block cylinder liner	18 Bolt	32 Hose clamp	47 Oil pressure switch
3 Front engine cover	19 Lockwasher spring	33 Oil cooler hose clamp	48 Drain plug
4 Oil filter cartridge	20 Bolt	34 Lock spring washer	49 Bearing oil seal
5 Connector	21 Bolt	35 Bolt	50 Crankcase oil seal
6 Lockwasher spring	22 Left-hand front cover gasket	36 Oil pan gasket	51 Taper plug
7 Bolt	23 Right-hand front cover gasket	37 Drain plug	52 Welch plug
8 Inlet water gasket	24 Water pump dowel	38 Drain plug washer	53 Timing chain cover dowel
9 Hose clamp	25 Water pump dowel	39 Oil pan assembly	54 Block-to-transmission case dowel
10 Rubber cap	26 Crankcase oil seal	40 Chain oil jet	55 Block dowel
11 Rubber cap	27 Washer	41 Crankcase baffle plate	56 Block dowel
12 Water inlet	28 Bolt	42 Crankcase net	57 Dowel
13 Lockwasher spring	29 Clamp spacer	43 Relief valve	58 Main bearing bolt
14 Indicator bolt	30 Tube clamp	44 Rear engine plate	59 Cylinder block assembly
15 Timing indicator		45 Oil level gauge	
16 Lockwasher spring			

with it in place in the car:

Removal and refitting of the camshaft
Removal and refitting of the cylinder head
Removal and refitting of the engine mountings
Removal and refitting of the sump and pistons (after disconnecting steering linkage) - not recommended
Removal and refitting of the flywheel - not recommended

3 Operations with engine removed

The following major operations must be carried out with the engine out of the car on a bench or floor.

Removal and refitting of the main bearings
Removal and refitting of the crankshaft

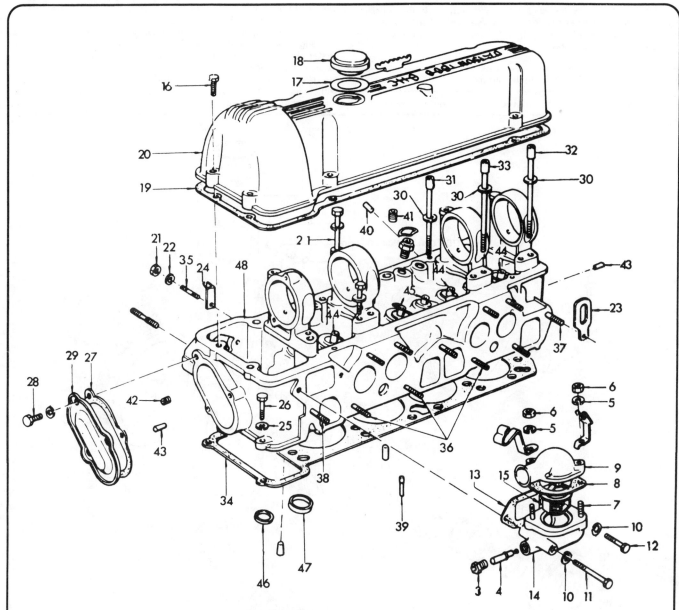

Fig. 1.2 Cylinder head components (Sec 1)

1	Cam bracket bolt	13	Thermostat gasket	25	Lockwasher spring	37	Stud
2	Cam bracket bolt	14	Thermostat housing	26	Bolt	38	Stud
3	Water temperature earth nut	15	Thermostat assembly	27	Front cover head gasket	39	Cylinder head oil jet
4	Water temperature gauge	16	Rocker cover bolt	28	Bolt	40	Taper plug
5	Spring washer	17	Oil cap packing	29	Front head cover	41	Cylinder blind plug
6	Nut	18	Oil filler cap	30	Washer	42	Cylinder blind plug
7	Stud	19	Rocker cover gasket	31	Cylinder head bolt	43	Oil gallery taper plug
8	Joint washer	20	Rocker cover	32	Cylinder head bolt	44	Exhaust valve guide
9	Water outlet	21	Nut	33	Cylinder head bolt	45	Intake valve guide
10	Spring washer	22	Spring washer	34	Cylinder head gasket	46	Exhaust valve insert
11	Bolt	23	Engine rear slinger	35	Stud	47	Intake valve insert
12	Bolt	24	Engine front slinger	36	Stud	48	Cylinder head

4 Methods of engine removal

There are two methods of engine removal: complete with clutch and gearbox , or without the gearbox. Both methods are described.

It is easier if a hydraulic trolley jack is used in conjunction with two axle-stands, so that the car can be raised sufficiently to allow easy access underneath. Overhead lifting tackle will be necessary in both cases.

NOTE: *We advise that cars fitted with automatic transmission necessitating engine and transmission removal, should have the transmission removed first as described in Chapter 6. The transmission even on its own, is very heavy.*

5 Engine - removal with manual gearbox

1   The complete unit can be removed easily in about four hours. It is essential to have a good hoist, and two strong axle - stands if an inspection pit is not available. Removal will be much easier if there is someone to assist, especially during the later stages.

2   With few exceptions, it is easier to lift out the engine with all ancillaries (alternator, distributor, carburettor, exhaust manifold) still attached and then remove them when the engine is on the bench. On vehicles equipped with air conditioning, take care not to disconnect any of the system connecting hoses, but remove the compressor drivebelt and the compressor retaining bolts only. Then tie the compressor to one side of the engine compartment (without straining the flexible hoses) so that it will not impede engine removal.

3   Before beginning work it is worthwhile to get all dirt cleaned off the engine at a garage equipped with steam or high pressure air and water cleaning equipment. This makes the job quicker, easier and of course much cleaner.

4   Using a pencil or scriber mark the outline of the bonnet hinge on either side to act as a datum for refitting. An assistant should now take the weight of the bonnet.

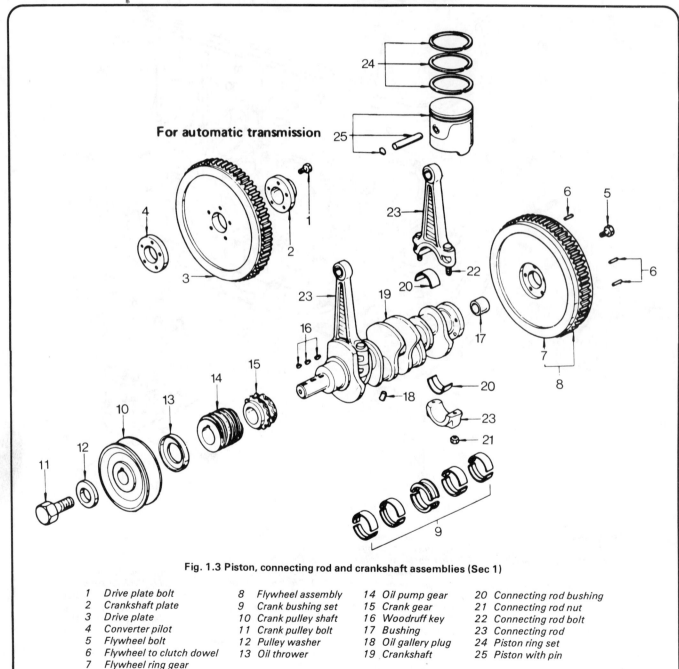

Fig. 1.3 Piston, connecting rod and crankshaft assemblies (Sec 1)

1 Drive plate bolt	8 Flywheel assembly
2 Crankshaft plate	9 Crank bushing set
3 Drive plate	10 Crank pulley shaft
4 Converter pilot	11 Crank pulley bolt
5 Flywheel bolt	12 Pulley washer
6 Flywheel to clutch dowel	13 Oil thrower
7 Flywheel ring gear	

14 Oil pump gear	20 Connecting rod bushing
15 Crank gear	21 Connecting rod nut
16 Woodruff key	22 Connecting rod bolt
17 Bushing	23 Connecting rod
18 Oil gallery plug	24 Piston ring set
19 Crankshaft	25 Piston with pin

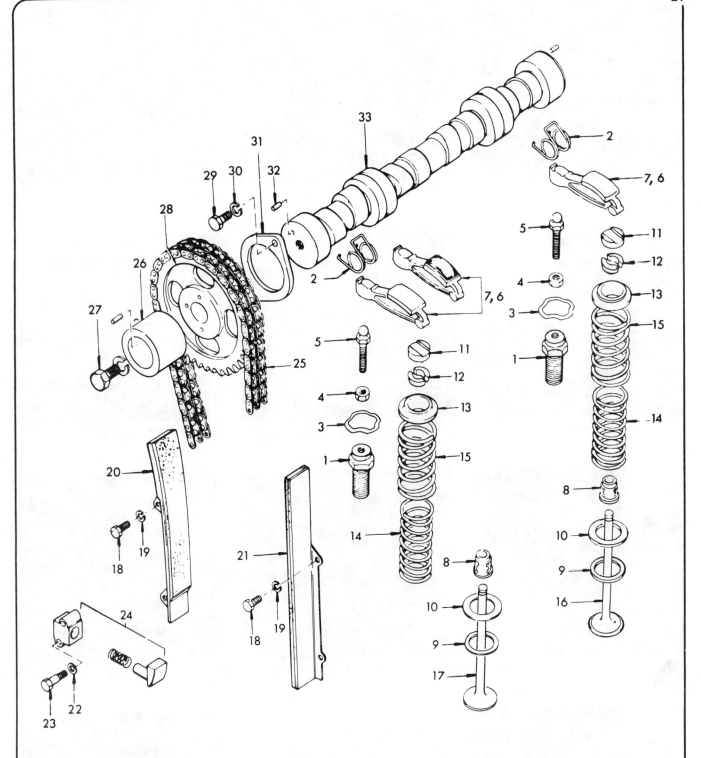

Fig. 1.4 Camshaft and valve assemblies (Sec 2)

1 Rocker bushing	10 Valve seat	18 Bolt	26 Fuel pump cam assembly
2 Rocker valve spring	11 Rocker valve guide	19 Spring washer	27 Cam gear bolt
3 Rocker retainer	12 Valve collet	20 Chain tension slack guide	28 Cam sprocket
4 Pivot locknut	13 Valve retainer	21 Chain tension side guide	29 Bolt
5 Valve rocker pivot	14 Valve spring	22 Washer	30 Spring washer
6 Valve rocker with pad	15 Valve spring	23 Bolt	31 Cam locking plate
7 Valve rocker	16 Exhaust valve	24 Chain tensioner	32 Camshaft dowel
8 Valve oil seal	17 Inlet valve	25 Camshaft chain	33 Camshaft
9 Inner valve spring seat			

5.11 Draining gearbox oil

5.13 Lifting away front grille panel

5.14 Slackening bottom hose clip

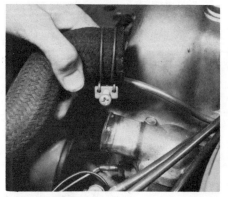
5.15 Detaching top hose

5.17 Removing radiator securing bolts

5.19 Lifting out the radiator

5.22 Detaching HT cables from rocker cover

5.23 Detaching HT cable from ignition coil

5.24 Removing air cleaner support bracket bolts

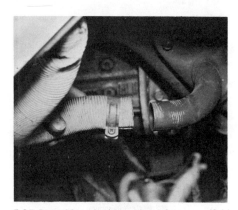
5.25 Detaching air cleaner hose from manifold adaptor

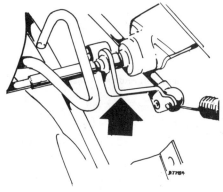
Fig. 1.5 Accelerator control bellcrank assembly (Sec 5)

5.29 Detaching choke control

5   Undo and remove the two bolts and washers that secure the bonnet to the hinge and carefully lift the bonnet up and then over the front of the car. Store in a safe place where it will not be scratched. Push down the hinges to stop accidents.

6   Disconnect the negative and then the positive battery terminal clamp bolts and detach them from the terminal posts.

7   Release the battery clamp securing nuts and lift away the clamp.

8   Lift the battery from the engine compartment

9   Place a container of at least 13 Imp pints under the drain tap and drain the radiator.

10   Place a container of at least 8 Imp pints under the engine sump drain plug. Unscrew the drain plug and allow the oil to drain out. Refit the drain plug.

11   Place a container of at least 4 Imp pints under the gearbox drain plug. Unscrew the drain plug and allow all the oil to drain out. Refit the drain plug (photo).

12   Remove the radiator shroud (if fitted), then undo and remove the screws securing the front grille panel to the body.

13   Carefully lift away the front grille panel (photo).

14   Slacken the bottom hose clip at the union end and detach the bottom hose from the radiator (photo).

15   Slacken the top hose clip at the thermostat end and detach the top hose (photo).

16   Detach the electric cable from the clips on the side of the radiator.

17   Working from the front of the car undo and remove the four bolts and washers securing the radiator assembly to the front panel (photo).

18   Move the radiator assembly rearward slightly.

19   Lift the radiator upward and away from the front of the car. Take care that the fan blades do not touch the matrix (photo).

20   Detach the LT cable from the side of the distributor. Also detach the vacuum pipe from the distributor vacuum unit.

21   Release the distributor cap clips and lift away the cap.

22   Move the HT cables from the clips on the top of the rocker cover (photo).

23   Release the HT cable from the ignition coil (photo).

24   Undo and remove the two bolts and spring washers securing the air cleaner stay to the inlet manifold (photo).

25   Slacken the clip securing the air cleaner hose to the warm air adaptor on the exhaust manifold. Detach the hose (photo).

26   Release the air cleaner from the top of the carburettor, lift upward and detach the two hoses located in the underside.

27   Slacken the hose clip on the side of the fuel pump and detach from the fuel pump. Plug the ends to stop loss of petrol or dirt ingress.

28   Detach the accelerator control from the bellcrank and bracket (Fig. 1.5).

29   Release the choke control from the bracket and control lever on the side of the carburettor (photo).

30   Slacken the clip and detach the hose from the rear of the inlet manifold.

31   Slacken the two clips and detach the bridge hose from the inlet manifold and metal pipe between the two manifolds (photo).

32   Make a note of the electrical connections at the rear of the starter motor solenoid and detach the cables (photo).

33   Detach the hose from the adaptor at the rear of number 4 spark plug.

34   Make a note of the electrical connections at the rear of the alternator and detach the cables.

35   Detach the cable from the water temperature sender unit and oil pressure switch.

36   Now working inside the car, untie the leather gaiter securing cord from the gear change lever.

37   Undo and remove the two console securing screws and washers (photo).

38   Lift the console from over the gear change lever.

39   Undo and remove the rubber gaiter retaining ring securing screw.

40   Lift the rubber gaiter up the gear change lever (photo).

41   Undo and remove the nut located at the bottom of the gear change lever (photo).

42   Lift the gear change lever up from the selector link,

43   Recover the upper and lower rubber bushes and washers (photo).

44   This photo shows the correct positions of the bushes and washers (photo).

45   Working under the car slacken the exhaust downpipe to silencer securing clip.

5.31 Disconnecting bridge hose

5.32 Starter motor cables attached to solenoid

5.37 Removing console securing screws

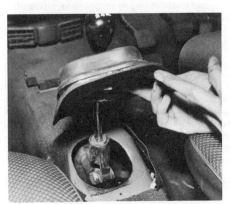
5.40 Rubber gaiter moved up gear lever

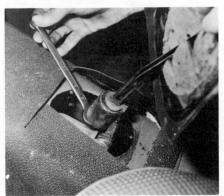
5.41 Removing the gear change lever lower nut

5.43 Removing the upper mounting bush

5.44 Gear change lever with bushes correctly fitted

5.47 Disconnecting the handbrake cable

5.48 Removing propeller shaft rear flange securing bolts

5.49 Disengaging the propellor shaft from the gearbox

46 Detach the exhaust downpipe from the exhaust manifold and move to one side.

47 Withdraw the split pin and remove the cotter pin retaining the handbrake cable to the relay lever (photo).

48 Mark the propeller shaft and final drive mating flanges to ensure correct reassembly and then undo and remove the four securing nuts, bolts and washers (photo).

49 Carefully lower the rear end of the propeller shaft and then draw the shaft rearward so disengaging from the rear of the gearbox (photo).

50 Undo and remove the two bolts and spring washers securing the clutch slave cylinder to the clutch bellhousing. Move the slave cylinder to one side (photo).

51 Unscrew the speedometer cable knurled nut and and detach the speedometer cable from the side of the gearbox (photo).

52 Detach the two cables from the reverse light switch.

53 Position a jack under the gearbox casing and take the weight of the unit from the rear mountings. Undo and remove the gearbox rear mounting securing bolt (photo).

54 Undo and remove the rear mounting crossmember securing bolts and washers (photo).

55 Move the crossmember to one side and lift away from under the car.

56 Check that all cables, and the exhaust system, are well out of the way before moving from under the car.

57 Undo and remove the engine mounting to front axle securing bolts

(photo).

58 Position an overhead hoist or crane over the engine and support the weight using chains or rope through the lifting eyes located on the right front, and left rear, of the cylinder head.

59 Check that all pipes, wires and controls are well out of the way and then slowly raising the engine and lowering the jack under the gearbox ease the complete unit up and over the engine compartment (photo).

60 When the sump is clear of the front body panel the rear of the gearbox can now be lifted by hand as the car is pushed rearward or the hoist is drawn away from the engine compartment. Lower the unit to the ground away from the car.

61 Check that the engine compartment and floor area around the car are clear of loose nuts and bolts as well as tools.

6 Engine - removal without gearbox

1 If it is necessary to remove only the engine, leaving the gearbox in position, the engine can be detached from the gearbox and then lifted away.

2 Follow the instructions given in Section 5, paragraphs 2-10, 12-35.

3 Detach the exhaust downpipe from the exhaust manifold.

4 Undo and remove the two bolts that secure the starter motor to

5.50 Removing clutch slave cylinder

5.51 Disconnecting speedometer cable from gearbox

5.53 Removing the gearbox rear mounting securing bolt

5.54 Rear mounting crossmember securing bolt removal

5.57 Removing engine mounting to front axle bolt

5.59 Lifting out the engine

the flywheel housing. Note that the battery earth cable is attached to the flywheel housing bottom bolt.Pull the starter motor forward and lift away.

5   Position an overhead hoist over the engine and support the weight using chains or rope through the lifting eyes located on the right front, and left rear, of the cylinder head.

6   Undo and remove the bolts and washers that secure the front engine mounting to the crossmember.

7   Undo and remove the remaining nuts and bolts that secure the engine to the gearbox bellhousing.

8   Check that no controls, cables or pipes have been left connected to the engine and that they are safely tucked to one side where they will not be caught, as the unit is being removed.

9   Raise the engine slightly to enable the engine mountings to clear their location on the front axle. Move it forward until the clutch is clear of the input shaft. Continue lifting the unit taking care not to damage the front body panel. Lower the engine to the floor.

10 To complete, clear out any loose nuts and bolts and tools from the engine compartment and the floor area.

7   Dismantling the engine - general

Keen DIY mechanics who dismantle a lot of engines will probably have a stand on which to put them, but most will make do with a work bench which should be large enough to spread around the inevitable bits and pieces and tools, and strong enough to support the engine weight. If the floor is the only place, try and ensure that the engine rests on a hard wood platform, or similar, rather than on concrete.

Spend some time on cleaning the unit. If you have been wise this will have been done before the engine was removed, at a service bay. Good water-soluble solvents will help to 'float' off caked dirt/grease under a water jet. Once the exterior is clean, dismantling may begin. As parts are removed clean them in petrol or paraffin (do not immerse parts with oilways in petrol or paraffin - clean them with a petrol soaked cloth and clear oilways with nylon pipe cleaners). If an air line is available use it for final cleaning off. Petrol or paraffin, which could possibly remain in oilways would dilute the oil for initial lubrication

after reassembly, must be blown out.

Always fit new gaskets and seals - but do *not* throw the old ones away until you have the new one to hand. A pattern is then available if they have to be made specially. Hang them up.

In general it is best to work from the top of the engine downward. In all cases support the engine firmly, so that it does not topple over when undoing stubborn nuts and bolts.

Always place nuts and bolts back with their components or place of attachment, if possible – it saves much confusion later. Otherwise put them in small, separate pots or jars so that their groups are easily identified.

If you have an area where parts can be laid down on sheets of paper, do so – putting the nuts and bolts with them. If you are able to look at all the components in this way it helps to avoid missing something on reassembly.

Even though you may be dismantling the engine only partly (possibly with it still in the car) the principles still apply. It is appreciated that most people prefer to do engine repairs, if possible, with the engine in position. Consequently an indication will be given as to what is necessary to lead up to carrying out repairs on a particular component. Generally speaking the engine is easy enough to get at as far as repairs and renewals of the ancillaries are concerned. When it comes to repair of the major engine components, however it is only fair to say that repairs with the engine in position are more difficult than with it out.

8   Engine ancillaries - removal

1   If you are stripping the engine completely or preparing to install a reconditioned unit, all the ancillaries must be removed first. If you are going to obtain a reconditioned 'short' motor (block, crankshaft, pistons and connecting rods) then obviously the cam box, cylinder head and associated parts will need retention for fitting to the new engine. It is advisable to check just what you will get with a reconditioned unit as changes are made from time to time.

2   The removal of all items connected with fuel, ignition and charging systems are detailed in their respective Chapters but for clarity they

are merely listed here.

> Distributor
> Carburettor (can be removed together with inlet manifold)
> Alternator
> Fuel pump
> Water pump
> Starter motor
> Thermostat

9 Engine mountings - removal and refitting

1   If the rubber insulator has softened because of oil contamination or failure of attachment, it will be necessary to fit a new mounting. Always cure the cause of the oil leak before fitting a new mounting.
2   Chock the rear wheels, apply the handbrake, jack up the front of the car and support on firmly based axle-stands.

Front mountings
3   Undo and remove the bolts that secure the engine mountings to the crossmember.
4   Position a piece of wood on the saddle of a jack and locate under the engine sump.
5   Carefully jack up the engine until the mounting is well clear of the crossmember.
6   Undo and remove the nuts and spring washers that secure each engine mounting to the engine mounting bracket.
7   Lift away the engine mounting.
8   Refitting of the front mounting is the reverse sequence to removal. The securing nuts and bolts should only be tightened to the specified torque wrench settings when the weight of the engine is on the mountings.

Rear mountings
9   Position a piece of wood on the saddle of a jack and locate under the transmission assembly.
10 Carefully raise the jack until the weight of the transmission assembly is supported by the jack.
11 Undo and remove the two bolts and spring washers that secure the mounting to the rear crossmember.
12 Undo and remove the four bolts and spring washers that secure the rear transmission crossmember to the underside of the body. Lift away the crossmember noting which way round it is fitted.
13 Undo and remove the bolts securing the rear engine mounting to the transmission extension housing. Lift away the mounting.
14 Refitting is the reverse sequence to removal. The following additional points should be noted:

> (a) Make sure that the mounting is correctly positioned before securing.
> (b) The securing nuts and bolts should only be tightened to the specified torque wrench settings when the weight of the transmission is on the mountings.

10 Oil filter - removal and refitting

1   The oil filter is a throwaway cartridge type which is changed regularly under service procedures.
2   To remove the filter grasp and turn in an anti-clockwise direction.
3   Smear the filter element sealing ring with engine oil before fitting to prevent binding and removal difficulty later.
4   Screw on the filter and tighten hand-tight only otherwise an oil leakage may occur.

11 Flywheel - removal, inspection and renovation

1   The flywheel is secured to the crankshaft rear flange by five bolts on L16 and L18 engines. The L20B has six securing bolts.
2   Undo and remove the bolts with a socket spanner and pull the flywheel off squarely. It is important not to damage the mating surfaces (photo).
3   The flywheel clutch friction surface should be shiny and unscored. Minor blemishes and scratches can be overlooked but deep grooves will probably cause clutch problems in time. Renewal may be advisable.

11.2 Flywheel securing bolts

4   If the starter ring gear teeth are badly worn the ring can be removed by first splitting it between two teeth with a chisel. Do not try to drive it off, because it rests in a shallow groove. If you have never fitted a new ring gear yourself it is best to have it done for you. It needs heating to a temperature of 200°C (392°F) evenly in order to shrink-fit it on the flywheel. The chamfers on the ring gear teeth must face the same way in which the original ring gear was fitted otherwise the starter motor will not engage correctly.

12 Rocker arms and pivots - removal

1   Slacken the clips and disconnect the hose to the air cleaner ventilation valve and thermostatic air bleed hose from the rocker cover.
2   Undo and remove the two bolts and spring washers that secure the air cleaner support bracket to the inlet manifold. Make a note of the electrical connections to the air cleaner temperature sensor unit and detach these.
3   Undo the wing nut at the top of the air cleaner and lift away the complete assembly.
4   Disconnect the HT leads at the spark plugs and tie back out of the way. It is important that when handling carbon filled HT leads they are treated with care otherwise the carbon insert will break down.
5   Undo and remove the six bolts and washers securing the rocker cover and gasket to the top of the cylinder head. Lift away the rocker cover and gasket. This gasket should be renewed on reassembly (photo).
6   Carefully unclip and then remove the small steady spring from each rocker arm. Note which way round the springs are fitted.
7   Unscrew the rocker pivot locknuts and then screw down the pivots as far as possible into the cylinder head.
8   Using a screwdriver push down on the top of each valve spring assembly and manipulate out each rocker arm. When this is being done the valve rocker guides located on the end of the valve stems must not be dislodged or lost. Also check that the cam heel for the rocker arm being removed is adjacent to its relevant arm before any attempt is made to compress the valve spring assembly.
9   As each rocker arm is removed place in order, so that they may be fitted in their original positions.
10 The rocker arm pivots may be unscrewed from the cylinder head. Lift away the rocker guides from each of the valve stem ends. Keep these in order as well.
11 Prior to inspecting the parts, wash in paraffin and wipe dry with a non-fluffy rag.
12 Inspect the rocker arm pivot head surface for wear or damage. Also inspect the rocker arm to pivot contact surfaces for wear or damage. Any parts that show wear must be renewed.

12.5 Lifting off the rocker cover

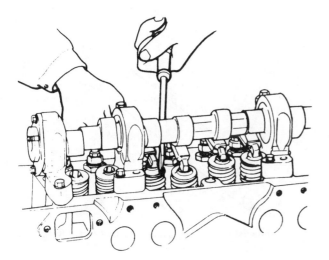
Fig. 1.6 Removing the rocker arms (Sec 12)

13.26 Removing sprocket securing bolt and cam

13 Cylinder head and camshaft - removal (engine in car)

1 Slacken the clips and disconnect the hose to the air cleaner ventilation valve and thermostatic air bleed hose from the rocker cover. Make a note of the electrical connections to the air cleaner temperature sensor unit and detach these.
2 Undo and remove the two bolts and spring washers that secure the air cleaner support bracket to the inlet manifold.
3 Undo the wing nut located at the top of the air cleaner and lift away the complete assembly.
4 Disconnect the fuel inlet pipe and fuel by-pass hose (if fitted) from the carburettor.
5 Detach the distributor vacuum feed pipe from the carburettor.
6 Disconnect the choke control cable from the carburettor.
7 Disconnect the throttle linkage from the carburettor throttle lever.
8 Undo and remove the four nuts and washers that secure the carburettor to the inlet manifold. Lift away the carburettor and its gasket.
9 Place a container of at least 13 Imp pints under the radiator bottom tank and open the tap. Allow the coolant to drain out.
10 Slacken the two hose clips and carefully detach the hose.
11 Slacken the clip and detach the heater hose from the rear of the cylinder head.
12 Disconnect the HT leads at the spark plugs. It is important that when handling carbon filled HT leads they are treated with care otherwise the carbon insert will break down.
13 Disconnect the HT lead from the centre of the ignition coil. Release the distributor cap retaining clips and lift away the cap and HT leads.
14 Slacken the clips and carefully detach the crankcase to inlet manifold ventilation hose.
15 Slacken the clips and detach the inlet manifold water pipe.
16 Slacken the battery terminal clamp bolts and remove the positive and then negative clamps from the terminal posts.
17 Disconnect the fuel inlet and outlet pipes from the fuel pump.
18 Undo and remove the two nuts and washers that secure the fuel pump to the cylinder head. Withdraw the fuel pump from the two studs and lift away together with the gasket and insulator block.
19 Undo and remove the exhaust manifold to downpipe flange nuts and washers. Detach the manifold from the downpipe and lift away from the side of the cylinder head.
20 Undo and remove the nuts and washers that secure the inlet manifold to the cylinder head. This must be done in a diagonal and progressive manner. Lift away the inlet manifold.
21 The inlet and exhaust manifold gaskets must not be used twice.
22 Undo and remove the six bolts and spring washers securing the rocker cover. Lift away the rocker cover and gasket. The gasket should be renewed upon reassembly.
23 Undo and remove the two external bolts which secure the front end of the cylinder head to the timing cover.
24 Slowly turn the crankshaft until the timing O-mark on the camshaft chain is in alignment and clearly visible with the timing mark dimple on the camshaft sprocket.
25 It should be observed that the timing mark number, which is stamped adjacent to the mark dimple, is number 1, 2 or 3, this depending on whether the camshaft chain has been previously readjusted due to stretch. These numbers are also stamped on the sprocket boss adjacent to the camshaft dowel locating holes. To quote an example: if a number 2 on the sprocket is found to be aligned with the camshaft chain O-mark, then the number 2 on the sprocket boss will be adjacent to the camshaft sprocket dowel locating hole and the camshaft dowel.
26 Undo and remove the camshaft sprocket retaining bolt and carefully lift away the little cam that operates the fuel pump actuating arm (photo).
27 Obtain a piece of soft wood and shape it so that it can be wedged between the right-hand side of the chain (when looking at it from the front) and the inner left-hand side of the chain. Make sure that the chain is not allowed to drop otherwise it will be necessary to remove the timing cover and sump so that the engine can be retimed (photo).
28 Carefully withdraw the camshaft sprocket from the end of the camshaft and detach the chain from the sprocket.
29 Refer to Fig 1.7 and slacken the bolts securing the cylinder head to the block. This must be done in a progressive manner to avoid distortion.
30 The cylinder head may now be lifted upward and away from the

13.27 Wooden wedge in position

13.30 Lifting off the cylinder head

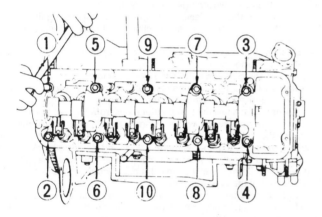

Fig. 1.7 Slackening sequence of cylinder head bolts (Sec 13)

Fig. 1.8 Special tool for removing cylinder head bolts (Sec 13)

cylinder block. Make sure that the camshaft chain is not disturbed. Recover the cylinder head gasket. Note, a new gasket will be necessary on reassembly (photo).
31 It may be found that a special tool is required to remove the cylinder head retaining bolts. If these bolts are fitted this tool is a necessity and will have to be obtained from the local Datsun dealer (Fig. 1.8).

14 Cylinder head and camshaft – removal (engine removed)

The sequence is very similar to that for removal when the engine is still in the car. Depending on the stage which the engine has already been dismantled, follow the instriuctions given in Section 13 disregarding those not applicable.

15 Camshaft - removal and inspection

1 The camshaft may be removed with the engine either in or out of the car. Follow the instructions given in Section 12 and remove the rocker arms.
2 Refer to Section 13 and follow the sequence given in paragraphs 24 to 28 inclusive.
3 Undo and remove the two bolts that secure the thrust plates and lift away the thrust plates.
4 Carefully draw the camshaft from the cylinder head ensuring that the cam lobes do not damage the camshaft bearings.

5 **Important** *Under no circumstances may the camshaft bearing bracket securing bolts be removed. Should this be done accidentally or otherwise it will be necessary to obtain a new cylinder head assembly.*
6 The bearing surfaces of the cam lobes should be flat and unpitted. If otherwise, you may expect rapid wear to occur in the future. Badly worn cam lobes hinder the opening of the valves and consequently engine performance.
7 If lack of lubrication has occurred the bearings may have become badly worn. In these circumstances, it will be necessary to renew the worn part, be it the bearings or the camshaft. Renewal of the bearings should be left to the local Datsun dealer.

16 Inlet and exhaust manifolds - removal and refitting

Inlet manifold
1 Slacken the clips and disconnect the rocker cover to air cleaner ventilation hose. Also disconnect the inlet manifold to air cleaner thermostatic air bleed hose when fitted.
2 Refer to Chapter 3 and remove the air cleaner assembly.
3 Slacken the clips and disconnect the fuel inlet pipe and by-pass hoses from the carburettor installation.
4 Detach the distributor vacuum feed pipe.
5 Detach the choke control cable and throttle linkage from the carburettor installation.
6 Undo and remove the four nuts and spring washers that secure the carburettor to the inlet manifold. Lift away the carburettor and recover the gasket.

7 Refer to Chapter 2, Section 2 and partially drain the cooling system.
8 Slacken the hose clips and detach the inlet manifold-to-crankcase ventilation hose. Also detach the water hose from the inlet manifold.
9 Progressively slacken and then remove the nuts and washers securing the inlet manifold to the side of the cylinder head. Lift away the inlet manifold taking care not to damage the combined inlet and exhaust manifold gasket.
10 Refitting the inlet manifold is the reverse sequence to removal.

Exhaust manifold
11 Remove the inlet manifold as described earlier in this Section.
12 Undo and remove the nuts that secure the exhaust downpipe to manifold flange. Carefully detach the downpipe and recover the flange gasket which should be discarded and a new one obtained ready for refitting.
13 Undo and remove the nuts and washers that secure the exhaust manifold to cylinder head studs. Lift away the exhaust manifold and recover the combined inlet and exhaust manifold gasket. This must be renewed upon reassembly.
14 Refitting the exhaust manifold is the reverse sequence to removal.

17 Cylinder head - dismantling, inspection and renovation

1 To remove the valves from the cylinder head requires a special G-clamp spring compressor. This is positioned with the screw head on the head of the valve and the claw end over the valve spring retainer. The screw is now turned until the two split collars round the valve stem are freed and can be removed. If the spring collars tend to stick so that the compressor cannot be tightened, tap the top of the spring (while the clamp is on) to free it.
2 Slacken off the compressor and the valve springs, retainers and collars will be released and can be lifted off. Slide off the oil seals and then recover the inner and outer spring seats. The seals should be renewed as a matter of course during reassembly.
3 Draw the valves out of the guides with care. Any tightness is probably caused by burring at the end of the stem, so clean this up before drawing the valves through. The guide will not then be scored.
4 Keep all parts in sets and in order so that they may be refitted in their original positions.
5 Valves, seats and guides should be examined in sets. Any valve which is cracked or burnt away at the edges must be discarded. Valves which are a slack fit in the guides should also be discarded if further rapid deterioration and poor seating are to be avoided. To decide whether a valve is a slack fit replace it in its bore and feel how much it rocks at the end. Then judge if this presents a deflection of more than 0.008 in (0.2 mm) at the collar end of the stem.
6 If the valves are obviously a very slack fit the remedy is to remove the old valve guides and fit new ones. This requires a 2 ton capacity press so renewal should be left to the local Datsun dealer.
7 If the valve stem and guide clearance is satisfactory measure the stem protrusion from the cylinder head. This should be 1.181 inch (30 mm). If this amount is exceeded the valve will have to be renewed as the valve head will be too thin at the seat area causing overheating and premature failure.
8 Where a valve has deteriorated badly at the seat the corresponding seat in the cylinder head must be examined. Light pitting or scoring may be removed by grinding the valve into the seat with carborundum paste. If worse, then the seat may need recutting with a special tool. This again is a job for the local Datsun dealer.
9 Before grinding-in valves it is best to remove all carbon deposits from the combustion chamber with a wire brush in a power drill. If no proper drill is available scrape the carbon off with an old screwdriver.
10 When grinding in valves to their seats all carbon must first be removed from the valve head and head end of the stem. This is effectively done by fitting the valve in a power drill chuck, clamping the drill in a vice and then scraping the carbon off the rotating valve with an old screwdriver. It is essential to protect the eyes with suitable goggles when doing this.
11 New valves must be ground into their seats. The procedure for grinding in valves is as follows: Obtain a tin of carborundum paste which contains coarse and fine grades, and a grinding tool consisting of a rubber suction cup on the end of a wooden handle. Smear a trace of coarse carborundum paste on the seat face and apply a suction grinder tool to the valve head. With a semi-rotary motion, grind the head to its seat, lifting the valve occasionally to redistribute the grinding paste. When a dull matt even surface is produced on both the valve seat and the valve, then wipe off the paste and repeat the process with fine carborundum paste, lifting and turning the valve to redistribute the paste as before. A light spring placed under the valve head will greatly ease this operation. When a smooth unbroken ring of light grey matt finish is produced, on both valve and valve seat faces, the grinding operation is complete (photo).
12 After grinding, check the valve head thickness as described in paragraph 7. If the protrusion now exceeds the maximum do not remedy this by grinding something off the valve stem end to rectify.
13 If valve seat inserts need to be renewed this must be done by the local Datsun dealer.
14 When the grinding in process has finished all traces of carborundum paste must be removed. This is best done by flushing the head with paraffin and hosing out with water.
15 If the reason for removal of the head has been a blown gasket, make sure that the surface is perfectly flat before it is refitted. This requires an accurate steel straight edge and a feeler gauge for checking. If there is any sign of warp over 0.003 in (0.0762 mm) it is worthwhile getting it machined flat.
16 Each valve has an inner and outer spring and these should, of course, not have any broken coils. The overall length of each spring must be no less than that specified and if it is, it must be discarded. The normal practice is to renew all springs when some are defective.

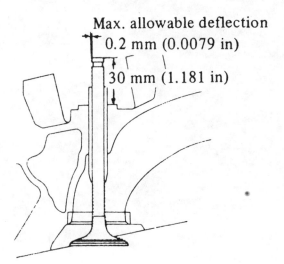

Max. allowable deflection
0.2 mm (0.0079 in)
30 mm (1.181 in)

Fig. 1.9 Valve stem and guide wear check (Sec 17)

17.11 Grinding in valves

18 Cylinder head - decarbonisation

1 This operation can be carried out with the engine either in or out of the car. With the cylinder head off, carefully remove, with a wire brush and blunt scraper, all traces of carbon deposits from the combustion spaces and the ports. The valve stems and valve guides should also be free from any carbon deposits. Wash the combustion spaces and ports down with petrol and scrape the cylinder head surface free of any foreign matter with the side of a steel rule or similar article. Take care not to scratch the surfaces.

2 Clean the pistons and top of the cylinder bores. If the pistons are still in the cylinder bores, it is essential that great care is taken to ensure no carbon gets into the bores as this could scratch the cylinder walls or cause damage to the piston and rings. To ensure that this does not happen first turn the crankshaft so that two of the pistons are at the top of the bores. Place clean non-fluffy rag into the other two bores, or seal them off with paper and masking tape. The water and oilways should also be covered with a small piece of masking tape to prevent particles of carbon entering the lubrication system and causing damage to a bearing surface.

3 There are two schools of thought as to how much carbon ought to be removed from the piston crown. One is that a ring of carbon should be left round the edge of the piston and on the cylinder bore wall as an aid to keeping oil consumption low. The other is to remove all traces of carbon during decarbonisation and leave everything clean.

4 If all traces of carbon are to be removed, press a little grease into the gap between the cylinder walls and the two pistons which are to be worked on. With a blunt scraper carefully scrape away the carbon from the piston crown, taking care not to scratch the aluminium. Also scrape away the carbon from the surrounding lip of the cylinder wall. When all carbon has been removed, scrape away the grease which will now be contaminated with carbon particles, taking care not to press into the bores. To assist prevention of carbon build up, the piston crown can be polished with a metal polish. Remove the rags or masking tape from the other two cylinders and turn the crankshaft so that those two pistons which were at the bottom are now at the top. Place a non-fluffy rag into the other two bores, or seal them with paper and masking tape. Do not forget the waterways and oilways as well. Proceed as previously described.

5 If a ring of carbon is going to be left around the piston, this can be helped by inserting an old piston ring into the top of the bore to rest on the piston and ensure that carbon is not accidentally removed. Check that there are no particles of carbon in the cylinder bores. Decarbonisation is now complete.

19 Oil pump - removal, inspection and refitting

1 The oil pump may be removed with the engine either in or out of the car.

2 Turn the crankshaft until the TDC mark on the crankshaft pulley is in alignment with the pointer located on the timing cover. Number 1 piston must be at the top of its compression stroke.

3 The TDC mark on the crankshaft pulley is the mark on the extreme left of the pulley when looking in from the front of the engine compartment. The graduated marks on the right-hand side of the TDC mark are in increments of 5°.

4 Disconnect the HT leads at the spark plugs. It is important that when handling carbon filled HT leads they are treated with care otherwise the carbon insert will break down.

5 Disconnect the HT lead from the centre of the ignition coil. Release the distributor cap retaining clips and lift away the cap and HT leads.

6 Disconnect the low tension lead from the side of the distributor body. Also detach the vacuum advance hose from the distributor.

7 Using a scriber, mark the distributor mounting bracket and timing cover to assist timing in refitting.

8 Undo and remove the two bolts and washers that secure the distributor and mounting bracket assembly to the timing cover and withdraw the assembly from the timing cover.

9 Use a pencil and make a mark across the timing cover to distributor assembly mounting flange in line with the offset driving dog on the drive gear spindle. The driving dog offset is towards the front of the engine.

10 Check the rear wheels, jack up the front of the car and support on firmly based stands. Remove the left-hand front wheel.

11 Place a container of at least 8 Imp pints under the engine sump drain plug. Remove the drain plug and allow the oil to drain out. Refit the drain plug.

12 Refer to Chapter 11 and remove the front anti-roll bar.

13 Undo and remove the screws securing the engine front splash shield and lift away the shield.

14 Undo and remove the four bolts and spring washers that secure the oil pump to the front cover. Carefully withdraw the oil pump and drive gear spindle (photo).

15 Wash the exterior of the oil pump and wipe dry with a clean non-fluffy rag. Withdraw the drive gear spindle.

16 Undo and remove the one small bolt and spring washer which retain the pump end cover. Detach the cover and gasket from the pump main body.

17 Wipe clean the face of the outer rotor and mark it so that it may be fitted correctly on reassembly.

18 Carefully withdraw the drive shaft and inner rotor assembly. Follow this with the outer rotor.

19 Unscrew and remove the cap bolt and washer from the end cover. Withdraw the spring and pressure relief valve noting which way round the parts are fitted.

20 Thoroughly clean all the component parts in petrol and then check the rotor endfloat and clearances.

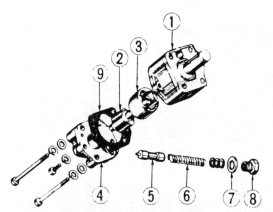

Fig. 1.10 Exploded view of oil pump (Sec 19)

1 Oil pump body	6 Regulator spring
2 Inner rotor and shaft	7 Washer
3 Outer rotor	8 Regulator cap
4 Oil pump cover	9 Cover gasket
5 Regulator valve	

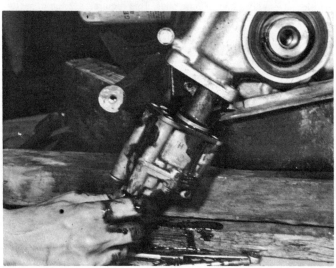

19.14 Removing oil pump

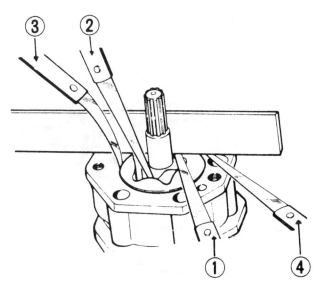

Fig. 1.11 Checking oil pump rotor clearances (Sec 19)

1 *Side clearance*
2 *Tip clearance*
3 *Outer rotor to body clearance*
4 *Rotor to bottom cover clearance*

21 Position the rotor and outer rotor in the pump body, and place the straight edge of a steel rule across the joint face of the pump. Measure the gap between the bottom of the straight edge and the top of the rotor and outer rotor.
22 Measure the clearances between the peaks of the lobes and peaks of the outer rotor with feeler gauges.
23 Measure the clearances between the outer rotor and the pump body.
24 Compare the results obtained with those given in the specifications at the beginning of this Chapter. If parts are worn the pump must be renewed as individual parts are not available.
25 Inspect the pressure relief valve for free-fitting in the bore, and for score marks in both the bore and valve plunger.
26 Reassembly of the pump is the reverse sequence to dismantling. Always use a new joint washer between the end cover and main body.
27 Refitting the oil pump is the reverse sequence to removal. The following additional points should be noted:

(a) *Make sure that the TDC marks are still in alignment at the crankshaft pulley and timing cover pointer.*
(b) *Smear a little jointing compound on either side of a new pump gasket. Make sure the mating surfaces are clean.*
(c) *Do not forget to refill the sump with oil and then check for oil leaks*

20 Engine sump - removal and refitting

1 Refer to Chapter 2, Section 2 and drain the cooling system.
2 Slacken the clips at either end of the top and bottom hoses and carefully disconnect these hoses. Also disconnect the heater hoses.
3 Disconnect the fuel inlet pipe from the fuel pump. Tape the end to stop dirt ingress.
4 Disconnect the throttle linkage from the carburettor.
5 *Automatic transmission:* Wipe the area around the torque converter cooling pipes at the lower radiator tank and then disconnect the pipes. Plug the ends to prevent entry of dirt or loss of transmission fluid.
6 Undo and remove the nuts and washers that secure the downpipe to the exhaust manifold flange. Detach the downpipe from the manifold.
7 Jack up the front and rear of the car and support on firmly based axle-stands. Alternatively position the car over a pit.
8 Place a container of at least 8 Imp pints under the engine sump

drain plug. Remove the drain plug and allow the oil to drain out. Refit the drain plug.
9 Remove the cover plate from the front of the clutch housing (manual gearbox) or torque converter housing (automatic transmission).
10 Refer to Chapter 11 and disconnect the steering connecting rod at the idler arm and steering box. Lower the linkage so that it is away from the vicinity of the sump.
11 Undo and remove the screws securing the engine front splash shield and lift away the shield.
12 Place a piece of wood on the saddle of a jack and support the weight of the engine.
13 Undo and remove the bolts that secure the front engine mountings to the front crossmember.
14 Jack up the front of the engine and position two pieces of wood between the engine mountings and front crossmember. Carefully lower the jack until the weight of the engine is on the blocks.
15 Undo and remove the bolts and washers securing the sump to the underside of the cylinder block and timing cover.
16 The sump may now be removed from the engine. If difficulty is experienced the engine must be raised. Recover the sump gasket.
17 Refitting the sump is the reverse sequence to removal. Remove all traces of old jointing compounds from the mating faces and always use a new gasket. Do not forget to refill the sump with oil.

21 Oil suction pipe and strainer - removal and refitting

1 The suction pipe and strainer can be removed from the underside of the cylinder block once the sump has been removed as described in Section 20.
2 Undo and remove the two bolts and spring washers that secure the flange to the cylinder block.
3 Carefully remove the pipe and strainer assembly. Recover the gasket.
4 Refitting the suction pipe and strainer is the reverse sequence to removal. Always use a new gasket to prevent air being drawn in at the joint.

22 Timing chain, tensioner and sprockets - removal and inspection

1 It is possible to remove the timing chain , tensioner and sprockets with the engine in the car although it should be appreciated that the working space will be a little restricted.
2 Refer to Chapter 2, Section 2 and drain the cooling system.
3 Slacken the top and bottom hose securing clips and detach the two hoses.
4 Refer to Chapter 2, Section 5 and remove the radiator.
5 Release the alternator mounting bolts, push the alternator towards the engine and lift away the fan belt. The alternator adjustment bracket should next be removed.
6 Undo and remove the four bolts that secure the fan and fan pulley to the water pump spindle. Lift away the fan and pulley.
7 Slacken the clips and detach the rocker cover to air cleaner ventilation hose and the thermostatic air bleed hose.
8 Make a note of the electrical connections to the air cleaner temperature sensor unit and detach these.
9 Undo and remove the two bolts which hold the air cleaner mounting bracket to the inlet manifold.
10 Undo the wing nut located at the top of the air cleaner and lift away the complete assembly.
11 Detach the HT leads at the spark plugs.
12 Disconnect the HT lead from the centre of the ignition coil. Release the distributor cap retaining clips and lift away the cap and HT leads.
13 Undo and remove the six bolts and spring washers securing the rocker cover. Lift away the rocker cover and gasket. The gasket should be renewed upon reassembly.
14 It will now be necessary to raise the front of the car or position the car on a ramp or over a pit. If jacking up the car, apply the handbrake, chock the rear wheels, jack up the front of the car and support on firmly based stands.
15 Place a container of at least 8 Imp pints under the engine sump drain plug. Remove the drain plug and allow the oil to drain out. Refit

the drain plug.

16 Refer to Section 20 and remove the sump as described in paragraph 9 onward.

17 Refer to Section 19 and remove the oil pump as described in paragraphs 2 and 3, 6 to 9 and 12 to 14.

18 Detach the inlet and outlet hoses from the fuel pump, Undo and remove the two securing nuts and spring washers and lift away the fuel pump.

19 Recheck the TDC mark on the crankshaft pulley is aligned with the pointer on the engine timing cover.

20 Undo and remove the crankshaft pulley securing bolt and washer and with a suitable universal puller draw the pulley from the crankshaft.

21 Undo and remove the five bolts and washers that secure the water pump to the front cover. Lift away the water pump and its gasket. A new gasket will be required on reassembly.

22 Locate then undo and remove the two bolts which secure the water pump protruding front portion of the cylinder head to the front cover.

23 Now undo and remove the remaining bolts that secure the front cover to the engine. Carefully tap the cover from its locating dowels in the cylinder block and lift away with extreme caution. This is because the gasket is also part of the cylinder head gasket. If necessary release any sticking areas with a sharp knife.

24 The oil slinger and worm drive gear may now be removed from the end of the crankshaft. Note which way round these two parts are fitted.

25 Before proceeding further inspect the timing chain and sprockets for correct markings. The two sprockets should be marked and these marks aligned with the O-marks on the timing chain links. Count the number of links between the O-marks - there should be 42.

26 Lock the camshaft sprocket with a metal bar and then unscrew the camshaft sprocket securing bolt. Lift away the bolt and fuel pump operating cam.

27 Inspect the camshaft sprocket and it will be seen that there are three timing marks on the outer radius. These marks are identified by the numbers 1,2 and 3 and corresponding numbers are stamped on the sprocket boss opposite the three camshaft dowel locating holes. These marks and additional dowel locating holes are used to compensate for chain stretch.

28 To check for stretch inspect the camshaft thrust plate located behind the camshaft sprocket, and find the small indent. The rear boss of the camshaft sprocket is also marked with three notches and one of the notches will be adjacent to the elongated indent depending on what timing mark (number 1, 2 or 3) on the sprocket outer periphery is aligned with the O-mark on the timing chain.

29 If the number 1 timing mark on the sprocket outer radius is aligned with the O-mark on the timing chain when the engine was dismantled, this indicates that the chain has not yet been adjusted.

30 Check once again that the engine is still set at the TDC position and then compare the alignment of the elongated indent on the camshaft thrust plate with the notch on the sprocket rear boss.

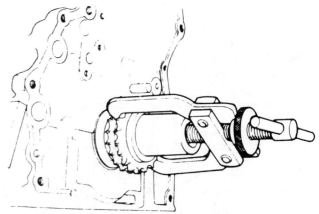

Fig. 1.12 Removing the crankshaft sprocket (Sec 22)

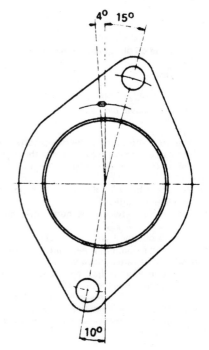

Fig. 1.13 Camshaft thrust plate (Sec 22)

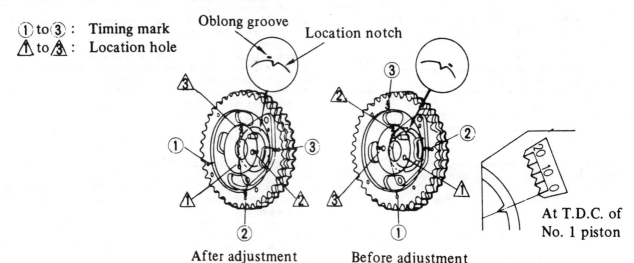

① to ③ : **Timing mark**

⚠ to ⚠ : **Location hole**

Oblong groove

Location notch

After adjustment   Before adjustment

At T.D.C. of No. 1 piston

Fig. 1.14 Camshaft sprocket location (Sec 22)

31 Should the notch on the sprocket rear boss be offset to the left-hand end (when looking from front of engine) of the elongated indent in the thrust plate, then it is an indication that the chain has stretched and will need adjusting.

32 The camshaft sprocket should be removed and repositioned so that the number 2 timing mark on the sprocket outer periphery is aligned with the O-mark on the timing chain link. The number 2 location hole in the camshaft boss should be engaged with the dowel in the camshaft.

33 Check for chain stretch again. Should the number 2 notch on the sprocket rear boss be to the left-hand end of the elongated indentation on the camshaft thrust plate, it will be necessary to remove and reposition the sprocket and check for stretch in the number 3 timing mark and number 3 location hole position.

34 Should the number 3 notch be beyond the left-hand side of the elongated indentation, then it is indicative that the chain has stretched and must be renewed.

35 Undo and remove the two bolts and plain washers and remove the timing chain tensioner assembly and gasket from the front face of the crankcase.

36 Undo and remove the four bolts and two plain washers that secure the two timing chain guides at either side of the timing chain.

37 Carefully ease the sprocket from the end of the camshaft and disengage the chain from the crankshaft sprocket. Remove the camshaft sprocket and chain from the engine.

38 Using a universal puller carefully draw the sprocket from the end of the crankshaft.

39 Thoroughly wash all components and wipe dry with a clean non-fluffy rag.

40 Carefully inspect the sprockets for wear on the teeth, and the timing chain for roller wear.

41 Inspect the two neoprene chain guides for wear or deep grooving. If evident they must be renewed.

42 The spring loaded tensioner should be dismantled and checked to ensure that the plunger is free in its bore. Inspect the spring to check that it has not distorted and the slipper head for wear or grooving.

43 Inspect the crankshaft pulley seal boss for grooving, should this be evident, the pulley will have to be renewed.

44 At this stage it is recommended that the front cover seal be removed and a new one fitted. To remove the old one and fit a new one use a drift of suitable diameter.

23 Pistons, connecting rods and bearings - removal

1 To remove the pistons and connecting rods, it is preferable that the engine be removed from the car and then the sump and cylinder head removed first as already described.

2 Should circumstances be that it is desired to keep the engine in the car, the following operations must be carried out first.

(a) Drain cooling system and engine oil
(b) Remove cylinder head.
(c) Remove engine sump and oil strainer.
(d) Remove front cover and timing chain.

3 It is possible to make a preliminary examination of the state of the pistons relative to the bores with the engine in the car after removal of the cylinder head, so bear this in mind where the inspection details are given in the next section.

4 Each connecting rod, bearing cap and piston is matched to each other and the cylinder, and must be refitted in the same position. Before removing anything mark each connecting rod near the cap with a light punch mark to indicate which cylinder it came from. There is usually a maker's number on the rod and cap so there should be no need to worry about mixing them up. If no numbers are apparent, then mark the cap as well.

5 It is also important to ensure that the connecting rods and pistons go back on the crankshaft the correct way round. The best way to record this is by noting which side of the engine block the marks you have made, or the existing numbers, face. Provided the pistons are not being renewed then they can be arrowed with chalk on the crown pointing to the front but if they are separated from the connecting rods you will still want to know which way round the rods go.

6 Having made quite sure that the positions are clear undo and remove the connecting rod cap securing nuts.

7 Carefully remove the bearing caps and shells and push the connecting rods and pistons through the top of the cylinder block (photo).

8 The shell bearings may be slid round to remove them from the connecting rods and caps.

9 To separate the pistons from the connecting rods a considerable pressure is needed to free the pins from the small ends. This is not possible with anything other than a proper press. Attempts with other methods will probably result in bent connecting rods or broken pistons. If new pistons are needed anyway it will need an experienced man to heat the connecting rods to fit the new gudgeon pins, so the same man may well take the old ones off. Leave this to the local Datsun dealer.

24 Pistons, piston rings and cylinder bores - inspection and renovation

1 Examine the pistons for signs of damage on the crown and around the top edge. If any of the piston rings have broken there could be quite noticeable damage to the grooves, in which case the piston must be renewed. Deep scores in the piston walls also call for renewal. If the cylinders are being rebored new oversize pistons and rings will be needed anyway. If the cylinders do not need reboring and the pistons are in good condition, only the rings need to be checked.

2 Unless new rings are to be fitted for certain, care has to be taken that rings are not broken on removal. Starting with the top ring first (all rings must be removed from the top of the piston) ease one end out of its groove and place a thin piece of metal behind it. Then move the metal strip carefully behind the ring, at the same time easing the ring upward so that it rests on the surface of the piston above until the whole ring is clear and can be slid off. With the second and third rings which must also come off the top, arrange the strip of metal to carry them over the other grooves. Note where each ring has come from (pierce a piece of paper with each ring showing 'top 1'.'middle 1' etc).

3 To check the existing rings, place them in the cylinder bore and press each down in turn to the bottom of the stroke. In this case a distance of 2½ inches (73 mm) from the top of the cylinder will be

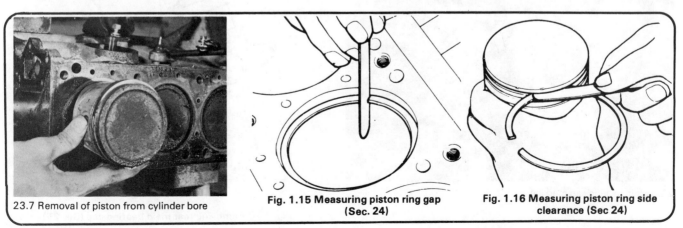

23.7 Removal of piston from cylinder bore

Fig. 1.15 Measuring piston ring gap (Sec. 24)

Fig. 1.16 Measuring piston ring side clearance (Sec 24)

satisfactory. Use an inverted piston to press them down square. With a feeler gauge measure the gap for each ring which should be as given in the specifications at the beginning of this Chapter. If the gap is too large, the rings will need renewal (Fig. 1.15).

4   Check that each ring gives a clearance in the piston groove according to specifications. If the gap is too great, new pistons and rings will be required if Datsun spares are used. However, independent specialist producers of pistons and rings can normally provide the rings required separately. If new Datsun pistons and rings are obtained it may be necessary to have the ridge ground away from the top of each cylinder bore. If specialist oil control rings are being obtained from an independent supplier the ridge removal will not be necessary as the top rings will be stepped to provide the necessary clearance. If the top ring, of a new set, is not stepped, it may hit the ridge made by the former ring and break (Fig. 1.16).

5   If new pistons are obtained the rings will be included, so it must be emphasised that the top ring may need to be stepped if fitted to an un-reground bore (or un-deridged bore).

6   The new rings should be placed in the bores and the gap checked on an un-reground bore. Check the gap above the line of the ridge. Any gaps which are too small should be increased by filing one end of the ring with a fine file. Be careful not to break the ring as they are brittle (and expensive). On no account make the gap less than specification. If the gap should close when under normal operating temperatures the ring will break.

7   The groove clearance of new rings in old pistons should be within the specified tolerances. If it is not enough, the rings could stick in the piston grooves, causing loss of compression. The piston grooves in this case will need machining out to accept the new rings.

8   Before putting new rings onto an old piston clean out the grooves with a piece of old broken ring.

9   Refit the new rings with care, in the same order as the old ones were removed. Note that some special oil control rings are supplied in three separate pieces. The cylinder bores must be checked for ovality, scoring, scratching and pitting. Starting at the top, look for a ridge where the top piston ring reaches the limit of its upward travel. The depth of this ridge will give a good indication of the degree of wear and can be checked with the engine in the car and the cylinder head removed.

10 Measure the bore diameter across the block and just below any ridge. This can be done with an internal micrometer or a vernier gauge. Compare this with the diameter of the bottom of the bore, which is not subject to wear. If no micrometer or measuring instruments are available, use a piston from which the rings have been removed and measure the gap between it and the cylinder wall with a feeler gauge.

11 If the difference in bore diameters at top and bottom is 0.010 inch (0.254 mm) or more, then the cylinders need reboring. If less than 0.010 inch (0.254 mm), then the fitting of new and special rings to the pistons can cure the defect.

25 Crankshaft - removal, inspection and renovation

1   With the engine removed from the car, the following parts should be removed as previously described:

    (a) Sump and oil pick-up pipe and screen.
    (b) Front cover
    (c) Timing sprockets and timing chain
    (d) Flywheel or adaptor plate (automatic transmission)

2   If the cylinder head is also removed so much the better as the engine can be stood firmly in an inverted position.

3   Remove the connecting rod bearing caps. This will already have been done if the pistons are removed.

4   Using a good quality socket wrench remove the two cap bolts from each of the five bearing caps.

5   Lift off each cap carefully. Each one should be marked with the bearing number. Note the raised arrow to show which way round the cap is fitted (photo).

6   The rear bearing cap will be tight and for removal it will be necessary to make up a puller. The official tool for this is shown in Fig 1.17.

7   The bearing cap shells will probably come off with the caps, in which case they can be removed by pushing them round from the end opposite the notch and lifting them out.

8   Note that the centre main bearing inserts have flanges on either side to take up endfloat of the crankshaft.

9   Grip the crankshaft firmly at each end and lift it out. Put it somewhere safe where it cannot fall. Remove the shell bearings from the inner housings.

10 Examine all the crankpins and main bearing journals for signs of scoring or scratching. If all surfaces are undamaged next check that all the bearing journals are round. This can be done with a micrometer or vernier, taking readings across the diameter at 6 or 7 points for each journal. If you do not own or know how to use one of these instruments, take the crankshaft to your local engineering works and request that they make a check for you.

11 If the crankshaft is ridged or scored it must be reground. If the ovality exceeds 0.002 inch (0.05 mm) on measurement, but there are no signs of scoring or scratching on the surfaces, regrinding may still be necessary. It would be advisable to ask the advice of the local engineering works to whom you entrust the work of regrinding in such instances.

12 Inspect the pilot bush in the end of the crankshaft and, if it is worn, it must be renewed. Remove the old bush, using a tap of suitable diameter and levering out or use a good fitting drift and grease to hydraulically drive it out.

13 Fit a new bush, using a stepped drift, so that it protrudes 0.177 to 0.197 in ((4.5 to 5.0 mm). Do not oil the bush.

25.5 Main bearing cap marking

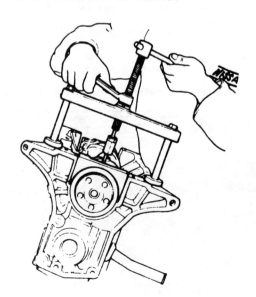

Fig. 1.17 Removing rear main bearing cap (Sec 25)

26 Main and big-end bearing shells - inspection and renewal

1   Big-end bearing failure is normally indicated by a pronounced knocking from the crankcase and a slight drop in oil pressure. Main bearing failure is normally accompanied by vibration, which can be quite severe at high engine speeds, and a more significant drop in oil pressure.

2   The shell bearing surfaces should be matt grey in colour with no sign of pitting or scoring. If they are obviously in bad condition it is essential to examine the crankshaft before fitting new ones.

3   Replacement shell bearings are supplied in a series of thicknesses dependent on the degree of regrinding that the crankshaft requires, which is done in multiples of 0.010 inch (0.250 mm). The engineering works regrinding the crankshaft will normally supply the correct shells with the reground crank.

4   If an engine is removed for overhaul regularly, it is worthwhile renewing big-end bearings every 30 000 miles (50 000 km) as a matter of course and main bearings every 50 000 miles (80 000 km). This will add many thousands of miles to the life of the engine before any regrinding of crankshaft is necessary. Make sure that bearing shells renewed are to standard dimensions, if the crankshaft has not been reground.

5   It is very important, if in doubt, to take the old bearing shells along if you want replacements of the same size. Some original crankshafts are 0.010 inch (0.250 mm) undersize on journals or crankpins and the appropriate bearings must be used. If dismantling a later model engine it may be found that completely plain main bearing shells are used which have no oil groove in the bearing face. Also, in order to improve engine performance, the connecting rod and main bearing shells have been modified in thickness allowance or standard thickness.

27 Lubrication system - general description

Oil is drawn from the engine sump through an oil strainer by a trochoid type oil pump. This is driven by a spindle which in turn is driven from the crankshaft. The upper end of the spindle drives the distributor. Oil is passed under pressure through a renewable canister type oil filter and onto the main oil gallery. It is then distributed to all the crankshaft bearings, chain tensioner and timing chain. The oil that is supplied to the crankshaft is fed to the connecting rod big-end bearings via drilled passages in the crankshaft. The connecting rod little ends and underside cylinder walls are lubricated from jets of oil issuing from little holes in the connecting rods.

Oil from the centre of the main gallery passes up to a further gallery in the cylinder head. This distributes oil to the valve mechanism and to the top of the timing chain. Drillings pass oil from the gallery to the camshaft bearings. Oil that is supplied to number 2 and 3 camshaft bearings is passed to the rocker arm, valve and cam lobe by two drillings inside the camshaft and small drillings in the cam base circle of each cam.

The oil pressure relief valve is located in the oil pump cover and is designed to control the pressure in the system to a maximum of 80 lbf/in^2 (5.6 kgf/cm^2).

28 Engine reassembly - general

To ensure maximum life with minimum trouble from a rebuilt engine, not only must everything be correctly assembled, but everything must be spotlessly clean; all the oilways must be clear, locking washers and spring washers must always be fitted where indicated and all bearings and other working surfaces must be thoroughly lubricated during assembly.

Before assembly begins renew any bolts or studs, the threads of which are in any way damaged, and whenever possible use new spring washers.

Apart from your normal tools, a supply of clean rag, an oil can filled with engine oil (an empty plastic detergent bottle thoroughly washed out and cleaned, will invariably do just as well), a new supply of assorted spring washers, a set of new gaskets, and a torque spanner should be collected together.

Sit down with a pencil and paper and list all those items which you intend to renew and acquire all of them before reassembly. If you have had experience of shopping around for parts you will appreciate that they cannot be obtained quickly. Do not underestimate the cost either; spare parts are relatively much more expensive now.

29 Crankshaft - refitting

1   Ensure the crankcase is thoroughly clean and that all the oilways are clear. A thin drill is useful for cleaning them out. If possible, blow them out with compressed air. Treat the crankshaft in the same fashion and then inject engine oil into the crankshaft oilways.

2   Install the main bearing shells by fitting the five upper halves of the main bearing shells to their location in the crankcase, after wiping the location clean. The centre bearing is the location for the flanged bearing shell (photo).

3   Note that on the back of each bearing is a tab which engages in locating grooves in either the crankcase or the main bearing cap housings.

4   New bearings are coated with protective grease; carefully clean away all traces of this with paraffin.

5   With the five upper bearing shells securely in place, wipe the lower bearing cap housings and fit the five lower shell bearings to their caps.

6   Generously lubricate the crankshaft journals, and the upper and lower main bearing shells, and carefully lower the crankshaft into position. Make sure it is the right way round (photos).

7   Fit the main bearing caps into position ensuring that the arrows are facing forward and are correctly located as indicated by the numbers noted or made during removal. The rear bearing cap location must be coated with a sealer (photos)

8   Refit the bearing cap securing bolts and tighten in a progressive manner to the final torque wrench setting which is given in the Specifications.

9   Test the crankshaft to ensure that it rotates freely. Should it be very stiff to turn, or possess high spots, a most careful inspection must be made, preferably by a skilled mechanic with a micrometer to trace the cause of the trouble. It is seldom that any trouble of this nature will be experienced when fitting the crankshaft.

29.2 The centre main bearing has a flanged shell bearing

29.6a Lubricating main bearings

29.6b Lowering crankshaft into position

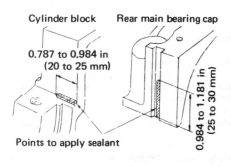

Fig. 1.18 Application of sealant (rear main bearing cap and cylinder block) (Sec 29)

Cylinder block   Rear main bearing cap

0.787 to 0.984 in
(20 to 25 mm)

0.984 to 1.181 in
(25 to 30 mm)

Points to apply sealant

29.7a Applying sealant to rear main bearing cap location

29.7b Fitting rear main bearing cap

29.8a Align rear main bearing cap with a straight edge ...

29.8b ... and fit the securing bolts

29.10 Checking crankshaft endfloat

29.11 Drifting rear oil seal into position

29.13 Fitting new side seals

10 The endfloat of the crankshaft may be checked. Using a screwdriver as a lever at one of the crankshaft webs and main bearing caps, move the crankshaft longitudinally as far as possible in one direction. Measure the gap between the side of the journal and the centre bearing flange. The thrust clearance should be 0.002 - 0.006 inch (0.05 - 0.15 mm) (photo).

11 Lubricate the rear oil seal and carefully refit the crankshaft rear flange into the rear main bearing cap and crankcase. A tubular drift of suitable diameter must be used for this (photo).

12 If during inspection it was noted that the crankshaft rear flange showed evidence of grooving where the original seal had previously run, it is permissible to fit a shim betweeen the seal and crankcase. This will allow the seal lip to operate on an unworn portion of the crankshaft.

13 Carefully tap new side seals down between the rear main bearing and crankcase (photo).

30 Piston and connecting rod - reassembly

1   If the same pistons are being used, then they must be mated to

the same connecting rod with the same gudgeon pin. If new pistons are being fitted it does not matter with which connecting rod they are used, but the gudgeon pin must be kept matched to its piston.

2   Upon reference to Section 23 it will be seen that special equipment, including a large press, is required to fit the piston to the connecting rod. This is a job for the local Datsun dealer. The notch mark on the piston crown must face towards the front of the engine when fitted and the oil jet hole in the connecting rod must face to the right-hand side of the engine.

3   Check that the piston pivots freely on the gudgeon pin and that it is free to slide sideways.

31 Piston rings - refitting

1   Check that the piston ring grooves and oilways are thoroughly clean and unblocked. Piston rings must always be fitted over the head of the piston and never from the bottom.

2   The easiest method to use when fitting rings is to wrap a long 0.002 inch feeler gauge round the top of the piston and place the rings, one at a time, starting from the bottom oil control ring.

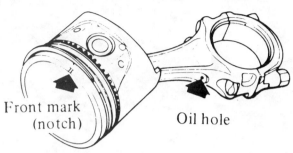

Fig. 1.19 Assembling piston and connecting rod (Sec 31)

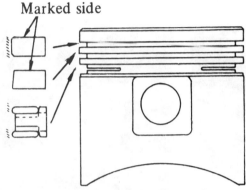

Fig. 1.20 Fitting piston rings (Sec 31)

3   Where a three-part oil control ring is fitted, fit the bottom rail of the oil control ring to the piston and position it below the bottom groove. Refit the oil control expander into the bottom groove and move the bottom oil control ring rail up into the bottom groove. Fit the top oil control rail into the bottom groove.
4   Ensure that the ends of the expander are butting, but not overlapping. Set the gaps of the rails and expander at 90° to each other.
5   Where a one-piece oil control ring is used fit this to the bottom groove. It can be fitted either way up.
6   Refit the lower and upper compression rings making sure that they are fitted the correct way up as marked on the top face.
7   Measure the ring to groove gap and the end gap to ensure that they are within specifications.

32 Piston and connecting rod assembly - refitting

The pistons complete with connecting rods can be fitted to the cylinder bores in the following sequence.
1   With a wad of clean non-fluffy rag wipe the cylinder bores clean.
2   The pistons, complete with connecting rods, are fitted to their bores from above.
3   Set the piston ring gaps so that the gaps are equidistant around the circumference of the piston.

4   Heavily lubricate the top of the piston and fit a ring compressor or a jubilee clip of suitable diameter (photo).
5   As each piston is inserted into its bore ensure that it is the correct piston/connecting rod assembly for that particular bore, that the connecting rod is the right way round, and that the front of the piston is toward the front of the bore. Lubricate the bore and piston well with engine oil.
6   The piston will slide into the bore only as far as the ring compressor. Gently tap the piston into the bore with a wooden or plastic hammer (photo).
7   Wipe clean the connecting rod half of the big-end bearing cap and the underside of the shell bearing, and fit the shell bearing in position with its locating tongue engaged with the corresponding groove in the connecting rod.
8   Never reuse old bearing shells.
9   Generously lubricate the crankpin journals with engine oil and turn the crankshaft so that the crankpin is in the most advantageous position for the connecting rod to be drawn onto it (photo).
10 Wipe clean the connecting rod bearing cap and back of the shell bearing and fit the shell bearing in position ensuring that the locating tongue at the back of the bearing engages with the locating groove in the connecting rod cap.
11 Generously lubricate the shell bearing and offer up the connecting rod cap to the connecting rod (photo).
12 Check that the big-end bolts are correctly located and then refit the cap retaining nuts. These should be tightened to a torque wrench setting of 33-40 lbf ft (4.5-5.5 kgf m).
13 Repeat the above described procedures for the three remaining piston/connecting rod assemblies.

33 Valves and valve springs - refitting

1   Rest the cylinder head on its side and insert each valve into its own guide. Refit the outer spring seat, inner spring seat inner and outer valve springs, oil seals and spring retainer (photos).
2   Fit the spring compressor with the base of the tool on the valve head and compress the valve springs until the collars can be slipped in place in the collar grooves in the valve stem (photo).
3   Gently release the valve spring and tap the valve stem end with a hammer to ensure that all parts are seated correctly.
4   Repeat this procedure until all eight valves and valve springs are fitted.

34 Cylinder head - refitting

1   After checking that both the cylinder block and cylinder head mating faces are perfectly clean, generously lubricate each cylinder bore with engine oil.
2   Always use a new cylinder head gasket as the old gasket will be compressed and not capable of giving a good seal. Never smear grease on either side of a gasket for when the engine heats up, the grease will melt and could allow pressure leaks to develop. Make sure the two locating dowels are in position.
3   Fit a new cylinder head gasket in position and carefully lower the cylinder head onto the cylinder block (photo).

32.4 Lubricating the piston rings

32.6 Fitting the piston and connecting rod assembly

32.9 Lubricate the crankpin journals

32.11 Fitting big end cap

33.1a Inserting valve into guide

33.1b Sliding on oil seal

33.1c Fitting inner and outer spring seats

33.1d Fitting valve springs and retainer

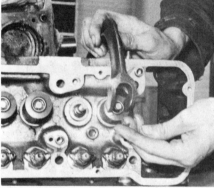
33.2 Inserting collars into groove in valve stem

34.3 Fitting the cylinder head

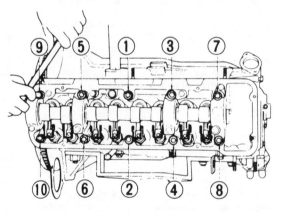
Fig. 1.21 Tightening sequence of cylinder head bolts (Sec 34)

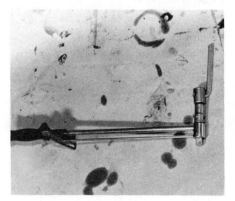
34.5 Using Allen key and socket set parts for tightening cylinder head bolts

35.3 Fitting camshaft thrust plate

36.1 Fitting crankshaft sprocket

4   Fit the cylinder head bolts and tighten finger-tight.
5   When all are in position tighten in a progressive manner to a final torque of 47-61 lbf ft (6.5-8.5 kgf m) in the sequence shown in Fig. 1.20. Where an Allen key is required fit it to a socket and T-bar adaptor from a socket set (photo).

35 Camshaft - refitting

1   Wipe the camshaft journals and bearings with a clean non-fluffy rag and then lubricate with engine oil.
2   Carefully insert the camshaft into the camshaft bearings making sure the sharp lobes do not damage the bearing surfaces.
3   Refit the camshaft thrust plate and secure with the two retaining screws (photo).

36 Timing chain, tensioner and sprocket - refitting

1   Fit the woodruff key to the crankshaft nose and then with a tubular drift of suitable diameter drive the crankshaft sprocket onto the crankshaft until the sprocket abuts the shoulder of the front main bearing journal. Make quite sure that the timing mark on the sprocket is facing outward (photo).
2   Offer up the timing chain to the crankshaft sprockets so that the lower timing O-mark on the chain is aligned with the mark on the crankshaft sprocket (photos).
3   Next engage the camshaft sprocket onto the upper part of the chain aligning the timing O-mark on the chain with the numbered timing mark on the periphery of the sprocket (photo).
4   Should a new timing chain be fitted, align the number 1 timing mark on the sprocket with the O-mark on the chain. When a used but serviceable timing chain is being refitted, align the mark 1,2 or 3, whichever is found most suitable for the degree of chain stretch (Section 22).
5   Refit the camshaft sprocket to the front of the camshaft, engaging the dowel on the camshaft with the applicable numbered hole in the

camshaft boss (photo).
6   Refit the fuel pump actuating cam and sprocket securing bolt and then tighten the latter to a torque of 87-116 lbf ft (12-16 kgf m)(photo).
7   Refit the timing chain guides and secure with the bolts and washers. The left-hand guide mounting holes are elongated to allow the movement required for adjustment. Press the guide inwards until the chain is tight and then tighten these two bolts (photos).
8   Assemble the tensioner, if apart, and then refit to the front face of the crankcase. Always use a new gasket. Secure with the two bolts and spring washers (photo).
9   Refit the second woodruff key to the crankshaft nose and slide on the worm drive gear. Refit the oil slinger, fitting it the correct way round as noted during dismantling (photos).
10 Generously lubricate the timing chain, sprockets, tensioner slipper pad and chain guide.

37 Front cover, drive spindle and oil pump - refitting

1   Wipe the mating faces of the front cover and cylinder block.
2   Apply some sealer to both sides of a new front cover gasket. Offer up the gasket to the dowels on the cylinder block. Also apply some sealer to the top face of the front cover (photo).
3   Carefully refit the front cover and hand tighten the securing bolts and spring washers.
4   Using a feeler gauge measure the gap (if any) between the cylinder block upper face and front cover upper face. This difference must be less than 0.0059 in (0.15 mm).
5   Tighten the securing bolts to the following torque wrench settings:

Size M8 (0.315 in)
7.2 - 11.6 lbf ft (1.0 - 1.6 kgf m)
Size M6 (0.236 in)
2.9 - 5.8 lbf ft (0.4 - 0.8 kgf m)

6   Lubricate the crankshaft pulley hub with a little high melting point

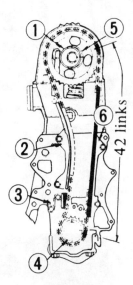

36.2a Fitting chain on crankshaft sprocket

36.2b Pulling chain up through front of cylinder head

**Fig. 1.22 Correct fitment of timing chain –
L16 and L18 engine shown (Sec 36)**

1   Fuel pump drive cam
2   Chain guide
3   Chain tensioner
4   Crank sprocket
5   Cam sprocket
6   Chain guide

NOTE: With the sprockets and chain correctly fitted, there should be 42 links between the timing marks on L16 and L18 engines, and 44 links on L20 engines

36.3 Chain engaged with camshaft sprocket

36.5 Sprocket fitted on camshaft

36.6 Tightening sprocket securing bolt

36.7a Fitting timing chain right-hand guide ...

36.7b ... and left-hand guide

36.8 Fitting timing chain tensioner

36.9a Fitting worm drive gear ...

36.9b ... and the oil slinger

37.2 Fitting the front cover

37.6 Tightening crankshaft pulley securing bolt

37.7 Inserting oil pump drive gear spindle

37.9 Fitting the oil pump

37.10 Fitting the fuel pump

37.11a Fitting the water pump ...

grease and slide on the crankshaft pulley. Secure the pulley with the bolt and washer and tighten to a torque wrench setting of 86.8 - 115.7 lbf ft (12 - 16 kgf m) (photo).

7 Align the TDC marks of the pulley and pointer with number 1 piston, on the compression stroke, and refit the oil pump and drive gear spindle to the front cover, not forgetting to use a new gasket. The offset dog on the gear spindle must be aligned with the pencil or crayon mark made on dismantling. The offset dog must face towards the front of the engine (photo).

8 If the mark is missing or new parts have been obtained, the dog must be set at the 11.25 o'clock position so that the smaller bow shape is toward the front of the engine.

9 Refit the four oil pump securing bolts and spring washers and tighten to a torque wrench setting of 8-10 lbf ft (1.1 - 1.5 kgf m) (photo).

10 Clean the mating faces of the fuel pump, spacer and front cover and refit the fuel pump. Do not forget to use new gaskets. Tighten the securing nuts and springwashers to a torque wrench setting of 8.7 - 13.0 lbf ft (1.2 - 1.8 kgf m) (photo).

11 At this stage of assembly the water inlet elbow, front engine lifting bracket and water pump may be refitted (photos)

38 Oil strainer and sump - refitting

1 Fit a new gasket to the oil strainer located in the crankcase and offer up the strainer assembly (photo).

2 Secure the pick-up pipe flange with the two bolts and spring washers.

3 Wipe the mating faces of the sump and crankcase and apply sealer to both sides of a new gasket.

4 Carefully fit the gasket to the crankcase and then offer up the sump (photo).

5 Refit bolts and spring washers that secure the sump and tighten in a diagonal and progressive manner to a final torque wrench setting of 4.3 - 6.5 lbf ft (0.6 - 0.9 kgf m).

39 Rocker arms and pivots - refitting

1 If the rocker pivot assemblies have been removed from the cylinder head these should be refitted to their original positions. Each assembly comprises a pivot, locknut, spring and seat.

2 Using a screwdriver compress the valve spring and insert the rocker arm. Make sure it is seating correctly and refit the small steady spring (photos).

3 Repeat the above sequence for each of the eight assemblies.

40 Valve clearances – adjustment

1 During routine servicing the valve clearances should be adjusted whilst the engine is **hot**. Remove the spark plug leads from the plugs, having identified their position. Slacken the clips and disconnect the hose to the air cleaner ventilation valve and thermostatic air bleed hose from the rocker cover.

2 Undo and remove the two bolts and spring washers that secure the air cleaner support bracket to the inlet manifold. Make a note of the electrical connections to the air cleaner temperature sensor unit and detach these.

3 Undo the wing nut at the top of the air cleaner and lift away the complete assembly. Undo and remove the six bolts and washers securing the rocker cover and gasket to the top of the cylinder head. Remove the rocker cover and gasket. Always use a new gasket on reassembly.

4 When rebuilding an engine after overhaul set the valve clearances to the specified value and recheck them having run the engine to normal working temperature.

5 Using a spanner on the crankshaft pulley bolt, rotate the crankshaft to bring No 1 piston to TDC on its compression stroke. This can be assessed by removing the spark plug from No 1 cylinder and placing a finger over the spark plug hole to feel the compression generated as the engine is turned. Alternatively, observe when both

37.11b ... and the water inlet elbow

38.1 Fitting the oil strainer ...

38.4 ... and then the oil sump

39.2a Fit the rocker arm ...

39.2b ... and then the small steady spring

40.9 Adjusting the valve clearance

the inlet and exhaust valves, for No 1 cylinder, are closed.
6   Adjustment of valves 1, 2, 3 and 5 may now be carried out. No 1 is at the timing chain end.
7   It should be noted that the clearances for inlet valves and exhaust valves are different. The order of the valves is as follows:

Exhaust – Inlet – Inlet – Exhaust – Exhaust – Inlet – Inlet – Exhaust

8   Using a feeler gauge of the specified thickness, measure the clearance between the cam lobe and the valve rocker. The gauge should be a sliding fit.
9   If the clearance is not as specified loosen the pivot locknut and turn the valve rocker pivot to provide the correct clearance (photo). See Fig. 1.4 to identify the parts.
10 When the correct setting has been obtained tighten the pivot lock nut and recheck the setting.
11 Having checked the four valve clearances mentioned in paragraph 3, rotate the crankshaft one complete revolution. The clearances for valves 4, 6, 7 and 8 can now be checked and, if necessary, adjusted.
12 Clean the rocker cover and cylinder head mating faces and, using a new gasket, refit the rocker cover, air cleaner with its hoses and electrical leads, spark plug leads and spark plugs.

41 Flywheel - refitting

1   This Section also applies where an adaptor plate is fitted instead of a flywheel when automatic transmission is used.
2   Fit the engine backplate, locating it on the dowels (photo).
3   Clean the mating faces of the crankshaft and flywheel (or adaptor plate).
4   Fit the flywheel (or adaptor plate) to the crankshaft and secure with the retaining bolts tightened to a torque of 101 - 116 lbf ft (14 - 16 kgf m) (photo).

42 Crankcase ventilation system - servicing

1   The closed type of crankcase ventilation system fitted to models covered by this manual draws air from the air cleaner and passes it through a mesh type flame trap to a hose connected to the rocker cover.
2   The air is then passed through the inside of the engine and back to the inlet manifold via a hose and regulating valve. This means that fumes in the crankcase are drawn into the combustion chamber, burnt and passed to the exhaust system.
3   When the car is being driven at full throttle conditions the inlet manifold depresssion is not sufficient to draw all fumes through the regulating valve and into the inlet manifold. Under these operating conditions the crankcase ventilation flow is reversed with the fumes drawing into the air cleaner instead of the inlet manifold.
4   To prevent engine oil being drawn into the inlet manifold a baffle plate and filter gauze pack is positioned in the crankcase.
5   Maintenance of the system simply involves inspection of the system and renewal of any suspect parts, Check the condition of the rocker cover to air cleaner hose and the crankcase to inlet manifold hose. Check for blockage, deterioration or collapse; should either be evident, new hoses should be fitted.
6   Inspect the seals on the engine oil filter cap and dipstick. If their condition has deteriorated renew the seals.
7   Operation of the ventilation regulation valve may be checked by running the engine at a steady idle speed and disconnecting the hose from the regulation valve. Listen for a hissing noise from the valve once the hose has been detached. Now place a finger over the inlet valve and a strong vacuum should be felt immediately as the finger is placed over the valve.
8   Should the valve prove to be inoperative it must be renewed as it is not practical to dismantle and clean it.
9   Other symtoms showing a faulty or inoperative valve are:

   (a) *Engine will not run smoothly at idle speed*
   (b) *Smoky exhaust*
   (c) *Engine idle speed rises and falls, but engine does not stop*
   (d) *Power loss at speeds above idle*

41.2 Positioning the engine backplate

41.4 Fitting the flywheel to the crankshaft

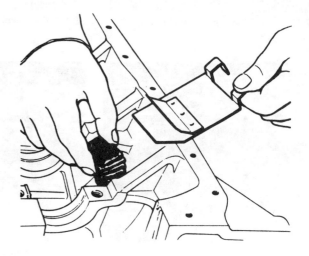
Fig. 1.23 Crankcase ventilation system baffle plate and filter gauze

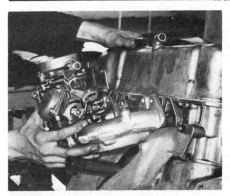

43a Fitting inlet manifold and carburettor assembly

43b Warm air deflector fitted on exhaust manifold

43c Fitting the water outlet and thermostat housing

43d Fitting the alternator ...

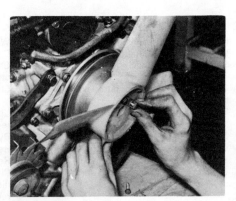

43e ... and the fan

43f Adjusting the fan belt tension

43 Engine ancillaries - refitting

With the basic engine completely assembled the ancillary equipment may now be refitted. The actual items will depend on whether the unit was stripped to the last nut and bolt. In all cases refitting of these parts is the reverse sequence to removal. Additional information will be found in the relevant Chapter or Section should this be found necessary (See photos).

44 Engine (and transmission) - refitting in car

1 Although the engine can be refitted by one man and suitable hoist, it is easier if two are present, one to control the hoist and the other to guide the unit into position so that it does not foul anything.
2 Generally speaking, refitting is a reversal of the procedure used when removing. Carefully lower the unit whilst an assistant guides it into position. Ensure that all loose leads, cables, etc are tucked out of the way. If not, it is easy to trap one and so cause additional work. When finally in position, refit or reconnect the following as applicable:

  (a) Mounting nuts, bolts and washers.
  (b) Reconnect engine to gearbox (or automatic transmission).
  (c) Speedometer drive cable.
  (d) Gear change lever (or selector mechanism).
  (e) Electrical connections to gearbox (or automatic transmission).
  (f) Clutch slave cylinder, check adjustment
  (g) Wires to oil pressure switch, temperature gauge thermal transmitter, ignition coil, distributor, alternator, air cleaner, emission system (as applicable)
  (h) Manifolds and carburettor, air cleaner
  (i) Propeller shaft and handbrake clamp
  (j) Exhaust system/down pipe to manifold
  (k) Starter motor and cables
  (l) Engine earth cable and battery
  (m) Heater and servo hoses
  (n) Vacuum advance and retard pipe
  (o) Distributor, cap and HT lead
  (p) Fuel pump and fuel pipes
  (q) Radiator and cooling system hoses
  (r) Bonnet and front grille

3 Check that the drain taps are closed and refill the cooling system with water. Full information will be found in Chapter 2.
4 Check the engine and transmission oil levels. Top-up or fill as necessary.

45 Engine - initial start-up after overhaul or major repair

1 Generally check all attachments to ensure that none have been forgotten during refitting.
2 Make sure that the battery is fully charged and that the oil, water and fuel are replenished.
3 If the fuel system has been dismantled it will require several revolutions of the engine on the starter motor to supply petrol to the carburettor.
4 As soon as the engine fires and runs, keep it going at a fast tickover only (not faster) and bring it up to normal working temperature.
5 As the engine warms up there will be odd smells and some smoke from parts getting hot and burning off oil deposits. The signs to look for are leaks of oil or water which will be obvious, if serious. Check also the connection of the exhaust downpipe to the manifolds as these do not always find their exact gas-tight position until the warmth and vibration having acted on them and it is almost certain that they will need tightening further. This should be done, of course, with the engine stopped.
6 When normal running temperature has been reached adjust the idling speed as described in Chapter 3.
7 Stop the engine and wait a few minutes to see if any lubricant or coolant is dripping out when the engine is stationary.
8 Road test the car to check that the timing is correct and giving the necessary smoothness and power. Do not race the engine - when new bearings and/or pistons and rings have been fitted, it should be run in at reduced revolutions for the first 500 miles (800 km).

46 Fault diagnosis – engine

Symptom	Reason/s	Remedy
Engine fails to turn over when starter button operated		
No current at starter motor	Flat or defective battery	Charge or renew battery. Push-start car (not automatics)
	Loose battery leads	Tighten both terminals and earth end of earth lead
	Defective starter solenoid or switch or broken wiring	Run a wire direct from the battery to the starter motor or by-pass the solenoid
	Engine earth strap disconnected	Check and retighten strap
Current at starter motor	Jammed starter motor drive pinion	Place car in gear and rock back and forward
	Defective starter motor	Remove and recondition
Engine turns over but will not start		
No spark at spark plug	Ignition damp or wet	Wipe dry the distributor cap and leads
	Ignition leads to spark plugs loose	Check and tighten at both ends
	Shorted or disconnected low tension leads	Check the wiring on the (-) and (+) terminals of the coil and to the distributor
	Dirty, incorrectly set, or pitted contact breaker points	Clean, file smooth, and adjust
	Faulty condenser	Check contact breaker points for arcing, renew if necessary
	Defective ignition switch	By-pass switch with wire
	Ignition leads connected wrong way round	Remove and refit in correct order
	Faulty coil	Remove and fit new coil
	Contact breaker point spring earthed or broken	Check spring is not touching metal part of distributor. Check insulator washers are correctly placed. Renew points if the spring is broken
No fuel at carburettor float chamber	No petrol in tank	Refill tank!
	Vapour lock in fuel line	Allow engine to cool, or apply a wet rag to the fuel line
	Blocked float chamber needle valve	Remove, clean and refit
	Fuel pump filter blocked	Remove, clean and refit
	Choked or blocked carburettor jets	Dismantle and clean
	Faulty fuel pump	Remove, overhaul, and refit
Excess of petrol in cylinder or carburettor flooding	Too much choke	Remove and dry spark plugs
	Float damaged or leaking or needle not seating	Remove, examine, clean and refit float and needle valve as necessary
	Float lever incorrectly adjusted	Remove and adjust correctly
Engine stalls and will not start		
No spark at spark plug	Ignition failure	See remedies under *Engine turns over*
No fuel at jets	No petrol in tank	Refill tank, check cap
	Sudden obstruction in carburettor	Check jets, filter, and needle valve in float chamber for blockage
Engine misfires or idles unevenly		
Intermittent sparking at spark plugs	Ignition leads loose	Check and tighten as necessary at spark plug and distributor cap ends
	Battery leads loose on terminals	Check and tighten terminal leads
	Battery earth strap loose on body attachment point	Check and tighten earth lead to body attachment point
	Engine earth lead loose	Tighten lead
	Low tension leads to terminals on coil loose	Check and tighten leads if found loose
	Low tension lead from coil to distributor loose	Check and tighten if found loose
	Dirty, or incorrectly gapped plugs	Remove, clean and regap.
	Dirty, incorrectly set, or pitted contact breaker points	Clean, file smooth, and adjust
	Tracking across inside of distributor cover	Remove and fit new cover
	Ignition too retarded	Check and adjust ignition timing
	Faulty coil	Remove and fit new coil

Symptom	Reason/s	Remedy

Engine misfires or idles unevenly (contd)

Symptom	Reason/s	Remedy
Fuel shortage at engine	Mixture too weak	Check jets, float chamber needle valve, and filters for obstruction. Clean. Carburettor incorrectly adjusted
	Air leak in carburettor	Remove and overhaul carburettor
	Air leak at inlet manifold to cylinder head	Test by pouring oil along joints. Bubbles, indicate leak. Renew manifold gasket
Mechanical wear	Incorrect valve clearances	Adjust to take up wear
	Burnt out exhaust valves	Renew defective valves
	Sticking or leaking valves	Renew valves as necessary
	Wear or broken valve springs	Check and renew as necessary
	Worn valve guides or stems	Renew valve guides and valves
	Worn pistons and piston rings	Dismantle engine, renew pistons and rings

Lack of power and poor compression

Symptom	Reason/s	Remedy
Fuel/air mixture leaking from cylinder	Burnt out exhaust valves	Remove cylinder head, renew defective valves
	Sticking or leaking valves	Renew valves as necessary
	Worn valve guides and stems	Renew valves and valve guides
	Weak or broken valve springs	Renew defective springs
	Blown cylinder head gasket	Remove cylinder head and fit new gasket
	Worn pistons and piston rings	Renew pistons and rings
	Worn or scored cylinder bores	Rebore, renew pistons and rings
Incorrect adjustments	Ignition timing wrongly set	Check and reset ignition timing
	Contact breaker points incorrectly gapped	Check and reset contact breaker points
	Incorrect valve clearances	Check valve clearances
	Incorrectly set spark plug gaps	Remove, clean and regap
	Carburation too rich or too weak	Tune carburettor for optimum performance
Carburation and ignition faults	Dirty contact breaker points	Remove, clean and replace
	Fuel filter blocked causing top end fuel starvation	Inspect, clean and refit all fuel filters
	Distributor automatic balance weights or vacuum advance and retard mechanisms not functioning correctly	Overhaul distributor, and check operation
	Faulty fuel pump	Remove

Excessive oil consumption

Symptom	Reason/s	Remedy
Oil being burnt by engine	Badly worn, perished or missing valve stem oil seals	Remove, fit new oil seals to valve stems
	Excessively worn valve stems and valve guides	Remove cylinder head and fit new valves and valve guides
	Worn piston rings	Fit oil control rings to existing pistons or purchase new pistons
	Worn pistons and cylinder bores	Fit new pistons and rings, rebore cylinders
	Excessive piston ring gap allowing blow-by	Fit new piston rings and set gap correctly
Oil being lost due to leaks	Leaking oil filter	Tighten or renew
	Leaking rocker cover gasket	Inspect and fit new gasket as necessary
	Leaking front cover gasket	Inspect and fit new gasket as necessary
	Leaking sump gasket and/or plug	Inspect gasket and plug

Chapter 2 Cooling system

Contents

Specifications

Type .... Pressurised system

Capacity (with heater)
160B/180B .... 1.43 gal (6.5 litre, 6.8 US qts)
610 .... 1.6 gal (7.4 litre, 7.8 US qts)

Thermostat .... Wax pellet
Location .... Top water outlet on cylinder head
Starts to open:
  Standard .... 82°C (180°F)
  Cold areas .... 88°C (190°F)
  Tropical areas .... 76.5°C (170°F)
Fully open:
  Standard .... 87°C (189°F)
  Cold areas .... 93°C (199°F)
  Tropical areas .... 81.5°C (179°F)
Maximum valve lift:
  Standard .... Above 0.315 in (8 mm) at 95°C (203°F)
  Cold areas .... Above 0.315 in (8 mm) at 100°C (212°F)
  Tropical areas .... Above 0.315 in (8 mm) at 90°C (194°F)

Radiator .... Corrugated fin
Automatic transmission .... Corrugated fin with integral oil cooler
Pressure cap opens .... 13 lbf/in² (0.91 kgf/cm²)
Test pressure .... 17 lbf/in² (1.2 kgf/cm²)

Fan belt tension .... 0.3 – 0.5 in (8 – 12 mm) deflection between alternator and fan pulleys

Water pump .... Rotary impeller
Drive .... V-belt from crankshaft

1 General description

The engine cooling water is circulated by a thermo-syphon, water pump assisted system. The coolant is pressurised to prevent primarily premature boiling in adverse conditions and to allow the engine to operate at its most efficient running temperature; this being just under the boiling point of water.

The radiator cap is set to a pressure of 13 lbf/in² (0.9 kgf/cm²) which increases the boiling point of the coolant to 230°F. If the water temperature exceeds this figure and the water boils, the pressure in the system forces the internal valve of the cap off its seat thus exposing the overflow pipe down which the steam from the boiling water escapes and so relieves the pressure. It is therefore important that the radiator cap is in good condition and that the spring behind the sealing washers has not weakened. Check that the rubber seal has not perished, and its seating in the neck is clean, to ensure a good seal.

The cooling system comprises the radiator top and bottom hoses, heater hoses, the centrifugal vane water pump (incorporated in the engine front cover, it carries the fan blades and is driven by the fan belt) and, the thermostat.

The system functions as follows: Cold water from the radiator circulates up the lower radiator hose to the water pump where it is pushed round the water passages in the cylinder block, helping to keep the cylinder bores and pistons cool.

The water then travels up into the cylinder head and circulates round the combustion spaces and valve seats absorbing more heat. Then, when the engine is at its normal operating temperature, the water travels out of the cylinder head, past the now open thermostat into the upper radiator hose and so into the radiator. The water passes down the radiator where it is rapidly cooled by the rush of cold air through the vertical radiator core. The water now cool reaches the bottom hose when the cycle is repeated.

When the engine is cold the thermostat (a valve which opens and

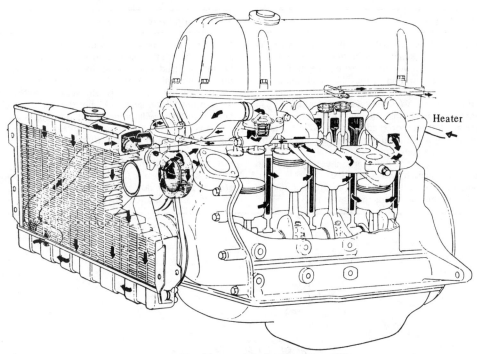

Fig. 2.1 Cooling system showing direction of flow

closes according to water temperature), maintains the circulation of the same water in the engine by returning it via the by-pass to the cylinder block water jacket. Only when the correct minimum operating temperature has been reached, as shown in the specifications, does the thermostat begin to open thus allowing water to return to the radiator.

On some models a torque coupling is fitted to the water pump to keep the fan speed at 2500 rpm or below. It also helps to reduce fan noise. On models with air conditioning the coupling keeps the fan speed at 1800 rpm or below.

If an automatic transmission is fitted, the hydraulic fluid is cooled by a heat exchanger inserted in the lower compartment of a modified radiator.

2   Cooling system – draining

1   With the car on level ground and the cooling system cold remove the radiator cap by turning anti-clockwise. If the engine is hot, then turn the filler cap very slightly until pressure in the system has had time to be released. Use a rag over the cap to protect your hand from escaping steam. If with the engine very hot the cap is released suddenly, the drop in pressure can result in the water boiling. With the pressure released, the cap can be removed.

2   If antifreeze is used in the cooling system, drain it into a bowl having a capacity of at least 13 Imp pints for re-use.

3   Open the drain plug at the bottom of the radiator. Also remove the engine drain plug on the right-hand side of the cylinder block. When a heater is fitted move the heater temperature control to the *hot* position (photos).

4   When the water has finished running, probe the orifices with a short piece of wire to dislodge any particles of rust or sediment which may be causing a blockage.

5   It is important to note that the heater cannot be drained completely during the cold weather so an antifreeze solution must be used. Always use an antifreeze with an ethylene glycol base.

2.3a Radiator drain plug

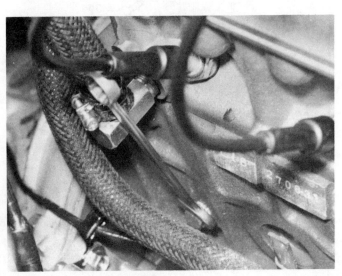

2.3b Removing engine drain plug

3 Cooling system – flushing

1   In time the cooling system will gradually lose its efficiency as the radiator becomes choked with rust, scale deposits from the water, and other sediment. To clean the system out, remove the radiator filler cap and drain plug and leave a hose running in the filler neck for ten to fifteen minutes.

2   In very bad cases, the radiator should be reverse flushed. This can be done with the radiator in position. The cylinder block plug is removed and a hose with a suitable tapered adaptor placed in the drain plug hole. Water under pressure is then forced through the radiator and out of the header tank filler cap neck.

3   It is recommended that some thin polythene sheeting is placed over the engine to stop water finding its way into the electrical system.

4   The hose should now be removed and placed in the radiator cap filler neck, and the radiator washed out in the usual manner.

4 Cooling system – filling

1   Refit the cylinder block and radiator drain plugs.

2   Fill the system slowly to ensure that no air lock develops. If a heater is fitted check that the control is set to the *hot* position, otherwise an air lock may form in the heater. The best type of water to use in the cooling system is rain water. Use this whenever possible.

3   Do not fill the system higher than 0.5 inch (12.7 mm) of the filler neck. Overfilling will merely result in wastage.

4   It is usually found that air locks develop in the heater radiator so the system should be vented during refilling by detaching the heater supply hose.

5   Pour coolant into the radiator filler neck whilst the end of the heater supply hose is held at the connection height. When a constant stream of water flows from the supply hose quickly refit the hose. If venting is not carried out it is possible for the engine to overheat.

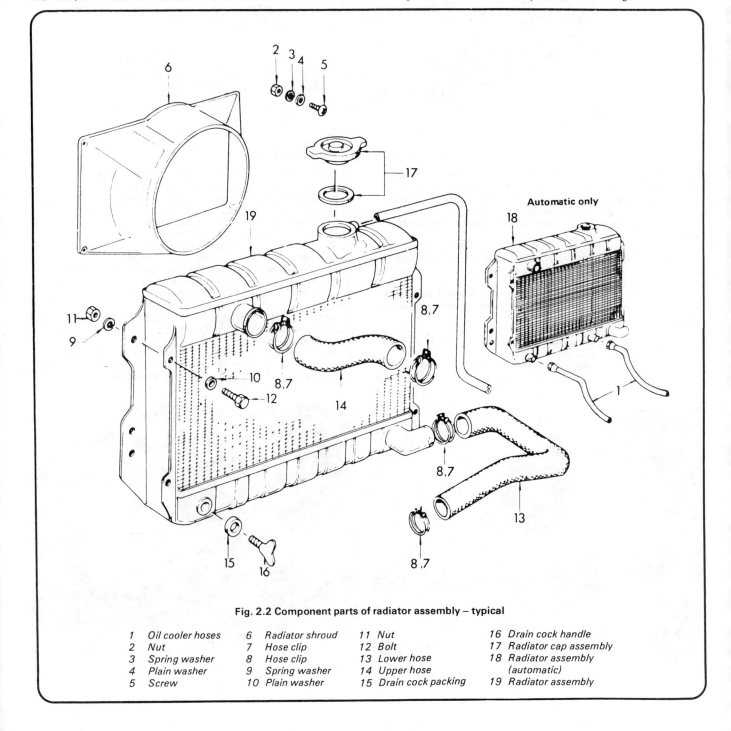

Fig. 2.2 Component parts of radiator assembly – typical

1 Oil cooler hoses	6 Radiator shroud	11 Nut	16 Drain cock handle
2 Nut	7 Hose clip	12 Bolt	17 Radiator cap assembly
3 Spring washer	8 Hose clip	13 Lower hose	18 Radiator assembly
4 Plain washer	9 Spring washer	14 Upper hose	(automatic)
5 Screw	10 Plain washer	15 Drain cock packing	19 Radiator assembly

Should the engine overheat for no apparent reason then the system should be vented before seeking other causes.
6   Only use antifreeze mixture with an ethylene glycol base.
7   Refit the filler cap and turn it firmly clockwise to lock in position.

5   Radiator – removal, cleaning, inspection and refitting

1   Drain the cooling system as described in Section 2.
2   Refer to Chapter 12 and remove the front grille.
3   Slacken the two clips which hold the top and bottom hoses to the radiator and carefully pull off the two hoses.
4   *Automatic transmission only:* Make up two pieces of tapered wood to insert into the ends of the two oil cooler pipes. Undo the two unions which hold the hydraulic fluid pipes to the radiator and carefully detach the two pipes. Plug the ends to stop syphoning of the hydraulic fluid and dirt ingress.
5   If a fan shroud is fitted, undo and remove the four bolts securing it to the radiator. Move the shroud rearward.
6   Undo and remove the four bolts and washers that secure the radiator to the side supports.
7   The radiator may now be lifted upward and away from the engine compartment.
8   Lift the radiator shroud (if fitted) away from the fan blades and remove from the engine compartment.
9   With the radiator away from the car any leaks can be soldered or repaired with fibreglass. Clean out the inside of the radiator by flushing as described earlier in this Chapter. When the radiator is out of the car it is advantageous to turn it upside down and reverse flush. Clean the exterior of the radiator by carefully using a compressed air jet or a strong jet of water to clear away any road dirt, flies etc.
10 When an oil cooler is fitted plug the union connections to stop water finding its way into the cooler department.
11 Inspect the radiator hoses for cracks, internal or external perishing and damage by overtightening of the securing clips. Also inspect the overflow pipe. Renew the hose if suspect. Examine the radiator hose clips and renew them if they are rusted or distorted.
12 The drain plug and washer should be renewed if leaking or with worn threads, but first ensure that the leak is not caused by a damaged washer.
13 Refitting the radiator is the reverse of the removal sequence.
14 If new hoses are being fitted, lubricate them with a little soap and they will be easier to fit.
15 Refill the cooling system as described in Section 4.

6   Thermostat – removal, testing and refitting

1   Partially drain the cooling system (usually 4 Imp pints is enough) as described in Section 2.
2   Slacken the top radiator hose at the thermostat housing and remove the hose.

3   Undo and remove the two nuts and washers that secure the thermostat housing to the cylinder head elbow.
4   Carefully lift the thermostat housing away from the elbow. Recover the joint washer adhering to either the housing or cylinder head elbow.
5   Using a screwdriver carefully ease the thermostat from its seating.
6   Test the thermostat for correct functioning by suspending it on a string in a saucepan of cold water. Also suspend a thermometer in the water. Heat the water and note the temperature at which the thermostat begins to open. Continue heating the water until the thermostat is fully open. Then let it cool down naturally. The readings taken should compare with those given in specifications at the beginning of this Chapter.
7   If the thermostat does not fully open in boiling water, or does not close down as the water cools, then it must be discarded and a new one obtained. Should the thermostat be stuck open when cold this will usually be apparent when removing it from the cylinder head.
8   Refitting the thermostat is the reverse sequence to removal. Always ensure that the thermostat housing and cylinder head elbow mating faces are clean and flat. If the thermostat housing or elbow is badly corroded fit a new housing. Always use a new gasket.
9   It is advantageous to fit a thermostat that does not open too early in the Winter months. If a Winter thermostat is fitted, provided the Summer one is still functioning correctly, it can be placed on one side and refitted in the Spring. Thermostats should last for two or three years before renewal becomes desirable.

7   Water pump – removal and refitting

1   Drain the cooling system as described in Section 2.
2   When a fan shroud is fitted undo and remove the four bolts securing it to the radiator and remove it.
3   Slacken the alternator mountings and push the unit towards the engine. Lift away the fan belt.
4   Undo and remove the four bolts and lock washers that secure the fan blade assembly and pulley to the hub. Lift them away.
5   Undo and remove the five bolts and washers securing the water pump to the front cover. Lift away the water pump and its gasket.
6   Refitting the water pump is the reverse sequence to removal. The following additional points should be noted:

   (a) Make sure the mating faces of the front cover and water pump are clean.
   (b) Refill the cooling system as described in Section 4.
   (c) Adjust the fan belt tension as described in Section 11.
   (d) Run the engine and check for water leaks.

8   Water pump – inspection and servicing

1   Inspect the body and vanes for signs of excessive corrosion. Also

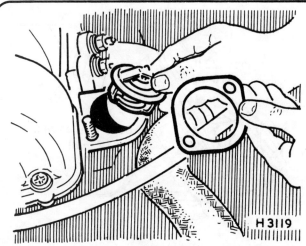

Fig. 2.3 Removal of gasket and thermostat (Sec 6)

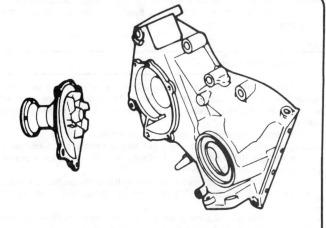

Fig. 2.4 Water pump and front cover (Sec 7)

check the bearings for signs of excessive endplay or roughness when
the spindle is being rotated.
2   Should the bearing condition be satisfactory and yet a rumble or
squeak is emitted when being driven by the fan belt, use a little water
pump seal lubricant to get rid of the noise.
3   If the bearings are worn or the pump leaking water a new pump
will have to be obtained and fitted as it is not possible to overhaul the
unit.

9   Torque coupling – general

1   This unit is filled with a special silicone oil which cannot be
replenished. If there is any sign of leakage the coupling must be
renewed.
2   Renewal of the torque coupling necessitates the renewal of the
water pump also as it cannot be separated.

10   Fan belt – removal and refitting

*If the fan belt is worn or stretched excessively it should be
renewed. The most usual reason for renewal is that the belt has
broken in service. It is recommended that a spare belt be always
carried in the car.*
1   Loosen the alternator mounting bolts and move the alternator
towards the engine.
2   Slip the old belt over the crankshaft, alternator and water pump
pulley wheels and lift it over the fan blades.
3   Put a new belt onto the three pulleys and adjust it as described in
Section 11. **NOTE**: *After fitting a new belt it will require adjustment
after 250 miles (400 km).*
4   Make a note of the car's engine number when buying a new belt.
Later models are fitted with larger pulleys and need a slightly larger fan
belt.

11   Fan belt tension – adjustment

1   It is important to keep the fan belt correctly adjusted and it is considered that this should be a regular maintenance task every 6000
miles (10 000 km). If the belt is loose it will slip, wear rapidly and
cause the alternator and water pump to malfunction. If the belt is too
tight the alternator and water pump bearings will wear rapidly, causing
premature failure of these components.
2   The fan belt tension is correct when a pressure of 22 lb (10 kg),
applied at the mid-point position between the alternator and fan
pulleys, deflects the belt 0.3 - 0.5 inch (8 - 12 mm) (photo).
3   To adjust the fan belt, slacken the alternator securing bolts and
move the alternator in or out until the correct tension is obtained. It is
easier if the alternator bolts are only slackened a little so it requires
some effort to move the alternator. In this way the tension of the belt
can be arrived at more quickly than by making frequent adjustments.
4   When the correct adjustment has been obtained fully tighten the
alternator mountings bolts.

12   Antifreeze precautions

1   In circumstances where it is likely that the temperature will drop
below freezing, it is essential that some of the water is drained and an
adequate amount of ethylene glycol antifreeze, added to the cooling
system.
2   Any antifreeze with an anti-corrosion additive can be left in the
cooling system for up to two years, but after six months it is advisable
to have the specific gravity of the coolant checked at your local dealer,
and thereafter every three months.
3   Coolant with a concentration of 30% will provide protection down
to a temperature of -15°C (5°F) and with a 50% concentration -35 °C
(-31°F).
4   Before adding antifreeze always check all hoses and the security
of their clips as it has a far greater searching effect than plain water.

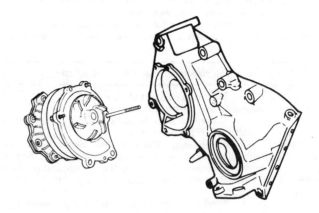

Fig. 2.5 Water pump (with torque coupling) and front cover (Sec 7)

11.2 Checking the fan belt tension

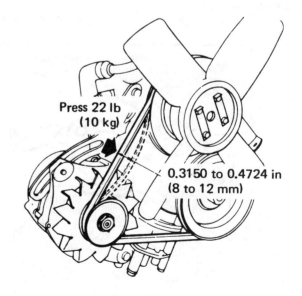

Press 22 lb
(10 kg)

0.3150 to 0.4724 in
(8 to 12 mm)

Fig. 2.6 Adjusting fan belt tension (Sec 11)

13 Fault diagnosis – cooling system

Symptom	Reason/s	Remedy
Overheating Heat generated in cylinder not being successfully disposed of by radiator	Insufficient water in cooling system	Top up radiator
	Fan belt slipping (accompanied by a shrieking noise on rapid engine acceleration)	Tighten fan belt to recommended tension or renew if worn
	Radiator core blocked or radiator grille restricted	Reverse flush radiator, remove obstructions
	Bottom water hose collapsed, impeding flow	Remove and fit new hose
	Thermostat not opening properly	Remove and fit new thermostat
	Ignition advance and retard incorrectly set (accompanied by loss of power and perhaps, misfiring)	Check and reset ignition timing
	Carburettor incorrectly adjusted (mixture too weak)	Tune carburettor
	Exhaust system partially blocked	Check exhaust pipe for constrictive dents and blockages
	Oil level in sump too low	Top up sump to full mark on dipstick
	Blown cylinder head gasket (Water/steam being forced down the radiator overflow pipe under pressure)	Remove cylinder head, fit new gasket
	Engine not yet run-in	Run-in slowly and carefully
	Brakes binding	Check and adjust brakes if necessary
Underheating Too much heat being dispersed by radiator	Thermostat jammed open	Remove and renew thermostat
	Incorrect grade of thermostat fitted allowing premature opening of valve	Remove and replace with new thermostat which opens at a higher temperature
	Thermostat missing	Check and fit correct thermostat
Loss of cooling water Leaks in system	Loose clips on water hoses	Check and tighten clips if necessary
	Top or bottom water hoses perished and leaking	Check and renew faulty hoses
	Radiator core leaking	Remove radiator and repair
	Thermostat gasket leaking	Inspect and renew gasket
	Pressure cap spring worn or seal ineffective	Renew pressure cap
	Blown cylinder head gasket (Pressure in system forcing water/steam down overflow pipe)	Remove cylinder head and fit new gasket
	Cylinder wall or head cracked	Dismantle engine, dispatch to engineering works for repair

Chapter 3
Fuel, carburation and emission control systems

Contents

Specifications

Fuel pump
Type	Mechanically operated
Pump pressure:	
Non-USA models	$2 \cdot 56 - 3 \cdot 41$ lbf/in² ($0 \cdot 18 - 0 \cdot 24$ kgf/cm²)
USA models	$3 \cdot 0 - 3 \cdot 8$ lbf/in² ($0 \cdot 21 - 0 \cdot 27$ kgf/cm²)
Delivery rate at 1000 rpm	$1 \cdot 76$ Imp pints/$2 \cdot 11$ US pints/1000 cc per minute

Carburettors (general)
Type
Single carburettor models (SC)	Nikki or Hitachi dual throat downdraught
Twin carburettor models (TC)	Hitachi to SU specifications

Application
SC models
1972 and 1973	
L16 manual transmission	Nikki 213282—331
automatic transmission	Nikki 213282—341
L18 (1972) manual transmission	Nikki 213304—361
automatic transmission	Nikki 213304—421
L18 (1973) manual transmission	Hitachi DCH340—2
automatic transmission	Hitachi DCH340—1

1974
    L16 manual transmission . . . .   Nikki 213282—332
        automatic transmission . . . .   Nikki 213282—341
    L18 manual transmission . . . .   Nikki 213304—362
        automatic transmission . . . .   Nikki 213304—421
    L20B manual transmission . . . .   Hitachi DCH340—15
        automatic transmission . . . .   Hitachi DCH340—14
1975
    L16 . . . .   Refer to data for 1974 models
    L18 . . . .   Refer to data for 1974 models
    L20B non-California:
        manual transmission . . . .   Hitachi DCH340—43
        automatic transmission . . . .   Hitachi DCH340—44
    L20B California:
        manual transmission . . . .   Hitachi DCH340—41
        automatic transmission . . . .   Hitachi DCH340—42
1976
    L16 . . . .   Refer to data for 1974 models
    L18 . . . .   Refer to data for 1974 models
    L20B non-California:
        manual transmission . . . .   Hitachi DCH340—43A
        automatic transmission . . . .   Hitachi DCH340—44A
    LB California:
        manual transmission . . . .   Hitachi DCH340—41A
        automatic transmission . . . .   Hitachi DCH340—42B
1977
    L16 . . . .   Refer to data for 1974 models
    L18 . . . .   Refer to data for 1974 models
TC models:
    1972 and 1973
    Manual and automatic transmission . . . .   Hitachi HJL38W6
    1974 onwards
    Manual and automatic transmission . . . .   Hitachi HJT38W7

Carburettor data
Nikki 213282—331, 213282—332 and 213282—341

	Primary	Secondary
Outlet diameter in (mm)	1·1024 (28)	1·2598 (32)
Venturi diameter in (mm)	0·8661 x 0·2756 (22 x 7)	1·1417 x 0·3937 (29 x 10)
Main jet	102	165
Main air bleed	60	60
1st slow air bleed in (mm)	0·0394 (1·0)	—
2nd slow air bleed	180	100
Slow economizer in(mm)	0·063 (1·6)	—
Power jet	45	
Float level in (mm)	0·8661 (22)	
Fuel pressure lbf/in² (kgf/cm²)	3·414 (0·24)	
Main nozzle in (mm)	0·0906 (2·3)	0·0984 (2·5)
Fast idle opening in (mm)	0·0512 (1·3)	
Interlock opening of primary and secondary throttle valve in (mm) .	0·291 (7·4)	

Nikki 213304—361, 213304—362 and 213304—421

	Primary	Secondary
Outlet diameter in (mm)	1·1811 (30)	1·3386 (34)
Venturi diameter in (mm)	0·9055 x 0·5512 x 0·2756 (23 x 14 x 7)	1·1811 x 0·3937 (30 x 10)
Main jet	102	170
Main air bleed	60	60
1st slow air bleed in (mm)	0·0394 (1·0)	—
2nd slow air bleed	210	100
Slow economizer in (mm)	0·063 (1·6)	—
Power jet	55	
Float level in (mm)	0·8661 (22)	
Fuel pressure lbf/in² (kgf/cm²)	3·414 (0·24)	
Main nozzle in (mm)	0·0906 (2·3)	0·1102 (2·8)
Fast idle opening in (mm)	0·0610 (1·55)	
Interlock opening of primary and secondary throttle valve in (mm)	0·248 (6·3)	

Hitachi DCH340—1 and DCH340—2

	Primary	Secondary
Outlet diameter in (mm)	1·181 (30)	1·339 (34)
Venturi diameter in (mm)	0·906 x 0·315 (23 x 8)	1·181 x 0·354 (30 x 9)
Main jet	97·5	170
Main air bleed	65	60
Slow jet	48	90
Slow air bleed	145	100
Slow economizer in (mm)		0·071 (1·8)
Power jet		53
Float level in (mm)		0·906 (23)
Fuel pressure lbf/in² (kgf/cm²)		2·42 (0·17)
Main nozzle – inner diameter x outer diameter in (mm)	0·098 x 0·138 (2·5 x 3·5)	0·098 x 0·157 (2·5 x 4)
Fuel level adjustment – clearance between valve stem and float seat in (mm)		0·059 (1·5)
Fast idle adjustment (fast idle cam, second step) – clearance between throttle valve and carburettor body:		
manual transmission in (mm)		0·035 – 0·039 (0·9 – 1·0)
automatic transmission in (mm)		0·044 – 0·048 (1·12 – 1·22)
Vacuum break adjustment – clearance between choke valve and carburettor body in (mm)		0·067 (1·7)
Choke unloader adjustment – clearance between choke valve and carburettor body in (mm)		0·173 (4·4)
Bi-metal setting – resistance between terminal and carburettor body at 21°C (70°F) ohms		9·8 – 10·2
Bi-metal setting		22°, centre of index marks
Interlock opening of primary and secondary throttle valves in (mm)		0·291 (7·4)
Dashpot adjustment (without loading)		1600 – 1800 rpm
BCDD set pressure:		
manual transmission in Hg (mm Hg)		– 19·7 ± 0·79 (– 500 ± 20)
automatic transmission in Hg (mm Hg)		– 18·9 ± 0·79 (– 480 ± 20)

Hitachi DCH340—14 and DCH340—15

	Primary	Secondary
Outlet diameter in (mm)	1·181 (30)	1·339 (34)
Venturi diameter in (mm)	0·906 x 0·315 (23 x 8)	1·181 x 0·354 (30 x 9)
Main jet	102	70
Main air bleed	60	60
Slow jet	46	160
Slow air bleed	145	100
Slow economizer in (mm)		0·071 (1·8)
Power jet		50
Float level in (mm)		0·906 (23)
Float pressure lbf/in² (kgf/cm²)		2·42 (0·17)
Main nozzle – inner diameter x outer diameter in (mm)	0·098 x 0·138 (2·5 x 3·5)	0·098 x 0·157 (2·5 x 4)
Fuel level adjustment – clearance between valve stem and float seat in (mm)		0·059 (1·5)
Fast idle adjustment (fast idle cam, second step) clearance between throttle valve and carburettor body:		
manual transmission in (mm)		0.035 – 0·039 (0·9 – 1·0)
automatic transmission in (mm)		0·044 – 0·048 (1·12 – 1·22)
Vacuum break adjustment – clearance between choke valve and carburettor body in (mm)		0·069 (1·7)
Choke unloader adjustment – clearance between choke valve and carburettor body in (mm)		0·173 (4·4)
Bi-metal setting – resistance at 21°C (70°F) ohms		6·0 – 6·4
Bi-metal setting		22° centre of index mark
Interlock opening of primary and secondary throttle valves in (mm)		0·291 (7·4)
Dashpot adjustment (without loading)		1600 – 1800 rpm
BCDD set pressure:		
manual transmission in Hg (mm Hg)		– 20·9 ± 0·787 (– 530 ± 20)

Hitachi DCH340—41 and DCH340—42

	Primary	Secondary
Outlet diameter in (mm)	1·181 (30)	1.341 (34)
Venturi diameter in (mm)	0·945 (24)	1·22 (31)
Main jet	99	160
Main air bleed	70	60

Slow jet 48
Power jet . . . .
Float level   in (mm) . . . .
Fuel pressure   lbf/in² (kgf/cm²) . . . .

48	80
	43
	0·906 (23)
	2·418 (0·17)

DCH340—41	DCH340—42

Float level adjustment – clearance between valve stem and float seat   in (mm)   →   0·059 (1·5)

Fast idle adjustment (fast idle cam, second step) clearance between throttle valve and carburettor body   in (mm) . . . .   →   0·040 – 0·048 (1·01 – 1·21) | 0·049 – 0·052 (1·23 – 1·33)

Vacuum break adjustment – clearance between choke valve and carburettor body   in (mm)   →   0·065 (1·65) | 0·065 (1·65)

Choke unloader adjustment – clearance between choke valve and carburettor body   in (mm)   →   0·096 (2·45) | 0·096 (2·45)

Bi-metal setting – resistance at 21°C (70°F)   ohms . . . .   →   3·7 – 8·9 | 3·7 – 8·9

Bi-metal setting . . . .   →   Centre of index mark

Interlock opening of primary and secondary throttle valve in (mm) . . . .   →   0·291 (7·38) | 0·291 (7·38)

Dashpot adjustment (without loading) . . . .   →   1900 – 2100 rpm | 1650 – 1850 rpm

BCDD set pressure   in Hg (mm Hg)   →   −20·8 ± 0·2 (−530 ± 5) | 20·0 ± 0·2 (−510 ± 5)

Hitachi DCH340—43 and DCH340—44

	Primary	Secondary
Outlet diameter in (mm)	1·181 (30)	1·341 (34)
Venturi diameter in (mm)	0·945 (24)	1·220 (31)
Main jet	97	160
Main air bleed	70	60
Slow jet	48	100
Power valve		40
Float level in (mm)		0·906 (23)
Fuel pressure lbf/in² (kgf/cm²)		2·408 (0·17)

DCH340—43	DCH340—44

Fuel level adjustment – clearance between valve stem and float seat in (mm)   →   0·051 – 0·067 (1·3 – 1·7) | 0·051 – 0·067 (1·3 – 1·7)

Fast idle adjustment (fast idle cam, second step) clearance between choke valve and carburettor body   in (mm) . . . .   →   0·040 – 0·048 (1·01 – 1·21) | 0·049 – 0·052 (1·23 – 1·33)

Vacuum break adjustment – clearance between choke valve and carburettor body   in (mm) . . . .   →   0·065 (1·65) | 0·065 (1·65)

Choke unloader adjustment – clearance between choke valve and carburettor body   in (mm) . . . .   →   0·096 (2·45) | 0·096 (2·45)

Bi-metal setting – resistance at 21°C (70°F)   ohms . . . .   →   3·7 – 8·9 | 3·7 – 8·9

Bi-metal setting . . . .   →   Centre of index mark

Interlock opening of primary and secondary throttle valve in (mm) . . . .   →   0·291 (7·38) | 0·291 (7·38)

Dashpot adjustment (without loading) . . . .   →   1900 – 2100 rpm | 1650 – 1850 rpm

BCDD set pressure   in Hg (mm Hg) . . . .   →   −208 ± 0·2 (−530 ± 5) | −200 ± 0·2 (−510 ± 5)

Hitachi DCH340—41A and DCH340—42B

	Primary	Secondary
Outlet diameter in (mm)	1·181 (30)	1·339 (34)
Venturi diameter in (mm)	0·945 (24)	1·220 (31)
Main jet	101	160
Main air bleed	70	60
Slow jet	48	80
Power valve		40
Float level in (mm)		0·906 (23)
Fuel pressure lbf/in² (kgf/cm²)		2·408 (0·17)

DCH340—41A	DCH340—42B

Fuel level adjustment – clearance between valve stem and float seat in (mm) . . . .   →   0·051 – 0·067 (1·3 – 1·7) | 0·051 – 0·067 (1·3 – 1·7)

Fast idle adjustment (fast idle cam, second step) clearance between valve and carburettor body   in (mm)   →   0·040 – 0·048 (1·01 – 1·21) | 0·049 – 0·052 (1·23 – 1·33)

Vacuum break adjustment – clearance between choke valve and carburettor body   in (mm)   →   0·059 (1·5) | 0·059 (1·5)

Choke unloader adjustment – clearance between choke valve and carburettor body   in (mm) . . . .   →   0·096 (2·45) | 0·096 (2·45)

Bi-metal setting – resistance at 21°C (70°F)   ohms . . . .   →   3·7 – 8·9 | 3·9 – 8·9

Bi-metal setting . . . .   →   Centre of index mark

Interlock opening of primary and secondary throttle valve in (mm) . . . .   →   0·291 (7·38) | 0·291 (7·38)

Dashpot adjustment (without loading) . . . .   →   1900 –2100 rpm | 1650 – 1850 rpm

BCDD set pressure   in Hg (mm Hg) . . . .   →   −20·8 ± 0·2 (−530 ± 5) | −200 ± 0·2 (−510 ± 5)

Hitachi DCH340—43A and DCH340—44A

	Primary	Secondary
Outlet diameter in (mm)	1·181 (30)	1·339 (34)
Venturi diameter	0·945 (24)	1·220 (31)
Main jet	99	160
Main air bleed	70	60
Slow jet	48	100
Power valve		43
Float level in (mm)		0·906 (23)
Fuel pressure lbf/in² (kgf/cm²)		2·408 (0·17)

	DCH340—43A	DCH340—44A
Fuel level adjustment – clearance between valve stem and float seat in (mm)	0·051 – 0·067 (1·3 – 1·7)	0·051 – 0·067 (1·3 – 1·7)
Fast idle adjustment (fast idle cam, second step) clearance between choke valve and carburettor body in (mm)	0·040 – 0·048 (1·01 – 1·21)	0·049 – 0·052 (1·23 – 1·33)
Vacuum break adjustment – clearance between choke valve and carburettor body in (mm)	0·056 (1·42)	0·056 (1·42)
Bi-metal setting – resistance a 21°C (70°F) ohms	3·7 – 8·9	3·7 – 8·9
Bi-metal setting		Centre of index mark
Interlock opening of primary and secondary throttle valve in (mm)	0·291 (7·38)	0·291 (7·38)
Dashpot adjustment (without loading)	1900 – 2100 rpm	1650 – 1850 rpm
BCDD set pressure in Hg (mm Hg)	−20·8 ± 0·2 (− 530 ± 5)	−20·0 ± 0·2 (−510 ± 5)

Hitachi HJL38W6

Bore in (mm)	1·4961 (38)
Piston lift in (mm)	1·1417 (29)
Jet needle	M-76
Nozzle jet diameter in (mm)	0·0921 (2·34)
Suction spring	23
Float chamber needle valve inner diameter in (mm)	0·0591 (1·5)
Float level in (mm)	0·9055 (23)
Float venting	Inner vent type
Fuel pressure lbf/in² (kgf/cm²)	3·4140 (0·24)
Throttle clearance at full throttle in (mm)	0·0236 (0·6)
Position at full throttle	6·5°

Hitachi HJT38W—7

Inlet diameter in (mm)	1·409 (35·8)
Outlet diameter in (mm)	1·5 (38)
Suction piston lift, max in (mm)	1·14 (29)
Jet needle	M87
Nozzle jet diameter in (mm)	0·0921 (2·34)
Suction spring in (mm)	0·91 (23)
Float needle valve in (mm)	0·059 (1·5)
Float level:	
Front in (mm)	0·98 (25)
Rear in (mm)	0·79 (20)
Fuel pressure lbf/in² (kgf/cm²)	3·4 (0·24)
Throttle valve opening in (mm)	0·024 (0·6)

Idle speed

L16S, L18S (manual)	600 rpm
L16S, L18S (automatic)	650 rpm in 'N' position
L18T (manual)	700 rpm
L18T (automatic)	750 rpm in 'N' position
L20B (manual)	750 rpm
L20B (automatic)	650 rpm in 'D' position

Fuel tank capacity

Saloon and Coupe models	13¼ Imp gal (15⅞ US gal/60 litres)
Estate models	12⅛ Imp gal (14½ US gal/55 litres)
Estate models (California)	11 Imp gal (13¼ US gal/50 litres)

Emission control data

Carburettor

Make	Hitachi DAF 328
Modified numbers	6 or 8
Primary vacuum jet	150
Secondary vacuum jet	130
Fast idle setting at full choke	16°
Primary slow air bleed	150

Air pump
Make . . . . Hitachi
Model . . . . ECP 140—1
Capacity . . . . 140 cc
Pulley ratio . . . . 118 : 103
Relief valve opening pressure . . . . 10 in Hg (254 mm Hg)

Flow guide valve
Make . . . . Hitachi
Model . . . . FGA—2 or FGA—1
Opening pressure . . . . 0·4 in Hg (10 mm Hg)

Check valve
Make . . . . Hitachi
Model . . . . CV 27—2
Opening pressure . . . . 5·90 in Hg (0·15 mm Hg)

Anti backfire valve
Make . . . . Hitachi
Type . . . . Gulp
Model . . . . AV 4—18
Duration time . . . . 1·5 – 1·9 secs.
Duration pressure . . . . 19·7 in Hg (500 mm Hg)

Speed detector and speed switch
Make . . . . Niles
Model . . . . Signex No. 570
Current flow commences . . . . 12·5 mph (20 kph)

Distributor (see also Chapter 4)
Make . . . . Hitachi
Model . . . . D 412—59
Capacitor capacity (advance) . . . . 0·22 mfd
        (retard) . . . . 0·05 mfd
Dwell angle . . . . 49 – 55°
Contact breaker points gap . . . . 0·020 in (0·508 mm)

Spark plugs (see also Chapter 4)
Make . . . . NGK
Model . . . . BP—6E
Gap . . . . 0·031 – 0·035 in (0·80 – 0·90 mm)

Torque wrench settings

	lbf ft	kgf m
Air gallery to injector nozzle	43·5	6·0
Gallery to exhaust manifold plug	43·5	6·0
Adjusting bar to cover (air pump)	9·5	1·3
Air pump adjustment bar	18	2·5
Air pump to cylinder block	9·5	1·3
Check valve to gallery	76	10·6
BCDD screws	1·5 to 3·0	0·2 to 0·4

1 General description

The fuel system consists of a fuel tank at the rear of the vehicle, a mechanical fuel pump located on the right-hand side of the engine front cover, and a single Hitachi or Nikki or twin SU-type, carburettors.

The fuel pump draws petrol from the fuel tank and delivers it to the carburettor. The level of petrol in the carburettor is controlled by a float operated needle valve. Petrol flows past the needle until the float rises sufficiently to close the valve. The pump will then freewheel under slight back pressure until the petrol level drops. The needle valve will then open and petrol continue to flow until the level rises again.

2 US Federal Regulations – servicing

It is important to appreciate that any adjustments made to the fuel system as well as the ignition system (see Chapter 4) will possibly result in the car failing to meet the legal requirements in respect of air pollution unless special test equipment is used at the same time as making the adjustments.

Information given in this Chapter is aimed specifically at the owner who is able to have the various settings and adjustments checked at the earliest possible opportunity. Full information on the exhaust emission control systems will be found at the end of this Chapter.

3 Air cleaner and element – removal and refitting

1 Undo and remove the wing nut located at the top of the air cleaner body.
2 Undo and remove the two bolts and spring washers that secure the air cleaner to its support bracket.
3 Unscrew the clip securing the air cleaner to the carburettor air intake.
4 Make a note of any electrical or hose connections to the air cleaner body and detach these.
5 The air cleaner assembly may now be lifted away from the engine.
6 To gain access to the filter element separate the body from the base and lift away the element. Note the location of the seals (photo).
7 Reassembling and refitting the air cleaner is the reverse sequence to removal (photos).

3.6 Removing the filter element

3.7a Air cleaner assembled to the engine

3.7b Summer or winter setting on the air cleaner

4   Automatic temperature control (ATC) type air cleaner – description and fault finding

1   This type of air cleaner incorporates a temperature sensor and a vacuum operated valve. The purpose of this type of air cleaner is to maintain air at the carburettor intake at a constant temperature level which will permit the use of a weaker mixture and also eliminate icing of the carburettor.

2   The action of the sensor and valve regulates the intake of engine compartment air and that drawn from a cover over the exhaust manifold so that a pre-determined air temperature level is maintained under all engine operating conditions.

3   This type of air cleaner provides the additional function by incorporating an idle compensator. This is essentially a thermostatic valve which compensates for excessively rich mixtures which can result from high engine compartment temperatures.

4   Vehicles equipped with an air conditioning unit have dual idle compensators.

5   Failure of the (hot air) vacuum operated valve may be indicated by poor performance in cold weather, excessive fuel consumption and a tendency to stall.

6   First check the security of the vacuum hoses and then with the engine switched off check that the valve is in the 'hot air closed' – 'engine compartment air intake open' mode. This condition can be observed by holding a mirror to the end of the air cleaner intake spout.

7   Disconnect the vacuum hose from the valve and substitute a spare length of hose. Suck the end of this hose with the mouth and check that the valve closes to 'engine compartment air' which proves the valve to be in good condition.

8   Any fault in the vacuum operated valve can only be rectified by renewing the complete air cleaner assembly.

5   ATC air cleaner – renewal of sensor

1   Remove the air cleaner cover.

2   Using a pair of pliers, flatten the tabs of the securing clip so that the vacuum hose can be disconnected. Mark the relative positions of the hoses before removing them.

3   Remove the sensor. **NOTE**: *The gasket is bonded to the air cleaner and should not be removed.*

4   Fit the sensor as shown in Fig. 3.2 and reconnect vacuum hoses.

6   ATC air cleaner idle compensator – checking and renewal

1   To remove the idle compensator, simply remove the air cleaner cover and unscrew the two compensator securing screws.

2   Check the correct opening of the valve by immersing the assembly in water at the temperatures as shown in Fig. 3.3.

3   To check for valve air leakage, alternatively blow and suck air at the valve orifice tube. The valve must be renewed if there is excessive leakage. Where dual valves are used (with air conditioner) hold each valve shut in turn while testing the one not held closed.

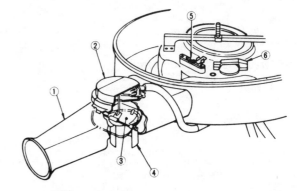

Fig. 3.1 Automatic temperature control air cleaner (Sec 4)

1 Intake spout	4 Hot air pipe
2 Vacuum capsule	5 Idle compensator
3 Air control valve	6 Sensor

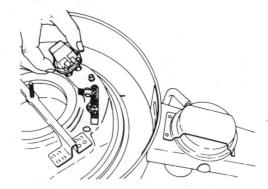

Fig. 3.2 Fitting the ATC air cleaner sensor (Sec 5)

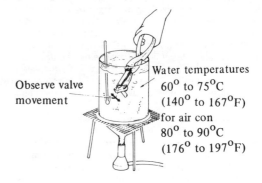

Observe valve movement

Water temperatures 60° to 75°C (140° to 167°F) for air con 80° to 90°C (176° to 197°F)

Fig. 3.3 Checking operation of idle compensator (Sec 6)

7 Fuel pump – general description

The mechanically operated fuel pump is actuated by a small cam located in front of the camshaft drive sprocket. One end of a rocker arm bears on the cam and the other end is attached to the diaphragm pull-rod. A spring is interposed between the underside of the diaphragm and the body to provide the upward motion for pumping action.

As the cam rotates the pivoted rocker arm moves outwards and this in turn pulls the diaphragm pull rod and diaphragm downward against the pressure of the diaphragm spring.

This creates sufficient vacuum in the pump chamber to draw in fuel from the tank through the gauze filter and non-return inlet valve.

The rocker arm is held in constant contact with the cam by an anti-rattle spring.

When the rocker arm is on the back of the cam the diaphragm spring is free to push the diaphragm upward thereby pushing the fuel in the pump chamber out to the carburettor through the non-return outlet valve.

When the float chamber in the carburettor is full the float chamber needle valve will close so preventing further flow of fuel from the fuel pump.

The pressure in the delivery line will hold the diaphragm downward against the pressure of the diaphragm spring and it will remain in this position until the needle valve in the float chamber opens to admit more petrol.

8 Fuel pump – removal and refitting

1   Disconnect the fuel pipes by disconnecting their unions on the fuel pump body. Plug the ends to stop dirt ingress (photo).
2   Undo and remove the two nuts, spring and plain washers that secure the fuel pump to the side of the front cover. Lift away the pump carefully noting the number of gaskets used between the pump and front cover mating faces.
3   Refitment is a straightforward reversal of removal. Always use new gaskets.

9 Fuel pump – dismantling, inspection and reassembly

1   Before dismantling, clean the exterior of the pump and then make a mark across the centre and base mating flanges so that they may be refitted in their original positions.
2   Undo and remove the four screws and spring washers that secure the cap to the upper body. Lift away the cap and gasket.
3   Undo and remove the five screws and spring washers that secure the upper body to the lower body casting. Carefully lift off the upper

body. It is possible for the diaphragm to stick to the mating flanges; if this happens, free with a sharp knife.
4   To release the diaphragm press down on its centre against the action of the diaphragm spring. Now tilt it until the end of the pull rod touches the inner wall of the body.
5   Carefully release the diaphragm and this will unhook the pull-rod from the rocker arm. Draw the pull rod through the oil seal.
6   Note the location of the inlet and outlet valves and then undo and remove the valve retainer securing screw. Lift away the retainer, inlet and outlet valves and small seals.
7   Finally unscrew the two pipe connectors from the side of the upper body.
8   To remove the oil seal from the lower body, note which way round it is fitted and then prise it out with a screwdriver.
9   Carefully examine the diaphragm for signs of splitting or cracking and obtain a new one if in any doubt.
10 If the valves are suspected of malfunctioning, they should be renewed.
11 Obtain a new oil seal ready for reassembly.

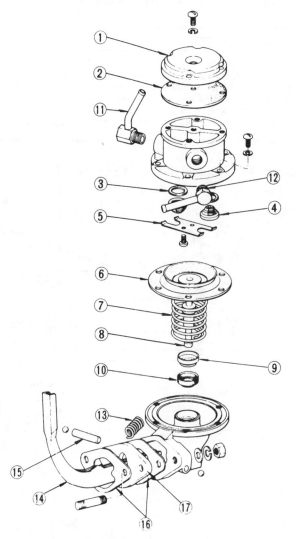

Fig. 3.4 Exploded view of fuel pump (Sec 9)

1 Fuel pump cap	10 Lower body seal
2 Cap gasket	11 Inlet connector
3 Valve packing assembly	12 Outlet connector
4 Fuel pump valve assembly	13 Rocker arm spring
5 Valve retainer	14 Rocker arm
6 Diaphragm assembly	15 Rocker arm side pin
7 Diaphragm spring	16 Fuel pump packing
8 Pull-rod	17 Spacer fuel pump to cylinder
9 Lower body seal washer	block

8.1 The fuel pump is mounted on the front right-hand side of the engine

12 Clean up the recesses where the valves are located and insert new gaskets into the valve location. Carefully position the valves so that the inlet valve has its spring facing the bottom of the pump. The outlet valve is positioned the other way up.

13 Secure the valves by refitting the retainer over them and refitting the two securing screws.

14 To refit the diaphragm first put a new oil seal into the lower body. Push the diaphragm pull-rod through the seal and locate the pull-rod in the rocker arm link.

15 Move the rocker arm until the diaphragm is level with the body flange and hold the arm in this position. Reassemble the two halves of the pump ensuring that the previously made marks on the flanges are adjacent to each other.

16 Refit the five screws and spring washers and tighten them down finger tight.

17 Move the rocker arm up and down several times to centralise the diaphragm, and then with the arm held down, tighten the screws securely in a diagonal and progressive manner.

18 Refit the cap gasket and the cap and secure with the four screws and spring washers. Refit the two pipe connectors.

10 Fuel pump – testing

If operation of the fuel pump is suspect, or it has been overhauled, it may be quickly dry-tested by holding a finger over the inlet pipe connector and operating the rocker lever through three complete strokes. When the finger is released a suction noise should be heard. Next hold a finger over the outlet nozzle and press the rocker arm fully. The pressure generated should hold for a minimum of fifteen seconds.

11 Carburettor (Nikki) – general description

The Nikki carburettor is a twin barrel down-draught type incorporating a primary and secondary system. These two systems are of the Zenith/Stromberg type. Upon inspection it will be seen that each system shares a common top cover assembly but has a separate main nozzle and throttle valve.

The function of the primary system is to supply a suitable petrol air mixture for low speeds, cruising speeds and acceleration. It will also provide the correct mixture for engine starting when the choke disc is in the closed position. There is a special power mechanism which will discharge fuel into the primary system under full load or acceleration.

The secondary system is similar in construction to the primary system but this provides mixtures for high speed and under full throttle opening conditions at low speeds.

A special diaphragm assembly controls the switch over time between the primary and secondary systems. This will occur at full throttle opening at high and low speeds.

12 Carburettor (Nikki) – removal and refitting

1 Open the bonnet and referring to Section 3, remove the air cleaner assembly.

2 Slacken the clip and detach the feed pipe from the carburettor body. If a fuel return pipe is fitted this must be detached also.

3 Detach the distributor vacuum advance pipe from the carburettor.

4 Disconnect the throttle control rod from the carburettor throttle

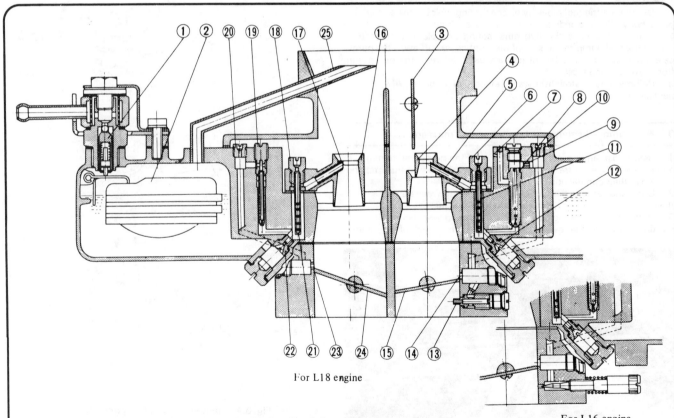

For L18 engine

For L16 engine

Fig. 3.5 Sectional view of carburettor (Sec 11)

1	Float valve	8	Slow jet	14	Bypass hole
2	Float	9	Slow economizer jet	15	Primary throttle valve
3	Choke valve	10	2nd slow air bleed	16	Secondary small venturi
4	Primary small venturi	11	Primary emulsion tube	17	Secondary main nozzle
5	Primary main nozzle	12	Primary main jet	18	Secondary main air bleed
6	Primary main air bleed	13	Idle nozzle	19	Step jet
7	1st slow air bleed				

20	Step air bleed
21	Secondary emulsion tube
22	Secondary main jet
23	Step hole
24	Secondary throttle valve
25	Air vent pipe

lever and then the choke control.

5   Undo and remove the four nuts and spring washers that secure the carburettor to the inlet manifold.

6   Carefully lift away the carburettor, discard the gaskets and recover any insulation packing used.

7   Refitting the carburettor is the reverse sequence to removal. Clean the mating faces free of any old gasket or jointing compound and always use new gaskets.

13 Carburettor (Nikki) – dismantling and reassembly

1   Wash the exterior of the carburettor and wipe dry with a clean non-fluffy rag. As the unit is dismantled note the location of each part and place in order on clean newspaper.

2   Using a small screwdriver or pointed pliers remove the small E-clip and detach the accelerator pump operating lever from the top cover assembly.

3   Disconnect the throttle lever return spring and then the primary to secondary interlock mechanism return spring.

4   Undo and remove the four screws and spring washers and partially lift away the top cover assembly. Detach the choke linkage and completely remove the top cover.

5   Disconnect the throttle vacuum chamber diaphragm rod from the secondary throttle lever.

6   Undo and remove the four screws and spring washers that secure the carburettor flange to the main body.

7   Unscrew the primary and secondary bore main air bleeds and emulsion tubes from each side of the carburettor body.

8   Unscrew the two plugs which cover the main jets. Carefully remove both main jets.

9   Unscrew and remove the primary and secondary slow air bleeds and then the primary and secondary slow running jets.

10 Undo and remove the two screws from the accelerator pump bore cover and carefully withdraw the accelerator pump plunger assembly.

11 Turn the carburettor body upside down and recover the lower spring and ball valve.

12 Carefully withdraw the small pin from the plunger assembly and if necessary dismantle the components. Take extra care on noting their locations and which way round each part is fitted.

13 Unscrew the pump injector securing bolt and lift away the injector and sealing washers. Turn the carburettor body upside down, and remove the small spring and ball from the injector bore.

14 Undo and remove the three screws securing the venturi to the secondary bore. Lift away the venturi and gasket.

15 On carburettors fitted with a fuel return assembly this should be removed next. This will give access to the needle valve and seat.

16 Using a box spanner unscrew and remove the needle valve and seat assembly.

17 Undo and remove the three float chamber securing screws and lift away the cover, glass and gasket. The spacer and float may now be removed from the chamber.

18 Undo and remove the three screws which secure the secondary throttle vacuum chamber assembly to the carburettor main body. Detach the assembly from the main body and recover the gasket.

19 Should it be necessary to dismantle the vacuum chamber, undo and remove the three screws on the outer cover. Carefully part the two halves of the assembly and lift away the diaphragm, spring and small check ball, and spring.

20 For carburettors fitted to engines of cars with automatic transmission, remove the dashpot assembly and its mechanism.

21 On carburettors fitted with a fuel return system, if the unit was functioning correctly before dismantling, leave well alone. If not it should be dismantled for further investigation. It is important that the bi-metal portion is kept intact.

22 The carburettor top cover may be dismantled if the choke valve and shaft require attention. Mark the relative position of the choke valve and cover to ensure correct reassembly.

23 Using a small file remove the peening from the ends of the choke valve retaining screws.

24 Disconnect the linkage from the end of the choke shaft.

25 Using a small screwdriver undo and remove the two choke valve securing screws. Withdraw the choke valve from the shaft.

26 Withdraw the choke valve shaft from the cover.

27 Should it be necessary to service the flange, first screw out and remove the idle mixture adjustment screw and spring.

28 Remove the throttle adjusting screw and spring.

29 Mark the relative positions of the primary and secondary throttle valves and their respective bores.

30 Using a small file remove the peening from the ends of the throttle plate securing screws.

31 Withdraw both throttle valves and then withdraw the throttle shafts from the flange.

32 Undo and remove the throttle lever and assembly retaining nut from the end of the primary throttle shaft.

33 The carburettor is now completely dismantled and, after cleaning, ready for inspection.

34 If a compressed air line is available carefully blow through all drillings. Do not use a wire probe to clean jets as it will only upset the calibration.

35 Lay a straight-edge across the top cover, main body and flange to ensure that no part is warped causing either air or fuel leaks.

36 Inspect all castings for signs of cracking and gasket surfaces for unevenness.

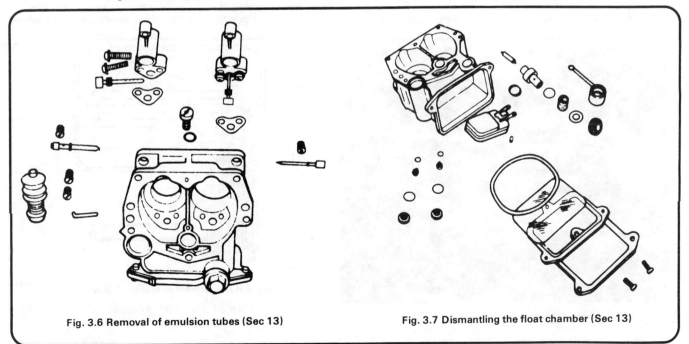

Fig. 3.6 Removal of emulsion tubes (Sec 13)   Fig. 3.7 Dismantling the float chamber (Sec 13)

37 Check the seating surface and the thread of the adjustment screw for damage.

38 Place the choke and throttle shafts back in their respective bores and check for an excessive clearance. If necessary obtain a new shaft or flange.

39 Reassembly of the carburettor is the reverse sequence to removal. Make sure that each part is clean for refitting and always use new gaskets. It will be necessary to check the fuel level in the float chamber as described in Section 14. The choke interlock fast idle opening adjustment will have to be set as described in Section 15. Also check the primary and secondary throttle interlock opening as described in Section 16. On models fitted with an automatic transmission the dashpot adjustment must be set as described in Section 17.

14 Carburettor (Nikki) – fuel level, check and adjustment

1 It will be observed that there is a horizontal line marked on the float chamber glass to indicate the correct fuel level. Should this level be correct before the carburettor was removed and overhauled and the original float and needle valve have been retained, it should not be necessary to re-adjust the fuel level (photo).

2 This check and adjustment may be carried out with the carburettor either on or off the inlet manifold.

3 With the float chamber cover glass removed invert the carburettor and allow the float seat to rest against the needle valve.

4 If the carburettor is on the inlet manifold lift the float with the fingers until the needle valve is closed.

5 Bend the float tab gently using a pair of long nosed pliers until the upper face of the float is in a horizontal position.

6 With the carburettor in the normal fitted position, allow the float to settle into its down position.

7 Measure the effective stroke of the float. This is the distance the float seat travels from the fully down to the fully up position. The travel should be as specified at the beginning of this Chapter.

8 If necessary bend the float stopper tab with a pair of long nosed pliers until the correct travel is obtained. Refit the float chamber gasket, glass and cover. Secure with the three retaining screws.

15 Carburettor (Nikki) fast idle opening – checking and adjustment

1 When the choke valve is in the fully closed position the primary throttle valve should be opened by a specified amount which will give a set throttle valve opening angle from the fully closed position.

2 Refer to Section 12 and remove the carburettor from the inlet manifold.

3 Move the choke operating lever by hand until the choke valve is in

the fully closed position.

4 Insert a rod of suitable diameter (see Specifications) between the throttle valve and throttle chamber inner wall, then adjust the linkage until the rod is a good sliding fit. Adjustment is made by bending the connecting link with a pair of pliers until the gauge just slides between the choke valve and the bore.

16 Primary and secondary throttle interlock opening – adjustment

1 Fig. 3.9 shows that the primary valve opens 50°. When the primary throttle valve opens 50°, the connecting link is contacted with the right-hand end of a groove on primary throttle arm (A).

2 When the throttle valve opens further, the locking arm is detached from the secondary throttle arm, permitting the start of the secondary system actuation.

3 The linkage between the primary and secondary throttles will operate properly if the distance 'G' between the throttle valve and the inner wall of the throttle chamber is as given in the Specifications.

4 Adjust if necessary by bending the connecting link.

17 Carburettor (Nikki) dashpot adjustment (automatic transmission models)

1 Proper contact between the throttle lever and dashpot stem provides normal dashpot performance.

2 If the normal setting cannot be obtained between the dashpot stem and throttle arm, loosen the locknut and rotate the dashpot, as necessary, so that the throttle arm touches the stem at 11° throttle valve opening.

3 The clearance 'B' in Fig. 3.10 should be as follows:

Model	'B' dimension
213304 – 421	0.0307 in (0.780 mm)
213282 – 341	0.0231 in (0.586 mm)

4 Tighten the locknut.

18 Carburettor (Nikki) idling speed – adjustment

1 Idling adjustment is made by throttle and idling adjustment screws as shown in Fig. 3.11.

2 Using a suitable screwdriver turn out the idle adjusting screw $2\frac{1}{4}$ (L16) or $1\frac{1}{2}$ (L18) turns, starting from the fully closed position. Turn in the throttle adjusting screw two or three turns and start the engine.

3 Turn out the throttle adjusting screw slowly until the specified

14.1 Fuel level sight glass

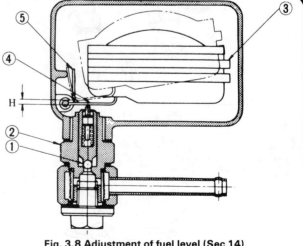

Fig. 3.8 Adjustment of fuel level (Sec 14)

1	Ball valve	4	Float arm
2	Valve seat	5	Float stopper
3	Float		

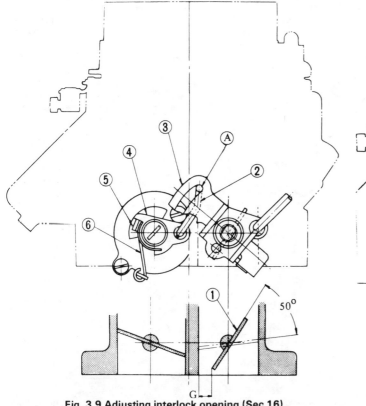

Fig. 3.9 Adjusting interlock opening (Sec 16)

1   Throttle valve   4   Rocking arm
2   Connecting link   5   Secondary throttle arm
3   Throttle arm   6   Rocking arm return spring

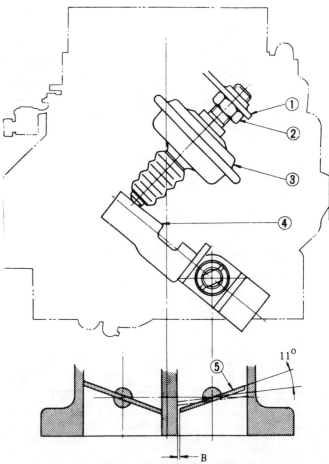

Fig. 3.10 Measuring dashpot operating clearance (Sec 17)

1   Dashpot bracket   4   Throttle lever
2   Locknut   5   Throttle valve
3   Dashpot

19 Carburettor (Nikki) choke control – removal and refitting

1   Disconnect the choke control wire from the choke control lever at the carburettor.
2   Detach the choke knob by holding the inner wire with a pair of pliers and pushing on the knob. Rotate through 90° and pull off the knob.
3   Undo and remove the nut and spacer securing the choke control outer cable and sleeve to the dash panel.
4   Push the outer cable sleeve through the hole in the dash and draw out the cable assembly.
5   Refitting the choke control assembly is the reverse sequence to removal. Lubricate the inner cable with engine oil to ensure free operation.

20 Carburettor (Nikki) accelerator control linkage – removal and refitting

1   Detach the accelerator rod ball joint from the pedal arm (Fig.3.12).
2   Undo and remove the two nuts, bolts and spring washers that secure the two accelerator shaft brackets to the engine bulkhead.
3   The linkage may be lifted away from the engine compartment once it is detached from the carburettor and return spring.
4   Refitting the linkage is the reverse sequence to removal. Lubricate the joint with engine oil to ensure free movement.

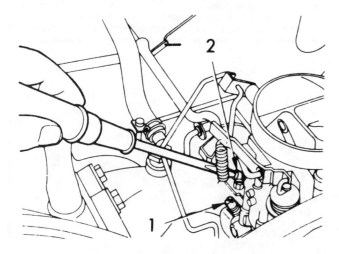

Fig. 3.11 Engine idle adjustment (Sec 18)

1   Throttle adjustment screw
2   Idle adjustment screw

idling speed is approximately obtained.
4   Turn the idle adjusting screw in or out until the engine runs smoothly at the highest speed.
5   Turn out the throttle adjusting screw until the specified engine speed is obtained.
6   Re-adjust the idle screw until the engine runs smoothly at the highest speed, then re-adjust the throttle screw until the specified engine idling speed is obtained.

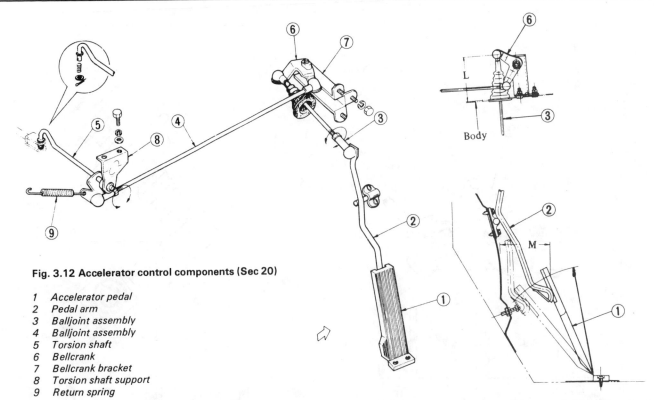

Fig. 3.12 Accelerator control components (Sec 20)

1   Accelerator pedal
2   Pedal arm
3   Balljoint assembly
4   Balljoint assembly
5   Torsion shaft
6   Bellcrank
7   Bellcrank bracket
8   Torsion shaft support
9   Return spring

21 Carburettor (TC models) – general description

1   The variable choke SU-type carburettor is a relatively simple instrument. It differs from most carburettors in that instead of having a number of various sized fixed jets for different conditions, only one variable jet is fitted to deal with all possible conditions.

2   Air passing rapidly through the carburettor draws petrol from the jet so forming the petrol/air mixture. The amount of petrol drawn from the jet depends on the position of the tapered carburettor needle, which moves up and down the jet orifice according to the engine load and throttle opening, thus effectively altering the size of jet so that exactly the right amount of fuel is metered for the prevailing driving conditions.

3   The position of the tapered needle in the jet is determined by engine vacuum. The shank of the needle is held at its top end in a piston which slides up and down the dashpot in response to the degree of manifold vacuum.

4   With the throttle fully open, the full effect of inlet manifold vacuum is felt by the piston which has an air bleed into the choke tube on the

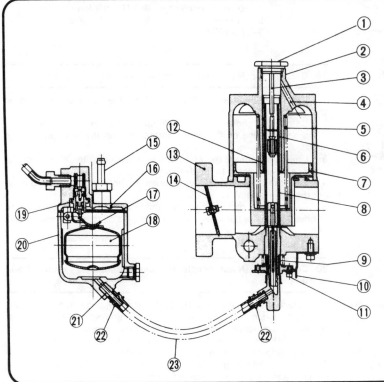

Fig. 3.13 Cross-sectional view of SU carburettor (Sec 21)

1   Oil cap nut
2   Suction chamber
3   Plunger rod
4   Transverse hole
5   Suction spring
6   Oil damper
7   Suction piston
8   Suction piston rod
9   Nozzle
10 Leaf spring
11 Idle adjusting nut
12 Suction guide
13 Throttle chamber
14 Throttle valve
15 Nipple
16 Float chamber cover
17 Float lever
18 Float
19 Needle valve
20 Float chamber
21 Sleeve
22 Clip
23 Fuel hose

outside of the throttle. This causes the piston to rise fully, bringing the needle with it. With the throttle partially closed, only slight inlet manifold vacuum is felt by the piston (although, of course, on the engine side of the throttle the vacuum is greater), and the piston only rises a little, blocking most of the jet orifice with the metering needle.

5   To prevent the piston fluttering and giving a richer mixture when the accelerator pedal is suddenly depressed, an oil damper and light spring are fitted inside the dashpot.

6   The only portion of the piston assembly to come into contact with the piston chamber or dashpot is the actual piston rod. All the other parts of the piston assembly, including the lower choke portion, have sufficient clearance to prevent any direct metal to metal contact which is essential if the carburettor is to function correctly.

22 Carburettor (TC) – removal and refitting

1   Disconnect and remove the complete air cleaner assembly from the carburettor air intake.

2   Slacken the clips and ease off the fuel feed pipes from the union on the float chamber cover. Plug the ends to prevent dirt ingress.

3   Slacken the clips and disconnect the float chamber breather hoses from their unions.

4   Disconnect the accelerator cable from the throttle linkage and the choke control cable from the choke levers.

5   Undo and remove the nuts and washers securing the carburettor body to the manifold studs. Lift away the complete carburettor installation.

6   Refitting the carburettors is the reverse sequence to removal. Always fit new gaskets to the inlet manifold flanges and one each side of the insulator block. Refer to the relevant Section and adjust the controls and carburettor settings.

23 Carburettors (TC) – dismantling

The SU-type carburettor with normally only two moving parts – the throttle valve and the piston assembly – makes it a straightforward instrument to service, but at the same time it is a delicate unit and clumsy handling can cause much damage. In particular it is easy to knock the finely tapered needle out of true, and the greatest care should be taken to keep all parts associated with the dashpot scrupulously clean.

1   Remove the oil dashpot plunger nut from the top of the dashpot.

2   Scribe marks on the suction chamber and carburettor body so that they may be refitted in their original positions. Undo and remove the four set screws and washers holding the suction chamber to the carburettor body, and lift away the suction chamber, light spring, piston and needle assembly (Fig.3.15).

3   To remove the metering needle from the choke portion of the piston unscrew the sunken retaining screw from the side of the piston choke and pull out the needle. When refitting the needle ensure that the shoulder is flush with the underside of the piston (Fig. 3.16).

4   Note which way round the front chamber cover is fitted and then undo and remove the four set screws and washers holding the cover to the main body. Lift away the float chamber cover and recover the float.

5   Normally it is not necessary to dismantle the carburettor further, but if, because of wear or for some other reason it is wished to remove the jet, this is easily accomplished by first detaching the jet operating lever from the jet head and then removing the jet by extracting it from the underside of the carburettor. The jet adjustment nut can then be unscrewed together with the jet adjusting nut locking spring and shim.

6   If the larger jet locking screw above the jet adjusting screw is removed, then the jet will have to be recentred when the carburettor is reassembled. With the jet screw removed it is an easy matter to

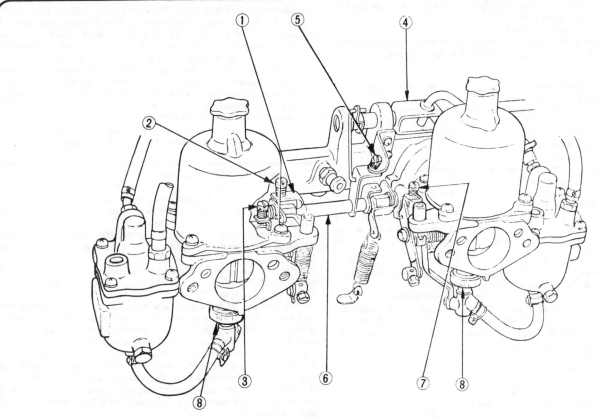

Fig. 3.14 Twin carburettor installation (Sec 22)

1	Throttle lever	5	Fast idle setting screw
2	Balance screw	6	Throttle shaft
3	Throttle adjusting screw (front)	7	Throttle adjusting screw (rear)
4	Auxiliary shaft	8	Idle adjusting nuts

remove the jet bearing and sealing washer.

7   To remove the throttle and actuating spindle, release the two screws holding the throttle in position in the slot in the spindle, slide the throttle out of the spindle (note which way round it is fitted) and then remove the spindle.

24 Carburettor (TC) float chamber – dismantling, examination and reassembly

1   To dismantle the float chamber, first disconnect the inlet pipe from the fuel pump at the top of the float chamber cover. Then disconnect the float chamber breather hose from the top of the float chamber cover.

2   Note the position of the float chamber cover and then undo and remove the four set screws. Lift away the float chamber cover.

3   Carefully insert a thin piece of bent wire under the float and lift it out. Check that the float is not cracked or leaking. If it is it must be repaired or renewed.

4   The float chamber cover contains the needle valve assembly which regulates the amount of fuel fed into the float chamber. One end of the float lever rests on top of the float, rising and falling with it, while the other pivots on a hinge pin which is held by two lugs. On the float chamber cover side of the float lever is a needle which rises and falls from its seating according to the movement of the lever. When the cover is in place the hinge pin is held in position by the walls of the float chamber. With the cover removed the pin is easily pushed out so freeing the float lever and the needle.

5   Examine the tip of the needle and the needle seating for wear. Wear is present when there is a discernible ridge in the chamfer of the needle. If this is evident then the needle and seating must be renewed.This is a simple operation and the hexagon head of the needle housing is easily screwed out. Never renew either the needle or the seating without renewing the other part as otherwise it will not be possible to get a fuel tight joint.

6   Clean the float chamber thoroughly.

7   Reassembly is the reverse sequence to removal. Before refitting the float chamber cover check that the fuel level setting is correct (Section 25).

25 Carburettor (TC) – fuel level adjustment

1   It is essential that the fuel level in the float chamber is always correct as otherwise excessive fuel consumption may occur. On reassembly of the float chamber check the fuel level before refitting the float chamber cover.

2   Invert the float chamber so that the needle valve is closed. It should be just possible to slide a 0.433 – 0.472 in (11 – 12 mm) bar between the curved portion of the float lever and the machined lip of the float chamber cover.

3   If the bar lifts the lever or if the lever stands proud of the bar then it is necessary to bend the lever at the point between the shank and the curved portion until the clearance is correct. Never bend the flat portion of the lever.

26 Carburettor (TC) – examination and repair

1   The SU-type carburettor generally speaking, is most reliable, but even so it may develop one of several faults which may not be readily apparent unless a careful inspection is carried out. The common faults which the carburettor is prone to are:

   (a)   Piston sticking
   (b)   Float needle sticking
   (c)   Float chamber flooding
   (d)   Water and dirt in the carburettor

2   In addition, the following parts are susceptible to wear after high mileages and as they virtually affect the economy of the engine should be checked and renewed where necessary every 24 000 miles (39 000 km).

   The carburettor needle. *If this has been incorrectly assembled at some time so that it is not centrally located in the jet orifice, then the metering needle will have a tiny ridge worn on it. If a ridge can be seen then the needle must be renewed. SU carburettor needles*

are made to very fine tolerances and should a ridge be apparent no attempt should be made to rub the needle down with fine emery paper. If it is wished to clean the needle it can be polished lightly with metal polish.

   The carburettor jet. *If the needle is worn it is likely that the rim of the jet will be damaged where the needle has been striking it. It should be renewed as otherwise fuel consumption will suffer. The jet can also be badly worn or ridged on the outside from where it has been sliding up and down between the jet bearings everytime the choke has been pulled out. Removal and renewal is the only answer here as well.*

   Check the edges of the throttle and the choke tube for wear. Renew if worn.

   The washers fitted to the base of the jet and to the float chamber may all leak after a time and can cause much fuel wastage. It is wisest to renew them automatically when the carburettor is stripped down.

   After high mileages the float chamber needle and seat are bound to be ridged. They are not an expensive item to renew and should be renewed as a set. They should never be renewed separately.

   Piston sticking. *The hardened piston rod which slides in the centre guide tube in the middle of the dashpot is the only part of the piston assembly (which comprises the jet needle, suction disc, and piston choke) that should make contact with the dashpot. The piston rim and the choke periphery are machined to very fine tolerances so that they will not touch the dashpot or the choke tube walls.*

   After high mileages, wear in the centre guide tube may allow the piston to touch the dashpot wall. This condition is known as sticking.

   If piston sticking is suspected or it is wished to test for this condition, rotate the piston about the centre guide tube at the same time sliding it up and down inside the dashpot. If any portion of the piston makes contact with the dashpot wall then that portion of the wall must be polished with metal polish until clearance exists. In extreme cases, fine emery cloth can be used.

   The greatest care should be taken to remove only the minimum amount of metal to provide the clearance, as too large a gap will cause air leakage and will upset the functioning of the carburettor. Clean down the walls of the dashpot and the piston rim and ensure that there is no oil on them. A trace of oil may be judiciously applied to the piston rod.

   If the piston is sticking under no circumstances try to clear it by trying to alter the tension of the light return spring.

27 Carburettor (TC) – jet centring

1   Remove the link between the jet head and lever. Remove the union holding the feed pipe to the base of the jet, together with the jet and jet adjusting nut securing spring.

2   Refit the jet and feed tube and press them up under the head of the large hexagonal jet locknut. Unscrew this nut slightly until the jet bearing can be turned.

3   Remove the damper securing nut and damper from the top of the dashpot and push the piston assembly right down so that the metering needle enters fully into the jet.

4   Tighten the jet locking nut and test the piston assembly to check that the needle is still quite free to slide in the jet orifice. On lifting the piston and then releasing it, the piston should hit the inside jet bridge with a soft metallic click, and the intensity of the click should be the same whether the jet is in its normal position or is fully lowered.

5   If the sound is different when the jet is fully lowered then the jet is not yet properly centralised and the process must be repeated.

6   When all is correct, remove the jet, refit the jet adjusting nut securing spring, the adjusting nut and jet, and the link between the jet head and the lever.

28 Carburettor (TC) – reassembly

1   With all parts clean reassembly begins by inserting the jet bearing into the carburettor body. Then fit the washer and locking nut.

2   Provided that care was taken during dismantling, reassembly is now the reverse sequence to dismantling. It will be necessary to centre

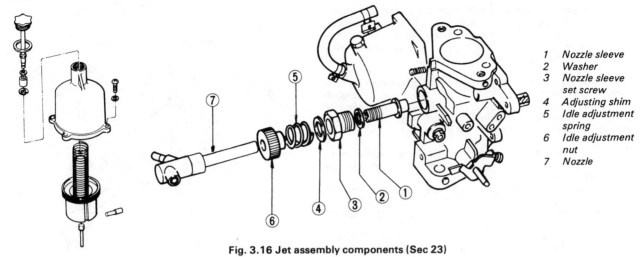

Fig. 3.15 Piston and suction
chamber assembly (Sec 23)

Fig. 3.16 Jet assembly components (Sec 23)

1 Nozzle sleeve
2 Washer
3 Nozzle sleeve
  set screw
4 Adjusting shim
5 Idle adjustment
  spring
6 Idle adjustment
  nut
7 Nozzle

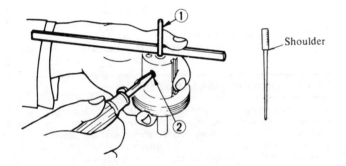

Fig. 3.17 Refitting jet needle to piston (Sec 23)

1 Jet needle   2 Jet needle setscrew

the jet assembly and check the float chamber fuel level. Full information will be found in earlier Sections.

29 Carburettor (TC) – tuning

1 The models covered by this manual which have twin carburettors have a twin SU-type carburettor installation and it is necessary for the carburettors to be correctly set as well as synchronizing them.
2 Start the engine and allow it to reach the normal operating temperature.
3 Check the carbon of the exhaust gas at idling speed with the choke fully in. If the exhaust tends to be black, and the tailpipe interior is also black it is a fair indication that the mixture is too rich. If the exhaust is colourless and the deposit in the exhaust pipe is very light grey it is likely that the mixture is too weak. This condition may also be accompanied by intermittent misfiring, while too rich a mixture will be associated with 'hunting'. Ideally the exhaust should be colourless with a medium grey exhaust pipe deposit.
4 Once the engine has reached its normal operating temperature remove the air cleaner installation and also disconnect the throttle linkage between the two instruments.
5 Only two adjustments are provided on the SU-type carburettor. Idling speed is governed by the throttle adjusting screw, and the mixture strength by the jet adjustment nut. The SU-type carburettor is correctly adjusted for the whole of its engine revolution range when the idling mixture strength is correct.
6 Idling speed adjusment is effected by the idling adjusting screw. To adjust the mixture set the engine to run around 1000 rpm by screwing in the idling screw for each carburettor.
7 Check the mixture strength by lifting the piston of the carburettor approximately 0.031 inch (0.8 mm) with a small screwdriver or using the small spring loaded pin located under the main body so as to disturb the air flow as little as possible. If:

(a) the speed of the engine increases appreciably, the mixture is too rich
(b) the engine speed immediately decreases, the mixture is too weak
(c) the engine speed increases very slightly, the mixture is correct

8 To enrich the mixture rotate the adjustment nut which is located at the bottom of the carburettor, downward. To weaken the mixture rotate the adjustment nut upward. Only turn the nut a little at a time and check the mixture strength between each turn.
9 It is likely that there will be a slight increase or decrease in rpm after the mixture adjustment has been made so the throttle idling adjusting screw should now be turned so that the engine idles at the recommended speed.
10 Once the two carburettors have been set it is now necessary to synchronize them. This means the idling suction must be equal on both.
11 It is best to use a vacuum synchronizing device but if one is not available it is possible to obtain fairly accurate synchronization by listening to the hiss made by the air flow into the inlet throats of each carburettor.
12 The aim is to adjust the throttle butterfly disc so that an equal amount of air enters each carburettor. With the two carburettors still disconnected from each other listen to the hiss from each carburettor and if a difference in intensity is noticed between them, then unscrew the throttle adjustment screw on the other carburettor until the hiss from both the carburettors is the same.
13 With a vacuum synchronizing device all that is necessary to do is place the instrument over the mouth of each carburettor in turn and adjust the adjusting screws until the reading on the gauge is identical for both carburettors.
14 Reconnect the two carburettors and refit the air cleaner assembly.

30 Carburettor (TC) – acclerator control linkage – removal and refitting

This is almost identical to that for single carburettor models with the exception of the actual connection to the carburettor installation. Refer to Sections 19 and 20 for further information.

31 Carburettor (Hitachi) – general description

The Hitachi DCH-340 carburettor is a twin barrel, downdraught type incorporating an economizer, an idle limiter, an electrically operated automatic choke, an anti-dieseling solenoid to eliminate run-on, and a power valve (vacuum actuated booster) to ensure high speed operation.

A boost controlled deceleration device is used with manual transmission models to reduce exhaust emission during coasting.

The carburettor incorporates a primary circuit for part-throttle operation and a secondary circuit for high-speed, full power operation. Both these circuits have Zenith/Stromberg type nozzles.

The carburettor is equipped with a piston type accelerator pump which is linked to the throttle valve.

The vacuum piston type power valve mechanism utilizes the vacuum below the throttle valve. During small throttle openings, the high vacuum in the intake manifold pulls the vacuum piston upwards and the power valve remains closed. Under full load or acceleration conditions, the lower vacuum conditions cause the piston to move down by the action of the spring and the power valve opens to admit additional fuel.

The anti-dieseling solenoid valve shuts off the fuel supply to the carburettor idling circuit to prevent the engine running on when the ignition is switched off.

A single float chamber is built into the carburettor and the chamber is internally vented.

The boost controlled deceleration device (BCDD) admits additional mixture into the inlet manifold during periods of deceleration and coasting when the manifold vacuum exceeds a pre-determined level. This action improves the combustion during this time and so reduces the emission of noxious exhaust fumes.

Admission of this additional mixture from a separate mixture passage in the carburettor is controlled by a vacuum controlled solenoid valve which in turn receives a signal from the speedometer needle as the vehicle speed falls below 10 mph (15 km/h).

The electrically-operated choke adjusts the position of the choke valve plate according to two factors: (i) the temperature of the engine coolant and (ii) the ambient temperature. These conditions are monitored by a modulator unit and ensure that the rich fuel/air mixture necessary for warming up is restored to normal as quickly as possible to keep exhaust fume emission to a minimum. A vacuum diaphragm opens the choke valve after starting the engine to regulate the air and fuel ratio.

Vehicles with automatic transmission are equipped with a dash pot device to allow the throttle valve to close slowly when the foot is released suddenly from the accelerator pedal (particularly when accompanied by heavy braking) and the engine might stall.

The Hitachi DAF 328 series carburettor is a twin barrel downdraught design and incorporates a primary and secondary system. The primary system operates on the Solex system whereas the secondary system is of the Zenith/Stromberg type.

The secondary system bore comprises a multiple venturi.

The change over between primary and secondary systems is controlled by a special diaphragm, one side of which is open to the atmosphere and the other side connected through a small drilling to air jets in both the primary and secondary systems.

When induction depression is increased at the venturis the diaphragm is pulled against its spring and to the secondary throttle valve via a linkage from the diaphragm. The secondary throttle valve now comes into operation.

Where the engine has been modified to comply with the Federal Regulations the fuel system has also been modified. Full information on the modifications and additional equipment required will be found later on in this Chapter.

32 Carburettor (Hitachi) – idle speed and mixture adjustment

On automatic transmission vehicles the check should be carried out in the 'D' position. **CAUTION:** *Be sure to engage the handbrake and chock all the roadwheels. Keep your foot on the brake pedal while depressing the accelerator to prevent the car moving forward. The use of a CO meter and an electric tachometer is essential.*

1   Remove the air hose between the 3-way connector and the air check valve. Plug the hose to prevent ingress of dirt.
2   Ensure that the ignition timing is correct according to the Specifications, and run the engine to the normal operating temperature.
3   Turn the throttle adjusting screw until the idling speed is 750 rpm (manual transmission) or 650 rpm (automatic transmission – in 'D' position).
4   Adjust the idle adjusting screw so that the CO percentage is $2\pm$1%.
5   Now re-adjust the throttle screw and idler screw to obtain the

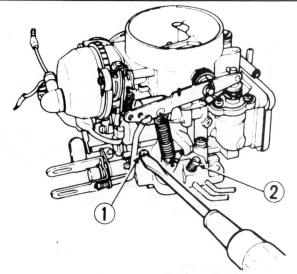

Fig. 3.18 Idle speed and mixture adjustment – DCH 340 carburettor (Sec 32)

1   Throttle adjusting screw   2   Idle adjusting screw

specified idle speed but still maintain the correct CO percentage.
6   Remove the plug and connect the air hose to the air check valve.

33 Carburettor (Hitachi) – fast idle adjustment

1   When starting the engine from cold, the choke valve plate will be closed and through a system of interconnnecting links, the throttle valve plate will be open to provide the correct fast idle speed.
2   Adjustment is carried out by turning the fast idle screw after releasing the locknut. With the carburettor in position on the manifold, the best method of adjustment is by trial-and-error method on successive cold starts. Where the carburettor is removed from the manifold then a twist drill will provide a suitable gauge to check the throttle valve plate opening (choke valve plate fully closed).

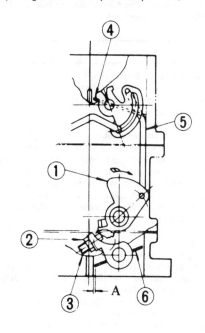

Fig. 3.19 Fast idle adjustment – DCH 340 carburettor (Sec 33)

1 Fast idle cam	*4 Choke valve plate*
2 Nut	*5 Connecting rod*
3 Fast idle screw	*6 Throttle valve*

34 Carburettor (Hitachi) – choke vacuum break adjustment

1   Remove the air cleaner cover.
2   Using a rod or twist drill as a gauge, 0.067 in (1.7 mm) in diameter, place it between the edge of the choke valve plate (in the closed position) and the carburettor body.
3   With the choke valve plate held in this position, the link rod should be located at the lower end of the slot in the choke piston lever. If necessary, bend the link rod to establish this condition.

35 Carburettor (Hitachi) – choke housing setting

1   Under normal conditions, the index mark on the thermostat cover should align with the centre line on the housing.
2   Where there is any tendency to over-choke, turn the cover not more than one graduation in a clockwise direction.

36 Carburettor (Hitachi) – choke unloader adjustment

1   Remove the air cleaner cover.
2   Using a rod or twist drill as a gauge, 0.173 in (4.4 mm) in diameter, place it between the edge of the choke valve plate (in the closed position) and the carburettor body.
3   Holding the choke valve plate in this position, the throttle lever should be able to be opened fully. If not, bend the unloader tongue.

37 Carburettor (Hitachi) – throttle valves interlock adjustment

1   The interlock mechanism operates correctly when the primary throttle valve plate is opened through 50° and the secondary throttle valve plate is about to open.
2   Where adjustment is required use a twist drill as a gauge 0.291 in (7.4 mm) in width and insert it between the edge of the primary throttle valve and the carburettor body. Bend the connecting link if necessary so that the secondary throttle valve plate is just about to open.

38 Carburettor (Hitachi) – dashpot adjustment

1   To set the position of the dashpot, first check that the carburettor idling speed and mixture settings are correct and that the engine is at normal operating temperature.
2   With the engine running, open the throttle until the engine speed is 1900 – 2100 rpm (manual transmission) or 1650 – 1850 rpm (automatic transmission).
3   Loosen the dashpot stem locknut and rotate the dashpot until the dashpot button just touches the throttle stop lever; then retighten the locknut.
4   Check that when the throttle is released suddenly, the engine speed drops smoothly from 2000 to 1000 rpm in about three seconds.

39 Carburettor (Hitachi) – removal and refitting

1   Remove the air cleaner.
2   Disconnect the fuel and vacuum lines from the carburettor.
3   Disconnect the automatic choke electrical leads also the lead from the anti-dieseling solenoid valve.
4   Disconnect the throttle linkage.
5   Unscrew and remove the four carburettor securing nuts and their washers and lift the carburettor from the inlet manifold. Remove the gasket.
6   Refitting is the reverse of removal procedure. Always use a new gasket.

40 Carburettor (Hitachi) – dismantling and reassembly

1   Using a soft brush and fuel, clean all dirt from the external surfaces of the carburettor.

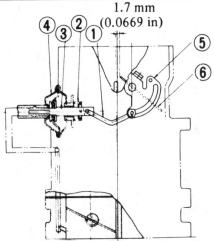

Fig. 3.20 Choke vacuum break adjustment – DCH 340 carburettor (Sec 34)

1	Link rod	4	Diaphragm
2	Spring	5	Piston lever
3	Piston	6	Choke valve plate

2   Detach the throttle return spring from the primary side of the unit.
3   Remove the accelerator pump level and rod.
4   Remove the fast idle cam connecting rod.
5   Unscrew the three screws which secure the thermostat housing cover of the automatic choke.
6   Unscrew the four securing screws and remove the automatic choke housing.
7   Detach the throttle return spring from the secondary side of the carburettor.
8   Unscrew the four securing screws and remove the float chamber.
9   Remove the diaphragm chamber and gasket.
10 Remove the fast idle cam, the cam spring and the counter lever.
11 Unscrew and remove the fuel inlet union hollow bolt, the banjo union, filter fuel inlet needle valve and stop plate.
12 Remove he accelerator pump components including the pump flexible boot, the piston, piston return spring and inlet valve.
13 Remove the accelerator pump injector and outlet valve assemblies.
14 Remove the primary and secondary venturis, the main air bleeds and the emulsion tubes.
15 Remove the slow jet and the slow air bleed.
16 Remove the primary and secondary main jets.
17 Remove the fuel level gauge cover, the float chamber level gauge, rubber seal, the float pivot shaft and the float.
18 Remove the power valve and the throttle lever and fast idle lever components.
19 Unscrew the anti-dieseling solenoid.
20 The boost controlled deceleration device can be removed after unscrewing the three securing screws (1). *On no account unscrew the screws (2). (Fig. 3.21).*
21 Clean all components in clean fuel and blow through internal

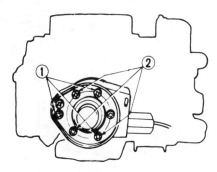

Fig. 3.21 BCDD screws (Sec 40)

1   Securing screws   2   Cover-to-body screws

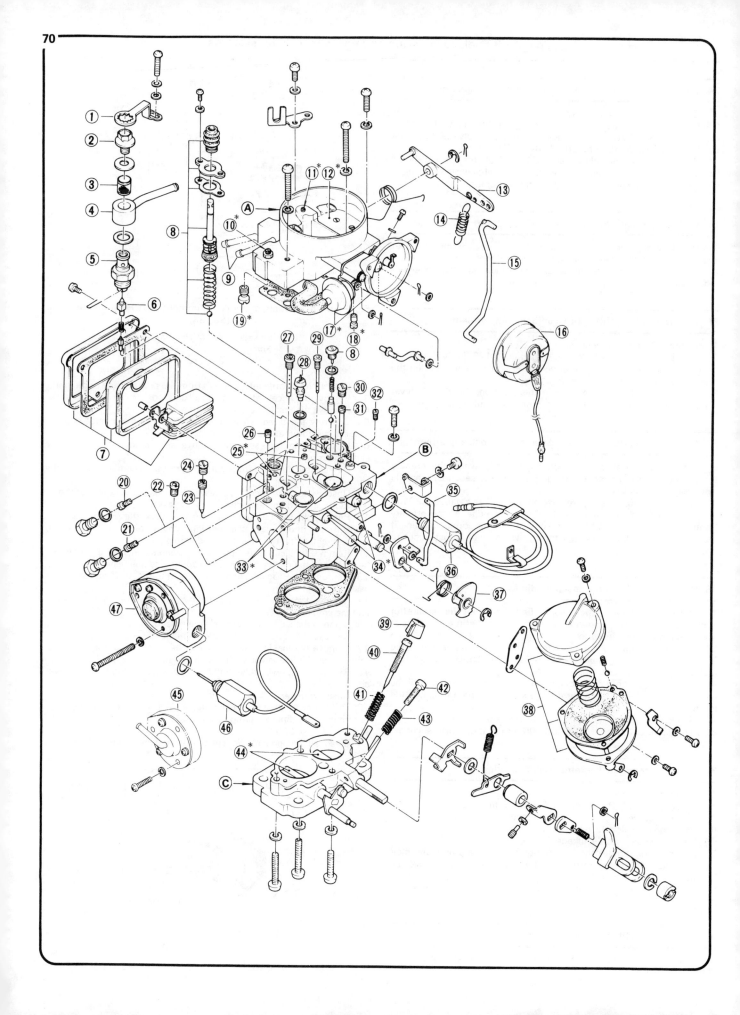

Fig. 3.22 Exploded view of DCH 340 carburettor

A   Choke chamber
B   Centre body
C   Throttle chamber
1   Lock lever
2   Filter set screw
3   Fuel filter
4   Fuel nipple
5   Needle valve body
6   Needle valve
7   Fuel chamber parts
8   Accelerating pump parts
9   Altitude compensator pipe (California)
10 *Coasting air bleed adjusting screw
11 *High speed enricher air bleed
12 *Choke valve
13 Accelerating pump lever
14 Throttle return spring
15 Accelerating pump rod
16 Automatic choke cover
17 *Automatic choke body and diaphragm chamber
18 *Richer jet
19 *Coasting air bleed I
20 Primary main jet
21 Secondary main jet
22 Secondary slow air bleed
23 Secondary slow jet
24 Plug
25 *Safe orifice
26 Coasting jet
27 Secondary main air bleed
28 Power valve
29 Primary main air bleed
30 Plug
31 Primary slow jet
32 No 2 primary slow air bleed
33 *Primary and secondary small venturi
34 *Venturi stopper screw
35 Choke connecting rod
36 Anti-dieseling solenoid
37 Fast idle cam
38 Diaphragm chamber parts
39 Idle limiter cap
40 Idle adjust screw
41 Idle adjust screw spring
42 Throttle adjust screw
43 Throttle adjust screw spring
44 *Primary and secondary throttle valve
45 BCDD (California)
46 Vacuum control solenoid
47 BCDD (except California)

Note: Do not remove the parts marked with an asterisk

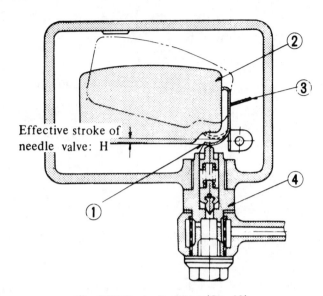

Effective stroke of needle valve: H

Fig. 3.23 Float adjustment (Sec 40)

1   Seat
2   Float
3   Float stop
4   Needle valve
H. = 0.051-0.067 in (1.3-1.7 mm)

passages and jets with air from a tyre pump. Never probe jets with wire or their calibration will be ruined.
22 Check the calibration marked on the jets with the figures shown in specifications in case any have been substituted by a previous owner.
23 Renew any worn parts and obtain new gaskets.
24 Reassembly is a reversal of dismantling but the following points must be observed.
25 Tighten the BCDD screws to the specified torque.
26 Smear the threads of the anti-dieseling solenoid with jointing compound.
27 When reassembling the float mechanism, pour some fuel into the float chamber through the fuel inlet union and then check the level in relation to the line on the sight glass. If the level is incorrect, bend the float seat and the float stopper to obtain the correct level and the correct float arm stroke (Fig. 3.23).
28 When the carburettor is fully assembled, carry out the checks and adjustments described in Sections 33 to 37.
29 When the carburettor is refitted on the engine, check the idle speed and mixture settings as described in Section 32.

41 Carburettor (Hitachi) accelerator control linkage – removal and refitting

1   This procedure is similar to that described in Section 20 except for minor differences in component design.
2   On cars equipped with automatic transmission, adjust the 'kick-down' switch so that the operating rod of the switch is fully engaged in the recess at the end of the accelerator pedal arm (accelerator pedal fully released) but without any pressure being exerted on the rod. When the adjustment is correct, tighten the switch locknut (Fig. 3.24).

42 Fuel filter – renewal

1   The disposable cartridge type fuel filter is located in the engine compartment. It cannot be cleaned and must be renewed at intervals of 24 000 mile (40 000 km).
2   Remove the filter by loosening the inlet and outlet hose clips and detaching the two hoses. Have a piece of tapered wood, such as a pencil, ready to plug the inlet pipe. Remove the filter from its securing clip (photo).
3   Fitting the new filter is the reverse of the removal sequence.

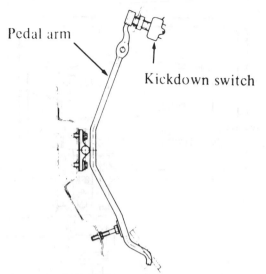

Fig. 3.24 'Kick-down' switch adjustment (automatic transmission)
(Sec 41)

42.2 Fuel filter is secured to the bulkhead by a spring clip

43 Fuel tank – removal and refitting

Two types of fuel tank are fitted to models covered by this manual. One type is used for Saloons whilst the other type is used on Estate Cars.

Models produced for the USA and Canadian markets have a reservoir tank as well as the Evaporative Emission Control System.

Saloon models

1   Open the boot lid and remove the compartment front finisher.
2   Remove the spare wheel and then place a suitable container under the fuel tank drain plug. Undo the drain plug and allow the contents to drain out. Refit the drain plug; keep the fuel in a closed metal drum for safety reasons.
3   Disconnect the fuel tank filler hose, ventilation hose, breather hose and outlet hose.

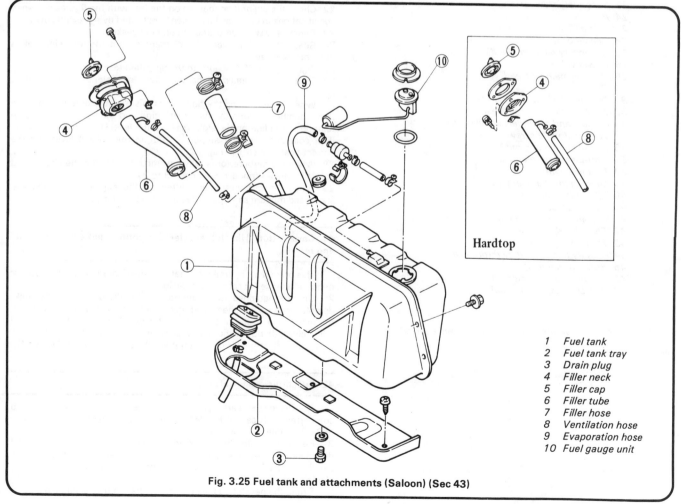

Hardtop

1   Fuel tank
2   Fuel tank tray
3   Drain plug
4   Filler neck
5   Filler cap
6   Filler tube
7   Filler hose
8   Ventilation hose
9   Evaporation hose
10   Fuel gauge unit

Fig. 3.25 Fuel tank and attachments (Saloon) (Sec 43)

4   For safety reasons disconnect the battery and then detach the leads from the sender unit. Note the location of each lead.
5   Remove the rear seat backrest and cushion.
6   Undo and remove the bolts securing the fuel tank to the body. There are two at the front and one on each side.
7   The fuel tank may be lifted away from the car.
8   Should it be necessary to remove the reservoir tank, unfasten the trim clips and detach the rear parcel shelf finisher.
9   Disconnect the three breather tubes from the reservoir.
10   Undo and remove the four bolts and washers securing the reservoir tank to the body. Lift away the reservoir tank.
11   Refitting the reservoir and fuel tank is the reverse sequence to removal.

Estate cars
12   Undo and remove the two self tapping screws securing the inspection cover to the rear floor. Lift away the inspection cover.
13   For safety reasons disconnect the battery. Detach the leads from the sender unit. Note the location of each lead.
14   Lift away the spare wheel and then place a suitable container under the fuel tank drain plug. Undo the drain plug and allow the contents to drain. Refit the drain plug; keep the fuel in a closed metal drum for safety reasons.
15   Disconnect the fuel tank filler hose, ventilation hose and outlet hose.
16   Undo and remove the four bolts and spring washers securing the fuel tank to the body and lift away the fuel tank.
17   Should it be necessary to remove the reservoir tank first remove the trim panel from the right-hand side of the rear body.
18   Detach the three ventilation hoses from the reservoir tank.
19   Carefully remove the grommet from the vapour hose and then detach the hose.
20   Undo and remove the two screws on the top face of the reservoir tank and then lift the tank up.

21   Release the latches at the lower flange section and slide out the reservoir tank.
22   Refitting the reservoir and fuel tank is the reverse sequence to removal.

Cleaning and repair
23   With time it is likely that sediment will collect in the bottom of the fuel tank. Condensation, resulting in rust and other impurities, is sometimes found in the fuel tank.
24   When the tank is removed, it should be vigorously flushed out and turned upside down, or if facilities are available, steam cleaned.
25   Repairs to the fuel tank to stop leaks are best carried out using resin adhesive and hardeners as supplied by most accessory shops. In cases of repairs being done to large areas, glass fibre mats or perforated zinc may be repaired to give the area support. If any soldering, welding or brazing is contemplated, the tank must be steamed out to remove any traces of petroleum vapour. It is dangerous to use naked flames on a fuel tank without this, even though it may have been lying empty for a considerable time.

44   Fuel gauge sender unit – fault finding

1   The sender unit is mounted on the fuel tank and access is gained once the tank has been removed on Saloon models, and on Estate models, after removal of the floor mounted inspection cover (photo).
2   If the fuel gauge does not work correctly then the fault is either in the sender unit, the gauge in the instrument panel, the wiring or the voltage regulator.
3   First test for operation, switch on the ignition and observe if the fuel and temperature gauges operate. If only one operates it can be assumed that the voltage regulator is satisfactory. However, if neither operates then check the regulator as described in Chapter 10.
4   To check the sender unit first disconnect the lead from the unit at the connector. Switch on the ignition and the gauge should read 'Empty'. Now connect the lead to earth and the gauge should read 'Full'. Allow 30 seconds for each reading.
5   If both the situations are correct then the fault lies in the sender unit.
6   If the gauge does not read 'Empty' with the lead disconnected from the sender unit, the lead should then also be disconnected from the gauge to the sender unit.
7   If the gauge still does not read 'empty' it is faulty and should be renewed. (For details see Chapter 10).
8   With the lead disconnected from the sender unit and earthed, if the gauge reads anything other than 'Full' check the rest of the circuit (see Chapter 10 for the wiring diagram).
9   To remove the unit first remove the tank from the car as described in Section 43 – Saloon models or remove the floor mounted inspection cover – Estate Car models.

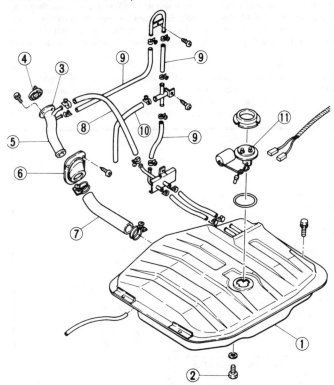

Fig. 3.26 Fuel tank and attachments (Estate) (Sec 43)

1	Fuel tank	7 Filler hose
2	Drain plug	8 Ventilation hose
3	Filler neck	9 Evaporation hose
4	Filler cap	10 Overflow hose
5	Filler tube	11 Fuel gauge unit
6	Filler hole grommet	

44.1 Fuel gauge sender unit – Saloon model

10 Using a screwdriver turn the lockplate in an anti-clockwise direction to release the bayonet catch and lift away the lock-plate, sender unit and gasket. Take care not to bend the lead arm.
11 Refitting the sender unit is the reverse sequence to removal. Always use a new gasket.

45 Emission control systems – general

Vehicles being operated in areas controlled by the US Federal Regulations on air pollution must have their engines and ancillary equipment modified and accurately tuned so that carbon monoxide, hydrocarbons and nitrogen produced by the engine are within finely controlled limits.

To achieve this there are several systems used. Depending on the pollution standard require, the systems may be fitted either singly or a combination of them all. The solution to the problem is achieved by modifying various parts of the engine and fuel supply system as will be seen in subsequent Sections.

46 Crankcase ventilation system – general description

This system draws clean air from within the air cleaner and passes it through a mesh flame arrester and into a hose which is connected to the top of the rocker cover. This air is then passed through the engine and into the inlet manifold via an oil separator, hose and regulating valve. This means any crankcase vapours are passed back into the combustion chambers and burnt.

The oil dipstick and filler cap are sealed to prevent the passing of vapours to the atmosphere.

The operation of this system is most efficient under part throttle conditions when there is a relatively high induction vacuum in the inlet manifold so as to allow the regulation valve to open and allow all crankcase vapours to be drawn from the crankcase. Under full throttle conditions the inlet manifold vacuum is not sufficient to draw all vapours from the crankcase and into the inlet manifold. In this case the crankcase ventilation air flow is reversed, with the fumes being drawn into the air cleaner instead of the inlet manifold.

Positioned within the crankcase is a baffle plate and filter mesh which will prevent engine oil from being drawn upwards into the inlet manifold.

Servicing information on this Section will be found in Chapter 1.

47 Exhaust emission control system – general

An air injection system is used with other engine modifications to reduce the amount of polluting gases being emitted by the exhaust system to atmosphere. 610 models for North America fitted with L20B engine also have an exhaust gas recirculation (EGR Control System). Models for California are equipped with a catalytic converter in the exhaust system.

48 Air injection system – general description

An air injection system is used with other engine modifications to reduce the amount of polluting gases being passed from the exhaust system to the atmosphere.

The principle of operation is that clean filtered air is injected into the exhaust port of each cylinder where unburnt carbon monoxide and hydrocarbons are present, a chemical reaction is able to take place which will bring the exhaust gases to an acceptable level.

Fitted in conjunction with this are a specially calibrated distributor and carburettor. The system comprises an air pump, air injection gallery and nozzle, check valve and anti-backfire valve plus various hoses and clips.

Clean air is drawn by the air pump and compressed by the two vanes of the pump and passed to the air injection gallery and nozzle assembly on the exhaust manifold. The air injector nozzle protrudes down at an angle into the exhaust manifold ports, in the area of the exhaust valves. The fresh air is injected into the manifold at these points. The air injection gallery and nozzle assembly is designed to ensure that an even distribution of air, which is drawn through a check valve, is passed to each exhaust manifold port.

The check valve is fitted in the delivery line at the injection gallery. The function of this valve is to prevent any exhaust gases passing into the air pump should the manifold pressure be greater than the pump injection pressure. It is designed to close against the exhaust manifold pressure should the air pump fail as a result, for example, of a broken drive belt.

To prevent backfiring in the exhaust system when the throttle is closed at high speed, and a coasting condition exists, a special anti-backfire valve is fitted between the inlet manifold and air delivery line. This valve supplies the inlet manifold with a certain amount of air which will burn completely in the combustion chamber and not in the

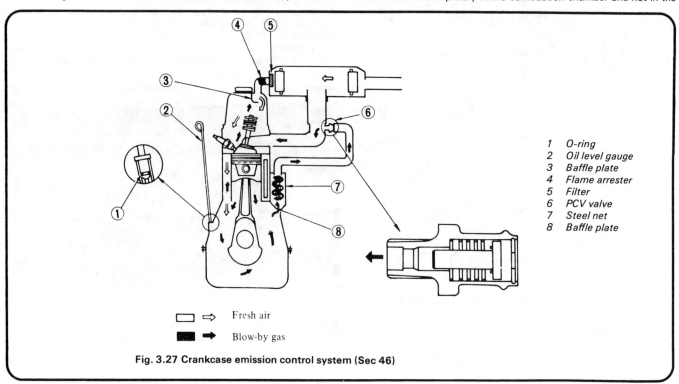

1	O-ring
2	Oil level gauge
3	Baffle plate
4	Flame arrester
5	Filter
6	PCV valve
7	Steel net
8	Baffle plate

☐ ⇨ Fresh air

■ ➡ Blow-by gas

Fig. 3.27 Crankcase emission control system (Sec 46)

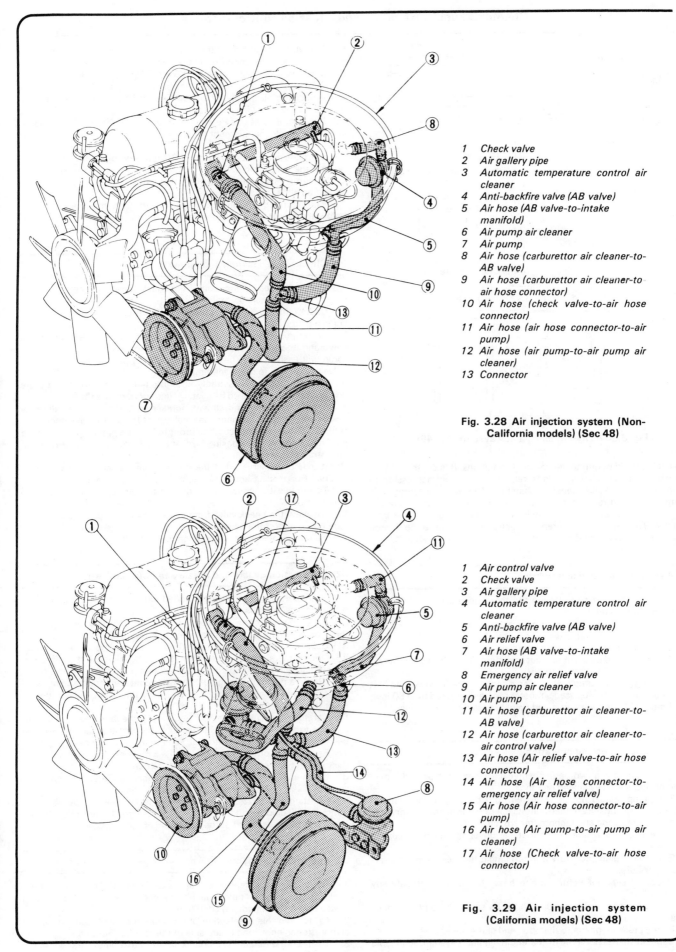

1 Check valve
2 Air gallery pipe
3 Automatic temperature control air cleaner
4 Anti-backfire valve (AB valve)
5 Air hose (AB valve-to-intake manifold)
6 Air pump air cleaner
7 Air pump
8 Air hose (carburettor air cleaner-to-AB valve)
9 Air hose (carburettor air cleaner-to-air hose connector)
10 Air hose (check valve-to-air hose connector)
11 Air hose (air hose connector-to-air pump)
12 Air hose (air pump-to-air pump air cleaner)
13 Connector

Fig. 3.28 Air injection system (Non-California models) (Sec 48)

1 Air control valve
2 Check valve
3 Air gallery pipe
4 Automatic temperature control air cleaner
5 Anti-backfire valve (AB valve)
6 Air relief valve
7 Air hose (AB valve-to-intake manifold)
8 Emergency air relief valve
9 Air pump air cleaner
10 Air pump
11 Air hose (carburettor air cleaner-to-AB valve)
12 Air hose (carburettor air cleaner-to-air control valve)
13 Air hose (Air relief valve-to-air hose connector)
14 Air hose (Air hose connector-to-emergency air relief valve)
15 Air hose (Air hose connector-to-air pump)
16 Air hose (Air pump-to-air pump air cleaner)
17 Air hose (Check valve-to-air hose connector)

Fig. 3.29 Air injection system (California models) (Sec 48)

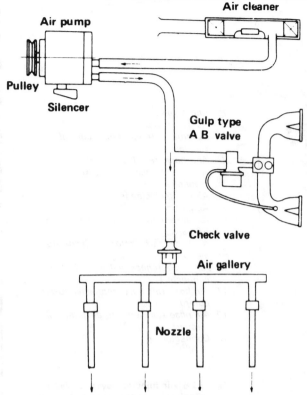

Fig. 3.30 Layout of air injection system (Sec 48)

exhaust manifold during these coasting conditions. It is controlled by a small sensor hose which is able to relay high manifold depression to the anti-backfire valve sensing chamber. The valve diaphragm is spring-loaded and reacts on this vacuum and is drawn downwards to open the air valve so as to supply air pump pressure to the inlet manifold. The valve will only remain open in proportion to the degree of depression felt by the diaphragm.

49 Air pump – removal and refitting

1   Open the bonnet and slacken the three hose clips at the pump cover end. Detach the hoses.
2   Slacken off the pump adjustment bracket bolt and mounting bolt and push the pump towards the cylinder block.
3   Lift the drivebelt from the pump pulley.
4   Remove the adjustment bracket and mounting bolts and lift the air pump from the engine compartment.
5   Refitting the air pump is the reverse sequence to removal. The belt should be sufficiently adjusted so that it can be depressed by 0.50 inch (12.7 mm) with the thumb at a mid point between the two pulleys.

50 Air pump – checking operation

1   The air pump is a two-vane positive displacement type and is permanently lubricated by sealed bearings.
2   The pump should not be removed from the engine for overhaul without first having ascertained that its operation is unsatisfactory. For this a pressure gauge and tachometer are required.
3   To test operation first check that the drivebelt tension is correct (Section 49).
4   Start the engine and allow it to run until it reaches normal operating temperature.
5   Check all clips for tightness and hoses for damage. Rectify any fault found.
6   Slacken the hose clip and detach the air supply hose at the check valve.
7   Fit the pressure gauge to the open end of the hose.
8   Connect the tachometer to the engine ignition system. A suitable

adaptor with a small hole in the side should be used. Run the engine at a constant fast idle speed of 1500 rpm and note the reading on the test gauge which should be at least 0.47 in Hg (12 mm Hg).
9   Should the air pressure readings be less than the required amount disconnect the air supply hose from the anti-backfire valve. Plug the hose and repeat test in paragraph 8.
10   Should the pressure readings be less than the required amount check the air cleaner element for blockage. Renew the element, do not clean it.
11   Start the engine and run at 1500 rpm and put a finger over the hole on the adaptor. If any air pressure can be felt or heard coming out of the pump relief valve then the valve can be considered faulty and should be either repaired or renewed.
12   After carrying out the above checks and the pump pressure is still below the recommended pressure then the air pump assembly should be renewed.

51 Check valve – testing and renewal

1   To test the correct function of the check valve start the engine and run until it reaches its normal operating temperature.
2   Check the hose connections for tightness and the hoses for serviceability. Rectify any fault found.
3   With the engine stationary, detach the air supply hose at the check valve and inspect the inside of the valve through the inlet aperture. A torch will assist here. The valve plate should bear lightly against the valve seat opposite to the inlet manifold.
4   Using a paper clip suitably straightened, unseat the valve plate and allow it to return onto its seating. If it sticks renew the valve.
5   Start the engine and slowly increase its speed to approximately 1500 rpm. Check for exhaust gas leakage at the check valve operation. A lighter flame will deflect when brought into the proximity of the hose junction. If the valve is leaking it must be renewed as it is a sealed unit and cannot be repaired.
6   It may be observed that the check valve may flutter or vibrate at engine idle speeds. Should this be the case it is quite normal.
7   To remove the check valve, detach the air supply hose from the check valve.
8   Unscrew the check valve from the air gallery flange taking extreme care not to distort the air gallery.
9   Refitting is the reverse sequence to removal.

52 Air injection gallery and nozzle – removal and refitting

1   This operation is not recommended unless it is vital. Pipe fracture would necessitate this.
2   Preferably soak the threaded sections of the injection nozzles in the exhaust manifold, overnight, with penetrating oil.
3   Using a small pipe wrench slacken the injection nozzle union nuts.
4   Detach the air supply hose from the check valve and then lift away the air gallery from the nozzles at the exhaust manifold.
5   Obtain a piece of strong but thin wire (coat hanger or fencing wire) and make a hook on one end in such a way that it is small enough to enter the nozzle bore.
6   Carefully insert the hooked end down the bore by a sufficient amount to allow the hook to engage on the nozzle lower lip. Grip the end of the wire with pliers and pull, so drawing out the nozzle.
7   Remove the other three nozzles in a similar manner. Keep them in their respective order so that they are not interchanged.
8   Use a small wire brush and clean the nozzles. Carefully inspect for signs of leaks, damage or fractures caused by heat.
9   Refitting the nozzles and air gallery is the reverse sequence to removal. All unions nuts must be tightened to the specified torque wrench settings as found at the beginning of this Chapter.

53 Special modifications (L18 engine) – general description

1   The engine modification system is to control the operation of the dual contact breaker point, distributor and carburettor deceleration device under certain driving conditions.
2   To achieve this a selection of switches are used to energise the carburettor solenoid and retard side of the special distributor.
3   To help understanding, models fitted with manual transmission,

the carburettor solenoid switch is only energised during deceleration when three conditions have arisen:

(a)   *The clutch pedal is not in operation*
(b)   *The accelerator pedal is not being depressed*
(c)   *A forward gear or reverse has actually been selected*

4   The retard function of the distributor is only energised so as to retard the timing by 10° when three conditions have arisen:

(a)   *The clutch pedal is not in operation*
(b)   *Third gear has been selected*
(c)   *The carburettor throttle valve is open within the range of 35° from idle and the throttle switch plunger is not being depressed*

54 Dual contact breaker point distributor – description and circuit check

1   For construction details see Chapter 4.
2   There are two sets of contact breaker points in the distributor and they are positioned opposite to each other. Both are mounted on the distributor breaker plate assembly independent of each other. One capacitor is used.
3   Both sets of contact breaker points are connected parallel in the primary ignition circuit and may be adjusted with the adjustment screws to achieve a 5° distributor rotor travel phase difference. This is 10° on the crankshaft pulley.
4   When the electrical relay for the retard set of contact breaker points is energised the engine operates on the advanced set of contact breaker points so as to achieve an initial advance of 10° BTDC.
5   When all the various switches are closed to complete the circuit to energise the relay, the engine will begin operating on the retard set of contact breaker points. The ignition timing will alter and the engine will now be running with a total retard of 10° in flywheel travel. In other words TDC.
6   There are six switches and a solenoid valve in the main circuits of the control system. They are as follows:

(a)   *Clutch*
(b)   *Accelerator*
(c)   *Neutral gear*
(d)   *Throttle*
(e)   *Speed switch*
(f)   *Transmission switches*
(g)   *Solenoid valve – carburettor*

If the operations of any one of these is suspect it is far better for the car to be taken to the local Datsun garage and have the complete system checked electronically rather than to try to trace the fault (other than a loose cable connection). The reason for this is that the function of the exhaust emission control system is dependent on the efficient operation of all parts of the system and if one fault occurs it can in fact give symptoms of another fault. Without experience of emission control systems and no test equipment, trouble-shooting is virtually impossible and considered inadvisable to attempt.

55 Exhaust gas recirculation (EGR) control system – general description

1   The system is based upon the principle of recirculating exhaust gases to the combustion chambers in order to reduce the combustion temperature and so reduce the noxious constituents of the combustion process.
2   Components of the system include a control valve, solenoid valve, engine coolant temperature sensor, modulator and the necessary interconnecting hoses.
3   The control valve admits exhaust gases to the combustion chambers but only under certain conditions.

(a)   *When the coolant temperature is between 87 and 105°F (31 and 41°C), the system is operational*
(b)   *Irrespective of coolant temperature, when the throttle valve is in the idling or fully open positions, the system is inoperative*

4   The EGR control valve regulates the intake of recirculated exhaust gas and operates by means of inlet manifold vacuum.
5   The EGR solenoid valve is attached to the EGR control valve for the purpose of opening or closing the vacuum source to the control valve. The solenoid valve is actuated by the coolant water temperature sensor operating through the modulator.
6   The water temperature sensor is installed in the engine cooling system thermostat housing and is additional to the water temperature gauge sensor installed in the cylinder block.

56 EGR system – inspection and maintenance

1   At 12 000 mile (20 000 km) intervals, the following operations should be carried out.
2   Inspect the entire EGR system, cleaning the external surfaces of the components and renewing any rubber hoses which show signs of deterioration.

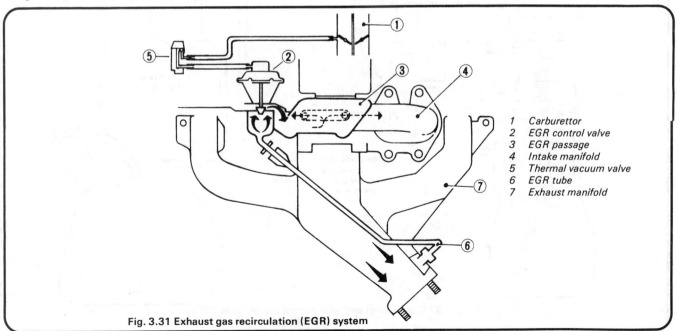

1   Carburettor
2   EGR control valve
3   EGR passage
4   Intake manifold
5   Thermal vacuum valve
6   EGR tube
7   Exhaust manifold

Fig. 3.31 Exhaust gas recirculation (EGR) system

3   Check the security of the electrical connections to the EGR solenoid valve.

4   Start the engine and increase its speed from idling to 3500 rpm and observe whether the control valve diaphragm and shaft move as the engine speed is increased. If they remain stationary, a fault exists.

5   Disconnect the leads from the solenoid valve and connect the valve directly to the battery terminals. Again increase the speed of the engine and note whether the control valve remains stationary. If it does, then it is in good condition.

6   With the engine running at normal idling speed, depress the EGR

control valve diaphragm by pushing in the bottom dished plate with the fingers. The engine will begin to run very unevenly if the valve is in good condition.

7   The water temperature sensor can only be satisfactorily checked for correct operation with an ohmmeter. Suspend the sensor in water which is being heated and having connected the ohmmeter to the sensor the following values should be indicated for a serviceable unit. Water temperature: 59 to 77°F (15 to 25°C) – 2300 to 3700 ohms 113 to 131°F (45 to 55°C) – 650 to 908 ohms.

8   As a regular maintenance operation at 12 000 mile (20 000 km)

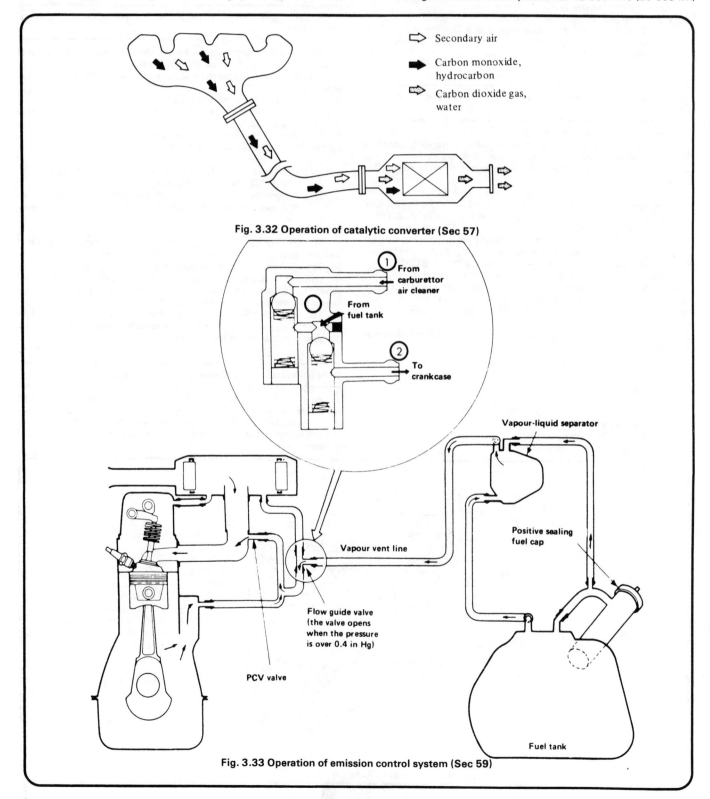

Fig. 3.32 Operation of catalytic converter (Sec 57)

Fig. 3.33 Operation of emission control system (Sec 59)

intervals, unbolt the control valve from the manifold and wire brush the seat of the valve to remove all deposits. Finally blow the seat clean with air from a tyre pump.

57 Catalytic converter – general description

610 models for California are equipped with a catalytic converter which is a device fitted to the exhaust system ahead of the silencer. It is made up of ceramic cores, coated with platinum or palladium, which act as catalysts to absorb combustible elements re,aining in the exhaust gases without being destroyed themselves.

A defective catalytic converter is indicated by excessive CO readings. It is renewed as a unit.

58 Catalytic converter – removal and refitting

1 Jack up the car and support it on axle stands.
2 Undo the catalytic converter lower guard plate securing bolts and remove the guard.
3 Remove the converter-to-exhaust pipe flange bolts and withdraw the converter.
4 Refitting is the reverse of the removal procedure. Tighten the securing bolts to 19 – 24 lbf ft (2.6 – 3.4 kgf m).

59 Evaporative emission control system – description

1 The system comprises the following items:

(a) Positive sealed fuel tank.
(b) Vapour liquid separator.
(c) Vapour vent line.
(d) Flow guide valve.

2 With the engine stationary fuel vapours through the natural process of evaporation will gradually fill the air space in the fuel tank, vapour liquid separator and vapour vent lines. Because the fuel tank is fitted with a sealing filler cap a pressure will build up in the system. When this occurs the flow guide valve will open at a pressure of 0.4 in Hg (10 mm Hg). Any excess vapours will then be bypassed into the crankcase via a hose.
3 When the engine is started, the vacuum created in the inlet manifold will open the positive crankcase ventilation valve and the crankcase side of the flow guide valve. Vapours which have been held in the crankcase, vent line, separator and fuel tank are then drawn into the inlet manifold and burnt in the combustion chamber.
4 When the vapour pressure in the system drops, the air cleaner side of the flow guide valve will open. This will allow atmospheric pressure to be directed from the air cleaner assembly to the fuel tank.

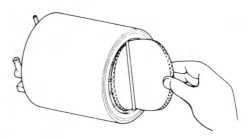

Fig. 3.34 Renewing the carbon canister filter (Sec 59)

Allowing this air into the system will prevent a vacuum being created in the system which could cause damage to the tank.
5 On some models a carbon canister, which absorbs the fuel vapours from the sealed fuel tank when the engine is at rest or idling, is incorporated in the system. When the engine speed is increased, the fuel vapours stored in the canister are drawn into the inlet manifold. The canister filter which can be removed from the bottom of the canister should be renewed every 25 000 miles (40 000 km).

60 Evaporative emission control system – checking

To carry out tests for efficient sealing requires the use of a manometer. As this type of equipment is not usually found amongst the belongings of a DIY motorist no further information is given in this Section. If it is suspected that there is a leak let the local Datsun garage test the system.

61 Exhaust system – general description

1 The exhaust system consists of a front pipe with pre-silencer assembly, centre pipe, rear pipe with main silencer, mounting insulators and brackets.
2 On Saloon models a protective heat shield is fitted over the main silencer to protect the luggage boot from the heat of the exhaust.
3 When fitting the exhaust system, ensure that it is routed correctly and that the clamps and securing bolts are tightened evenly. Components subject to stress and strain are liable to fracture.
4 When any one part of the system requires renewal, consideration should be given to renewing the complete system as, apart from accidental damage, when one part fails the rest of the system is not likely to last long.

See overleaf for 'Fault diagnosis – fuel system'

62 Fault diagnosis – fuel system

Symptom	Reason/s	Remedy
Fuel consumption excessive	Air cleaner choked and dirty giving rich mixture	Remove, clean, renew element and replace air cleaner
	Fuel leaking from carburettor, fuel pump or fuel lines	Check for and eliminate all fuel leaks. Tighten fuel line union nuts
	Float chamber flooding	Check and adjust float level
	Generally worn carburettor	Remove, overhaul and replace
	Distributor condenser faulty	Remove and fit new unit
	Balance weights or vacuum advance mechanism in distributor faulty	Remove and overhaul distributor
	Carburettor incorrectly adjusted, mixture too rich	Tune and adjust carburettor
	Idling speed too high	Adjust idling speed
	Contact breaker gap incorrect	Check and reset gap
	Valve clearances incorrect	Check rocker arm to valve stem clearances and adjust as necessary
	Incorrectly set spark plugs	Remove, clean and re-gap
	Tyres under-inflated	Check tyre pressures and inflate if necessary
	Wrong spark plugs fitted	Remove and replace with correct units
	Brakes dragging	Check and adjust brakes
Insufficient fuel delivery or weak mixture due to air leaks	*Petrol tank air vent restricted	Remove petrol cap and clean out air vent
	Partially clogged filters in pump and carburettors	Remove and clean filters. Remove and clean out float chamber and needle valve assembly
	Incorrectly seating valves in fuel pump	Remove, and overhaul or fit a new fuel pump
	Fuel pump diaphragm leaking or damaged	Remove, and overhaul or fit a new fuel pump
	Gasket in fuel pump damaged	Remove, and overhaul or fit new fuel pump
	Fuel pump valves sticking due to petrol gumming	Remove and overhaul or thoroughly clean fuel pump
	Too little fuel in fuel tank (prevalent when climbing steep hills)	Refill fuel tank
	Union joints on pipe connections loose	Tighten joints and check for air leaks
	Split in fuel pipe on suction side of fuel pump	Examine, locate and repair
	Inlet manifold to head or inlet manifold to carburettor gasket leaking	Test by pouring oil along joints - bubbles indicate leak. Renew gasket as appropriate

* Not applicable where evaporative emission control system is fitted

Chapter 4 Ignition system

Contents

Specifications

Spark plugs
Make . . . . NGK
Applied engine:
    L16 and L18 (single carburettor) BP5ES
    L18 (twin carburettor) BP6ES
    L20B California . . . . BP6ES - 11
    L20B Non-California BP6ES
Plug gap:
    L16, L18 and L20B (Non-California) . . . . 0.031 - 0.035 in (0.8 - 0.9 mm)
    L20B (California) . . . . 0.039 - 0.043 in (1.0 to 1.1 mm)

Firing order . . . . 1 – 3 – 4 – 2

Ignition coil
Make . . . . Hitachi or Hanshin
Type:
    L16 and L18 . . . . 6R200
    L20B (Non-California) . . . . C6R - 607, H5 - 15 - 10
    L20B (California) . . . . CIT - 17, STC - 10
Primary voltage . . . . 12 volts
Spark gap . . . . More than 0.275 in (7 mm)

Distributor
Non-USA Models
Make . . . . Hitachi
Rotation . . . . Anti-clockwise
Ignition timing
    L16S and L18S . . . . 10° BTDC/600 rpm (manual transmission)
                                           10° BTDC/650 rpm (automatic transmission)
    L18T (up to 1973) . . . . 14° BTDC/650 rpm (manual transmission)
                                             14° BTDC/700 rpm (automatic transmission)
    L18T (1973 onwards) . . . . 10° BTDC/700 rpm (manual transmission)
                                             10° BTDC/750 rpm (automatic transmission)
Dwell angle . . . . 49° - 55°
Condenser capacity . . . . 0.22 to 0.44 mfd
Points gap . . . . 0.018 to 0.022 in (0.45 to 0.55 mm)

USA models

	Non-California	California
Make	Hitachi	[Anti-clockwise]
Type		
Non-California	D4A4-04 (Manual transmission), D4A4-06 (Automatic transmission)	
California	D4F4-03	
Rotation		
Dwell angle	40° - 55°	–
Points gap	0.018 - 0.022 in	–
	(0.45 - 0.55 mm)	
Air-gap		0.008 - 0.016 in
		(0.2 - 0.4 mm)
Condenser capacity	0.20 - 0.24 mfd	–
Ignition timing		
Manual transmission	12° BTDC/750 rpm	
Automatic transmission	12° BTDC/650 rpm (in D position)	

Torque wrench settings

	lbf ft	kgf m
Spark plugs	11 - 18	1.5 - 2.5

1   General description

In order that the engine can run, it is necessary for an electrical spark to ignite the fuel/air mixture in the combustion chamber at exactly the right moment in relation to engine speed and load. The ignition system is based on feeding low tension voltage from the battery to the ignition coil where it is converted to high tension voltage. The high tension voltage is powerful enough to jump the spark plug gap in the cylinder many times a second under high compression, providing that the system is in good condition and that all adjustments are correct.

The conventional ignition system is divided into two circuits, the low tension circuit (LT) and high tension circuit (HT).

The low tension circuit (sometimes known as the primary circuit), consists of the battery, leads interconnecting to the ignition switch, voltage regulator, fuse box, ignition coil, low tension windings, distributor contact breaker points and condenser.

The high tension circuit consists of the high tension or secondary coil windings, the heavy duty ignition lead from the centre of the coil to the centre of the distributor cap, the rotor arm, and the spark plug leads and spark plugs. The system functions in the following manner:

Low tension voltage is changed in the coil into high tension voltage by the opening and closing of the contact breaker points in the low tension circuit. High tension voltage is then fed via the contact in the centre of the distributor cap to the rotor arm of the distributor. The rotor arm revolves inside the distributor cap and each time it comes in line with one of the four metal segments in the cap, which are connected to the spark plug leads, the opening and closing of the contact breaker points causes the high tension voltage to build up, jump the gap from the rotor arm to the appropriate metal segment and so via the spark plug lead to the spark plug, where it finally jumps the spark plug gap before going to earth.

The ignition timing is advanced and retarded automatically, to ensure the spark occurs at just the right moment for the particular load at the prevailing engine speed.

The ignition advance is controlled by a mechanically operated system which comprises two weights which move out from the distributor shaft as the engine speed rises due to centrifugal force. As they move outward they rotate the cam relative to the distributor shaft, and so advance the spark timing. The weights are held in position by two light springs and it is the tension of the springs which is largely responsible for correct spark advancement.

From 1975, California models are equipped with a breakerless type of distributor. In the conventional distributor the ignition timing is detected by the cam and breaker arm, while in the transistorised ignition it is detected by the reluctor on the shaft and the pick-up coil, provided in place of the contact breaker. An electric signal, generated in the pick-up coil is conducted to a transistor ignition unit and breaks the primary circuit; this generates high voltage in the secondary circuit, which is the same as in the conventional ignition system. The breakerless type distributor has the conventional centrifugal and vacuum advance mechanism.

2   Contact breaker points – adjustment

1   To adjust the contact breaker points be they of the single or double type, first release the two clips securing the distributor cap to the distributor body, and lift away the cap. Clean the cap inside and out with a dry cloth. It is unlikely that the four segments will be badly burned or scored, but if they are the cap will have to be renewed.

2   Push in the carbon brush located in the top of the cap once or twice to make sure that it moves freely.

3   Gently prise the contact breaker points open to examine the condition of their faces. If they are rough, pitted or dirty, it will be necessary to remove them for resurfacing, or for new points to be fitted.

4   Presuming that the points are satisfactory, or that they have been cleaned and refitted, measure the gap between the points by turning the engine over until the contact breaker arm is on the peak of one of the four cam lobes (photo).

5   A 0.018 - 0.022 in (0.45 - 0.55 mm) feeler gauge should now just fit between the points.

6   If the gap measurement differs from the figure given, ie is too great or too small, slacken the contact breaker plate securing screw.

7   Using the adjuster screw adjust the contact gap. Tighten the securing screw and check the gap again (photo).

8   A revised type of distributor has been used on later models that does not have an adjuster screw.

9   To adjust the points gap, loosen the contact breaker plate set screws. Move the plate around the pivot pin to achieve the specified contact breaker gap. Tighten the contact breaker plate screws.

10   Refit the rotor arm and distributor cap and clip the spring blade retainers into position.

3   Contact breaker points – removal and refitting

1   If the contact breaker points are burned, pitted or badly worn they must be removed and either renewed, or their faces must be filed smooth.

2   To remove the points of either a single or dual contact distributor, remove the rotor.

3   Slacken the screws at the contact breaker point arm and the primary lead connection. Do not however remove the screws.

4   Carefully pull up on the primary lead to disconnect the terminal from the contact arm.

5   Slacken the cheese head screw that holds the earth wire to the contact breaker points assembly and detach the earth wire.

6   Undo and remove the two screws securing the points assembly to the distributor breaker plate. Lift away the assembly from the distributor.

7   To reface the points, rub their faces on a fine carborundum stone or on fine emery paper. It is important that the faces are rubbed flat and parallel to each other so that there will be complete face to face contact when the contact breaker points are closed. One of the points will be pitted and the other will have deposits on it.

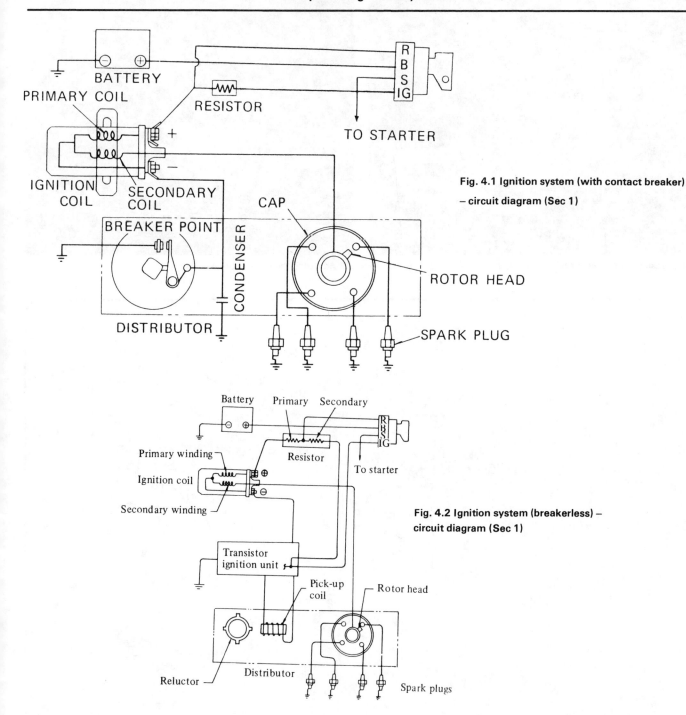

Fig. 4.1 Ignition system (with contact breaker) – circuit diagram (Sec 1)

Fig. 4.2 Ignition system (breakerless) – circuit diagram (Sec 1)

8 It is necessary to completely remove the built-up deposits, but not necessary to rub the pitted point right down to the stage where all the pitting has disappeared, though obviously if this is done it will prolong the time before the operation of refacing the points has to be repeated.
9 Refitting the contact breaker points is the reverse sequence to removal. The gap should be reset as described in the previous Section.
10 Finally refit the rotor arm and then the distributor cap.

---

4 Condenser – removal, testing and refitting

1 The purpose of the condenser (capacitor) is to ensure that when the contact breaker points open there is no sparking across them which would waste voltage and cause wear.
2 The condenser is fitted in parallel with the contact breaker points. If it develops a short circuit, it will cause ignition failure as the points will be prevented from interrupting the low tension circuit.
3 If the engine becomes very difficult to start or begins to miss after several miles of running and the breaker points show signs of excessive burning, then the condition of the condenser must be suspect. A further test can be made by separating the points by hand with the ignition switched on. If this is accompanied by a flash it is possible that the condenser has failed.
4 Without special test equipment the only sure way to diagnose condenser trouble is to renew the suspect unit and note if there is any improvement.
5 To remove the condenser from the distributor, remove the distributor cap and the rotor arm.
6 Disconnect the condenser lead from the breaker plate assembly and then undo and remove the bolt, spring and plain washers securing the condenser to the distributor body.
7 Note that on the dual contact breaker points assembly two condensers are fitted. Inspection and removal is similar to that for the

2.4 Checking the contact breaker points gap

2.7 Adjusting the contact breaker points

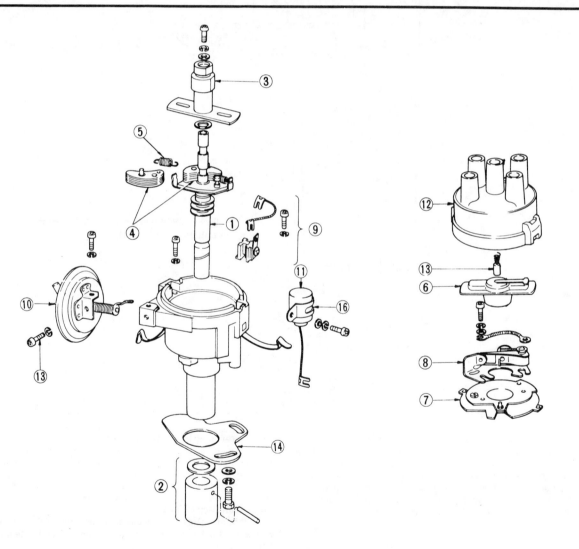

Fig. 4.3 Single contact breaker distributor – component parts (Sec 7)

1	Shaft assembly		assembly	8	Contact set	12 Distributor cap assembly
2	Collar set assembly	5	Governor spring	9	Terminal assembly	13 Carbon point assembly
3	Cam assembly	6	Rotor head assembly	10	Vacuum control assembly	14 Fixing plate
4	Governor weight	7	Breaker assembly	11	Condensor assembly	

single contact breaker points distributor.

8   Refitment is simply a reversal of the removal process.

5 Distributor – lubrication

1   It is important that the distributor is regularly lubricated at the mileages recommended in Routine Maintenance.

2   Release the two clips retaining the distributor cap; lift away the cap and the rotor arm.

3   Smear a trace of petroleum jelly (vaseline) on the distributor cam. On L20B engine a wick is provided for lubricating the cam.

4   Apply two drops of engine oil onto the cam assembly securing screws. This will run down the spindle when the engine is hot and lubricate the bearings.

5   To lubricate the automatic timing control allow a few drops of oil to pass through the hole in the breaker plate assembly through which the four sided cam emerges. Apply not more than one drop of oil to the pivot post and remove any excess.

6 Distributor – removal and refitting

1   To remove the distributor from the engine, start by pulling the terminals off each of the spark plugs. Release the low tension lead from the ignition coil on the side of the distributor.

2   Turn the crankshaft until the timing marks are in the 10°, 12° or 14° BTDC position depending on the model, number 1 cylinder on the compression stroke. The contact breaker points should be just opening.

3   Undo and remove the bolt and washer securing the clamping plate to the distributor support casting.

4   The distributor may now be withdrawn from its support.

5   Refitment is a reversal of the above process, providing that the engine has not been turned in the meantime. If the engine has been disturbed it will be best to retime the ignition (Section 12).

7 Distributor – dismantling

The instructions given in this Section are applicable to the single contact breaker type distributor. The twin contact breaker type is, however, basically similar. Therefore if these instructions are followed for the latter type of distributor, the reader will find that most of the content of this Section is applicable (Figs. 4.3 and 4.4).

1   With the distributor removed from the car and on the bench, remove the distributor cap and lift off the rotor arm. If very tight, lever it off gently with a screwdriver.

2   Remove the contact breaker points as described in Section 3.

3   Undo and remove the bolt, spring and plain washer securing the fixing plate to the underside of the distributor body. Lift away the fixing plate.

4   Undo and remove the two screws and spring washers that secure the vacuum control assembly to the side of the distributor body. Withdraw the vacuum assembly. It will be necessary to lift the operating link clear of the pin on the breaker plate.

5   Detach the condenser lead from the breaker plate assembly. Undo and remove the bolt, spring and plain washers securing the condenser to the side of the distributor body. Lift away the condenser.

6   Withdraw the low tension terminal block from the side of the distributor housing.

7   Undo and remove the cheese head screw and then slacken the breaker plate securing screws. Remove the clips that hold the breaker assembly in position and lift away the breaker assembly from the distributor body.

8   It is important that the breaker plate is not further dismantled. It consists of an upper and lower member which run on steel balls positioned between the breaker plate and breaker springs. Check that the ball bearings are in position and retain them by tightening the two setscrews until reassembly.

9   Using a parallel pin punch of suitable diameter remove the pin that secures the collar to the shaft. Remove the collar and thrust washer.

10   Again using the parallel pin punch remove the pin securing the skew gear to the shaft. Remove the skew gear.

11   The shaft and action plate may now be withdrawn from the distributor body. Recover the upper thrust washer.

12   Undo and remove the set screw located at the top of the shaft. Mark the relative position of the cam and shaft and separate the two parts.

13   Note the location of the weights and springs and separate the parts from the action plate.

14   The distributor is now completely dismantled.

8 Distributor – inspection and renovation

1   Wash all parts in petrol and allow to dry.

2   Check the contact breaker points as described in Section 3. Check the distributor cap for signs of tracking, indicated by a thin black line between the segments. Renew the cap if any signs of tracking are found.

3   If the metal portion of the rotor arm is badly burned or loose, renew the rotor arm. If slightly burnt clean the arm with a fine file.

4   Check that the carbon brush moves freely in the centre of the distributor cover.

5   Examine the balance weights and pivot pins for wear and renew the weights or cam assembly if a degree of wear is found.

6   Examine the shaft and teeth of the cam assembly on the shaft. If the clearance is excessive compare the parts with new and renew either, or both, if they show signs of excessive wear.

7   If the shaft is a loose fit in the distributor bushes and can be seen to be worn, it will be necessary to fit a new shaft and bushes. The bushes are simply pressed out. **NOTE**: *Before inserting a new bush it should be stood in engine oil for at least 24 hours.*

8   Examine the length of the centrifugal weight springs and compare them with new springs. If they have stretched they must be renewed.

9   Inspect the skew gear for signs of wear, and, if evident obtain a new gear.

9 Distributor – reassembly

1   Reassembly is a straightforward reversal of the dismantling process but there are several points which should be noted in addition to those already given in the Section on dismantling:

   (a)   Lubricate with engine oil the centrifugal weights and other parts of the mechanical advance mechanism, the cam and the shaft and action plate.

   (b)   Always use a new upper and lower thrust washer if they show signs of wear or if endfloat is more than 0.002 - 0.005 inch (0.0508 - 0.1270 mm).

   (c)   On reassembling the cam driving pins with the centrifugal weights, check that they are in the correct position as noted on removal (Fig. 4.5).

   (d)   Check the action of the weights in the fully advanced and fully retarded positions and ensure they are not binding.

   (e)   Finally set the contact breaker gap to 0.018 - 0.022 inch (0.45 - 0.55 mm) as described in Section 2. Reset the governor springs and cam.

10 Breakerless distributor – dismantling and reassembly

1   Refer to Fig. 4.6. Take off the cap and remove the rotor head.

2   Remove the two securing screws and detach the vacuum controller.

3   Undo the pick-up coil securing screws and remove the coil assembly.

4   Using two screwdrivers, lever the reluctor from the shaft. Take care not to distort or damage the teeth of the reluctor. Remove the roll pin.

5   Remove the breaker plate setscrews and lift out the breaker plate assembly.

6   Remove the collar by driving out the roll pin and then remove the rotor shaft and driveshaft assembly.

7   Match-mark the rotor shaft and driveshaft, then remove the packing from the top of the rotor shaft and unscrew the rotor shaft securing setscrew.

8   Mark one of the governor springs and its bracket, also one of the

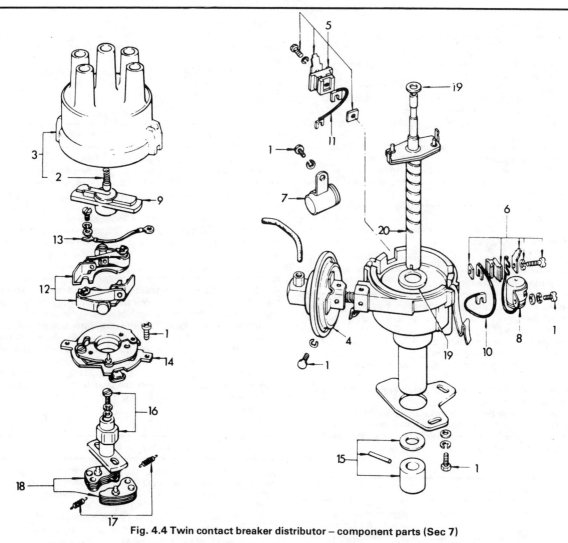

Fig. 4.4 Twin contact breaker distributor – component parts (Sec 7)

1	Set screw	6	Terminal assembly	11	Lead wire assembly	16	Cam assembly set
2	Carbon brush assembly	7	Condenser assembly	12	Contact set	17	Governor spring set
3	Cap assembly	8	Condenser assembly	13	Earth wire assembly	18	Governor weight
4	Vacuum control assembly	9	Rotor head assembly	14	Breaker plate assembly	19	Thrust washer set
5	Terminal assembly	10	Lead wire assembly	15	Collar set	20	Shaft assembly set

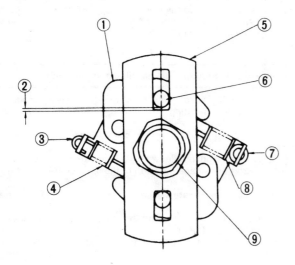

Fig. 4.5 Setting governor spring and cam (Sec 9)

1	Governor weight	5	Cam plate
2	0.0004-0.0018 in (0.01-0.046 mm)	6	Weight pin
		7	Circular hook
3	Rectangular hook	8	Governor spring (A)
4	Governor spring (B)	9	Rotor positioning tip

governor weights and its pivot pins, so that they can be refitted in the same positions.

9   Carefully unhook and remove the governor weights.

10   Reassembly is the reverse of the dismantling procedure. Make sure that the match-marks are aligned so that parts are refitted in their original positions.

11   If the contactor is removed from the breaker plate, adjust the cam-to-contactor clearance to 0.012 in (0.3 mm) as shown in Fig. 4.7.

12   When fitting the reluctor, drive in the roll pin with its slit towards the outer end of the shaft.

13   Lightly grease the top of the rotor shaft.

14   Adjust the air-gap, by loosening the pick-up coil screws, to 0.008 - 0.016 in (0.2 - 0.4 mm).

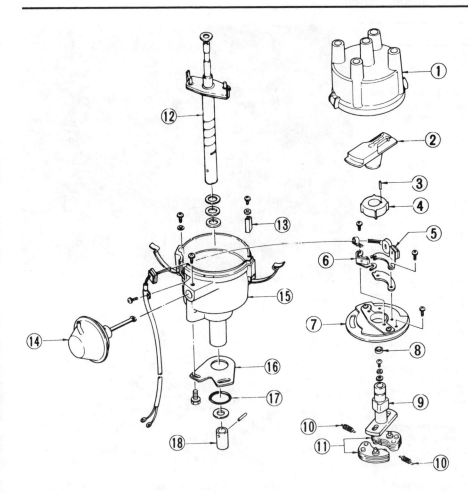

Fig. 4.6 Exploded view of breakerless distributor (Sec 10)

1   Cap assembly
2   Rotor head assembly
3   Roll pin
4   Reluctor
5   Pick-up coil
6   Contactor
7   Breaker plate assembly
8   Packing
9   Rotor shaft
10 Governor spring
11 Governor weight
12 Shaft assembly
13 Cap setter
14 Vacuum controller
15 Housing
16 Fixing plate
17 O-ring
18 Collar

11 Transistor ignition unit – removal and refitting

The transistor ignition unit, which makes and breaks the primary circuit, is highly reliable; however, should a fault develop, the entire assembly must be renewed. The unit is located on the left-hand dash side panel in the passenger compartment.

1   Disconnect the earth lead from the battery negative terminal.
2   Disconnect the wiring harness from the unit.
3   Undo the two securing screws and remove the unit.
4   Refitting is the reverse of the removal sequence. Ensure that the wiring is connected correctly, as shown in Fig. 4.9. If it is wired incorrectly the unit will be damaged.

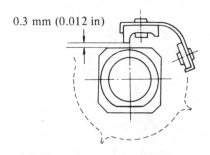

0.3 mm (0.012 in)

Fig. 4.7 Adjusting the cam-to-contactor (Sec 10)

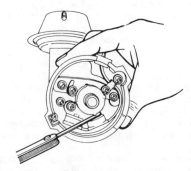

Fig. 4.8 Checking the air gap (Sec 10)

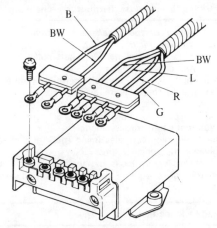

Fig. 4.9 Transistor ignition unit wiring connections (Sec 11

12 Ignition timing

1   If the distributor has been removed for overhaul or other reason first turn the crankshaft until number 1 piston is on the compression stroke.

2   Turn the crankshaft further until the notch on the pulley is in line with the mark on the front cover scale. Refer to specifications for the particular model in question. Make all settings when looking at it from the front of the engine (photo).

3   Set the rotor until the contact is towards the segment for number 1 spark plug lead in the distributor cap.

4   Fit the distributor into its support bracket taking care to engage the drive gear correctly.

5   If difficulty is experienced in refitting the distributor, back off the oil pump bolts and pull the oil pump away from the front cover by about 0.25 inch (6 mm) to keep it clear of the distributor shaft dog. Then partially insert the distributor into the support bracket and turn the shaft anti-clockwise by about 30° before the skew gear is meshed to the crankshaft. Push the distributor fully home. This will turn the rotor back to the correct position.

6   Refit the adjusting plate securing screw and rotate the distributor to obtain the exact point of opening of the contact breaker points. Should adjustment not be possible withdraw the distributor and try again using the next thread of the skew gear.

7   Remesh the oil pump drive dog if necessary turning the crankshaft to bring the two ends into line. Retighten the oil pump securing bolts.

8   The opening of the contact breaker points can be accurately gauged by connecting a timing light between No 1 spark plug and its HT lead. Disconnect the vacuum line and, with the engine idling, shine the light on the crankshaft pulley and timing cover mark.

9   To check the phase difference on distributors with twin contact breaker points, proceed as follows, using a dwell meter:

(a)   *Disconnect the wiring harness of the distributor from the engine harness and connect a wire between B (black) of engine harness and B of distributor harness (advance side).*

(b)   *With the engine idling, adjust the ignition timing by rotating the distributor to the specified setting.*

(c)   *Disconnect the wire from B of the distributor harness and connect it to Y (yellow) of the distributor harness (retard side).*

(d)   *With the engine still idling check that the phase delay is seven degrees in terms of crankshaft angular movement.*

12   To adjust the phase difference, refer to Fig. 4.11 and turn out the adjuster plate setscrew ½ to 2 turns. The screw is located at the contact set on the retard side. Using the notch in the adjuster plate as a hold, turn the adjuster plate as required until the correct delay is obtained. The ignition timing is retarded when the plate is turned anti-clockwise. Tighten the adjuster plate setscrews after adjustment.

13   Check that the ignition timing of the advance side is as specified.

14   After adjustment remove the connecting wire and reconnect the distributor wiring harness to the engine harness.

13 Ignition timing (breakerless distributor) – checking

Note: *Ignition timing of the breakerless distributor can only be checked using a stroboscopic timing light.*

1   Clean the timing mark on the crankshaft pulley and the timing indicator on the front cover.

2   Warm the engine to the normal operating temperature, then connect a timing light to the No 1 cylinder spark plug cable. Fit a tachometer.

3   Set the idling speed to approximately 750 rpm for manual and 650 rpm for automatic transmission models.

4   Shine the timing light on the timing mark and check that the timing is as given in the Specifications.

5   Adjust, if necessary, by loosening the distributor setscrew and rotating the distributor as required to obtain the correct setting.

14 Spark plugs and leads

1   The correct functioning of the spark plugs is vital for the correct

12.2 Timing marks – typical

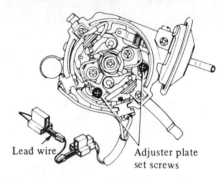

Lead wire   Adjuster plate set screws

Fig. 4.10 Connecting both primary terminals (Sec 12)

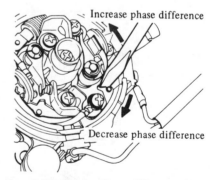

Increase phase difference

Decrease phase difference

Fig. 4.11 Adjusting the phase difference (Sec 12)

running and efficiency of the engine.

2   At the intervals recommended in Routine Maintenance the plugs should be removed, examined, cleaned, and if the electrodes are worn excessively, renewed. The condition of the spark plug will also tell much about the overall condition of the engine.

3   If the insulator nose of the spark plug is clean and white, with no deposits, this is indicative of a weak mixture, or too hot a plug. (A hot plug transfers heat away from the electrodes slowly - a cold plug transfers it away quickly).

4   The plugs fitted as standard are those given in the Specifications at the beginning of this Chapter. If the top and insulator nose is covered with hard black looking deposits, then this is indicative that the mixture is too rich. Should the plug be black and oily, then it is likely that the engine is fairly worn, as well as the mixture being too rich.

5   If the insulator nose is covered with light tan to greyish brown deposits, the mixture is correct and it is likely that the engine is in good condition.

Measuring plug gap. A feeler gauge of the correct size (see ignition system specifications) should have a slight 'drag' when slid between the electrodes. Adjust gap if necessary

Adjusting plug gap. The plug gap is adjusted by bending the earth electrode inwards, or outwards, as necessary until the correct clearance is obtained. Note the use of the correct tool

Normal. Grey-brown deposits, lightly coated core nose. Gap increasing by around 0.001 in (0.025 mm) per 1000 miles (1600 km). Plugs ideally suited to engine, and engine in good condition

Carbon fouling. Dry, black, sooty deposits. Will cause weak spark and eventually misfire. Fault: over-rich fuel mixture. Check: carburettor mixture settings, float level and jet sizes; choke operation and cleanliness of air filter. Plugs can be re-used after cleaning

Oil fouling. Wet, oily deposits. Will cause weak spark and eventually misfire. Fault: worn bores/piston rings or valve guides; sometimes occurs (temporarily) during running-in period. Plugs can be re-used after thorough cleaning

Overheating. Electrodes have glazed appearance, core nose very white – few deposits. Fault: plug overheating. Check: plug value, ignition timing, fuel octane rating (too low) and fuel mixture (too weak). Discard plugs and cure fault immediately

Electrode damage. Electrodes burned away; core nose has burned, glazed appearance. Fault: pre-ignition. Check: as for 'Overheating' but may be more severe. Discard plugs and remedy fault before piston or valve damage occurs

Split core nose (may appear initially as a crack). Damage is self-evident, but cracks will only show after cleaning. Fault: pre-ignition or wrong gap-setting technique. Check: ignition timing, cooling system, fuel octane rating (too low) and fuel mixture (too weak). Discard plugs, rectify fault immediately

6   If there are any traces of long brown tapering stains on the outside of the white portion of the plug, then the plug will have to be renewed, as this shows that there is a faulty joint between the plug body and the insulator, and compression pressure is being allowed to leak past.

7   Spark plugs should be cleaned by a sand blasting machine, which will free them from carbon more thoroughly than cleaning by hand. The machine will also test the condition of the plugs under compression. Any plug that fails to spark at the recommended pressure should be renewed.

8   The spark plug gap is of considerable importance as, if it is too large or too small the size of the spark and its efficiency will be seriously impaired. The spark plug gap should be set to that given in the Specifications.

9   To set the gap, measure with a feeler gauge and then bend open, or close, the outer electrode until the correct gap is achieved. The centre electrode must never be bent as this may crack the insulation and cause plug failure, if nothing worse.

10   Refit the leads from the distributor in the correct firing order (see Specifications).

11   The plug leads require no routine attention other than being kept clean and wiped over regularly. Inspect for signs of damage or deterioration of the leads and check for security of all connections.

15 Ignition system – fault finding

By far the majority of breakdowns and running troubles are caused by faults in the ignition system, either in the low tension or high tension circuits. Fault finding must be carried out in a systematic manner otherwise a considerable amount of time will be wasted.

16 Ignition system – faulty symptoms

There are two main symptoms indicating ignition faults, either the engine will not fire, or the engine is difficult to start and misfires. If it is a regular misfire, ie the engine is running on only two or three cylinders the fault is almost sure to be in the secondary, or high tension circuit. If the misfiring is intermittent, the fault could be in either the high or low tension circuits. If the car stops suddenly or will not start at all it is likely that the fault is in the low tension circuit. Loss of power and overheating, apart from faulty carburation are normally due to faults in the distributor or incorrect ignition timing.

17 Fault diagnosis – engine fails to start

1   If the engine fails to start and the car was running normally when it was last used, first check there is fuel in the petrol tank. If the engine turns over normally on the starter motor and the battery is evidently well charged, then the fault may be in either the high or low tension circuits. First check the HT circuit. **NOTE**: *If the battery is known to be fully charged, the ignition light comes on, and the starter motor fails to turn the engine, check the tightness of the leads of the battery terminals and the secureness of the earth lead to its connection to the body. It is quite common for the leads to have worked loose, even if they look and feel secure. If one of the battery terminal posts gets very hot when trying to work the starter motor this is a sure indication of a faulty connection to that terminal.*

2   One of the commonest reasons for bad starting is wet or damp spark plugs, leads and distributor. Remove the distributor cap. If condensation is visible internally, dry the cap with a rag and wipe over the leads. Refit the cap.

3   If the engine still fails to start, check that current is reaching the plugs, by disconnecting each plug lead in turn at the spark plug end, and holding the end of the cable about 0.2 inch (5.0 mm) away from the cylinder block. Spin the engine on the starter motor by pressing the rubber button on the starter motor solenoid switch (under the bonnet).

4   Sparking between the end of the cable and the block should be fairly strong with a regular blue spark. (Hold the lead with rubber to avoid electric shocks). If current is reaching the plugs, then remove them, clean and regap them to that given in the Specifications. The engine should now start.

5   Switch on the ignition and remove the lead from the centre of the distributor and holding it within rubber spin the engine as before; a rapid succession of blue sparks between the end of the lead and the

block indicates that the coil is in order, and that either the distributor cap is cracked, the carbon brush is stuck or worn, the rotor arm is faulty, or the contact points are burnt, pitted or dirty. If the points are in bad shape, clean and reset them as described in Section 3.

6   If there are no sparks from the end of the lead from the coil then check the connections of the lead to the coil and distributor cap, and if they are in order, check out the low tension circuit starting with the battery.

7   Switch on the ignition and turn the crankshaft so that the contact breaker points have fully opened. Then with either a 12 volt voltmeter or bulb and length of wire, check that current from the battery is reaching the starter solenoid switch. No reading indicates that there is a fault in the cable to the switch, or in the connections at the switch or at the battery terminals. Alternatively the battery earth lead may not be properly earthed to the body.

8   Refer to the applicable wiring diagram and with the ignition switched on systematically test the circuit at all points to the ignition coil. If no reading is obtained at any point recheck the last test point and this will show the wire or terminal failure.

9   Check the CB or – terminal on the coil (this is the one connected to the distributor) and if no reading is recorded on the voltmeter then the coil is broken and must be renewed. The engine should start when a new coil has been fitted.

10   If a reading is obtained at the distributor cable connection at the coil, then check the low tension terminal on the side of the distributor. If no reading is obtained then check the wire for loose connections etc. If a reading is obtained then the final check on the low tension circuit is across the contact breaker points. No reading means a broken condenser which when renewed will enable the car to finally start.

18 Fault diagnosis – engine misfires

1   If the engine misfires regularly, run it at a fast idling speed, and short out each of the plugs in turn by placing a short screwdriver across from the spark plug terminal to the cylinder head. Ensure the screwdriver has a *wooden* or *plastic insulated handle.*

2   No difference in engine running will be noticed when the plug in the defective cylinder is short circuited. Short circuiting the working plugs will accentuate the misfire.

3   Remove the plug lead from the end of the defective plug and hold it about 0.20 inch (5.0 mm) from the cylinder head. Restart the engine. If sparking is fairly strong and regular the fault must lie in the spark plug.

4   The plug may be loose, the insulation may be cracked, or the points may have burnt away giving too wide a gap for the spark to jump. Worse still, one of the points may have broken off. Either renew the plug, or clean it, reset the gap, and then test it.

5   If there is no spark at the end of the plug lead or if it is weak and intermittent check the ignition lead from the distributor to the plug. If the insulation is damaged renew the lead. Check connections at the distributor cap.

6   If there is still no spark, examine the distributor cap carefully for tracking. This can be recognised by a very thin black line running between two or more electrodes or between an electrode and some other part of the distributor. These lines are paths which now conduct electricity across the cap thus letting it run to earth. The only answer is to fit a new distributor cap.

7   Apart from the ignition timing being incorrect, other causes of misfiring have already been dealt with under the Section dealing with the failure of the engine to start (Section 17).

8   If the ignition timing is too far retarded, it should be noted that the engine will tend to overheat and there will be quite a noticeable drop in power. If the engine is overheating and the power is down, and the ignition timing is correct, then the carburettor should be checked, as it is likely that this is where the fault lies. See Chapter 3 for details of this.

19 Fault diagnosis – breakerless ignition system

Checking the HT circuit is the same as for the conventional ignition system. Checking the primary circuit, however, needs special test equipment which, if wrongly connected in the system will result in damage to the transistor ignition unit. Therefore it is recommended that this work is done by your local Datsun garage.

Chapter 5 Clutch

Contents

Specifications

Type	Diaphragm spring, single plate
Clutch disc	
Facing size (o.d x i.d x thickness)	7·87 x 5·12 x 0·138 in (200 x 130 x 3·5 mm)
Thickness of disc assembly	0·307 in (7·8 mm)
Minimum depth of rivet head from surface	0·012 in (0·3 mm)
Allowable free-play of spline	0·016 in (0·4 mm)
Clutch pedal	
Height	
RH drive	6·61 in (168 mm)
LH drive	6·91 in (175·5 mm)
Free-play	0·04 – 0·20 in (1 –5 mm)
Full stroke	5·31 in (135 mm)
Master cylinder diameter	0·6248 in (15·88 mm)
Slave cylinder diameter	0·750 in (19·05 mm)

Torque wrench settings	lbf ft	kgf m
Clutch-to-flywheel	12 – 16	1·6 –2·2
Pedal locknuts	6 – 9	0·8 – 1·2
Master cylinder securing bolts	6 – 9	0·8 – 1·2
Slave cylinder securing bolts	22 – 30	3·0 – 4·1
Pedal fulcrum bolt	22 – 30	3·0 – 4·1

1 General description

The models covered by this manual are fitted with a diaphragm spring clutch operated hydraulically by a master and slave cylinder.

The clutch comprises a steel cover which is bolted and dowelled to the rear face of the flywheel and contains the pressure plate and clutch disc or driven plate.

The clutch disc is free to slide along the splined gearbox input shaft and is held in position between the flywheel and pressure plate by the pressure of the diaphragm spring.

Friction lining material is riveted to the clutch disc which has a spring cushioned hub to absorb transmission shocks and to help ensure a smooth take off.

The pendant clutch pedal is connected to the clutch master cylinder and hydraulic fluid reservoir by a short pushrod. The master cylinder and hydraulic reservoir are mounted on the engine side of the bulkhead in front of the driver.

Depressing the clutch pedal moves the piston in the master cylinder forward so forcing hydraulic fluid through the clutch hydraulic pipe to the slave cylinder.

The piston in the slave cylinder moves rearward on the entry of the fluid and actuates the clutch release arm by a short pushrod. The opposite end of the release arm is forked and carries the release bearing assembly.

As this pivoted clutch release arm moves rearward it pushes the release bearing forward to bear against the diaphragm spring and pushes forward so moving the pressure plate backward and disengaging the pressure plate from the clutch disc.

When the clutch pedal is released the pressure plate is forced into contact with the high friction linings on the clutch disc and at the same time pushes the clutch disc a fraction of an inch forward on its splines so engaging the clutch disc with the flywheel. The clutch disc is now firmly sandwiched between the pressure plate and the flywheel so the drive is taken up.

As the friction linings on the clutch disc wear, the pressure plate automatically moves closer to the disc to compensate and eliminates the necessity for frequent adjustment.

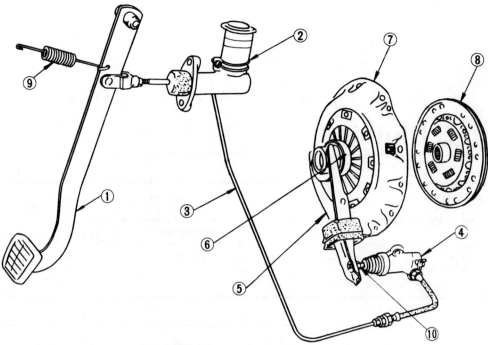

Fig. 5.1 Clutch operating system

1	Clutch pedal	4	Clutch slave cylinder	7	Clutch cover
2	Clutch master cylinder	5	Withdrawal lever	8	Clutch disc
3	Clutch piping	6	Release bearing	9	Return spring
				10	Push rod

2   Hydraulic system – bleeding

1   Gather together a clean glass jar, a length of rubber or plastic tubing which fits tightly over the bleed nipple on the slave cylinder, a tin of hydraulic brake fluid and someone to help.
2   Check that the master cylinder is full. If it is not, fill it and cover the bottom two inches of the jar with hydraulic fluid.
3   Remove the rubber dust cap from the bleed nipple on the slave cylinder, and with a suitable spanner open the bleed nipple approximately three quarters of a turn.
4   Place one end of the tube over the nipple and insert the other end in the jar so that the tube orifice is below the level of the fluid.
5   The assistant should now depress the pedal and hold it down at the end of its stroke. Close the bleed screw and allow the pedal to return to its normal position.
6   Continue this series of operations until clear hydraulic fluid without any traces of air bubbles emerges from the end of the tubing. Be sure that the reservoir is checked frequently to ensure that the hydraulic fluid does not drop too far, thus letting air into the system.
7   When no more air bubbles appear tighten the bleed nipple on the downstroke.
8   Refit the rubber dust cap over the bleed nipple.

3   Clutch pedal – removal and refitting

1   Working inside the car carefully withdraw the clutch pedal-to-pushrod clevis pin spring pin. The cotter pin may now be withdrawn from the pushrod yoke.
2   Detach the clutch pedal return spring from the pedal.
3   Undo and remove the fulcrum bolt securing nut, spring washer and plain washer. Carefully withdraw the fulcrum bolt.
4   On some models it may be necessary to slacken the handbrake lever support bracket securing bolts.
5   The pedal may now be lifted away from the bracket. Recover the two half bushes from the pedal fulcrum.
6   Inspect the pedal bushes, if wear is evident, obtain new bushes.
7   Refitting the pedal is the reverse of the removal procedure. Lubricate the pedal bushes and shaft.
8   Adjust the pedal height and free play as described in Section 4.

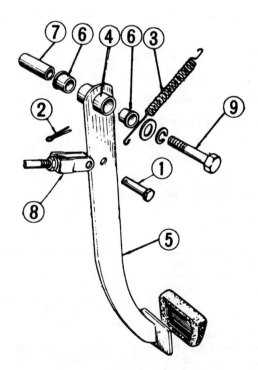

Fig. 5.2 Exploded view of clutch pedal assembly (Sec 3)

1	Clevis pin	6	Bush
2	Cotter pin	7	Sleeve
3	Return spring	8	Push rod
4	Pedal boss	9	Fulcrum pin
5	Pedal assembly		

4 Clutch pedal – adjustment

1 The pedal height is adjusted at the stop by slackening locknut A (refer to Fig. 5.3) and screwing the stop in or out until the specified height is obtained. Tighten the locknut.

2 Slacken the pushrod locknut, B in Fig. 5.3, and rotate the pushrod to adjust the clutch pedal play to 0.04 – 0.20 in (1 – 5 mm). Tighten the locknut.

3 Check that the pedal operates through the recommended stroke.

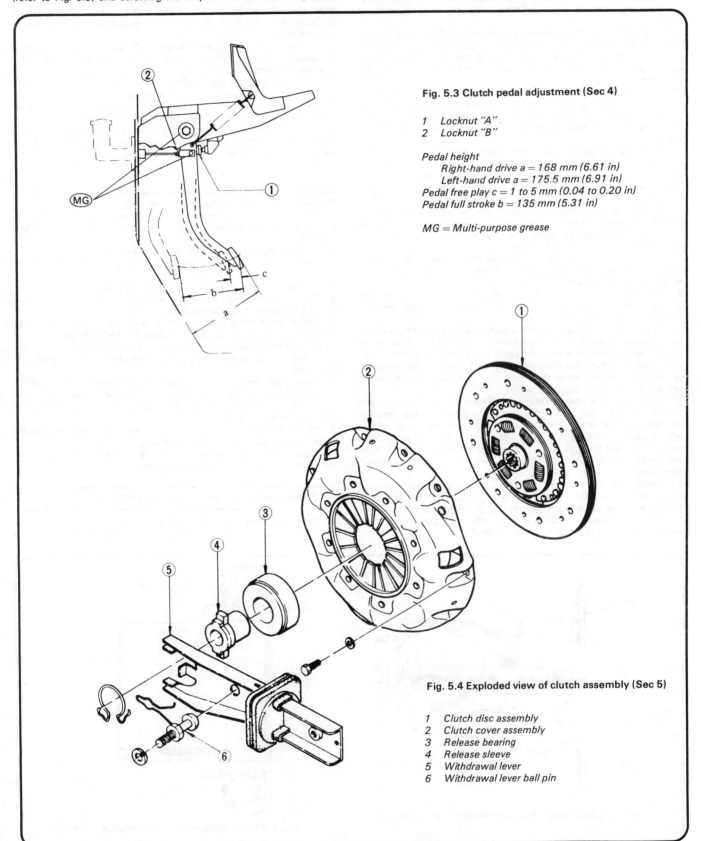

Fig. 5.3 Clutch pedal adjustment (Sec 4)

1 Locknut "A"
2 Locknut "B"

Pedal height
   Right-hand drive a = 168 mm (6.61 in)
   Left-hand drive a = 175.5 mm (6.91 in)
Pedal free play c = 1 to 5 mm (0.04 to 0.20 in)
Pedal full stroke b = 135 mm (5.31 in)

MG = Multi-purpose grease

Fig. 5.4 Exploded view of clutch assembly (Sec 5)

1 Clutch disc assembly
2 Clutch cover assembly
3 Release bearing
4 Release sleeve
5 Withdrawal lever
6 Withdrawal lever ball pin

5 Clutch – removal and refitting

1   Remove the gearbox as described in Chapter 6.
2   With a scriber, or file, mark the relative position of the clutch cover and flywheel to ensure correct refitting if the original parts are to be used.
3   Remove the clutch assembly by unscrewing the six bolts holding the cover to the rear face of the flywheel. Unscrew the bolt diagonally half a turn at a time to prevent distortion of the cover flange, also to prevent an accident caused by the cover flange binding on the dowels and suddenly flying off.
4   With the bolts and spring washers removed, lift the clutch assembly off the locating dowels. The driven plate or clutch disc will fall out at this stage, as it is not attached to either the clutch cover assembly or the flywheel. Carefully make a note of which way round it is fitted.
5   It is important that no oil or grease gets on the clutch disc friction linings, or the pressure plate and flywheel faces. It is advisable to handle the parts with clean hands and to wipe down the pressure plate and flywheel faces with a clean dry rag before inspection or refitting commences.
6   To refit the clutch plate place the clutch disc against the flywheel with the larger end of the hub away from the flywheel. On no account should the clutch disc be refitted the wrong way round as it will be found impossible to operate the clutch.
7   Refit the clutch cover assembly loosely on the dowels. Refit the six bolts and spring washers and tighten them finger tight so that the clutch disc is gripped but can still be moved.
8   The clutch disc must now be centralised so that when the engine and gearbox are mated, the gearbox input shaft splines pass through the splines in the centre of the hub.
9   Centralisation can be carried out quite easily by inserting a round bar or long screwdriver through the hole in the centre of the clutch, so that the end of the bar rests in the small hole in the end of the crankshaft containing the input shaft bearing bush. Moving the bar sideways or up and down will move the clutch disc in whichever direction is necessary to achieve centralisation.
10   Centralisation is easily judged by removing the bar or screwdriver and viewing the driven plate hub in relation to the hole in the centre of the diaphragm spring. When the hub is exactly in the centre of the release bearing hole, all is correct. Alternatively, if an old input shaft can be borrowed this will eliminate all guesswork as it will fit the bush and centre of the clutch hub exactly, obviating the need for visual alignment.
11   Tighten the clutch bolts firmly in a diagonal sequence to ensure the cover plate is pulled evenly, and without distortion of the flange. Tighten the bolts to the recommended torque wrench setting.
12   Refit the gearbox, bleed the slave cylinder if the pipe was disconnected and check the clutch for correct operation.

6 Clutch – inspection and renovation

1   In the normal course of events clutch dismantling and reassembly is the term used for simply fitting a new clutch pressure plate and friction disc. Under no circumstances should the pressure plate assembly be dismantled. If a fault develops in the assembly an exchange unit must be fitted.
2   If a new clutch disc is being fitted it is false economy not to renew the release bearing at the same time. This will preclude having to fit it at a later date when wear on the clutch linings is very small.
3   Examine the clutch disc friction linings for wear or loose rivets and the disc for rim distortion, cracks and worn splines.
4   Examine the hub splines for wear and make sure that the centre hub is not loose or that any of the torsion springs are broken.
5   Check the machined faces of the flywheel and the pressure plate. If either is badly grooved it should be machined until smooth, or a new component fitted. If the pressure plate is cracked or split it must be renewed.

7 Release bearing – removal and refitting

1   To gain access it is necessary to remove the gearbox as described in Chapter 6.
2   Remove the dust cover from the clutch housing.
3   Detach and remove the clutch release lever from the clutch housing.
4   Release the retainer spring clip from the withdrawal lever.
5   Remove the release bearing, bearing sleeve and holder spring from the clutch housing as one complete assembly.
6   Check the bearing for signs of overheating, wear or roughness. Should such conditions be apparent, the old bearing should be drawn off the bearing sleeve, using a universal two leg extractor.
7   Using a bench vice and suitable packing, press a new bearing onto the sleeve.
8   Apply high melting point grease to the contact surfaces of the release lever, lever ball pin and bearing sleeve. Also the contact surfaces of the gearbox front cover. Pack grease into the inner recess of the bearing sleeve (Fig. 5.6).
9   Fit the retainer spring to the release lever. Also fit the holder spring to the release bearing and sleeve assembly.
10   Refit the release bearing assembly to the release lever and fit to the gearbox bellhousing. Refit the dust cover.

8 Clutch master cylinder – removal and refitting

1   Drain the fluid from the clutch master cylinder reservoir by attaching a rubber tube to the slave cylinder bleed nipple. Undo the

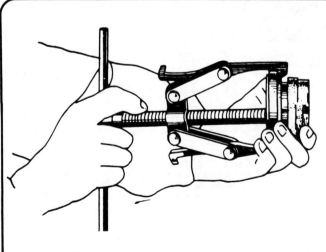

Fig. 5.5 Removing release bearing from carrier (Sec 7)

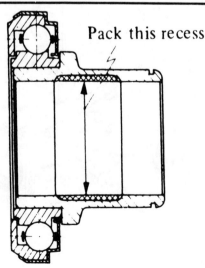

Pack this recess

Fig. 5.6 Lubricating recess of bearing sleeve (Sec 7)

nipple approximately three quarters of a turn and then pump the fluid into a suitable container by operating the clutch pedal. Note that the pedal must be held in against the floor at the completion of each stroke and the bleed nipple tightened before the pedal is allowed to return. When the pedal has returned to its normal position loosen the bleed nipple and repeat the process, until the reservoir is empty.

2   Place a rag under the master cylinder to catch any hydraulic fluid that may be spilt. Unscrew the union nut from the end of the metal pipe where it enters the clutch master cylinder and gently pull the pipe clear.

3   Withdraw the spring clip retaining the pushrod yoke to pedal clevis pin and remove the clevis pin.

4   Undo and remove the two bolts and spring washers that secure the master cylinder to the bulkhead. Lift away the master cylinder taking care not to allow hydraulic fluid to come into contact with the paintwork, as it acts as a solvent (photo).

5   Refitting the master cylinder is the reverse sequence to removal. Bleed the system as described in Section 2 of this Chapter.

8.4 The clutch master cylinder

9   Clutch master cylinder – dismantling, examination and reassembly

Note: *Two makes of master cylinder are available, Nabco and Tokico. Parts are not interchangeable, so take care that the correct items are obtained for any repair.*

1   Ease back the rubber dust cover from the pushrod end.

2   Using a pair of circlip pliers release the circlip retaining the pushrod assembly. Lift away the pushrod complete with rubber boot and shaped washer.

3   By shaking hard, the piston assembly may be removed from the cylinder bore.

4   Carefully straighten the lip on the spring seat and separate the spring seat, spring and valve assembly from the piston.

5   Slide the valve end spring seat down the valve rod and carefully remove the seal. Also remove the piston cup from the piston noting which way round it is fitted.

6   Thoroughly clean the parts in brake fluid or methylated spirit. After drying the items inspect the seals for signs of distortion, swelling, splitting or hardening although it is recommended new rubber parts be fitted after dismantling as a matter of course.

7   Inspect the bore and piston for signs of deep scoring. If scoring is evident, fit a new cylinder. Make sure the port at the bottom of the bore is clear by poking gently with a piece of wire.

8   As the parts are refitted to the cylinder bore make sure that they are thoroughly wetted with clean hydraulic fluid.

9   Refit the valve seal to the end of the valve and slide on the spring seat.

10 Fit the seal to the piston so that the lip faces away from the main part of the piston.

11 Assemble the spring to the valve end spring seat and then the second spring seat to the other end of the valve stem.

12 Fit the valve rod and spring seat to the piston and lock by depressing the spring seat lip.

13 Carefully fit the piston and valve assembly to the bore making sure the piston seal does not roll over as it enters the bore.

14 Smear a little grease, to the correct specification onto the ball end of the pushrod and refit the pushrod assembly. Slide down the washer and secure in position with the circlip.

15 Pack the rubber dust cover with the same type of grease and place over the end of the master cylinder.

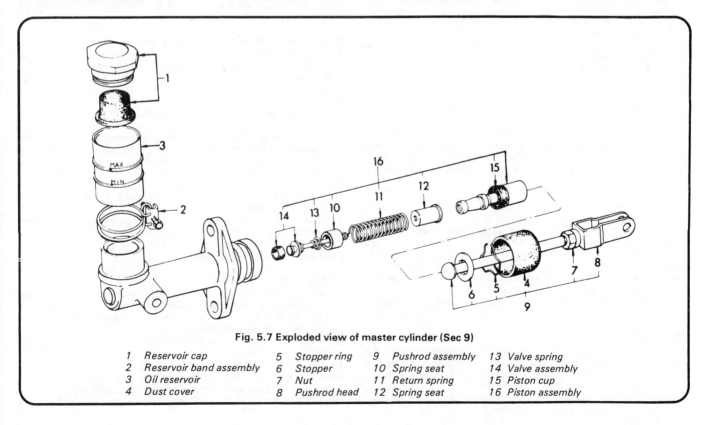

Fig. 5.7 Exploded view of master cylinder (Sec 9)

1 Reservoir cap	5 Stopper ring	9 Pushrod assembly	13 Valve spring
2 Reservoir band assembly	6 Stopper	10 Spring seat	14 Valve assembly
3 Oil reservoir	7 Nut	11 Return spring	15 Piston cup
4 Dust cover	8 Pushrod head	12 Spring seat	16 Piston assembly

10 Slave cylinder – removal and refitting

1   Wipe the top of the master cylinder reservoir and unscrew the cap.
Place a piece of polythene sheet over the top of the reservoir and refit
the cap. This will stop hydraulic fluid syphoning out during subsequent
operations.
2   Wipe the area around the flexible pipe-to-metal pipe union and
disconnect the flexible pipe.
3   Undo and remove the two bolts and spring washers securing the
slave cylinder to the clutch housing. Lift away the slave cylinder
(photo).
4   Refitting the slave cylinder is the reverse sequence to removal. It
will be necessary to bleed the hydraulic system as described in Section
2.

11 Slave cylinder – dismantling, inspection and reassembly

Note: *Two makes of slave cylinder are available, Nabco and Tokico.
Parts are not interchangeable, so take care that the correct items are
obtained for any repair.*
1   Clean the outside of the slave cylinder before dismantling.
2   Pull off the rubber dust cover and by shaking hard, the piston, seal
and spring should come out of the cylinder bore.
3   If they prove stubborn carefully use a foot pump air jet on the
hydraulic hose connection and this should remove the internal parts,
but do take care as they will fly out. It is recommended that a plastic
bag be placed over the dust cover end to catch the parts.
4   Remove the seal from the piston noting which way round it is
fitted.
5   Wash all internal parts with either brake fluid or methylated spirit
and dry using a non-fluffy rag.
6   Inspect the bore and piston for signs of deep scoring. Fit a new
cylinder.
7   Carefully examine the rubber components for signs of swelling,
distortion, splitting, hardening or other wear. Should any such condition exist it is recommended that new parts be fitted.
8   All parts should be reassembled wetted with clean hydraulic fluid.
9   Fit a new seal to the piston and place the smaller diameter end of
the spring onto the piston projection.
10   Insert the spring and piston into the bore taking care not to roll the
lip of the seal.
11   Apply a little grease to the correct specification, to either end of
the pushrod and pack the dust cover.
12   Fit the dust cover over the end of the slave cylinder engaging the
lips over the groove in the body.
13   Fit the pushrod to the slave cylinder by pushing through the hole in
the dust cover.

12 Fault diagnosis – clutch

1   There are four main faults to which the clutch and release
mechanism are prone. They may occur by themselves, or in conjunction with any of the other faults. They are clutch squeal, slip, spin and
judder.

Clutch squeal
2   If on taking up the drive or when changing gear, the clutch
squeals, this is indicative of a badly worn clutch release bearing.
3   As well as regular wear due to normal use, wear of the clutch
release bearing is much accentuated if the clutch is ridden or held
down for long periods in gear, with the engine running. To minimise
wear of this component the car should always be taken out of gear at
traffic lights and for similar traffic hold ups.
4   The clutch release bearing is not an expensive item but difficult to
get at.

Clutch slip
5   Clutch slip is a self-evident condition which occurs when the
clutch friction plate is badly worn, oil or grease have got onto the
flywheel or pressure plate faces, or the pressure plate itself is faulty.
6   The reason for clutch slip is that due to one of the faults above,
there is insufficient pressure from the pressure plate, or insufficient

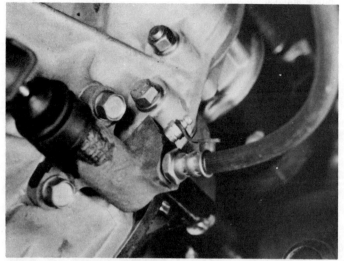

10.3 The clutch slave cylinder

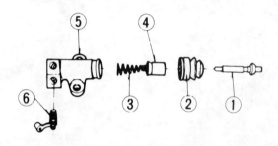

Fig. 5.8 Exploded view of slave cylinder (Sec 11)

1 Pushrod	4 Piston
2 Dust cover	5 Body
3 Piston spring	6 Bleed screw

friction from the friction plate to ensure solid drive.
7   If small amounts of oil get onto the clutch, they will be burnt off
under the heat of the clutch engagement, and in the process, gradually
darken the linings. Excessive oil on the clutch will burn off leaving a
carbon deposit which can cause quite bad clutch slip, or fierceness,
spin and judder.
8   If clutch slip is suspected, and confirmation of this condition is
required, there are several tests which can be made.
9   With the engine in second or third gear and pulling lightly sudden
depression of the accelerator pedal may cause the engine to increase
its speed without any increase in road speed. Easing off on the
accelerator will then give a definite drop in engine speed without the
car slowing.
10   In extreme cases of clutch slip the engine will race under normal
acceleration conditions.
11   If slip is due to oil or grease on the linings a temporary cure can
sometimes be effected by squirting carbon tetrachloride into the
clutch. The permanent cure is, of course, to renew the clutch driven
plate, and trace and rectify the oil leak.

Clutch spin
12   Clutch spin is a condition which occurs when there is a leak in the
clutch hydraulic actuating mechanism, there is an obstruction in the
clutch either in the first motion shaft or in the operating lever itself, or
the oil may have partially burnt off the clutch lining and have left a
resinous deposit which is causing the clutch disc to stick to the pressure plate or flywheel.
13   The reason for clutch spin is that due to any, or a combination of,
the faults just listed, the clutch pressure plate is not completely freeing
from the centre plate even with the clutch pedal fully depressed.
14   If clutch spin is suspected, the condition can be confirmed by

extreme difficulty in engaging first gear from rest, difficulty in changing gear, and very sudden take up of the clutch drive at the fully depressed end of the clutch pedal travel as the clutch is released.

15 Check the clutch master cylinder, slave cylinder and the connecting hydraulic pipe for leaks. Fluid in one of the rubber dust covers fitted over the end of either the master or slave cylinder is a sure sign of a leaking piston seal.

16 If these points are checked and found to be in order then the fault lies internally in the clutch, and it will be necessary to remove the clutch for examination.

Clutch judder

17 Clutch judder is a self-evident condition which occurs when the gearbox or engine mountings are loose or too flexible, or when there is oil on the face of the clutch friction disc.

18 The reason for clutch judder is that due to one of the faults just listed, the clutch pressure plate is not freeing smoothly from the friction disc and is snatching.

19 Clutch judder normally occurs when the clutch pedal is released in first or reverse gears, and the whole car shudders as it moves forward or backward.

Chapter 6
Manual gearbox and automatic transmission

Contents

Specifications

Manual transmission

Type .... 3-speed R3W65, 4-speed F4W63 or F4C63 and 5-speed FS5W63 all with synchromesh on all forward gears

Synchromesh type

3-speed	Warner
4-speed	
F4W63	Warner
F4C63	Servo
5-speed	Warner

Gear ratios

	3-speed	4-speed	5-speed
1st	3.263 : 1	3.382 : 1	3.382 : 1
2nd	1.458 : 1	2.013 : 1	2.013 : 1
3rd	1.000 : 1	1.312 : 1	1.312 : 1
4th	–	1.000 : 1	1.000 : 1
5th	–	–	0.854 : 1
Reverse	3.570 : 1	3.365 : 1	2.182 : 1

Gear backlash

All gears	0.0020 – 0.0055 in (0.05 – 0.14 mm)

Gear endplay

	3-speed	4-speed	5-speed
1st	0.0020–0.0087 in (0.05–0.22 mm)	0.0020–0.0059 in (0.05–0.15 mm)	0.0126–0.0165 in (0.32–0.42 mm)
2nd	0.0039–0.0087 in (0.10–0.22 mm)	0.0020–0.0059 in (0.05–0.15 mm)	0.0087–0.0126 in (0.22–0.32 mm)
3rd	–	0.0020–0.0059 in (0.05–0.15 mm)	0.0020–0.0059 in (0.05–0.15 mm)
5th	–	–	0.0020–0.0059 in (0.05–0.15 mm)

Reverse idler	0.0059–0.0157 in (0.15–0.40 mm)	0.0039–0.0118 in (0.10–0.30 mm)	0.0079–0.0157 in (0.20–0.40 mm)
Laygear	–	0.0020–0.0059 in (0.05–0.15 mm)	0.0016–0.0047 in (0.04–0.12 mm)
Clearance between baulk ring and clutch gear	All types　0.0472–0.0630 in (1.2–1.6 mm)		

Refill capacities
3-speed	3 Imp pt (3$\frac{5}{8}$ US pt, 1.7 litre)
4-speed	3$\frac{1}{2}$ Imp pt (4$\frac{1}{4}$ US pt, 2.0 litre)
5-speed	3$\frac{1}{2}$ Imp pt (4$\frac{1}{4}$ US pt, 2.0 litre)

Automatic transmission

Type ....
3-speed 3N71B (Jatco)

Gear ratios
1st	2.458 : 1
2nd	1.458 : 1
3rd	1.000 : 1
Reverse	2.182 : 1

Converter range ....
2.0 : 1 to 1.0 : 1

Oil type ....
Automatic transmission fluid, *Dexron* type

Oil capacity ....
4$\frac{7}{8}$ Imp qt (5$\frac{7}{8}$ US qt, 5.5 litre)

Torque wrench settings
Manual transmission

	lbf ft	kgf m
Reverse light switch	14–22	2.0–3.0
Front cover bolt	5.8–7.2	1.1–1.8
Rear extension bolt	12–18	1.6–2.5
Mainshaft nut (4-speed)	65–80	9–11
(5-speed)	101–123	14–17
Transmission-to-engine bolt	29–35	4.0–4.8
Crossmember mounting bolt	20–27	2.7–3.7

Automatic transmission

Drive plate-to-converter bolt	29–36	4–5
Oil pipe-to-casing	22–36	3–5
Selector range lever-to-shaft	22–29	3–4

Manual Gearbox

1　General description

The manual gearbox fitted to models covered by this manual is of the three-, four- or five-speed forward and reverse, type with synchromesh action on all forward gears.

The forward gears are of a helical gear formation and the reverse gear a sliding mesh type using spur gears.

jthe main driveshaft gear is meshed with the counter drive gear. The forward speed gears on the countershaft are in constant mesh with the main gears. Each of the main gears rides on the mainshaft on needle roller bearings, rotating freely.

When the gearchange lever is operated the relevant coupling-sleeve is caused to slide on the synchronizer hub and engages its inner teeth with the outer teeth formed on the mainshaft gear. The synchronizer hub is splined to the mainshaft so enabling them to rotate in unison.

The gearbox fitted can be one of two types, Warner or Servo, the difference being that on the Warner baulk rings synchronize the coupling sleeve with the mainshaft gear whilst on the Servo type this action is achieved by a synchroniser ring.

Moving the gearchange lever to the reverse gear position moves the mainshaft reverse gear into engagement with the reverse idle gear.

The gearbox casing is of two parts, the main casing with all gears and gear shafts, and the rear extension.

The Warner and Servo type gearboxes are similar with the exception of the synchromesh units only. The procedures for removal, dismantling, inspection and reassembly are similar but where necessary information will be found covering any differences.

With the three-speed gearbox a remote gearchange system mounted on the steering column is used. Rods connect the gearchange lever to the operating levers on the side of the gearbox casing. Movement is transferred to the gear synchronizer sleeves by

rods and shift forks. The gear selector mechanism for the four and five-speed gearbox is mounted on the floor. Gearchange lever movement is transferred through a striking rod to special gates which are located on the shaft rods. Movement is then via shift forks in contact with the synchronizer sleeves.

Information on the automatic transmission will be found later in this Chapter.

2　Gearbox – removal and refitting

1　The procedure for removing the three-, four-, and five-speed gearboxes is very similar with the exception of disconnecting the gearchange lever.

2　The best method of removing the gearbox is to separate the gearbox bellhousing from the engine and to lower the gearbox away from the underside of the car. It is recommended that during the final stages of removal assistance is obtained because of the weight.

3　Disconnect the battery, raise the car and place on axle-stands if a ramp is not available. The higher the car is off the ground the easier it will be to work underneath.

4　Undo the gearbox drain plug and drain the oil into a clean container. When all the oil has drained out refit the drain plug.

5　Refer to Chapter 9 and disconnect the handbrake cable at the equaliser pivot.

6　Detach the speedometer cable from the gearbox extension housing. Tie the cable back out of the way.

7　To give better access the exhaust system pre-silencer should be rotated. Slacken the two centre pipe clamps and turn the pre-silencer to the left.

8　On pick-up models the exhaust downpipe must be detached from the exhaust manifold.

9　Refer to Chapter 7 and remove the propeller shaft.

10 Locate the electrical cable connections to the neutral gear switch, third gear switch and reverse gear switch. Make a note of the cable colour coding and detach.

11 Disconnect the gearchange rods from the operating levers and relay shaft on column gearchange models.

12 On floor gearchange models disconnect the gearchange lever from the control arm.

13 Disconnect the relay shaft from between the gearbox and side plate.

14 Refer to Chapter 10 and remove the starter motor.

15 Refer to Chapter 5 and remove the clutch slave cylinder from the clutch housing.

16 Using a garage hydraulic jack support the weight of the gearbox. The jack saddle must not rest on the drain plug. Position a block of soft wood between the saddle and cover plate.

17 Undo and remove the two bolts and spring washers that secure the gearbox extension housing to the rear mounting.

18 Place a second jack under the engine sump to take the weight of the engine.

19 Remove the bolts and spring washer securing the crossmember to the underside of the body. Lift away the crossmember.

20 Undo and remove the bolts and spring washers that secure the clutch bellhousing to the rear of the engine.

21 Check that all gearbox attachments have been released and then with the help of a second person take the weight of the gearbox.

22 Lower both jacks slightly until there is sufficient room for the bellhousing flange to clear the underbody panels.

23 Ease the gearbox rearward ensuring that the weight of the unit is not supported on the input shaft which is easily bent.

24 Finally lift the gearbox away from under the car.

25 Before any work is carried out on the gearbox it should be thoroughly washed in paraffin or a water-soluble solvent, and dried using a non-fluffy rag.

26 Refitment is the reverse sequence to removal. Do not forget to refill the gearbox with the recommended grade of oil.

3 Gearbox (3 speed) – dismantling

1 Place the complete unit on a firm bench and ensure that you have the following tools (in addition to a normal range of spanners etc) available.

(a) Good quality circlip pliers; 2 pairs, (1 expanding and 1 contracting)
(b Copper head mallet, at least 2 lbs (1 kg)
(c) Drifts, steel $\frac{3}{8}$ inch (9 mm) and brass $\frac{3}{8}$ inch (9 mm)
(d) Small containers for needle rollers
(e) Engineer's vice mounted on firm bench

Any attempt to dismantle the gearbox without the foregoing is not necessarily impossible, but will certainly be very difficult and inconvenient resulting in possible injury to the person or damage to the gearbox. Read the whole of this Section before starting work.

Take care not to let the synchromesh hub assemblies come apart before you want them to. It accelerates wear if the splines of hub and sleeve are changed in relation to each other. As a precaution it is advisable to make a line up mark with a dab of paint.

Before finally going ahead with dismantling first ascertain the availability of spare parts – particularly shims and selective circlips, which could be difficult.

2 Withdraw the clutch release lever rubber boot from the aperture in the gearbox bellhousing.

3 Release the retaining spring and disconnect the release lever and bearing.

4 Turn the gearbox upside down, undo and remove the fourteen bolts and spring washers securing the cover plate to the main casing. Lift away the cover plate and gasket.

5 Undo and remove the speedometer pinion assembly retaining bolt and lockplate from the extension housing.

6 Withdraw the speedometer pinion assembly.

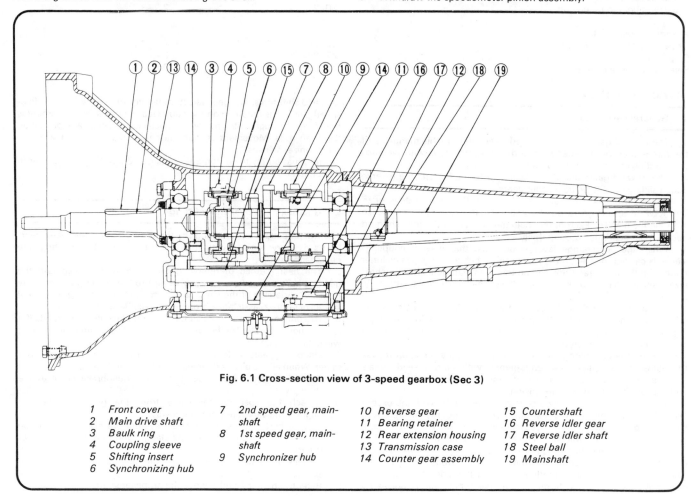

Fig. 6.1 Cross-section view of 3-speed gearbox (Sec 3)

1 Front cover	7 2nd speed gear, main-shaft	10 Reverse gear	15 Countershaft
2 Main drive shaft		11 Bearing retainer	16 Reverse idler gear
3 Baulk ring	8 1st speed gear, main-shaft	12 Rear extension housing	17 Reverse idler shaft
4 Coupling sleeve		13 Transmission case	18 Steel ball
5 Shifting insert	9 Synchronizer hub	14 Counter gear assembly	19 Mainshaft
6 Synchronizing hub			

7 Undo and remove the bolts and spring washers that secure the extension housing to the main casing. The extension housing may now be drawn rearward from the main casing. Recover the gasket.
8 Using a pair of circlip pliers remove the circlips retaining the gearshaft cross-shaft.
9 Undo and remove the two nuts and spring washers holding the cross-shaft cotter pins. Carefully tap out the cotter pins.
10 The two cross-shafts may now be carefully tapped out from the main casing. Recover the shift fork lever and thrust washers from the end of the cross-shafts.
11 Undo and remove the bolts and spring washers that secure the input shaft front bearing cover to the front of the main casing. Lift away the cover and oil seal.
12 Using a soft metal drift carefully tap out the layshaft. The laygear cluster and thrust washers may now be lifted away from the main casing. Note the locations and which way round the thrust washers are fitted.
13 Bend back the tab washer, undo and remove the bolt and the washer securing the reverse idler shaft to the main casing.
14 Using a small drift tap out the shaft and lift away the reverse idler gear noting which way round it is fitted.
15 Undo and remove the plug from the interlock hole and remove the spring and detent ball. If a reverse light switch is fitted, this should be removed next.
16 Using a small parallel pin punch tap out the spring pins that secure the shift fork to the shift rods.
17 The shift rods may now be tapped out using a soft metal drift. Note which way round each shift rod is fitted.
18 The interlock plunger fitted in the main casing between the shift rods should now be recovered.
19 Remove the detent ball and spring from the blanked hole above the first/reverse shift rod.
20 The complete mainshaft assembly may now be withdrawn from the main casing.
21 Using a soft faced hammer carefully tap out the input shaft and bearing assembly from the front of the gear case.
22 The gearbox main casing is now stripped out. Thoroughly flush out the interior of the casing with paraffin and wipe clean with a non-fluffy rag.

4 Input shaft (3-speed) – dismantling

1 The shaft and bearing are located in the front of the main casing by a large circlip in the outer track of the bearing.
2 To renew the bearing first remove the selective-fit circlip and washer from the front end of the bearing.
3 Place the outer track of the race on the top of a firm bench vice and drive the input shaft through the bearing. Note that the bearing is

fitted with the circlip groove toward the forward end of the input shaft. Lift away the bearing.
4 Recover the spigot bearing from the mainshaft end of the input shaft.

5 Mainshaft (3-speed) – dismantling

1 Remove the circlip from the front of the mainshaft and detach the top gear baulk ring and synchronizer assembly from the mainshaft.
2 Slide the second gear baulk ring and intermediate gear from the mainshaft.
3 Remove the circlip at the rear of the mainshaft and detach the speedometer drive gear ball bearing and spacer from the mainshaft.
4 Place the rear mainshaft bearing and retainer on the jaws of a firm bench vice and drive the mainshaft through the assembly.
5 Remove the first/reverse synchromesh assembly together with the first gear baulk ring and first gear from the mainshaft.

6 Synchro hubs (3-speed) – dismantling and inspection

1 The synchro hubs are only too easy to dismantle – just push the centre out and the whole assembly flies apart. The point is to prevent this happening, before you are ready. Do not dismantle the hubs without reason and do not mix up the parts of the two hubs.
2 It is most important to check backlash in the splines between the outer sleeve and inner hub. If any is noticeable the whole assembly must be renewed.
3 Mark the hubs and sleeve so that you may reassemble them on the same splines. With the hub and sleeve separated, the teeth at the end of the splines which engage with corresponding teeth of the gearwheels, must be checked for damage and wear.
4 Do not confuse the keystone shape at the ends of the teeth. This shape matches the gear teeth shape and it is a design characteristic to minimise jump-out tendencies.
5 If the synchronising cones are being renewed it is sensible also to renew the sliding keys and springs which hold them in position.

Note: *From transmission number 5102481 a revised design of baulk ring, shifting insert and spread springs has been used. These are interchangeable with older units, but only as a set.*

7 Synchro hubs (3-speed) – reassembly

1 The hub assemblies are not interchangeable so they must be reassembled with their original or identical new parts.
2 The splines on the sliding keys are offset and must be assembled

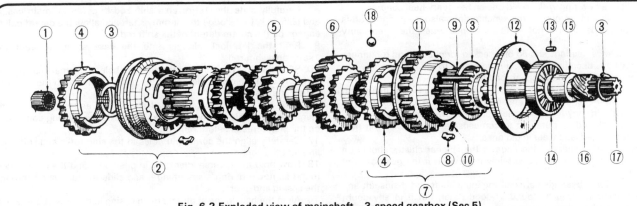

Fig. 6.2 Exploded view of mainshaft – 3-speed gearbox (Sec 5)

1 Pilot bearing	7 1st synchromesh assembly	13 Locking peg
2 2nd and 3rd synchromesh assembly	8 Shifting insert	14 Mainshaft bearing
3 Snap ring	9 Synchromesh hub	15 Distance piece
4 Baulk ring	10 Synchromesh spring	16 Speedometer drive gear
5 2nd speed gear, mainshaft	11 Reverse gear	17 Mainshaft
6 1st speed gear, mainshaft	12 Bearing retainer	18 Steel ball

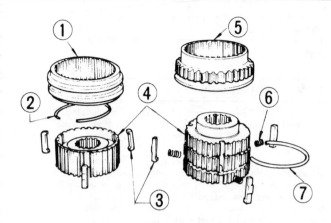

Fig. 6.3 Component parts of synchromesh assembly (Sec 6)

1	Coupling sleeve	5	Reverse gear
2	Spread spring	6	Synchro spring
3	Shifting insert	7	Stopper ring
4	Synchro hub		

to both hubs so that the offset is towards the spigoted end of the hub.
3   One slotted key is assembled to each hub for locating the turned out end of the key spring.
4   It should be noted that the clutch keys for each synchromesh unit are of slightly different lengths.
5   The turned out end of each spring must locate in the slotted key and be assembled to the hub in an anti-clockwise direction as viewed from either side of the hub.

8   Gearbox components (3-speed) – inspection

1   It is assumed that the gearbox has been dismantled for reasons of excessive noise, lack of synchromesh action on certain gears or for failure to stay in gear. If anything more drastic than this (total failure, seizure or main casing cracked) it would be better to leave it alone and look for a replacement, either secondhand or an exchange.
2   Examine all gears for excessively worn, chipped or damaged teeth. Any such gears should be renewed.
3   Check all synchromesh rings for wear on the bearing surfaces, which normally have clear machined oil reservoir lines in them. If these are smooth or obviously uneven, renewal is essential. Also, when the rings are fitted to their gears – as they would be when in operation – there should be no rock. This would signify ovality or lack of con-centricity. One of the most satisfactory ways of checking is by compar-ing the fit of a new ring with an old one on the gearwheel cone.
4   The teeth and cut outs in the synchro rings also wear, and for this reason also it is unwise not to fit new ones when the opportunity avails.
5   All ball race bearings should be checked for chatter and roughness after they have been flushed out. It is advisable to renew these anyway even though they may not appear too badly worn.
6   Circlips which are all important in locating bearings, gears and hubs should be checked to ensure that they are undistorted and undamaged. In any case a selection of new circlips of varying thicknesses should be obtained to compensate for variations in new components fitted, and wear in old ones.
7   The thrust washers at the ends of the laygear cluster should be renewed, as they will almost certainly have worn if the gearbox is of any age.
8   Needle roller bearings between the input shaft and mainshaft and in the laygear are usually found in good order, but if in any doubt renew the needle rollers as necessary.
9   For details of inspection of the synchro hub assemblies refer to Section 6.

9   Input shaft (3-speed) – reassembly

1   The bearing can be driven onto the shaft with a piece of tube of

suitable diameter to go over the shaft and abut against the inner race of the bearing. Do not drive the bearing on by the outer race. The circlip groove is offset and should be toward the forward end of the shaft.
2   Make sure the bearing is driven fully up to the gear.
3   Put the circlip onto the bearing outer track.
4   Refit the washer and selective-fit circlip to retain the bearing on the shaft. There should be no endfloat.

10   Mainshaft (3-speed) – reassembly

1   Fit the 1st gear on the rear of the mainshaft with its cone towards the rear end of the shaft. Place one baulk ring over the gear cone.
2   Fit the 1st/reverse synchronizer assembly with the plain end of the sleeve towards the rear end of the mainshaft.
3   Fit the spacer washer and then, using a bench vice and soft faced hammer, drive the mainshaft bearing and retainer assembly onto the mainshaft.
4   Refit the distance piece, ball bearing and speedometer drive gear and secure by fitting a circlip to the mainshaft.
5   A circlip should be selected so that 1st gear has an endfloat of 0.002 – 0.0087 inch (0.05 – 0.22 mm) and may be checked by feeler gauges between the face of the 1st gear and mainshaft flange.
6   Refit 2nd gear onto the front of the mainshaft so that the cone is towards the front end of the shaft. Place a baulk ring over the gear cone.
7   Refit the 2nd/top synchronizer assembly onto the mainshaft and secure with a circlip.
8   A circlip should be selected so that 2nd gear has an endfloat of 0.004 – 0.0087 inch (0.10 – 0.22 mm) and may be checked by feeler gauges between the face of 2nd gear and the mainshaft flange.

11   Gearbox (3-speed) – reassembly

1   Lubricate the needle roller bearing with a little gearbox oil and fit into the end of the input shaft.
2   Fit the input shaft into the front face of the gearbox and place a baulk ring over the gear cone.
3   Carefully insert the mainshaft assembly into the main casing taking care to engage the mainshaft spigot end into the rear of the input shaft.
4   Position the bearing retainer into the main casing.
5   Place the main casing on the bench in such a manner that the interlock hole faces upward.
6   Insert the detent spring and ball bearing into the blank ended hole. Hold it in position against spring pressure so that a drummy shaft of the same diameter as the shift rod can be inserted into the 1st/reverse shift rod hole.
7   Place the shaft forks on the synchronizer sleeves.
8   Carefully slide the 1st/reverse shift rod through the main casing and shift fork, to dislodge the dummy shaft and allow the detent ball to engage on the centre detent of the shift rod.
9   Refit the interlock plunger into the case so as to abut the 1st/reverse shift rod.
10   Slide the 2nd/top shift rod through the hole in the main casing and shift fork until the centre detent on the rod is aligned with the interlock hole in the main casing.
11   Refit the remaining detent ball and spring and secure with the plug. It is advisable to smear a little non-hardening sealing compound on the plug threads before refitting.
12   Carefully align the spring pin holes in the shift forks and shift rods and refit the spring pins.
13   Now hold the reverse idler gear in position – and the correct way round as noted during dismantling – and slide the idler shaft through the casing and gear.
14   Align the hole in the shaft and main casing and screw in the retain-ing screw. Lock the screw with the lockplate.
15   Fit the needle roller bearings in each end of the laygear, place the laygear in the main casing with the thrust washers held in position on either end with grease.
16   Slide the layshaft through the casing, thrust washer and laygear.
17   Using feeler gauges check the laygear endfloat. This should be 0.0016 – 0.0047 in (0.04 – 0.12 mm). If necessary adjust by fitting thicker or thinner thrust washers.

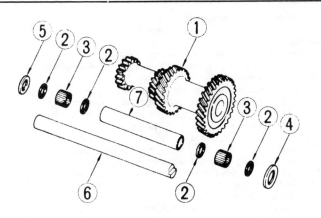

Fig. 6.4 Exploded view of laygear assembly – 3-speed gearbox (Sec 11)

1	Laygear	5	Washer
2	Washer	6	Layshaft
3	Bearing	7	Spacer
4	Washer		

18 Place the shift levers in the main casing so as to engage with the shift forks.

19 Slide new oil seals onto the cross-shafts and insert the shafts through the casing, thrust washers and shift levers.

20 Hold the thrust washers against the side of the casing and fit the circlips to the grooves in the cross-shafts.

21 Carefully align the notches in the cross-shafts with the cotter pin holes in the shift levers. Insert the cotter pins and secure with the washers and nuts.

22 Always fit a new oil seal to the input shaft bearing cover and retainer. The lip must face inward.

23 Refit the cover and new gasket to the front of the main casing and secure with the retaining bolts and spring washers.

24 Fit a new gasket to the extension housing mating face and offer the extension housing up the the main casing.Secure with the retaining bolts and spring washers.

25 Insert the speedometer pinion assembly into the extension housing and secure with the bolt and lockplate.

26 If a reverse light switch was fitted it should now be refitted.

27 Lubricate all gears, shafts and parts of the selector mechanism to ensure adequate lubrication.

28 Fit a new cover plate gasket and refit the cover plate. Secure in position with the fourteen bolts and spring washers. These must be tightened in a diagonal and progressive manner to stop distortion.

29 Refit the clutch release lever, bearing, retainer spring and rubber dust cover.

30 The gearbox is now ready for refitting to the car. Do not forget to refill the gearbox with the recommended grade oil.

12 Gearchange lever assembly (3-speed) – removal and refitting

1   Refer to Chapter 11 and remove the horn ring, steering wheel and steering columnshell and suitable assembly.

2   Using a pair of circlip pliers remove the circlip located at the control rod top support bracket.

3   Slacken the support bracket clamp screw. Lift away the support bracket.

4   Withdraw the control rod insert, bush and spring.

5   Again with circlip pliers remove the circlip and clevis pin that retains the column gearchange lever to the control rod and disconnect the lever.

6   Now turning to the steering gearbox end of the linkage, disconnect the gearchange rods from the control levers. This is done by removing the split pin and plain and spring washer on each rod trunnion.

7   Undo and remove the lower support bracket retaining bolts and disconnect the lower clamp and control rod levers retainer.

8   Disconnect the 2nd/top gear change lever, then the lower support

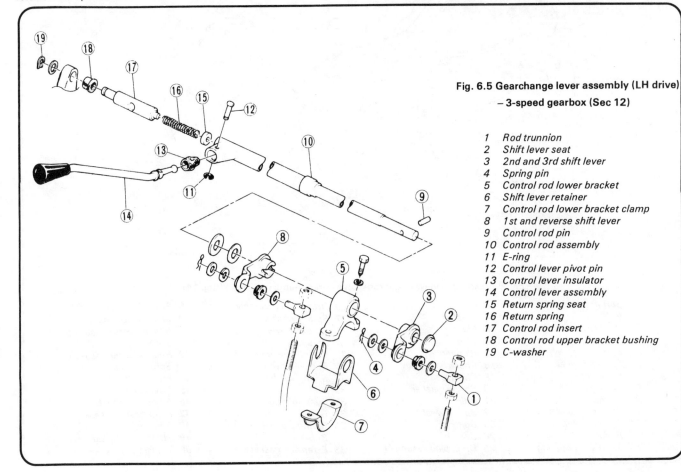

Fig. 6.5 Gearchange lever assembly (LH drive) – 3-speed gearbox (Sec 12)

1	Rod trunnion
2	Shift lever seat
3	2nd and 3rd shift lever
4	Spring pin
5	Control rod lower bracket
6	Shift lever retainer
7	Control rod lower bracket clamp
8	1st and reverse shift lever
9	Control rod pin
10	Control rod assembly
11	E-ring
12	Control lever pivot pin
13	Control lever insulator
14	Control lever assembly
15	Return spring seat
16	Return spring
17	Control rod insert
18	Control rod upper bracket bushing
19	C-washer

bracket and finally the 1st/reverse lever from the control rod end.

9   The control rod may now be pulled out with care.

10 Should it be necessary to dismantle even further, detach the gearchange rods from the operating lever and relay shaft. Slacken and remove the relay shaft from between the gearbox and side plate.

11 Reassembling and refitting is the reverse sequence to removal and dismantling. To ensure ease of operation lubricate all moving parts with a little grease.

12 It will be necessary to adjust the linkage as described in Section 13.

13 Gearchange lever assembly (3-speed) – adjustment

1   Move the gearchange lever to the neutral position.

2   Clean off any dirt on the control levers and look for a groove on the top edge of each lever. Also locate a ridge on the control rod lower bracket.

3   When the linkage is correctly adjusted and the gearchange lever is in the neutral position, all three marks will line up.

4   Should adjustment be necessary either shorten or lengthen the gearchange rods as necessary at the adjusting nuts located above and below the trunnions.

14 Gearbox (4-speed) – dismantling

1   Refer to Section 3, paragraphs 1 – 3 inclusive.

2   Release the thrust bearing assembly from the clutch arm (photo).

3   Lift the clutch arm from the bellhousing.

4   Unscrew the reverse light switch from the side of the extension housing.

5   Unscrew and remove the bolt and lockplate securing the speedometer pinion and housing assembly to the extension housing. Withdraw the assembly.

6   Using a pair of circlip pliers, remove the circlip and clevis pin that holds the striking rod to the gearchange lever socket (photo).

7   Undo and remove the fourteen bolts and spring washers that secure the cover plate to the main casing.

8   Lift away the cover plate and its gasket.

9   Undo and remove the screws and spring washers securing the input shaft bearing cover to the main casing (photo).

10 Undo and remove the extension housing bolts and spring washers.

11 Carefully withdraw the extension housing by a sufficient amount to disengage the striking rod lever from the shift rod gates (photo). Alternatively the striking rod lever may be left in position until later (paragraph 14).

12 Remove the extension housing and striking rods as an assembly.

13 If the extension housing oil seal showed signs of leaking the old seal should be levered out using a screwdriver and a new seal fitted using a suitable diameter drift (photo).

14 This photo shows the striking rod lever in position in the shift rod gates. Detach the striking rod now if it was left in position (paragraph 11). Using a screwdriver move the synchronizer sleeves into gear so as to lock up the mainshaft. Unscrew and remove the mainshaft end nut. Return the synchronizer sleeves to their neutral position. It is easier to remove this nut now rather than later.

15 Using a suitable diameter drift, tap out the layshaft towards the

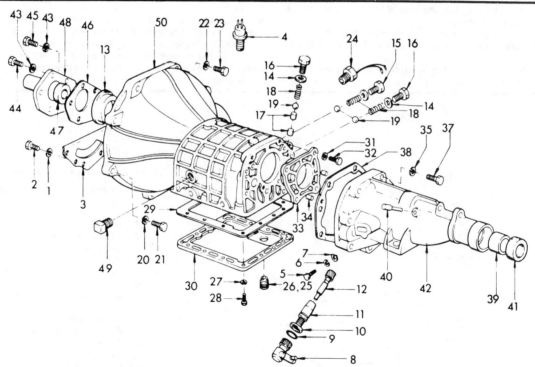

Fig. 6.6 Exploded view of gearbox case components (4-speed) (Sec 14)

1 Spring washer	retainer	26 Drain plug assembly	39 Extension bushing
2 Bolt	14 Washer	27 Spring washer	40 Breather assembly
3 Dust cover	15 Plug	28 Bottom cover	41 Rear extension housing
4 Neutral switch	16 Plug	hexagonal bolt	seal
5 Bolt	17 Plunger	29 Bottom cover gasket	42 Rear extension housing
6 Spring washer	18 Check ball spring	30 Bottom cover	43 Spring washer
7 Lock plate	19 Check ball	31 Spring washer	44 Fixing bolt
8 Retainer	20 Spring washer	32 Bolt	45 Fixing bolt
9 O-ring	21 Bolt	33 Bearing retainer	46 Front cover gasket
10 Sleeve oil seal	22 Spring washer	34 Dowel pin	47 Front cover oil seal
11 Pinion sleeve	23 Bolt	35 Spring washer	48 Front cover
12 Pinion	24 Switch	37 Bolt	49 Thread taper plug
13 Main shaft bearing	25 Drain plug assembly	38 Extension gasket	50 Transmission case

14.2 Detaching thrust bearing assembly from clutch arm

14.6 Removing the clevis pin

14.9 Removing the input shaft bearing cover

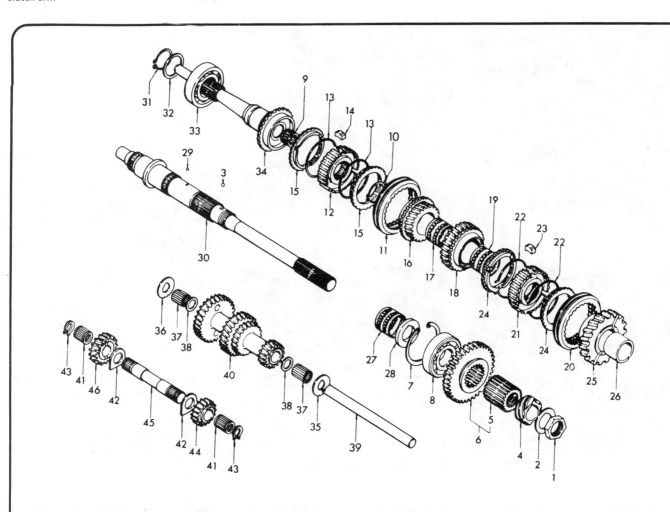

Fig. 6.7 Gearbox gear components (4-speed) (Sec 14)

1 Main shaft nut	12 Synchro hub	24 Baulk ring	36 Thrust washer
2 Main shaft lock washer	13 Spread spring	25 Main shaft first gear	37 Needle bearing assembly
3 Steel ball	14 Shifting insert	26 Main shaft bushing	38 Counter spacer
4 Speedometer gear	15 Baulk ring	27 Main shaft needle bearing	39 Counter shaft
5 Reverse hub main shaft	16 Third speed gear	28 Thrust washer	40 Counter gear
6 Reverse main gear and hub set	17 Main shaft needle bearing	29 Steel ball	41 Reverse gear needle bearing
7 Main shaft snap ring	18 Second gear assembly	30 Main shaft	42 Thrust washer
8 Main shaft bearing	19 Main shaft needle bearing	31 Main drive snap ring	43 Snap ring
9 Main shaft pilot bearing	20 Coupling sleeve	32 Main drive spacer	44 Reverse gear
10 Snap ring	21 Synchronise hub	33 Main drive bearing	45 Reverse shaft
11 Sleeve coupling	22 Spead spring	34 Main drive gear	46 Reverse gear
	23 Shifting insert	35 Thrust washer	

14.11 Withdrawing the extension housing

14.13 Lever out the oil seal with a screwdriver

14.14 Location of striking rod lever in shift rod gates

14.15 Removal of layshaft

14.16 Lifting out the lay-gear

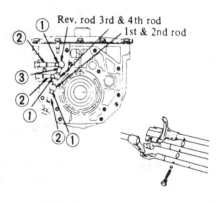
Fig. 6.8 Layout of check balls and interlock plungers (4-speed) (Sec 14)

1 Checking ball
2 Checking ball spring
3 Interlock plunger

14.17 Removing the check ball and spring retaining plug

14.19a Lift away the shift fork and ...

14.19b ... withdraw the fork rod

14.22 Removing the 3rd and 4th shift rod

14.23 Driving out the spring pin

front. Note location of spring pin as it must engage with the input shaft bearing cover on assembly (photo).
16 Lift away the laygear and thrust washers noting which way round they are fitted (photo).
17 Unscrew the lowermost plug retaining the spring and check ball and recover the spring and check ball (photo).
18 Carefully drive out the spring pin located in the hub of the reverse speed shift fork.
19 Lift away the shift fork and withdraw the fork rod (photos).
20 Unscrew the second plug retaining the spring and check ball and recover the spring and check ball.
21 Carefully drive out the spring pin securing the 3rd and 4th shift fork to the shift rod.
22 Withdraw the 3rd and 4th shift rod (photo).
23 Carefully drive out the spring pin securing the 1st and 2nd shift fork to the shift rod (photo).
24 Unscrew the plug located at the top of the main casing and recover the spring and check ball (photo).
25 Withdraw the 1st and 2nd shift rod (photo).
26 Lift away the 1st and 2nd shift fork (photo).
27 Lift away the 3rd and 4th shift fork (photo).
28 Using a pair of circlip pliers remove the circlip from the inner end of the reverse idler shaft.
29 Lift away the thrust washer and reverse gear.
30 Withdraw the reverse shaft assembly rearward from the main

casing (photo).
31 Undo and remove the four bolts and spring washers that secure the mainshaft rear bearing retainer to the main casing.
32 The mainshaft assembly may now be withdrawn from the rear of the main casing (photo).
33 Using a soft faced hammer tap out the input shaft assembly (photo).
34 Lift away the caged needle roller bearing from the rear of the input shaft.

15 Input shaft (4-speed) – dismantling

1   The shaft and bearing are located in the front of the main casing by a large flanged sleeve pressed onto the bearing outer track.
2   To remove the bearing first remove the selective-fit circlip and washer from the front end of the bearing.
3   Place the outer track of the race on the top of a firm bench vice and drive the input shaft through the bearing. Note which way round the bearing is fitted. Lift away the bearing.
4   Using a suitable diameter drive remove the bearing from the flange sleeve.
5   If not already done, recover the spigot bearing from the mainshaft end of the input shaft.

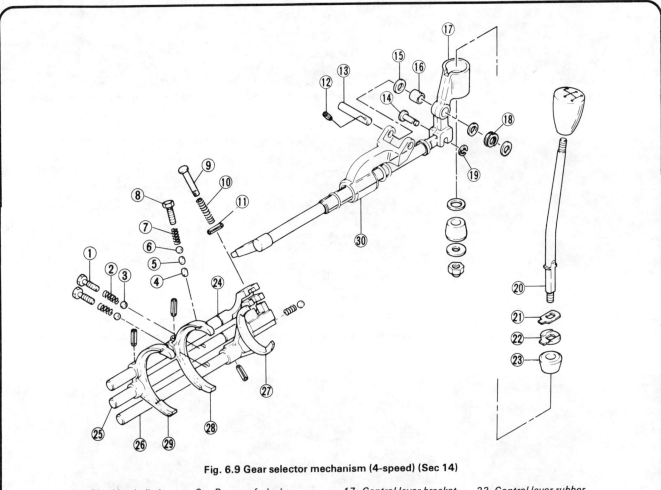

Fig. 6.9 Gear selector mechanism (4-speed) (Sec 14)

1 Checking ball plug	9 Reverse fork pin	17 Control lever bracket	23 Control lever rubber
2 Checking ball spring	10 Reverse pin return spring	18 Control spring	24 1st and 2nd fork rod
3 Checking ball	11 Roller pin	19 Striking pin C-ring	25 3rd and 4th fork rod
4 Interlock plunger	12 Retaining pin	20 Control lever	26 Reverse fork rod
5 Interlock plunger	13 Control arm pin	21 Control lever upper washer	27 Reverse shift fork
6 Checking ball	14 Striking rod pin	22 Control lever upper washer	28 1st and 2nd shift fork
7 Checking ball spring	15 Thrust washer		29 3rd and 4th fork rod
8 Checking ball plug	16 Control bushing		30 Control arm

14.24 Removal of the third check ball retaining plug

14.25 Removing 1st and 2nd shift rod

14.26 Lifting out 1st and 2nd shift fork

14.27 Removing 3rd and 4th shift fork

14.30 Withdrawing reverse shaft assembly

14.32 Removing the mainshaft assembly

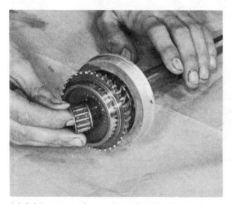
14.34 Input shaft needle roller bearing

16.1 Removing circlip from front of mainshaft

16.2 Slide off the 3rd/top gear synchronizer ...

16.4 ... and the 3rd gear and needle bearing

16.5 Removal of nut and lock plate

16.7 Reverse gear and splined hub removal

16.10 Removal of 1st gear and needle roller bearing

16.11a Removal of sleeve ...

16.11b ... and 1st/2nd gear synchronizer assembly

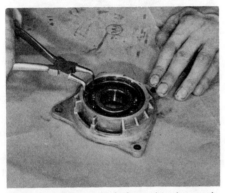

16.13 Removing mainshaft rear bearing retaining circlip

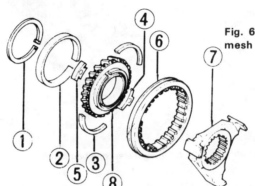

Fig. 6.10 Component parts of synchro-mesh assembly – (F4C63 gearbox) (Secs 17 and 18)

1   Circlip
2   Synchro ring
3   Brake band
4   Thrust block
5   Anchor block
6   Coupling sleeve
7   Synchro hub
8   Clutch gear

16 Mainshaft (4-speed) – dismantling

1   Using a pair of circlip pliers remove the circlip from the front of the mainshaft (photo).
2   Slide off the 3rd/top gear synchronizer assembly from the mainshaft (photo).
3   Note that a baulk ring is located on both ends of the syncrhonizer.
4   Slide off the 3rd gear complete with needle bearings (photo).
5   Undo and remove the nut and lockplate from the rear of the mainshaft. If it has not already been slackened off take care to hold the mainshaft securely as it is very tight (photo).
6   Remove the speedometer drive gear and ball bearing from the mainshaft (photo 16:5).
7   The reverse gear and splined hub may now be withdrawn from the mainshaft (photo).
8   Place the mainshaft in a vice and with a soft metal hammer drive the mainshaft through the rear bearing and retainer assembly.
9   Slide the thrust washer off the mainshaft.
10 Slide off the 1st gear and needle roller bearing (photo).
11 Using a soft faced hammer carefully drift off the sleeve and remove the 1st/2nd gear synchronizer assembly and 2nd gear and needle roller bearing (photos).
12 Again note that a baulk ring is located on either end of the synchronizer.
13 Remove the circlip from the mainshaft rear bearing retainer and drive out the bearing from the retainer (photo).

17 Synchro hubs (4-speed) – dismantling and inspection

Refer to Section 6.

18 Synchro hubs (4-speed) – reassembly

Refer to Section 7.

19 Gearbox components (4-speed) – inspection

Refer to Section 8.

20 Input shaft (4-speed) – reassembly

1   Fit the bearing into the retainer. This is easily done by pressing together between soft faces in a bench vice. Make sure the bearing is the correct way round.
2   The bearing can be driven onto the shaft with a piece of tube of suitable diameter to go over the shaft and butt against the inner race of the bearing. Do not drive the bearing on by the outer race. Make sure the bearing and retainer are the correct way round.
3   Make sure the bearing is driven fully up to the gear.
4   Refit the washer and selective-fit circlip to retain the bearing on the shaft. There should be no endfloat.

21 Mainshaft (4-speed) – reassembly

1   Press the mainshaft rear bearing into the retainer and secure with the circlip. This is easily done by pressing together between soft faces in a bench vice. Make quite sure the bearing is the correct way round.
2   Hold the mainshaft vertically and fit the 2nd gear and needle roller bearing assembly (photo).
3   Place a baulk ring onto the gear cone (photo).
4   Fit the 1st/2nd gear synchronizer sleeve and hub assembly taking care that the synchronizer shift plate ends engage in the 2nd gear baulk ring notches (photo).
5   Slide the sleeve onto the mainshaft (photo).
6   Fit the second baulk ring into the synchromesh unit (photo).
7   Fit the 1st gear together with the needle roller bearing onto the sleeve (photo).
8   Position the ball bearing in the mainshaft and place the thrust washer over the ball bearing and mainshaft (photo).

21.2 Fit the 2nd gear and needle roller bearing assembly ...

21.3 ... and then the baulk ring on the gear cone

21.4 Fit 1st/2nd gear synchronizer sleeve and hub assembly

21.5 Sliding the sleeve onto the mainshaft

21.6 Fitting the second baulk ring ...

21.7 ... and then 1st gear and needle roller bearing

21.8 Locating thrust washer on mainshaft

21.9 Fitting mainshaft rear bearing retainer

21.10 Placing shim on mainshaft

21.11 Fitting 3rd gear and needle roller bearing ...

21.12 and then the baulk ring over the gear cone

21.13 Fitting 3rd/top gear synchronizer sleeve and hub assembly

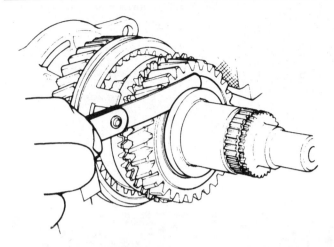

Fig. 6.11 Measuring gear endplay (Sec 21)

9 Place the mainshaft rear bearing and retainer on the top of a firm bench vice and with a soft faced hammer drive the mainshaft onto the bearing. Alternatively place on a firm bench and with a drift on the inner track drive the bearing into position (photo).
10 Apply a little grease to the shim and place on the mainshaft (photo).
11 Now fit the 3rd gear together with the needle roller bearing on the front of the mainshaft (photo).
12 Place a baulk ring over the gear cone (photo).
13 Fit the 3rd/top gear synchronizer sleeve and hub assembly making sure the synchronizer shift plate ends engage in the 3rd gear bulk ring notches (photo).
14 Fit a selective circlip which gives a minimum clearance between the end face of the hub and ring groove.

22 Gearbox (4-speed) —reassembly

1 Insert the mainshaft assembly into the main casing (photo).
2 Line up the retainer bolt holes, then with a soft faced hammer drive the mainshaft and retainer into position.
3 Refit the rear bearing retainer bolts and spring washers.
4 Fit the splined hub and reverse gear onto the mainshaft so that he large boss on the gear is towards the rear of the mainshaft (photo).
5 Place the drive ball bearing into the mainshaft and slide the speedometer drive gear into position over the ball bearing (photo).
6 Fit the retaining nut lockplate and then the nut. Screw the latter up finger tight (photo).
7 Fit the top gear baulk ring over the gear cone (photo).
8 Fit the caged needle roller bearing to the rear of the input shaft (photo).
9 Carefully insert the input shaft through the front of the main casing and engage the needle roller bearing onto the mainshaft spigot. Make sure that the notches in the baulk ring locate over the synchronizer shift plate ends (photo).
10 Fit the reverse idler gear to the end of the idler shaft with the longest spline. Secure with a circlip.
11 Place a thrust washer onto the reverse shaft so that it abuts the gear then fit the shaft through the gear case from the rear (photo).
12 Place a thrust washer on the front of the shaft followed by the reverse idler driven gear. This is the one with the helical teeth (photo).
13 Secure with a selective circlip to give an endfloat of 0·004 – 0.0118 in (0.10 – 0.30 mm).
14 The laygear must now be fitted with needle rollers. Insert a spacer in the laygear shaft bore (photo).
15 Insert the laygear shaft guide (photo).
16 Pack the needle roller bearing aperture with grease and assemble the needle rollers into the grease.
17 Invert the laygear and fit the second spacer needle rollers.
18 With the needle roller bearings and spacers correctly fitted into the laygear, fit the laygear into the main casing (photo).
19 Slide a thrust washer into approximate position between the

22.1 Fitting the mainshaft assembly into casing

22.4 Fitting the reverse gear

22.5 Sliding the speedometer drive gear over ball bearing

22.6 Fitting the retaining nut

22.7 Fitting the baulk ring over the gear cone

22.8 Insert needle roller bearing in rear of input shaft ...

22.9 ... and then fit the shaft in the main casing

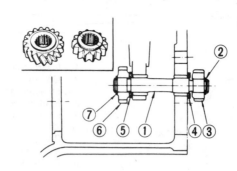

Fig. 6.12 Reverse idler gear assembly
(Sec 22)

1　Reverse idler shaft
2　Circlip
3　Idler driving gear
4　Thrust washer
5　Thrust washer
6　Idler gear
7　Circlip

22.11 Fitting the reverse shaft ...

22.12 ... then the thrust washer and reverse idler gear

22.14 Inserting spacer into laygear

22.15 Sliding in laygear shaft guide

22.18 Positioning the laygear in the casing

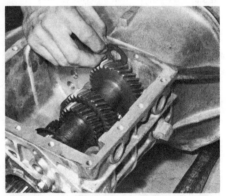

22.19 Locating the front thrust washer ...

22.20 ... and the rear thrust washer

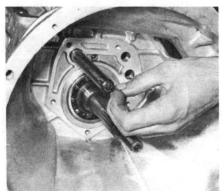

22.21 Fitting the laygear shaft

22.22 Measuring the endfloat

laygear and front main casing (photo).
20 Slide a thrust washer into approximate position between the laygear and rear main casing (photo).
21 Carefully insert the layshaft through the main casing thrust washers and laygear (photo).
22 Check the laygear endfloat with feeler gauges. It should be 0·002 – 0·006 in (0·05 – 0·15 mm). Adjust if necessary using thicker or thinner thrust washers (photo).
23 Place the shift forks onto the synchronizer sleeves in the positions noted during dismantling.
24 Slide the 1st/2nd gear shift rod through the case and shift fork until the centre detent on the rod is aligned with the detent ball hole (photo).
25 Fit the interlock into the case so as to abut the 1st/2nd shift rod (photo).
26 Slide the 3rd/top shift rod through the main case and shift fork making sure that the interlock pin is in position in the shift rod then push the rod through the hole until the centre detent is aligned with the detent ball hole (photo).

27 Fit the second ball into the upper hole.
28 Hold the reverse gear shift fork in position on the reverse gear and slide the shaft rod through the fork and main casing (photo).
29 Align the spring pin hole in the shift forks and rods and carefully refit the spring pins (photo).
30 Fit the three detent balls and springs and secure with the three plugs. The plug threads should be smeared with a little non-setting sealing compound before refitting (photo).
31 This photo shows all selector rods and plugs fitted.
32 Fit a new gasket to the extension housing face and partially slide over the mainshaft. Engage the striking rod lever in the shift rod gates. Push fully home and secure with bolts and spring washers (photo).
33 Fit a new oil seal to the front mainshaft bearing cover. The lip must face inward.
34 Fit a new gasket to the main casing and then refit the cover.Tighten the retaining bolts and spring washers (photo).
35 Align the holes in the striker rod and insert the clevis pin that holds the striking rod to the gearchange lever socket. Secure with the circlip (photo).

22.24 Inserting 1st/2nd gear shift rod

22.25 Inserting interlock ball bearing

22.26 Fitting 3rd/top shift rod

22.28 Fitting the reverse gear shift rod

22.29 Driving in the spring pins

22.30 Fitting detent balls

22.31 Selector rods and plugs fitted to main casing

22.32 Fitting the extension housing

22.34 Fitting the front cover

22.35 Inserting the clevis pin securing the striking rod

22.36 Fitting the speedometer drive pinion assembly

22.38 Assembling clutch arm and release bearing

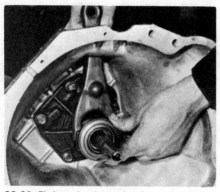

22.39 Fitting clutch arm and release bearing assembly

22.40 Fitting the main casing cover-plate

36 Insert the speedometer drive pinion assembly into the extension and secure with the lockplate and bolt (photo).

37 Refit the reverse light switch to the extension housing.

38 Reconnect the clutch withdrawal arm to the release bearing (photo).

39 Refit the clutch withdrawal arm and release bearing to the bellhousing. Refit the rubber grommet in the withdrawal arm aperture of the bellhousing (photo).

40 Fit a new cover-plate gasket and then the cover-plate. Secure with the fourteen bolts and spring washers which should be tightened in a progressive and diagonal manner (photo).

23 Gearbox (5-speed) – dismantling

1 Refer to Section 14, paragraphs 1–5 inclusive.

2 Remove the front cover securing bolts, take off the cover and collect the countershaft front bearing shim.

3 Using a pair of circlip pliers, remove the main drive bearing circlip.

4 Remove the reverse select return plug, spring and plunger from the rear extension.

5 Undo the rear extension securing bolts and withdraw the extension using a puller. Separate the gearbox casing from the adaptor plate, using a soft hammer.

24 Gear assembly (5-speed) – dismantling

1 Secure the gear assembly in a vice with the countershaft upwards. Fig. 6.13 shows the assembly mounted with the Datsun adaptor setting plate.

2 Drive out the retaining pins from each fork rod with a parallel pin punch.

3 Remove three check balls plugs, and drive out the fork rods from the adaptor plate by lightly tapping on the front end. Collect the checkballs, springs and interlock plungers.

4 Remove the reverse idle gear and shaft.

5 From the end of the mainshaft remove the rear circlip, the

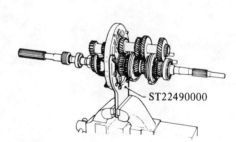

Fig. 6.13 Gear assembly (5-speed) mounted in vice (Sec 23)

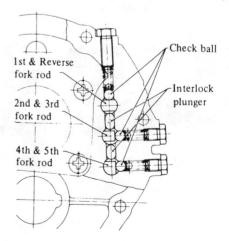

Fig. 6.14 Location of check balls and interlock plungers (5-speed) (Sec 23)

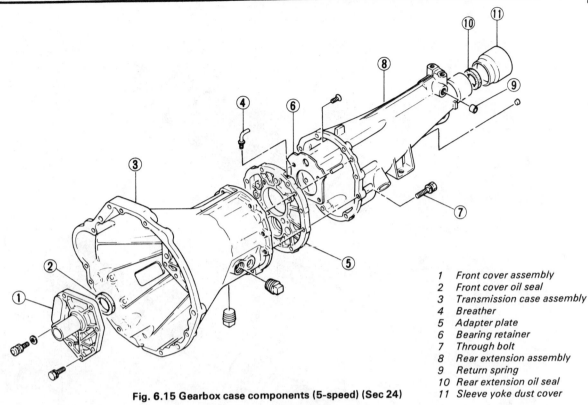

1 Front cover assembly
2 Front cover oil seal
3 Transmission case assembly
4 Breather
5 Adapter plate
6 Bearing retainer
7 Through bolt
8 Rear extension assembly
9 Return spring
10 Rear extension oil seal
11 Sleeve yoke dust cover

Fig. 6.15 Gearbox case components (5-speed) (Sec 24)

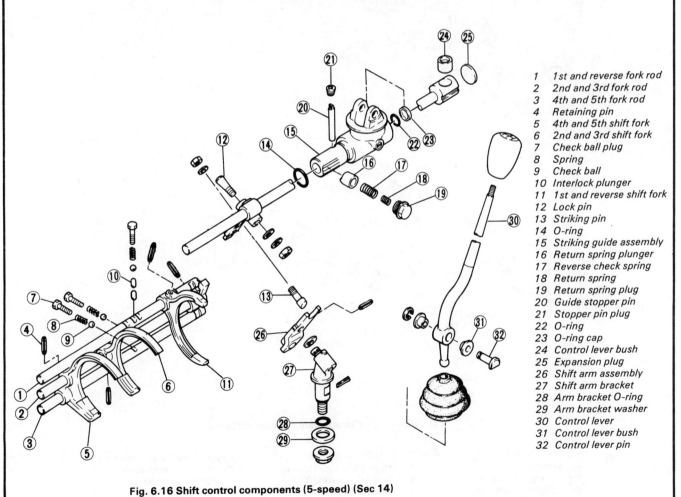

1 1st and reverse fork rod
2 2nd and 3rd fork rod
3 4th and 5th fork rod
4 Retaining pin
5 4th and 5th shift fork
6 2nd and 3rd shift fork
7 Check ball plug
8 Spring
9 Check ball
10 Interlock plunger
11 1st and reverse shift fork
12 Lock pin
13 Striking pin
14 O-ring
15 Striking guide assembly
16 Return spring plunger
17 Reverse check spring
18 Return spring
19 Return spring plug
20 Guide stopper pin
21 Stopper pin plug
22 O-ring
23 O-ring cap
24 Control lever bush
25 Expansion plug
26 Shift arm assembly
27 Shift arm bracket
28 Arm bracket O-ring
29 Arm bracket washer
30 Control lever
31 Control lever bush
32 Control lever pin

Fig. 6.16 Shift control components (5-speed) (Sec 14)

116

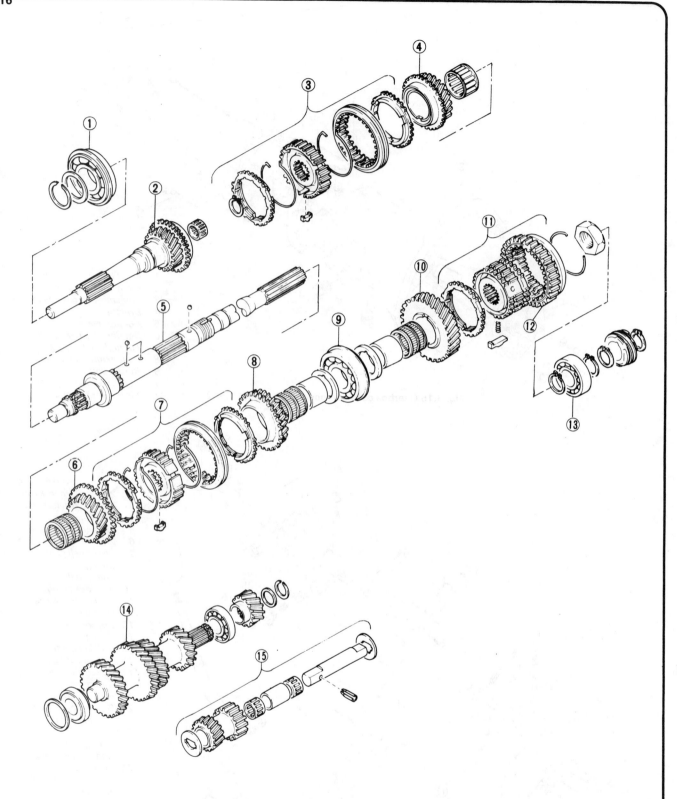

Fig. 6.17 Gearbox internal components (5-speed) (Sec 24)

1	Main drive bearing	6	3rd gear, mainshaft	11	Reverse and 1st synchronizer
2	Main drive gear	7	3rd and 2nd synchronizer	12	Reverse gear, mainshaft
3	4th and OD synchronizer	8	2nd gear, mainshaft	13	Mainshaft end bearing
4	OD gear, mainshaft	9	Main shaft bearing	14	Counter gear assembly
5	Mainshaft	10	1st gear, mainshaft	15	Idler gear assembly

speedometer drive gear and then the other circlip.
6   Remove the circlip from the mainshaft end bearing and using a puller remove the bearing.
7   Mesh the 1st and 2nd gears at the same time. Release the staking of the mainshaft nut and remove the nut.
8   Remove the synchro hub with reverse gear, then 1st gear together with needle bearing and bush, thrust washer and steel ball.
9   From the rear end of the countergear remove the circlip and thrust washer. Using a puller withdraw the 1st countergear.
10   Using a puller drive out the mainshaft, while holding the front of the mainshaft gear assembly and countergear assembly, approximately 0·40 in (10 mm) and then remove the main drive gear and countergear.
11   Remove the mainshaft gear assembly.

25 Mainshaft (5-speed) – dismantling

1   Remove the 2nd gear thrust washer and steel ball, then the 2nd gear and needle bearing.
2   Using a press remove the 2nd gear mainshaft bush, the 3rd gear then 2nd and 3rd speed synchronizer.
3   Remove the circlip on the front end of the mainshaft and withdraw the 4th and 5th speed synchronizer and the 5th gear.

26 Main drive gear and countergear (5-speed) – dismantling

Do not remove the bearings unless any parts are defective. If the

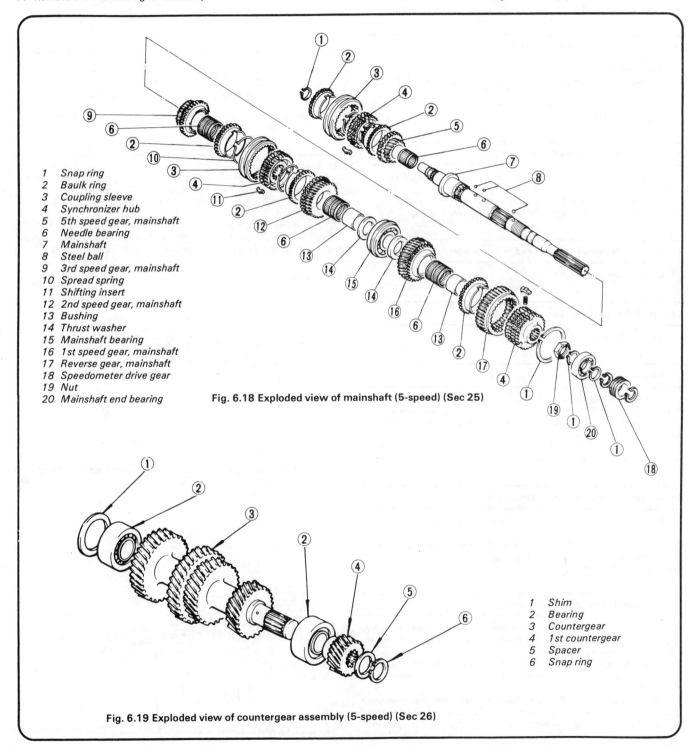

1   Snap ring
2   Baulk ring
3   Coupling sleeve
4   Synchronizer hub
5   5th speed gear, mainshaft
6   Needle bearing
7   Mainshaft
8   Steel ball
9   3rd speed gear, mainshaft
10 Spread spring
11 Shifting insert
12 2nd speed gear, mainshaft
13 Bushing
14 Thrust washer
15 Mainshaft bearing
16 1st speed gear, mainshaft
17 Reverse gear, mainshaft
18 Speedometer drive gear
19 Nut
20 Mainshaft end bearing

Fig. 6.18 Exploded view of mainshaft (5-speed) (Sec 25)

1   Shim
2   Bearing
3   Countergear
4   1st countergear
5   Spacer
6   Snap ring

Fig. 6.19 Exploded view of countergear assembly (5-speed) (Sec 26)

drive gear bearing is renewed, fit a selective circlip of a thickness that will eliminate endplay.

27 Reverse idler gear (5-speed) – dismantling and reassembly

1   Dismantle and reassemble the reverse idler gear in the order shown in Fig. 6.20.
2   When fitting the thrust washers on the shaft, ensure that the brown surfaces are facing toward the gears.

28 Synchro hubs (5-speed) – dismantling and inspection

Refer to Section 6.

29 Rear extension (5-speed) – dismantling

1   Remove the screw and stopper pin.
2   Remove the lock pin from the striking lever and withdraw the striking rod.
3   Do not remove the bush; if the bush is worn the rear extension housing must be renewed.

30 Adaptor plate (5-speed) – dismantling

1   Using an impact driver undo the four bearing retainer securing screws and remove the bearing retainer.
2   Remove the mainshaft bearing from the rear extension side.
3   Use a brass drift to tap out the countergear rear bearing.

31 Gearbox components (5-speed) – inspection

Refer to Section 8.

32 Synchro hubs (5-speed) – reassembly

Refer to Section 7.

33 Rear extension (5-speed) – reassembly

1   Fit a new oil seal in the housing.
2   Apply multi-purpose grease to the O-ring and plunger grooves in the striking rod. Insert the striking rod with the striking rod guide through the rear extension.
3   Fit the striking lever on the front end of the striking rod, then fit the stopper pin and retaining screw.

34 Adaptor plate (5-speed) – reassembly

1   Fit the countergear rear bearing outer race by tapping it into position using a brass drift.
2   Fit the mainshaft bearing and tap it home using a plastic hammer.
3   Fit the bearing retainer and securing screws. Stake the screws at two places with a centre punch.

35 Mainshaft (5-speed) – reassembly

When assembling the mainshaft, use selective circlips of suitable thickness to obtain the endplay given in the Specifications at the beginning of this Chapter.
1   Fit the 5th gear needle bearing, mainshaft 5th gear and baulk ring with 4th and 5th speed synchronizer on the front of the mainshaft. Fit the selective circlip.
2   Fit the 3rd gear needle roller bearings, 3rd gear, 3rd gear baulk ring, 2nd and 3rd speed synchronizer in that order, then fit the 2nd gear bush and mainshaft bearing thrust washer by tapping lightly with a plastic hammer.

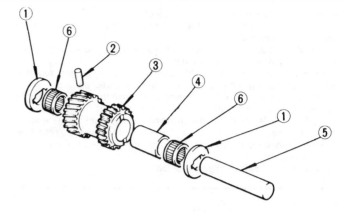

Fig. 6.20 Exploded view of reverse idler gear (5-speed) (Sec 27)

1	*Reverse washer*	4	*Needle bearing spacer*
2	*Retaining pin*	5	*Reverse idler shaft*
3	*Reverse idler gear*	6	*Needle bearing*

3   Fit the 2nd gear baulk ring, needle bearing, 2nd gear, steel ball and thin thrust washer.

36 Gear assembly (5-speed) – reassembly

1   Mount the adaptor plate in a vice; refer to Fig. 6.13.
2   Fit the mainshaft assembly to the adaptor plate and fit the mainshaft nut.
3   Pull the mainshaft assembly into the adaptor plate with a suitable puller, (Fig. 6.22 shows the official Datsun tool) until the thrust washer-to-bearing clearance is approximately 0·39 in (10 mm).

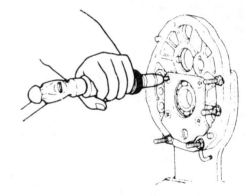

Fig. 6.21 Removing the adaptor plate bearing retainer (5-speed) (Sec 36)

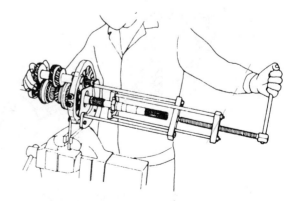

Fig. 6.22 Fitting the mainshaft to adaptor plate (5-speed) (Sec 36)

4   Position the baulk ring on the cone surface of the main drive gear. Oil the mainshaft pilot bearing and fit it on the shaft. Fit the main drive gear assembly on the front end of the mainshaft and then the countergear assembly on the front end of the mainshaft and main drive gear.
5   Hold the gear in position and pull the mainshaft assembly into the adaptor plate together with the main drive gear and countergear. Remove the mainshaft nut.
6   Press the 1st countergear onto the countershaft.
7   Fit the spacer on the rear end of the 1st countergear and secure it with a selective circlip.
8   Now fit the steel ball, thick thrust washer, 1st gear bush, needle bearing, 1st gear, 1st gear baulk ring, 1st speed synchronizer together with reverse main gear and mainshaft nut on the rear end of the mainshaft, in that order.
9   Mesh 1st and 2nd gears at the same time and tighten the mainshaft nut to a torque of 101 – 123 lbf ft (14 –17kgf m). Stake the nut into the groove on the mainshaft.
10 Check that the gear endplay is within the specification.
11 Fit a 0·043 in (1·1 mm) thick circlip to the front of the mainshaft end bearing.
12 Fit the mainshaft end bearing and then a selective circlip to the rear side of the bearing to eliminate any endplay.
13 Fit the speedometer drive front circlip, then the speedometer drive and rear circlip.
14 Fit the reverse idler gear assembly.
15 Place the three shift forks in the groove in each coupling sleeve. Fit the 1st and reverse fork rod through the 1st and reverse shift fork and the adaptor plate and secure with a new retaining pin.
16 Fit the check ball, spring and plug. Apply a non-setting sealing compound to the thread of the plug. Align the centre notch in the 1st and reverse fork rod with the check ball. The plug for the 1st and reverse fork is longer than the other two plugs, see Fig. 6.14.
17 Fit the interlock plunger on the adaptor plate.
18 Insert the 2nd and 3rd fork rod through the adaptor plate , fit the 2nd and 3rd shift fork, and 4th and 5th shift fork. Secure with a new retaining pin.
19 Fit the check ball and spring, then the ball plug with the thread coated with a sealant. Align the centre notch in the 2nd and 3rd fork rod with the check ball.
20 Fit the interlock plunger on the adaptor plate. Insert the 4th and 5th fork rod through the adaptor plate and fit the 4th and 5th shift fork, secured with a new retaining pin.
21 Fit the check ball and spring, then the check ball plug with the

thread coated with a sealant. Tighten the check ball plugs to 12 – 16 lbf ft (1·6 – 2·2 kgf m).
22 Oil all the sliding surfaces and check that the shift rods operate correctly and that the gears engage smoothly.

37 Gearbox (5-speed) – reassembly

1   Ensure that the mating faces of the adaptor plate and rear extension are clean and coat the faces with a sealing compound.
2   Position the fork rods in 5th gear and gradually slide the rear extension onto the adaptor plate. Fit the shift arm on to the 4th and 5th fork rod and then fit the striking lever pin into the other fork rods. Check that the shift rods operate correctly.
3   Ensure that the mating faces of the adaptor plate and gearbox casing are clean, then coat the faces with a sealing compound.
4   Slide the gearbox casing onto the adaptor plate and tap it home with a plastic hammer.
5   Fit the main drive bearing and countershaft front bearing. Check that the mainshaft rotates freely.
6   Fit the through-bolts and washers, and tighten to a torque of 9 – 13 lbf ft (1·3 – 1·8 kgf m).
7   Fit the main drive bearing circlip in the groove in the bearing.
8   To determine the thickness of the countershaft front bearing shim before fitting the front cover, a Datsun counter bearing setting gauge (ST 22500000) is required.
9   Support the gearbox with its front end uppermost. Place the setting gauge on the countershaft front bearing and turn the main driveshaft until the bearing is settled down.
10 Measure the clearance, (B) as shown in Fig. 6.25, between the setting gauge and the front end of the casing with a feeler gauge. The depth (H) can be obtained from the formula: H = A – B.

H: Depth from front end of casing to countershaft front bearing.
A: Figure marked on setting gauge.
B: Measured value using feeler gauge.

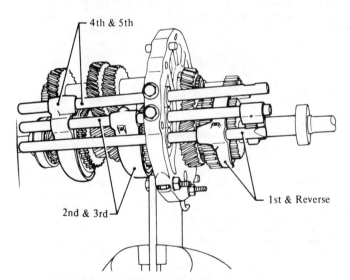

Fig. 6.24 Fitting shift forks and fork rods (5-speed) (Sec 36)

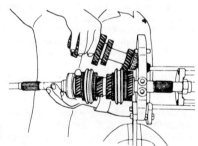

Fig. 6.23 Fitting the main drive gear and counter gear (5-speed) (Sec 36)

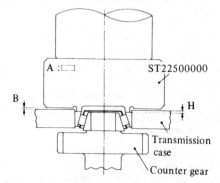

Fig. 6.25 Determining thickness of countershaft front bearing shim (5-speed) (Sec 37)

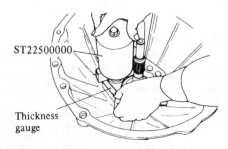

Fig. 6.26 Measuring clearance 'B' (Fig. 6.25) (Sec 37)

11 Select the correct shim from the following table:

No.	"H" mm (in)	Thickness of countershaft front bearing shim mm (in)
1	1·185 to 1·210 (0·0467 to 0·0476)	1·200 (0·0472)
2	1·210 to 1·235 (0·0476 to 0·0486)	1·225 (0·0482)
3	1·235 to 1·260 (0·0486 to 0·0496)	1·250 (0·0492)
4	1·260 to 1·285 (0·0496 to 0·0506)	1·275 (0·0502)
5	1·285 to 1·310 (0·0506 to 0·0516)	1·300 (0·0512)
6	1·310 to 1·335 (0·0516 to 0·0526)	1·325 (0·0522)
7	1·335 to 1·360 (0·0526 to 0·0535)	1·350 (0·0531)
8	1·360 to 1·385 (0·0535 to 0·0545)	1·375 (0·0541)
9	1·385 to 1·410 (0·0545 to 0·0555)	1·400 (0·0551)
10	1·410 to 1·435 (0·0555 to 0·0565)	1·425 (0·0561)
11	1·435 to 1·460 (0·0565 to 0·0575)	1·450 (0·0571)
12	1·460 to 1·485 (0·0575 to 0·0585)	1·475 (0·0581)
13	1·485 to 1·510 (0·0585 to 0·0594)	1·500 (0·0591)
14	1·510 to 1·535 (0·0594 to 0·0604)	1·525 (0·0600)
15	1·535 to 1·560 (0·0604 to 0·0614)	1·550 (0·0610)
16	1·560 to 1·585 (0·0614 to 0·0624)	1·575 (0·0620)
17	1·585 to 1·610 (0·0624 to 0·0634)	1·600 (0·0630)
18	1·610 to 1·635 (0·0634 to 0·0644)	1·625 (0·0640)
19	1·635 to 1·660 (0·0644 to 0·0654)	1·650 (0·0650)

12 Clean the mating faces of the front cover and gearbox case, then apply a sealing compound to both faces. Apply grease to the selected shim so that it will stick to the countershaft front bearing, and fit the front cover.

13 Apply a sealing compound to the threads of the front cover securing bolts, fit the bolts and tighten to 9 – 13 lbf ft (1·3 – 1·8 kgf m).

14 Grease the reverse select return plunger and fit it in the rear extension. Fit the reverse select return spring and plug. Coat the plug thread with a sealing compound and tighten to 6 – 7 lbf ft (0·8 – 1·0 kgf m).

15 Fit the speedometer pinion assembly on the rear extension, check that the lock plate is lined-up with the groove in the speedometer pinion sleeve and fit the securing bolts.

16 Fit the reverse light switch.

17 Apply a light coat of multi-purpose grease to the withdrawal lever, release the bearing and bearing sleeve, then fit them on the clutch housing. Fit the dust cover on the clutch housing.

18 Fit the control lever temporarily and check through all the gears for smooth operation.

Automatic transmission

38 Automatic transmission – general description

A type 3N71B automatic transmission is fitted and provides a range of six selector positions: P – R – N – D – 2 – 1.

The gear sets are of the Sympson planetary type and are controlled by two multiple-disc clutches, a brake band and multiple-disc brake.

Gear changing is fully automatic in relation to vehicle speed and engine torque input. The vehicle speed and engine manifold vacuum signals are constantly fed to the transmission to provide the appropriate gear ratio for maximum efficiency and performance at all throttle openings.

The unit includes a three element hydrokinetic torque converter coupling capable of torque multiplication at an infinitely variable ratio between 2 : 1 and 1 : 1. The torque converter is of a welded construction and cannot be dismantled for servicing.

Due to the complexity of the automatic transmission unit, if performance is not up to standard, or overhaul is necessary, it is imperative that this be undertaken by the local Datsun garage who will have special equipment for accurate fault diagnosis and rectification. It is important that the fault is diagnosed before the unit is removed from the car.

The contents of the following sections are therefore solely general and servicing information.

39 Automatic transmission – fluid level

It is important that only a recommended grade of automatic transmission fluid is used when topping up or changing the fluid (See Specifications).

1 With the car standing on level ground, open the bonnet and clean around the top of the filler tube and dipstick.

2 Move the selector lever to the P (Park) position and firmly apply the handbrake.

3 Start the engine and allow it to run at a fast idle speed until the engine and transmission unit reach their normal operating temperature.

4 With the engine running at the normal idle speed withdraw the dipstick, wipe, quickly return and withdraw again.

5 If necessary add sufficient fluid to the transmission unit via the filler tube to bring the level to the 'full' mark on the dipstick. Do not overfill the unit.

40 Automatic transmission – removal and refitting

1 Any suspect faults must be referred to the local Datsun garage before unit removal as with this type of transmission its fault must be confirmed, using special equipment, before it is removed from the car.

2 As the automatic transmission is relatively heavy it is best if the car is raised from the ground on ramps but it is possible to remove the unit if the car is placed on high axle stands. Two people will be required during the later stages of removal.

3 Disconnect the battery positive and negative terminals.

4 Refer to Chapter 10 and remove the starter motor.

5 Place a large container under the drain plug, remove the drain plug and allow all the fluid to drain. Refit the drain plug. If the car has recently been driven take care because the fluid will be very hot and can easily burn.

6 Remove the filler tube and dipstick from the transmission casing.

7 Disconnect the oil cooler pipes and plug the unions to prevent the ingress of dirt.

8 Disengage the torsion shaft from the accelerator linkage.

9 Remove the propeller shaft, as described in Chapter 7, and blank-off the opening in the rear extension to prevent any oil leaking out.

10 Disconnect the exhaust downpipe.

11 Disconnect the selector range lever from the manual shaft.

12 Disconnect the speedometer cable from the rear extension.

13 Make a note of the electrical connections at the inhibitor switch and downshift solenoid. Disconnect the wiring.

14 Disconnect the vacuum tube from the vacuum diaphragm.

15 Disconnect the oil charging pipe and plug the opening.

16 Place a piece of wood on the saddle of a hydraulic jack, position it under the engine sump and take the weight of the engine. Place a second jack under the transmission.

17 Remove the engine rear plate rubber plug and, working through the opening, remove the bolts securing the torque converter to the engine adaptor plate. Scribe match-marks on the converter and adaptor plate so that they can be reconnected in their original positions.

18 Remove the rear engine mounting bolts and crossmember securing bolts and lift away the mounting assembly.

19 Remove the bolts securing the transmission to the engine.

20 With the help of a second person carefully withdraw the assembly rearwards, so as to clear the converter from the adaptor plate, and

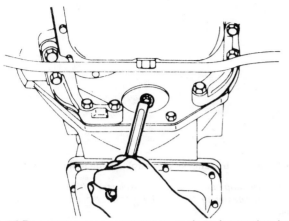

Fig.6. 27 Removing torque converter-to-engine adaptor plate bolts (Sec 40)

lower the transmission taking care that the torque converter does not become separated from the front of the transmission.

21 Refitting the transmission is the reverse of the removal procedure. The following additional points should be noted:

    (a) *Line-up the notch in the torque converter with that in the oil pump.*

    (b) *Ensure that the match-marks on converter and adaptor plate are aligned.*

    (c) *Refill the transmission with the correct amount of the recommended oil. (See Specifications).*

    (d) *Check the adjustment of the selector lever and inhibitor switch as described in Section 43.*

41 Shift linkage (automatic transmission) – adjustment

Floor shift

1 Refer to Fig. 6.28. Before fitting the control knob, set dimension 'A' to 0·433 – 0·472 in (11 – 12 mm).

2 Fit the control knob on the lever; at the same time check the dimension 'B' and adjust it to 0·0039 – 0·0433 in (0·1 – 1·1 mm) by turning the pushrod (1).

3 Loosen the adjusting nuts (3). Set the control lever and selector lever (5) in the 'N' position, and adjust the clearance 'C' to 0·039 in (1 mm) by turning the adjusting nuts, as required at the trunnion (2) which connects with the selector rod (4).

Column shift

4 Refer to Fig. 6.29. Loosen the trunnion adjusting nuts (9).

5 Place the control lever and selector range lever in the 'N' position.

6 Set the clearance 'D' between the select lever stopper pin (6) and position the plate (7) to 0·02 – 0·039 in (0·5 – 1·0 mm) by turning the adjusting nuts in or out at the trunnion (8).

7 Check that the linkage operates correctly; if necessary, re-adjust or renew the parts as required.

42 Kickdown switch and solenoid – checking and adjusting

1 Failure of the transmission to downshift from 3rd to 2nd speed may be due to too high a road speed, incorrect adjustment of the accelerator pedal switch or a faulty solenoid.

2 The kickdown switch should be adjusted so that when the pedal is depressed to about $\frac{7}{8}$ of its stroke, the switch will be heard to close with a distinct click.

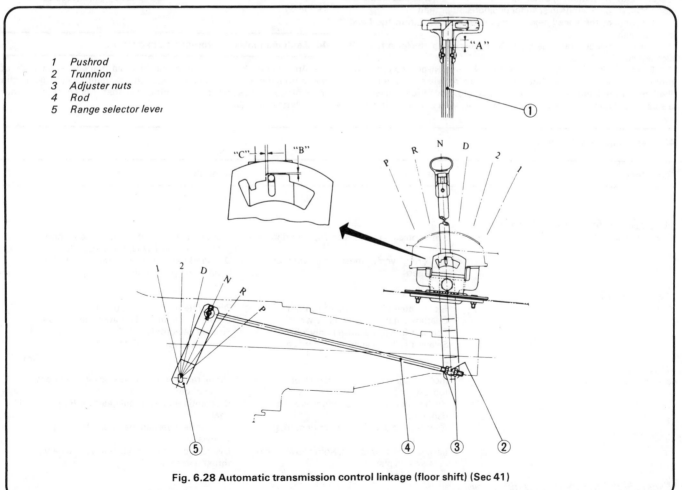

1 Pushrod
2 Trunnion
3 Adjuster nuts
4 Rod
5 Range selector lever

Fig. 6.28 Automatic transmission control linkage (floor shift) (Sec 41)

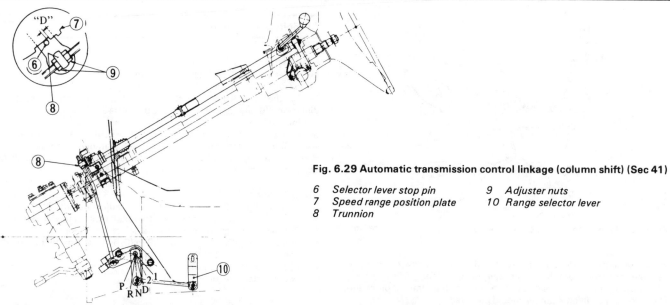

Fig. 6.29 Automatic transmission control linkage (column shift) (Sec 41)

6   Selector lever stop pin   9   Adjuster nuts
7   Speed range position plate   10   Range selector lever
8   Trunnion

3   Apart from checking the electrical leads to the solenoid for continuity and security, any other malfunction must be due to a faulty solenoid which must be renewed as a unit.

43 Selector linkage and inhibitor switch – adjustment

1   Failure of the switch will be indicated by incorrect operation of the starter motor (actuation in other than 'N' or 'P' positions) and illumination of the reverse lamps in selector positions other than 'R'.
2   Disconnect the speed selector remote control rod from the hand control lever.
3   Turn the selector range lever to 'N'. In this mode, the lever to shaft slot will appear vertical.
4   Place the hand control lever in the 'N' position and connect the remote control rod to it so that the joint trunnion will enter the hole at the base of the hand lever without any need to move the hand lever in a sideways direction. If necessary, release the two control rod locknuts

at the trunnion to achieve perfect alignment.
5   Check all the speed selector positions and note that a distinct 'click' should be heard at each detent.
6   Remove the two switch body securing bolts and then unscrew the screw located beneath the body. Insert a thin rod 0·059 in (1·5 mm dia) into the screw hole so that it passes into the hole in the internal rotor of the switch. Tighten the switch body bolts, remove the rod and refit the screw.
7   Check the operation of the switch, if it is still faulty, renew it complete.

44 Fault diagnosis – automatic transmission

An accurate knowledge and considerable practical experience of the automatic transmission is required for fault diagnosis. If the transmission is suspect it is recommended that it is checked by your local Datsun garage.

45 Fault diagnosis – manual transmission

Symptom	Reason/s	Remedy
Weak or ineffective synchromesh		
General wear	Synchronising cones worn, split or damaged	Dismantle and overhaul gearbox. Fit new gear wheels and synchronising cones
	Baulk ring synchromesh dogs worn, or damaged	Dismantle and overhaul gearbox. Fit new baulk ring synchromesh
Jumps out of gear		
General wear or damage	Broken gear change fork rod spring	Dismantle and replace spring
	Gearbox coupling dogs badly worn	Dismantle gearbox. Fit new coupling dogs
	Selector fork rod groove badly worn	Fit new selector fork rod
	Selector fork rod securing pin loose	Remove cover, and tighten pin
Excessive noise		
Lack of maintenance	Incorrect grade of oil in gearbox or oil level too low	Drain, refill, or top up gearbox with correct grade of oil
General wear	Bush or needle roller bearings worn or damaged	Dismantle and overhaul gearbox. Renew bearings
	Gear teeth excessively worn or damaged	Dismantle, overhaul gearbox. Renew gearwheels
	Laygear thrust washers worn allowing excessive end play	Dismantle and overhaul gearbox. Renew thrust washers
Excessive difficulty in engaging gear		
Clutch not fully disengaging	Clutch pedal adjustment incorrect	Adjust clutch pedal correctly

Chapter 7 Propeller shaft

Contents

Specifications

Type	One- or two-piece shaft
Spider journal axial play	Less than 0·0008 in (0·02 mm)

Circlip thickness availability

White	0·0788 in (2·00 mm)
Yellow	0·0795 in (2·02 mm)
Red	0·0803 in (2·04 mm)
Green	0·0811 in (2·06 mm)
Blue	0·0819 in (2·08 mm)
Light brown	0·0827 in (2·10 mm)
No paint	0·0835 in (2·12 mm)
Pink	0·0843 in (2·14 mm)

Torque wrench settings

	lbf ft	kgf m
Shaft-to-companion flange bolt (differential carrier end)	17 – 24	2·4 – 3·3
Companion flange nut	145 – 174	20 – 24
Flange yoke (rear shaft)-to-companion flange (front shaft) bolt	17 – 24	2·4 – 3·3
Centre bearing bracket fixing nuts	6 – 8	0·79 – 1·06
Centre bearing bracket-to-body bolts	37 – 50	5·1 – 6·9

1 General description

A tubular propeller shaft transmits the drive from the gearbox to the rear axle. Due to the variety of angles caused by the up-and-down movement of the rear axle in relation to the gearbox, universal joints are fitted to each end of the shaft to convey the drive through the constantly varying angles.

To accommodate fore-and-aft movement of the rear axle due to road spring or power unit movement on its mountings, a sliding joint of the reverse spline type is used.

Each universal joint comprises a centre spider, four needle roller bearing assemblies and two yokes. The bearings are lubricated and sealed for life during manufacture.

610 series Saloon models having independent rear suspension are equipped with a two-joint type of propeller shaft and on Estate Cars

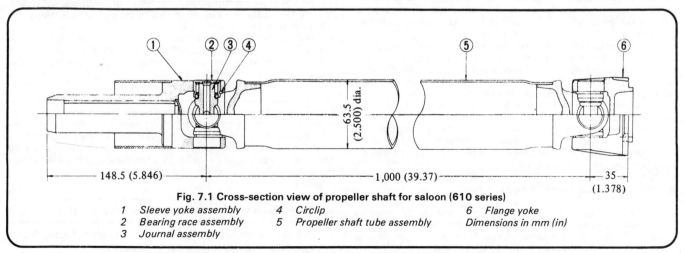

Fig. 7.1 Cross-section view of propeller shaft for saloon (610 series)

1 Sleeve yoke assembly	4 Circlip	6 Flange yoke
2 Bearing race assembly	5 Propeller shaft tube assembly	Dimensions in mm (in)
3 Journal assembly		

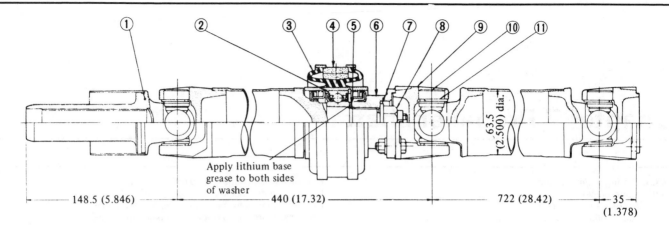

Apply lithium base
grease to both sides
of washer

Fig. 7.2 Cross-section view of propeller shaft for Estate Car (610 series)

1 Sleeve yoke assembly	4 Cushion rubber	7 Plain washer	10 Bearing race assembly
2 Centre bearing	5 Washer	8 Locking nut	11 Circlip
3 Centre bearing insulator	6 Companion flange	9 Flange yoke	Dimensions in mm (in)

with rigid axle, the shaft is a three-joint type. The 810 series models are equipped with the three-joint two-piece type shaft.

2 Propeller shaft – testing for wear whilst on the car

1   To check for wear, grasp each unit of the universal joint, and with a twisting action, determine whether there is any play or slackness in the joint. This will indicate any wear in the bearings. Do not be confused by backlash between the crownwheel and pinion.
2   Try an up-and-down rocking movement which will indicate wear of the thrust faces on the spiders and those inside the cups.
3   On centre bearing type propeller shafts, check the resilience of the rubber by grasping either side of the bearing and lifting up and down. An easy action indicates the rubber has probably been contaminated by oil or tired through age.
4   Wear in the needle roller bearings is characterised by vibration in the transmission, 'clonks' on taking up the drive, and, in extreme cases of lack of lubrication, metallic squeaking, and ultimately grating and shrieking sounds as the bearings break up.

3 Propeller shaft – removal and refitting

1   One-piece propeller shaft. Slacken the end clamps of the centre tube and pre-silencer and move to the left. Chock the front wheels, jack up the rear of the car and support on firmly based stands. Remove the left-hand rear wheel. Undo and remove the handbrake rear cable adjusting nut from the adjuster and disconnect the left-hand cable from the handbrake adjuster. This will give sufficient room to remove the propeller shaft.
2   With a scriber or file mark the propeller shaft coupling flanges at the rear so that they may be refitted in their original position.
3   Two-piece propeller shaft. Support the weight of the propeller shaft at the centre. Undo and remove the two bolts and washers securing the centre bearing support bracket to the crossmember.
4   Undo and remove the four nuts, bolts and washers that secure the rear coupling flanges.
5   Place a container under the rear of the gearbox to catch oil that will issue from the end. Carefully lower the rear of the propeller shaft, draw rearward to detach the splined end from the gearbox and lift away from the underside of the car.
6   Refitting the propeller shaft is the reverse sequence to removal but the following additional points should be noted:

  (a) Ensure that the mating marks scratched on the propeller shaft and differential pinion flanges are in alignment.
  (b) Tighten the companion flange bolts and centre bearing support bracket bolts to the specified torque.

4 Universal joints – inspection and repair (one-piece)

1   Before dismantling make sure that a repair kit is available otherwise an exchange unit must be obtained.
2   Mark all parts to ensure that, if they are refitted they are in their original positions.
3   Clean away all traces of dirt and grease from the area around the universal joint.
4   Remove the four circlips from the journal assembly using a screwdriver.
5   Hold the propeller shaft and using a soft faced hammer, tap the universal joint yoke so as to remove the bearing cups by 'shock' action.
6   Remove all four bearing cups in the manner described and then free the propeller shaft from the spider.
7   Thoroughly clean out the yokes and journals.
8   Check to see if the journal diameter has worn. If it has it must be renewed.
9   Renew the spider seal rings if there is evidence of damage.
10 Inspect the sleeve yoke spline to gearbox main shaft splines for wear. The sleeve yoke must be renewed if backlash is evident.
11 If vibrations from the propeller shaft have been experienced, check the run-out at the centre by rotating on V-shaped blocks and a dial indicator gauge at the centre. The run-out must not exceed 0.0236 in (0.6 mm).
12 To reassemble, fit new oil seals and retainers on the spider journals, place the spider on the propeller shaft yoke and assemble the needle rollers into the bearing cups, retaining them with some thick grease.
13 Fill each bearing cup about $\frac{1}{3}$ full with high melting point grease. Also fill the grease holes in the journal spider with grease taking care that all air bubbles are eliminated.
14 Refit the bearing cups on the spider and tap the bearings home so that they lie squarely in position. Secure with the circlips. Seven different thickness circlips (see the Specifications) are available to give an axial play of less than 0.0008 in (0.02 mm).

5 Universal joints – inspection and repair (two-piece)

The sequence is virtually identical with that for the one piece type. To overhaul the middle universal joint it will be necessary to part the two halves. This is done by marking the two flanges and then removing the four nuts, bolts and spring washers.

6 Centre bearing – removal and refitting (two piece)

1   Remove the propeller shaft assembly as outlined in Section 3.
2   Part the two halves as described in Section 5.

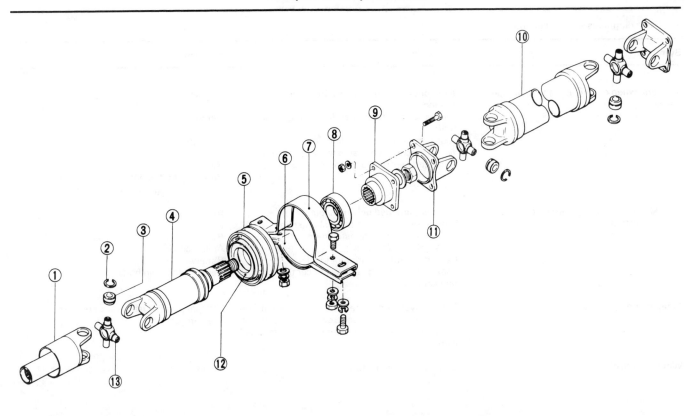

Fig. 7.3 Exploded view of propeller shaft (810 series)

1   Sleeve yoke assembly
2   Circlip
3   Bearing race assembly
4   Front propeller shaft

5   Cushion rubber
6   Centre bearing support
7   Centre bearing bracket

8   Centre bearing
9   Companion flange
10 Rear propeller shaft

11 Flange yoke
12 Centre bearing insulator
13 Journal assembly

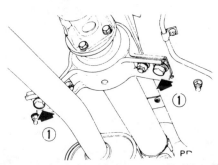

Fig. 7.4 Removing centre bearing bracket (Sec 6)

3   With a scriber or file, mark the relationship of the companion flange to the propeller shaft.
4   It will now be necessary to hold the companion flange in a vice or wrench. Using a socket wrench undo and remove the retaining nut and plain washer. This nut will be very tight.
5   Using a soft metal drift or a puller remove the centre bearing assembly.
6   Check the centre bearing by rotating the race. If it feels rough or is noisy it must be discarded. Also check the inner track for 'rock' which ideally should not be evident.
7   Before fitting a rear bearing assembly, check that it compares exactly with the old one removed. It is not necessary to lubricate the bearing as it is sealed during manufacture.
8   Reassembly and refitting is the reverse sequence to removal.

See overleaf for 'Fault diagnosis – propeller shaft'

7   Fault diagnosis – propeller shaft

Symptom	Reason/s	Remedy
Vibration when driving at medium or high speed	Worn or damaged universal joint needle bearing	Renew
	Unbalance due to bent or dented propeller shaft	Renew
	Loose propeller shaft installation	Retighten
	Worn transmission rear extension bushing	Renew
	Damaged centre bearing or insulator	Renew
		Renew joint if unable to free up or if joint feels rough when rotated by hand
Knocking sound during starting or noise during coasting	Worn or damaged universal joint	Renew
	Worn sleeve yoke and main shaft spline	Renew
	Loose propeller shaft installation	Retighten
	Loose joint installation	Adjust circlip
	Damaged centre bearing or insulator	Renew
	Loose or missing bolts at centre bearing bracket-to-body	Renew or tighten bolts
Scraping noise	Dust cover on sleeve yoke rubbing on transmission rear extension. Dust cover on companion flange rubbing on differential carrier	Straighten out dust cover to remove interference
Whine or whistle	Damaged centre bearing	Renew

Chapter 8 Rear axle

Contents

Specifications

Type designation	R160	H165B	H190

Final gear ratio	**R160**	**H165B**	**H190**
	3·900 : 1	3·700 : 1	4·375 : 1
	4·111 : 1	3·889 : 1	
	4·375 : 1	4·111 : 1	

Drive pinion preload

Adjusted by	Shim	Collapsible spacer	Shim

Oil capacity:

Imp pt (US pt, litre)	1¾ (1¾, 0·8)	2 (2⅜, 1·1)	1¾ (2⅛, 1·0)

Drive pinion

Preload: lbf in (kgf cm)

Without oil seal	6·1 – 8·7 (7 – 10)	—	8·7 – 11 (10 – 13)
With oil seal	6·9 – 9·5 (8 – 11)	6·1 – 8·7 (7 – 10)	9·5 – 12 (11 – 14)

At companion flange bolt hole lb (kg):

Without oil seal	4·4 – 6·4 (2·0 – 2·9)	—	6·4 – 8·4 (2·9 – 3·8)
With oil seal	5·1 – 7·1 (2·3 – 3·2)	4·4 – 6·4 (2·0 – 2·9)	7·1 – 9 (3·2 – 4·1)

Thickness of pinion height-adjusting washer:

R160 and H165B .... 0·1217 in (3·09 mm) to 0·1441 in (3·66 mm) in increments of
0·0012 in (0·03 mm)

H190 .... 0·1016 in (2·58 mm) to 0·1252 in (3·18 mm) in increments of
0·0012 in (0·03 mm)

Thickness of drive pinion bearing adjusting washer:

R160 .... 0·0909 in (2·31 mm) to 0·1020 in (2·59 mm) in increments of
0·0008 in (0·02 mm)

H190 .... 0·1500 in (3·81 mm) to 0·1620 in (4·09 mm) in increments of
0·0008 in (0·02 mm)

Length of pinion bearing adjusting spacer:

R160 .... 2·2126 in (56·2 mm) to 2·2520 in (57·20 mm) in increments of
0·0008 in (0·02 mm)

H165B .... 2·1457 in (54·50 mm) to 2·2047 in (56·0 mm) in increments of

H190 .... 0·012 in (0·3 mm)

Side gear

	R160	H165B	H190
Side gear thrust washers: in (mm)	0.0295 – 0.0315 (0.75 – 0.80)	0.0309 (0.785)	0.0295 – 0.0315 (0.75 – 0.80)
	0.0315 – 0.0335 (0.80 – 0.85)	0.0329 (0.835)	0.0315 – 0.0335 (0.80 – 0.85)
	0.0335 – 0.0354 (0.85 – 0.90)	0.0348 (0.885)	0.0335 – 0.0354 (0.85 – 0.90)
		0.0407 (1.035)	0.0354 – 0.0374 (0.90 – 0.95)
		0.0467 (1.185)	

Sidegear to thrust washer clearance .... 0.0039 – 0.0079 in (0.10 – 0.20 mm)

Crownwheel

	R160	H165B	H190
Crownwheel to pinion backlash in (mm)	0.0039 – 0.0079 (0.10 – 0.20)	0.0039 – 0.0059 (0.10 – 0.15)	0.0059 – 0.0079 (0.15 – 0.20)
Thickness of side retainer adjusting shim in (mm)	0.0020 (0.05)	—	—
	0.0028 (0.07)	—	—
	0.0039 (0.10)	—	—
	0.0079 (0.20)	—	—
	0.0197 (0.50)	—	—
Thickness of side bearing adjusting shim in (mm)	—	0.0020 (0.05)	—
	—	0.0028 (0.07)	—
	—	0.0039 (0.10)	—
	—	0.0079 (0.20)	—
	—	0.0197 (0.50)	—
Side bearing preload at ring gear bolt lb (kg)	3.3 – 6.2 (1.5 – 2.8)	3.1 – 6.0 (1.4 – 2.7)	2.2 – 6.2 (1.7 – 2.8)
Side bearing standard width in (mm)	0.7874 (20.00)	0.7283 (18.50)	0.7874 (20.00)

Torque wrench settings:

	lbf ft	kgf m
Drive pinion nut:		
R160	123 – 145	17.0 – 20.0
H165B	101 – 217	14.0 – 30.0
H190	101 – 123	14.0 – 17.0
Ring gear bolt	51 – 58	7.0 – 8.0
Side retainer bolt (R160)	7 – 9	0.9 – 1.2
Rear cover bolt (R160)	14 – 19	1.9 – 2.6
Rear cover to mounting nut (R160)	43 – 58	6.0 – 8.0
Differential to driveshaft bolt (R160)	36 – 43	5.0 – 6.0
Differential mounting nut (R160)	51 – 72	7.0 – 10.0
Side bearing cap bolt:		
H165B	36 – 43	5.0 – 6.0
H190	29 – 36	4.0 – 5.0
Differential carrier to axle case nut, H165B and H190	14 – 18	2.0 – 2.5
Companion flange bolts	17 – 24	2.4 – 3.3
Side yoke securing bolt	23 – 31	3.2 – 4.3

1 General description

Three different types of differential unit are fitted to the models covered by this manual. Saloon and Hardtop models having independent rear suspension (IRS) are equipped with the type R160 differential carrier. Estate Cars having leaf spring rear suspension are equipped with a rigid rear axle (RA) and the differential unit may be the type 165B or H190.

Saloon models

The main rear axle component is the hyphoid final drive and differential unit which is fixed to the body shell at the rear using a bracket located on rubber mountings. The front of the differential unit is mounted on a nose piece, bolted to a sub-frame.

Splined swing-axle drive shafts, pivoting at their inner ends on universal joints attached to the differential drive flanges, transfer the drive to the rear hubs which are mounted on the trailing ends of suspension arms.

The crownwheel and pinion each run on opposed tapered roller bearings, the bearing pre-load and meshing of the crownwheel and pinion being controlled by shims. Spring loaded oil seals, of the type normally found at the front of the differential nose piece, prevent loss of oil from the differential at the end of the pinion shaft and driveshaft flanges.

Estate Car

The rear axle is semi-floating and is held in place by semi-elliptic springs. These springs provide the necessary lateral and longtitudinal location of the axle. The rear axle incorporates a hyphoid crownwheel and pinion, and a two-pinion differential. All repairs can be carried out to the component parts of the rear axle without removing the axle casing from the car.

The crownwheel and pinion together with the differential gears are mounted in the differential unit which is bolted to the front face of the banjo type axle casing.

Adjustments are provided for the crowneheel and pinion backlash; pinion depth of mesh; pinion shaft bearing pre-load; and backlash between the differential gears. All these adjustments may be made by varying the thickness of the various shims and thrust washers.

The axle or halfshafts (easily withdrawn) are splined at inner ends to fit into the splines in the differential wheels. The inner wheel bearing races are mounted on the outer ends of the axle casing and are secured by nuts and lock washers. The rear bearing outer races are located in the hubs.

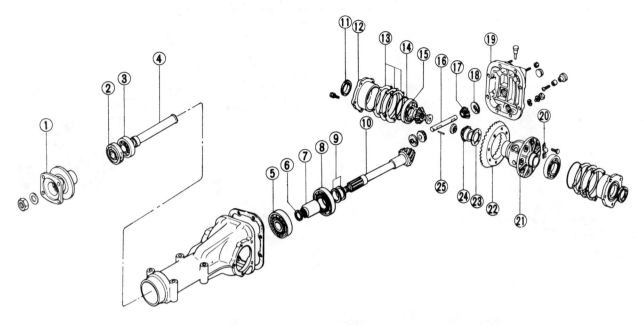

Fig. 8.1 Exploded view of differential gear carrier – type H160

1 Companion flange	spacer	13 Side retainer adjusting	19 Rear cover
2 Oil seal	8 Pinion rear bearing	shim	20 Lock strap
3 Pilot bearing	9 Pinion height adjusting	14 O-ring	21 Differential gear case
4 Pilot bearing spacer	washer	15 Side bearing	22 Ring gear
5 Pinion front bearing	10 Drive pinion	16 Pinion mate shaft	23 Thrust washer
6 Pinion bearing adjusting	11 Oil seal	17 Pinion mate	24 Side gear
washer	12 Side retainer	18 Thrust washer	25 Lock pin
7 Pinion bearing adjusting			

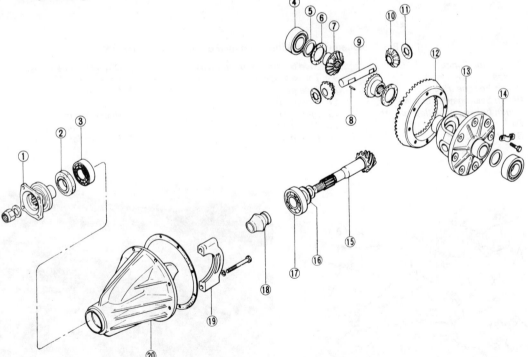

Fig. 8.2 Exploded view of differential gear carrier – type H165B

1 Companion flange	6 Thrust washer	12 Ring gear	washer
2 Oil seal	7 Side gear	13 Differential gear case	17 Pinion rear bearing
3 Pinion front bearing	8 Lock pin	14 Lock strap	18 Collapsible spacer
4 Side bearing	9 Pinion mate shaft	15 Drive pinion	19 Side bearing cap
5 Side bearing adjusting	10 Pinion	16 Pinion height adjusting	20 Differential housing
shim	11 Thrust washer		

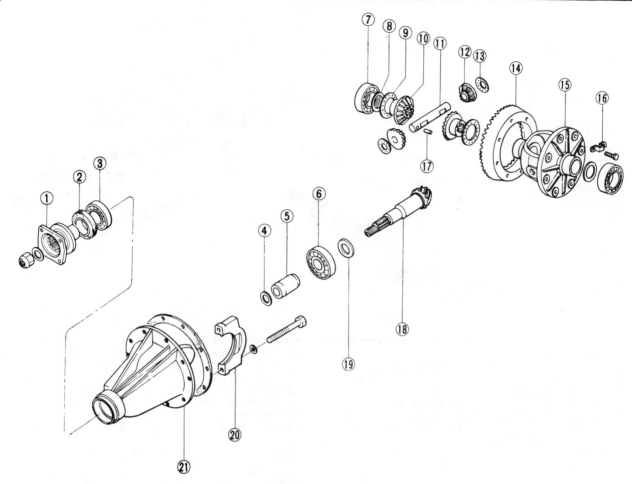

Fig. 8.3 Exploded view of differential gear carrier – type H190

1	Companion flange	8	Side bearing adjusting washer	15	Differential gear case
2	Oil seal	9	Thrust washer	16	Lock strap
3	Pinion front bearing	10	Side gear	17	Lock pin
4	Pinion bearing adjusting washer	11	Pinion mate shaft	18	Drive pinion
5	Pinion bearing adjusting spacer	12	Pinion mate	19	Pinion height adjusting washer
6	Pinion rear bearing	13	Thrust washer	20	Side bearing cap
7	Side bearing	14	Ring gear	21	Differential housing

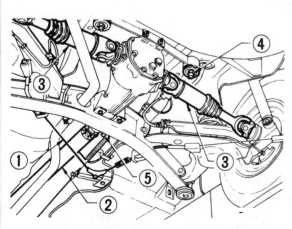

Fig. 8.4 Removing the differential carrier (IRS) (Sec 2)

1	Handbrake cable	4	Attaching nuts
2	Propeller shaft	5	Attaching bolts
3	Driveshaft		

2.5 Remove final drive mounting member securing nuts

2   Final drive casing and differential unit (IRS) – removal and refitting

1   Refer to Chapter 9 and detach the handbrake cable.
2   Scribe marks on the propeller shaft and drive shaft flanges so that they may be refitted in their original positions.
3   Undo and remove the securing nuts and bolts as applicable. Tie the shafts back out of the way.
4   Using a jack support the centre of the final drive casing.
5   Undo and remove the nuts securing both ends of the final drive mounting member (photo).
6   Undo and remove the four bolts that secure the final drive to the rear suspension member.
7   Carefully draw the unit rearward and then lower to the ground. Remove it from under the car.
8   Using pieces of wood or bricks, support the weight of the suspension member so that the rubber mountings are not damaged.
9   Refitting is the reverse of the removal procedure. Do not forget to refill the unit with the correct oil.

3   Final drive casing and differential unit (IRS) – dismantling, inspection and reassembly

Most garages will prefer to fit a complete set of gears, bearings, shims and thrust washers rather than renew parts which may have worn. To do the job properly requires the use of special and expensive tools which the majority of car owners do not have.

The primary object of these special tools is to enable the mesh of the crownwheel to the pinion to be set very accurately and thus ensure that noise is kept to a minimum. If any increase in noise cannot be tolerated (provided that the final drive unit is not already noisy due to a defective part) then it is best to allow a Datsun garage to carry out repairs.

Final drive units have been rebuilt without the use of special tools so if the possibility of a slight increase in noise can be tolerated then it is quite possible for any do-it-yourself mechanic to successfully set-up this unit without special tools.

The final drive unit should first be removed from the car as described in Section 2 and then proceed as follows:
1   Wash down the exterior to remove all traces of dirt and oil. Wipe dry with a non-fluffy rag.
2   Undo and remove the drain plug and allow the oil to drain into a suitable container having a capacity of 2 Imp pints (1.136 litres 2.402 US pints). Refit the drain plug.
3   Undo and remove the eight bolts and spring washers that secure the rear cover to the main casing. Lift away the rear cover and gasket.
4   Undo and remove the two long side bolts securing the side flanges. Lift away the two bolts and washers.
5   The side flanges should next be removed. Ideally a slide hammer is required but it is possible to remove these using a soft metal drift and hammer or universal puller.
6   Undo and remove the five bolts and spring washers that secure the side bearing retainer to the main casing. Mark the retainer and main casing so that they may be refitted in their original positions.
7   Using a universal two leg puller and metal thrust block inserted into the side bolt hole carefully draw the side bearing retainers from the main casing.
8   Note the location of any shims which may have been used to set the bearing preload.
9   The differential assembly may now be withdrawn from the rear of the main casing.
10 Hold the pinion flange, either with a large wrench or in a firm bench vice and then undo and remove the flange retaining nut and washer.
11 Using a universal two leg puller and thrust pad withdraw the pinion flange.
12 Using a drift carefully remove the dust cover and oil seals.
13 The pinion shaft may now be drifted from the casing using a soft faced hammer. It will be observed that when the pinion shaft is removed the rear bearing inner races, bearing spacers and shims will also be released.
14 The oil seal should be removed next from the main casing using a screwdriver.
15 Using a metal drift carefully tap out the front bearing inner race.

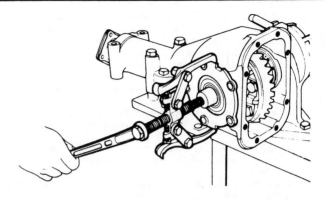

Fig. 8.5 Using universal puller to remove the side flange (Sec 3)

16 To remove the rear bearing inner race from the pinion can present a few problems. If it has to be renewed then it may be dismantled with a hammer and chisel. If it is still serviceable, then leave well alone. Alternatively take the pinion shaft to the local Datsun garage who will have a press and special tool necessary.
17 Using a metal drift, and working through the main casing, carefully tap out the front and rear bearing outer races.
18 Using a strong universal puller draw the right-hand bearing inner race from the differential case.
19 The left-hand bearing inner race may be removed once the crownwheel has been detached (paragraph 20).
20 If the crownwheel is to be removed, mark its relative position on the differential case and bend back the lock tabs. Slacken the securing bolts in a progressive and diagonal manner. Remove the bolts, tab washers and the crownwheel.
21 Using a small parallel pin punch carefully tap out the differential pinion shaft lock pin located on the crownwheel side of the differential case. It may be observed that this pin hole is caulked over in which case the hole must be cleaned out with a small chisel.
22 Tap out the differential pinion shaft from the differential case. Lift out the pinion gears, side gears and thrust washers taking care to keep the gears and thrust washers in their mated positions so that unless parts are to be renewed they may be refitted in their original positions.
23 The final drive assembly is now dismantled and should be washed and dried with a clean non-fluffy rag ready for inspection.
24 Carefully inspect all the gear teeth for signs of pitting or wear and if evident new parts must be obtained. The crownwheel and pinion are a matched pair so if one of the two requires renewal a new matched pair must be obtained. If wear is evident on one or two of the differential pinion gears or side gears it is far better to obtain all four gears rather than just renew the worn one.
25 Inspect the thrust washers for score marks and wear, and if evident obtain new ones.
26 Before the differential case side bearings were removed they should have been inspected for signs of wear. Usually if one bearing is worn it is far better to fit a complete new set. When the new parts have been obtained as required, reassembly can begin. First fit the thrust washers to the side gears and place them in position in the differential housing.
27 Place the thrust washers behind the differential pinion gears and mesh these two gears with the side gears through the two apertures in the differential housing. Make sure they are diametrically opposite to each other. Rotate the differential pinion gears through 90° bringing them into line with the pinion gears shaft bore in the housing.
28 Insert the pinion gear shaft with the locating pin hole in line with the pin hole.
29 Using feeler gauges measure the endfloat of each side gear. The correct clearance is 0.004 to 0.008 in (0.1-0.2 mm). If this figure is exceeded new thrust washers must be obtained. Dismantle the assembly again and fit new thrust washers (Fig. 8.6).
30 Lock the pinion gear shaft using the pin which should be tapped fully home using a suitable diameter parallel pin punch. Peen over the end of the pin hole to stop the pin working its way out.
31 The crownwheel may next be refitted. Wipe the mating face of the crownwheel and differential housing and, if original parts are being used, place the crownwheel into position with the previously made marks aligned. Refit new bolts and new lock washers that secure the crownwheel, and tighten these in a progressive and diagonal manner

to a final torque wrench setting of 51 - 58 lbf ft (7.0-8,0 kgf m).

32 If new bearings are to be fitted to each side of the differential housing, measure the assembled thickness by placing on a flat metal surface with a 5.5 lb (2.5 kg) weight on the top of the bearing. The bearing width should be 0.787 inch (20.00 mm).

33 Using a suitable diameter drift on the inner track, carefully refit the bearings. The smaller diameter of the taper must face outwards. The bearing cage must not be damaged in any way.

34 Using a suitable diameter drift carefully fit the taper roller bearing behind the pinion shaft head. The larger diameter must be next to the pinion head.

35 Using suitable diameter tubes, fit the two taper roller bearing cones into the final drive housing making sure that they are fitted the correct way round.

36 Slide the shims and bearing spacers onto the pinion shaft and insert into the final drive housing.

37 Refit the second taper roller bearing onto the end of the pinion shaft and follow this with a new oil seal. Before the seal is actually fitted, apply some grease to the inner face between the two lips of the seal.

38 Apply a little jointing compound to the outer face of the seal.

39 Using a tubular drift of suitable diameter carefully drive the oil seal into the final drive housing. Make quite sure it is fitted squarely into the housing.

40 Refit the drive pinion flange and hold securely in a bench vice. Fit the plain washer and new self-locking nut. Tighten the nut firmly. For H165B type differential, refer to Section 5 for adjustment of the preload of a drive pinion with the collapsible spacer.

41 Refit the differential carrier assembly into the final drive housing.

42 Check that the O-ring is correctly located on each side retainer and then with the differential carrier assembly held in its approximate fitted position, refit the two side retainers. Do not forget to refit the shim packs noted during assembly. The arrows cast in the retainers should be positioned at the bottom.

43 Refit the side retainer securing bolts and spring washers.

44 Carefully slide in the two side flange assemblies and secure in position with the plain washer, spring washer and bolt. Tighten to a torque wrench setting of 6.5-8.7 lbf ft (0.9-1.2 kgf m).

45 If possible mount a dial indicator gauge so that the probe is resting on one of the teeth of the crownwheel and determine the backlash between the crownwheel and pinion. The backlash may be varied by adjusting the thickness of the shim packs.

46 The best check to be made to ascertain the correct meshing of the crownwheel and pinion, is to smear a little engineer's blue onto the crownwheel and pinion, and rotate the pinion. The contact mark should appear right in the middle of the crownwheel teeth. Refer to Fig. 8.10 where the correct tooth pattern is shown. Also given are the incorrect tooth patterns and the method of obtaining the correct pattern. Obviously this will take time and further dismantling but will be well worth while.

47 If a dial indicator gauge is available check the run-out of the crownwheel. This should not exceed 0.004-0.008 in (0.10-0.20 mm). If the result is in excess, the unit must be dismantled again and a check made for dirt between the crownwheel and differential housing mating faces. If clean, further investigation will have to be made to see whether the crownwheel or differential housing is distorted.

48 Before refitting the rear cover make quite sure that the mating faces are free from traces of the old gasket or jointing compound.

49 Fit a new gasket and then the rear cover, and secure with the eight bolts and spring washers; tighten these bolts in a diagonal and progressive manner.

50 The unit is now ready for refitting to the car. Do not forget to refill with the correct oil.

---

4   Pinion oil seal (type R160 and H190 differential) - renewal

The pinion oil seal may be renewed with the final drive unit in or out of the car.

1 Place a container of suitable capacity under the final drive assembly and remove the drain plug. Allow all oil to drain out and refit the drain plug.

2 Chock the front wheels, jack up the rear of the car and support on firmly based stands. Remove the road wheels to give better access.

3 Refer to Chapter 9 and disconnect the handbrake left-hand rear cable.

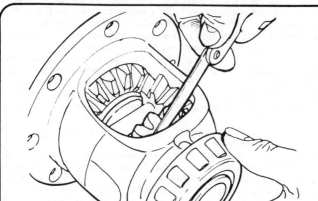
Fig. 8.6 Measuring clearance between side gear and thrust washer (Sec 3)

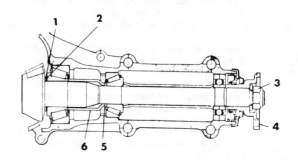
Fig. 8.7 Sectional view of drive pinion (Sec 3)

1 Adjustment shim   4 Companion flange
2 Adjustment washer 5 Adjustment washer
3 Nut   6 Bearing spacer

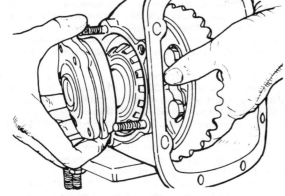
Fig. 8.8 Refitting side retainer (Sec 3)

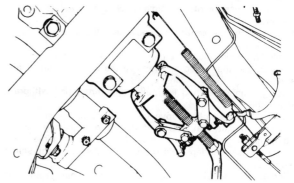
Fig. 8.9 Removing the pinion shaft flange (Sec 4)

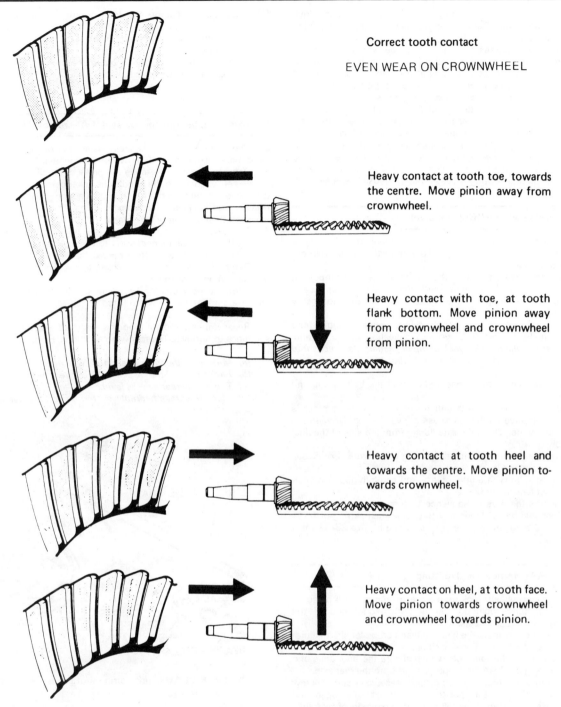

Correct tooth contact

EVEN WEAR ON CROWNWHEEL

Heavy contact at tooth toe, towards the centre. Move pinion away from crownwheel.

Heavy contact with toe, at tooth flank bottom. Move pinion away from crownwheel and crownwheel from pinion.

Heavy contact at tooth heel and towards the centre. Move pinion towards crownwheel.

Heavy contact on heel, at tooth face. Move pinion towards crownwheel and crownwheel towards pinion.

Fig. 8.10 Crownwheel tooth marking (Sec 3)

4   The exhaust and silencer assembly will have to be moved to allow the propeller shaft to be lowered to the floor. Slacken the U bolt securing the nuts and turn the pre-silencer chamber through 90°.
5   Mark the mating flanges of the propeller shaft and final drive to ensure correct refitting.
6   Undo and remove the propeller shaft flange securing bolts and carefully lower the propeller shaft. Swing to one side.
7   Undo and remove the pinion shaft flange securing nut and washer.
8   Using a universal puller and suitable thrust pad draw off the pinion shaft flange.
9   The old oil seal may be removed by disintegrating in situ with a chisel or screwdriver taking great care not to damage its seating.
10   Smear the seal lip with a little grease and carefully tap into position. The lip must face inward.
11   Reassembly is the reverse sequence to removal.

5   Pinion oil seal (type H165B differential) - removal

1   The pinion oil seal cannot be renewed without removing the differential carrier, as the collapsible spacer must be renewed whenever the front oil seal is renewed.
2   Having removed the differential carrier as described in Section 2, take off the side bearing caps and withdraw the differential gear case assembly.
3   Remove the drive pinion nut and withdraw the drive pinion assembly. Lever out the oil seal.
4   Fit a new oil seal and locate a new collapsible spacer on the drive pinion. Insert the companion flange into the oil seal and hold it firmly against the pinion front bearing cone. From the rear of the carrier, insert the drive pinion into the companion flange.

5   Make sure that there is no grease or oil on the threads of the drive pinion and the new nut. Tighten the nut carefully until all pinion endplay is eliminated.

6   From this point, increased torque must be applied since the collapsible spacer must be compressed. The nut must be tightened to provide a turning torque at the companion flange bolt holes of between 4.4 and 6.4 lb (2.0 and 2.9 kg). This can be checked with a suitably calibrated torque wrench or a spring balance.

7   Tighten the nut carefully until the correct pinion bearing preload is obtained. The preload of a used bearing is the same value as that of a new bearing. The tightening torque of the pinion nut will usually exceed 100 lbf ft (14 kgf m) before the specified preload is achieved.

8   If the pinion nut is overtightened, the spacer will have to be renewed, as loosening the nut will release the compression between the pinion front and rear bearing cones and the collapsible spacer.

6 Final drive side oil seal (IRS) - renewal

1   Place a container of suitable capacity under the final drive assembly and remove the drain plug. Allow all of the oil to drain out and refit the drain plug.

2   Chock the front wheels, jack up the rear of the car and support on firmly based axle-stands. Remove the road wheel to give better access.

3   Mark the mating flanges of the shafts and final drive to ensure correct refitting.

4   Undo and remove the driveshaft flange securing bolts and carefully detach the driveshaft. Lower the driveshaft to the ground. NOTE: *On later models the side yoke of the driveshaft fits directly into the differential unit and is retained by a central bolt which must be removed.*

5   Hold the driveshaft flange; undo and remove the bolt, spring and plain washers.

6   To remove the side flange is difficult unless a slide hammer is available. An alternative method is to use a lever placed between the flange and side retainer. Draw the side flange from the side of the final drive assembly.

7   Remove the old seal by dismantling using a screwdriver or chisel. Take care not to damage its seating.

8   Smear the seal lip with a little grease and carefully tap into position. The lip must face inward.

9   Reassembly is the reverse sequence to removal. The side flange retaining bolt should be tightened to a torque wrench setting of 13.7-18.8 lbf ft (1.9-2.6 kgf m) or side yoke securing bolt to 23-31 lbf ft (3.9-4.3 kgf m)

7 Rear axle (RA) - removal and refitting

1   Chock the front wheels, jack up the rear of the car and place on firmly based axle-stands located under the body and forward of the rear axle. Remove the rear wheels.

2   With a scriber or file mark the final drive and propeller shaft so that they may be refitted in their original positions.

3   Undo and remove the four bolts which secure the final drive and propeller shaft flanges. Move the propeller shaft from the rear axle.

4   Wipe the top of the brake master cylinder reservoirs and unscrew the cap. Place a piece of thin polythene sheet over the top of the reservoir cap. Refit the cap. This will prevent syphoning of hydraulic fluid during subsequent operations.

5   Wipe the area around the union nut on the brake feed pipe at the rear axle and unscrew the union nut.

6   Undo and remove the locknut and washer from the flexible hose.

7   Detach the flexible hose from its support bracket.

8   Refer to Chapter 9 and detach the handbrake linkage from the rear axle at the balance lever.

9   Using axle-stands, or other suitable means, support the weight of the rear axle.

10   Undo and remove the eight U-bolts locknuts and remove the U-bolts.

11   Detach the shock-absorber mounting brackets and move to one side. If necessary tie back with string or wire.

12   Detach the rubber bump stop and mounting.

13   The rear axle may now be lifted over the rear springs, and drawn away from one side of the car.

14   Refitting the rear axle is the reverse sequence to removal. The

following additional points should be noted:

    (a) *Tighten the U-bolts nuts when the weight of the car is on the wheels*

    (b) *It will be necessary to bleed the brake hydraulic system as described in Chapter 9.*

8 Axleshaft, bearing and oil seal (RA) - removal and refitting

1   Chock the front wheels, jack up the rear of the car and place on firmly based axle-stands. Remove the rear wheel.

2   Refer to Chapter 9 remove the brake drum, disconnect the pipe to the wheel cylinder and the handbrake linkage from the backplate.

3   Undo and remove the four nuts and spring washers that secure the retainer and backplate to the axle casing. There are two holes in the axleshaft flange to allow for access.

4   The axleshaft assembly may now be withdrawn from the axle casing. If tight it will be necessary to use a slide hammer or tyre levers to ease the wheel bearing from the axle casing.

5   Remove the bearing collar by splitting with a chisel; a new one will be required on reassembly!

6   Should a new bearing be required this job should be left to the local Datsun garage. They are fitted under a force of between 4 and 5 tons, and a press is necessary.

7   Reassembling and refitting the axleshaft assembly is the reverse sequence to removal. The following additional points should be noted:

    (a) *Make sure the wheel bearing is well packed with grease.*

    (b) *Pack the lip of the oil seal with a little grease.*

    (c) *Top up the rear axle oil level.*

    (d) *Bleed the brake hydraulic system as described in Chapter 9.*

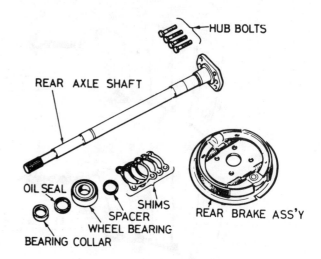

Fig. 8.11 Axleshaft component parts (RA) (Sec 8)

Fig. 8.12 Cutting bearing retainer collar (Sec 8)

9   Pinion oil seal (RA) - renewal

The procedure for renewing the pinion oil seal is basically the same as the procedure described in Sections 4 or 5 appropriate.

10   Differential unit (RA) - removal and refitting

1   If it is wished to overhaul the differential carrier assembly or to exchange it for a reconditioned unit, first remove the axleshafts as described in Section 8.
2   Mark the propeller shaft and pinion flange to ensure that they are refitted in the same relative position.
3   Undo and remove the four bolts from the flanges. Separate the two parts and lower the propeller shaft to the ground.
4   Place a container under the differential unit assembly and remove the drain plug. Allow all the oil to drain out and then refit the plug.
5   Undo and remove the nuts and spring washers securing the differential unit assembly to the axle casing.
6   Draw the assembly forward from over the studs on the axle casing. Lift away from under the car. Recover the paper joint washer.
7   Refitting the differential assembly is the reverse sequence to removal. The following additional points should be noted:

(a) Always use a new joint washer and make sure the mating faces are clean
(b) After refitting do not forget to refill the rear axle with the recommended oil

11   Differential unit (RA) - dismantling, inspection and reassembly

1   Hold the differential unit vertically in a vice and then, using a scriber or dot punch, mark the bearing cap and adjacent side of the differential carrier so that the bearing caps are refitted to their original positions.
2   Cut the locking wire; undo and remove the four bolts and spring washers securing the end caps. Lift away the bearing caps and any shims previously used. Keep the shims in their pairs so that they are not interchanged during reassembly.
3   The sequence for dismantling is now basically identical to that for the independent rear suspension type. Read through the instructions given in Section 3 paragraph 9-50 making a note of any differences that are not relevant in the description or found on the unit being dismantled. Provided care is taken, no troubles will occur.

12   Fault diagnosis – rear axle

Symptom	Reason/s
Noise on drive, coasting or overrun	Shortage of oil Incorrect crownwheel to pinion mesh Worn pinion bearings Worn side bearings Loose bearing cap bolts
Noise on turn	Differential side gears worn, damaged or tight
Knock on taking up drive or during gearchange	Excessive crownwheel to pinion backlash Worn gears Worn axleshaft splines Pinion bearing preload too low Loose drive coupling nut Loose securing bolts or nuts within unit Loose roadwheel nuts or elongated wheel nut holes Loose driveshaft flange Worn differential flexible mountings Worn or damaged driveshaft universal joint
Oil leakage	Defective gaskets or oil seals possibly caused by clogged breather or oil level too high

Chapter 9 Braking system

Contents

Specifications

Type	Hydraulically operated. Drum or disc front, drum rear. Mechanically-operated handbrake to rear wheels. Servo assistance on models with front disc brakes

Front drum brake

	610 series	810 series
Drum diameter	9·00 in (228·6 mm))	
Out-of-round (max)	0·0008 in (0·02 mm)	
Maximum recondition diameter	9·055 in (230 mm)	
Wheel cylinder diameter	0.8125 in (20.638 m)	0.8751 in (22.23 mm)
Lining dimensions:		
Width	1·575 in (40 mm)	
Thickness	0·177 in (4·5 mm)	
Length	8·642 in (219·5 mm)	
Minimum lining thickness	0·059 in (1·5 mm)	

Rear drum brake

Specification as for front drum brakes with the following exception:

	610 series	810 series
Wheel cylinder diameter	0.875 in (22.225 mm)	0.8125 in (20.64 mm)

Front disc brake

	610 series	810 series
Disc diameter	9.130 in (232 mm)	9.98 in (253.5 mm)
Maximum run-out	0.0024 in (0.06 mm)	0.0047 in (0.12 mm)
Standard disc thickness	0.394 in (10.0 mm)	0.492 in (12.5 mm)
Minimum disc thickness	0.331 in (8.4 mm)	0.413 in (10.5 mm)
Caliper cylinder diameter	2.000 in (50.8 mm)	2.125 in (53.98 mm)
Pad dimensions:		
Width	1.563 in (39.7 mm)	2.083 in (52.9 mm)
Thickness (new)	0.354 in (9.00 mm)	0.362 in (9.2 mm)
Length	3.386 in (86.0 mm)	3.00 in (76.2 mm)
Minimum thickness	0.04 in (1.0 mm)	0.08 in (2.0 mm)

Master cylinder

	610 series	810 series
Inner diameter	0.75 in (19.05 mm)	0.812 in (20.64 mm)
Maximum piston clearance	0·0059 in (0·15 mm)	

Brake pedal

	610 series	810 series
Free height	7.28 in (185 mm)	7.09 in (180 mm)
Full stroke of pedal pad	5.71 in (145 mm)	5.81 in (147.5 mm)
Pedal play	0.2–0.6 in (5–15 mm)	0.04–0.20 in (1–5 mm)

Handbrake
Normal stroke:

Rigid axle – centre lever type	5 to 6 notches
– stick lever type	9 to 11 notches
IRS	5 to 6 notches

Servo unit
Type . . . . Master-Vac M45–4.5 in (114.3 mm) diameter
or M60–6.0 in (152.4 mm) diameter

Torque wrench settings

	lbf ft	kgf m
Master cylinder attaching nut	5.8–8.0	0.8–1.1
Brake tube flare nut	11–13	1.5–1.8
Brake hose connector	12–14	1.7–2.0
Air bleed valve	5.1–6.5	0.7–0.9
Fulcrum pin of brake pedal	26–30	3.6–4.2
Pedal stopper locknut	5.8–8.0	0.8–1.1
Connector mounting bolt:		
6 mm diameter bolt	3.6–5.1	0.5–0.7
8 mm diameter bolt	5.8–8.0	0.8–1.1
Wheel cylinder mounting bolts:		
Front – stud bolt side	3.6–5.1	0.5–0.7
– hexagon bolt side	10–13	1.4–1.8
Rear (810 models)	4–6	0.6–0.8
Caliper fixing bolt	53–71	7.3–9.9
Disc securing bolt	28–38	3.9–5.3

1 General description

The braking system fitted to models covered by this manual may be one of two types or a combination depending on the particular model and destined market. To avoid confusion each system is described individually.

The all drum brake models are fitted with two leading type brake shoes to the front wheels and the rear brakes of the leading and trailing type. The hydraulic system is of the dual line type whereby the front brakes and rear brakes are operated by individual hydraulic circuits so that if a line should fail, braking action will still be available on two wheels.

Most models have disc brakes fitted to the front wheels and drum brakes of the leading and trailing type to the rear . A dual line hydraulic circuit is used. Pedal pressure is assisted by a Master-Vac servo unit.

The handbrake is a mechanical type which brakes the rear wheels. It is engaged or released through a stick-type lever or a centre-type lever. When the handbrake is applied, a warning lamp on the instrument panel will come on to indicate that the handbrake is engaged.

The drum brakes are of the internally expanding type whereby the shoes are moved outwards into contact with the brakedrum. Two wheel cylinders are fitted to each front brake unit and one to each rear unit.

The front disc brakes are of the rotating disc and semi-rigid-mounted caliper design. The disc is secured to the flange of the hub, and the caliper is mounted on the steering swivel. Two types of caliper are fitted, a single cylinder type and one with two cylinders.

On the single cylinder type a single piston moves outwards in its bore, as hydraulic pressure is applied and pushes one pad onto the face of the disc. At the same time a reaction is created on the yoke (which carries the cylinder) and effort is transferred to the second side of the disc, also pushing a second pad onto the other face of the disc and so creating a clamping or squeezing action.

On the two-cylinder type, when the brake is operated, the inner pad is directly pushed against the disc by piston B, see Fig. 9.4. and the outer pad is indirectly pushed by piston A. The yoke and cylinder body slide through the grippers and there is no metallic contact. The pad-to-disc clearance is automatically adjusted due to the elasticity of the piston seal.

The mechanically operated stoplight switch is secured by the pedal mounting plate inside the car and is operated by the pedal arm.

2 Front drum brake - adjustment

1   Chock the rear wheels, apply the handbrake, jack up the front of the car and support on firmly based axle-stands.
2   Depress the brake pedal several times to centralise the shoe.

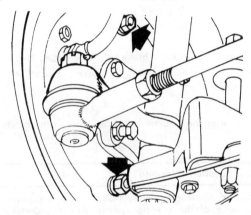

Fig. 9.1 Front drum brake adjustment (Sec 2)

3   Locate the adjusters at the top and bottom of the brake backplate and apply a little penetrating oil.
4   Turn the cam adjusters clockwise (right drum) or anti-clockwise (left drum) until the drum is locked. Now turn the adjusters back until the wheel is free to rotate.
5   Spin the wheel and apply the brakes hard to centralise the shoes. Re-check that it is not possible to turn the adjuster further without locking the wheel.
6   A rubbing noise when the wheel is spun is usually due to dust on the brake drum and shoe lining. If there is no obvious slowing down of the wheel due to brake binding there is no need to slacken off the adjusters until the noise disappears. It is far better to remove the drum and clean, taking care not to inhale any dust.
7   Repeat this process for the second front drum.

3 Rear drum brake - adjustment

1   Only one adjuster is fitted and is located towards the top of the backplate. To take up clearance rotate the adjuster clockwise as viewed from inboard of the brake backplate (Fig. 9.2).
2   Do not forget to release the handbrake before commencing. Normally adjustment of the rear brake will also adjust excessive movement of the handbrake except where the cables have stretched. In this instance it will be necessary to adjust the linkage as described later in this Chapter.
3   On 810 models adjustment is not normally necessary as the brake drum-to-shoe clearance is automatically compensated for by operating the handbrake. When the drum-to-shoe clearance is correct, the

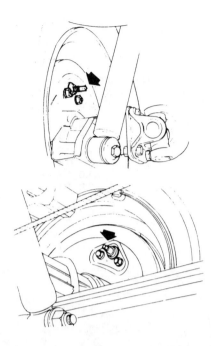

Fig. 9.2 Rear drum brake adjustment (Sec 3)

Top – Saloon and Hardtop   Bottom – Estate Car

operating noise of the adjuster is not heard when the handbrake is operated.

---

4 Hydraulic system - bleeding

1   Removal of all air from the hydraulic system is essential to the correct working of the braking system. Before undertaking this, examine the fluid reservoir cap to ensure that the vent hole is clear. Check the level of fluid in the reservoir and top up if required. The tandem master cylinders have two reservoirs.
2   Check all brake line unions and connections for seepage, and at the same time check the condition of the rubber hoses which may be perished.
3   If the condition of the caliper or wheel cylinder is in doubt, check for signs of fluid leakage.
4   If there is any possibility that incorrect fluid has been used in the system, drain all the fluid out and flush through with methylated spirits. Renew all piston seals and cups since they will be affected and could fail under pressure.
5   Gather together a clean glass jar, a 12 inch length of tubing which fits tightly over the bleed screws and a tin of the correct brake fluid.
6   The first thing which should be bled is the master cylinder.
7   Remove the dust caps from the bleed screws. Clean the bleed screws and fit the rubber tube over one of them.
8   With the free end of the tube in a jar of fluid, sufficient to cover the end of the tube, open the bleed screw $\frac{1}{4}$ of a turn, with a spanner, and have an assistant depress the brake pedal. Tighten the screw and allow the pedal to return. Repeat this operation on the other master cylinder bleed screw until no air is visible in the emerging fluid. At intervals make certain that the reservoir is kept topped up, otherwise air will enter again.
9   The brakes are bled in the same way as described for the master cylinder. Start at the rear left-hand wheel and continue with the right rear wheel, then the left front wheel, and finish with the right front wheel (photo).
10 When completed check the level of the fluid in the reservoir and then check the feel of the brake pedal, which should be firm and free from any 'spongy' action, which is normally associated with air in the system. If necessary, repeat the bleeding procedure.

4.9 Bleed hose connected to front brake

---

5 Front disc brake - pad renewal

1   Chock the rear wheels, jack up the front of the car and support it on axle-stands. Remove the front roadwheels.

Single cylinder type (refer to Fig 9.3)
2   Carefully remove the anti-rattle clip from the caliper plate and inspect the lining thickness. When the lining has worn down to 0.04 in (1 mm) or less the pad must be renewed (photos)
3   To remove the pads ease the caliper plate outwards away from the engine compartment so as to allow the piston to retract into its bore by approximately 0.157 in (4 mm)
4   The outer pad may now be withdrawn using a pair of long nose pliers.
5   Move the caliper plate inward towards the engine compartment and withdraw the inner pad and anti-squeal shim (if fitted) (photo).
6   Carefully clean all traces of dirt or rust from the recesses in the caliper in which the pads lie, and the exposed face of the piston.
7   Use a piece of wood or screwdriver to fully retract the piston with the caliper cylinder (photo).
8   Pads must always be renewed in sets of four and not singly. Also pads must not be interchanged side to side.
9   Fit new friction pads and secure with the anti-rattle clip. The clip must be fitted the correct way round as indicated by the sticker on the outer face of the clip.

Two cylinder type (refer to Fig. 9.4)
10 Remove the retaining clip, pad pins and anti-squeal springs (photos).
11 Remove the pads. If the lining is less than 0.08 in (2 mm) the pads must be renewed (photo).
12 Clean piston ends and around the gripper.
13 Loosen the bleed screw and push piston B (outer) into the cylinder until the dust seal groove of piston B lines up with the end of the retaining ring on the dust seal, then tighten the bleed screw and fit the inner pad. Take care not to push the piston in too far as the piston seal will be damaged. If it should be pushed in too far remove the caliper assembly and dismantle it (See Section 8).
14 Push piston A (inner) into the cylinder, by pulling the yoke, and fit the outer pad.
15 Refit the anti-squeal spring, pad pins and retaining clip.
16 Depress the brake pedal several times to settle the pads in position.
17 Check the brake fluid level in the reservoir, and top-up as necessary (photo).
18 Refit the roadwheels and lower the car to the ground.

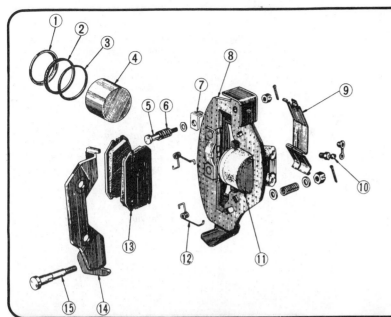

Fig. 9.3 Exploded view of brake caliper
(single cylinder type) (Sec 5)

1   Retainer
2   Wiper seal
3   Piston seal
4   Piston
5   Holddown pin
6   Spring
7   Support bracket
8   Caliper plate
9   Clip
10 Bleeder screw
11 Cylinder
12 Torsion spring
13 Pad
14 Mounting bracket
15 Pivot pin

5.2a Anti-rattle clip on caliper plate

5.2b Pad linings ready for checking

5.5 Removing the inner pad assembly

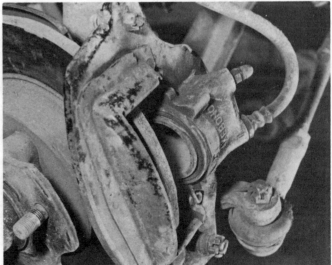

5.7 Piston to be retracted into cylinder

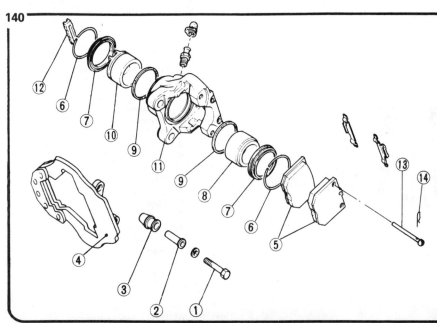

Fig. 9.4 Exploded view of brake caliper (two-cylinder type) (Sec 5)

1 Fix bolt
2 Collar
3 Gripper
4 Yoke
5 Pad
6 Retainer ring
7 Dust seal
8 Piston B
9 Piston seal
10 Piston A
11 Cylinder body
12 Yoke holder
13 Pad pin
14 Clip

5.10a Remove the retaining clips ...

5.10b ... and the pad pins

5.11 Removing the brake pads

5.17 Checking the brake fluid level

6   Front disc brake caliper -removal and refitting

1   Chock the rear wheels. Jack up the front of the car and support it on axle-stands. Remove the front roadwheel.
2   Disconnect the flexible hose from the caliper. Plug the end of the hose to prevent fluid flowing out.
3   Remove the brake pads as described in Section 5.
4   Undo and remove the two bolts securing the caliper to the steering knuckle. Lift off the caliper.
5   Refitting is the reverse of the removal procedure. Bleed the hydraulic system as described in Section 4.

7   Brake caliper (single cylinder) - dismantling and reassembly

1   Remove the caliper as described in Section 6.
2   To remove the piston, the air jet from an air line or foot pump should be used. Tighten the bleed screw and apply the jet to the hydraulic pipe aperture in the cylinder body. The piston assembly should now be ejected.
3   Carefully remove the rubber seal from the groove in the cylinder bore.
4   Carefully remove the wiper seal and retainer from the open end of the cylinder.
5   Unscrew and remove the bleed screw. Further dismantling should not be necessary unless it is obvious that a part has worn. If damage exists the assembly must be renewed as a whole.
6   Thoroughly clean all parts and wipe with a clean non-fluffy rag. The seals must be renewed.
7   Check the cylinder bore and piston for signs of deep scoring; if evident, a new assembly must be obtained.
8   To reassemble, first fit the wiper seal into its recess in the cylinder and follow this with the retainer.
9   Carefully insert the piston into the cylinder bore until the piston rim is nearly flush with the wiper seal retainer.
10 Position the cylinder to the caliper plate and secure with the two tension springs.
11 Refit the caliper as described in Chapter 6.

8   Brake caliper (two-cylinder) - dismantling and reassembly

1   Remove the caliper as described in Section 6.
2   Remove the securing bolts from the cylinder body and separate the yoke and cylinder body.
3   Remove the yoke holder from the piston.
4   Remove the retaining rings and dust seals from the ends of both pistons.
5   Force out the pistons, using an air line or foot pump. Remove the piston seals. Remove the gripper only if necessary.
6   Clean all the parts and check the cylinder bores and pistons for signs of scoring or damage. Renew all seals.
7   Fit the piston seals. Apply brake fluid to the sliding parts and insert the pistons in the cylinders. Fit piston A in the direction shown by the arrow Q1 and piston B in the direction of the arrow Q2 as shown in Fig 9.5. When inserting the pistons take care not to insert them too far. Fit piston A so that its yoke groove lines up with the yoke groove of the cylinder.
8   Apply brake grease to the sealing surface of the dust seals. Fit the dust seal and clamp securely with the retainer ring.
9   Fit the yoke holder to piston A.
10 Fit the gripper to the yoke. Apply a 1% soap/water solution to the inner wall of the gripper and drive in the gripper collar.
11 Fit the yoke to the yoke holder and, supporting the end of piston B, press the yoke into the yoke holder with a force of 44-66 lb (20-30 kg). Make sure that there is no clearance between the piston and yoke.
12 Tighten the gripper securing bolts to 12-15 lbf ft (1.6 - 2.1 kgf m).
13 Refit the caliper as described in Section 6.

9   Front brake disc - removal and refitting

1   Chock the rear wheels, apply the handbrake, jack up the front of the car and support on firmly based stands. Remove the roadwheel (photo).

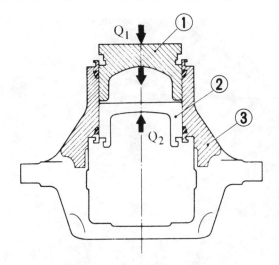

Fig. 9.5 Fitting the pistons (Sec 8)

1   Piston A   3   Cylinder body
2   Piston B

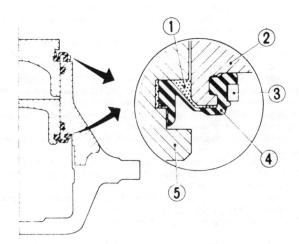

Fig. 9.6 Fitting the dust seal (Sec 8)

1   Grease   4   Dust seal
2   Cylinder body   5   Piston
3   Retaining ring

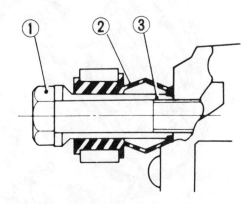

Fig. 9.7 Fitting the gripper (Sec 8)

1   Fix bolt   3   Collar
2   Gripper

9.1 Front brake disc

2   Refer to Section 5 and remove the pads.

3   Undo and remove the caliper securing bolts and spring washers. Lift the caliper from the disc and suspend on a piece of wire so that the flexible hose is not strained.

4   Using a screwdriver remove the grease cap from the hub.

5   Straighten the ears and withdraw the split pin locking the castellated nut to the stub axle.

6   Tighten the castellated nut and with a dial indicator gauge on the outer circumference or feeler gauges and suitable packing measure the run-out. This must not exceed the figure given in the Specifications at the beginning of this Chapter. If this figure is exceeded the surface must be refaced or a new disc obtained.

7   Undo and remove the castellated nut, thrust washer and outer hub bearing.

8   The hub and disc assembly may now be drawn from the stub axle. Should it be necessary to renew the hub bearings further information will be found in Chapter 11.

9   Mark the relative positions of the disc and hub so that they may be refitted in their original positions.

10 Undo and remove the four bolts and separate the hub from the disc.

11 Thoroughly clean the disc and inspect for signs of deep scoring or excessive corrosion. If these are evident the disc may be reground to within the specified limits.

12 Refitting the disc is the reverse sequence to removal. Tighten the disc retaining bolts to a torque wrench setting of 38.3 lbf ft (5.3 kgf m).

13 Refer to Chapter 11 and adjust the hub bearings.

14 Recheck the disc run-out. If a new disc was fitted and the run-out is excessive check the hub flange for run-out and for dirt trapped between the mating faces, rectify by either cleaning or fitting a new hub.

10 Front drum brake shoes - removal and refitting

1   Chock the rear wheels, apply the handbrake, jack up the front of the car and support on firmly based stands. Remove the roadwheel.

2   Refer to Section 3 and back off the brake adjusters.

3   The drum may now be removed from the wheel studs. If it is tight, use a soft faced hammer and tap outwards on the circumference, rotating the drum whilst completing this operation. Alternatively screw two bolts of suitable thread into the drum and draw off the drum.

4   The brake linings should be renewed if they are so worn that the rivet heads are flush with the surface of the linings. If bonded linings are fitted, they must be renewed when the lining material has worn down to 0.06 in (1.5 mm) at its thinnest point.

5   Where brake shoe anti-rattle springs are fitted, use a pair of pliers and rotate the retainer through 90° and lift away the retainer, spring, seat and pin.

6   Make a note of the locations of the shoe return springs and which way round they are fitted. Carefully ease the shoes from the slots in the wheel cylinders.

7   Lift away the shoes and return springs.

8   If the shoes are to be left off for a while, do not depress the brake pedal otherwise the pistons will be ejected from the cylinders causing unnecessary work.

9   Thoroughly clean all traces of dust from the shoes, backplate and brake drums using a stiff brush.

10 Check that the pistons are free to move in the cylinders, that the rubber dust covers are undamaged and in position, and that there are no hydraulic fluid leaks.

11 Apply a drop of oil to the adjuster threads.

12 Prior to reassembly, smear a trace of brake grease to the steady platforms and shoe locations on the cylinders. Do not allow any grease to come into contact with the linings or rubber parts.

13 Refit the shoes in the reverse sequence to removal. The pull off springs should preferably be renewed every time new shoes are fitted, and must be refitted in their original web holes. Position them between the web and backplate.

14 Back off the adjuster and refit the brake drum. Refit the roadwheel.

15 Adjust the front brake and lower the car to the ground and finally, road test.

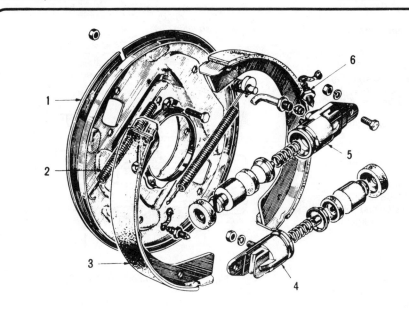

Fig. 9.8 Front drum brake assembly (Sec 10)

1   Backplate
2   Return spring
3   Brake shoe assembly
4   Wheel cylinder (fore)
5   Wheel cylinder (aft)
6   Bleeder

11 Front drum brake wheel cylinder - removal, overhaul and refitting

1 Remove the brake drum and shoes as described in Section 10.
2 Clean down the rear of the backplate to catch any hydraulic fluid which may issue from the open pipe or wheel cylinder.
3 Wipe the top of the brake master cylinder reservoirs and unscrew the caps. Place a piece of thick polythene over the top of the reservoirs and refit the caps. This is to stop hydraulic fluid syphoning out. On models with a fluid level indicator it will be necessary to plug the open ends of the pipe to prevent loss of hydraulic fluid.
4 Disconnect the flexible hose and bridge pipe using an open ended spanner.
5 Unscrew the bleed screw, then undo and remove the cylinder securing nut and washer. Also remove the nut, bolt and spring washer securing the cast extension to the backplate. Lift away the wheel cylinder.
6 To dismantle the wheel cylinder first remove the rubber boot and then withdraw the piston, and seal assembly and spring from the cylinder bore. Take care to note which way round and in what order the parts are removed.
7 Inspect the inside of the cylinder for score marks. If any are found, the cylinder and piston will require renewal. **NOTE:** *If the wheel cylinder requires renewal always ensure that the replacement is exactly the same as the one removed.*
8 If the cylinder is sound, thoroughly clean it out with fresh hydraulic fluid.

Fig. 9.9 Exploded view of front wheel cylinder (Sec 11)

1	Dust cover	5	Spring
2	Piston	6	Cylinder
3	Piston cup	7	Bleeder
4	Spring retainer	8	Bleed cap

9 The old rubber seal will probably be swollen and visibly worn.
10 Smear all internal parts with fresh hydraulic fluid and reassemble into the cylinder in the reverse order to removal.
11 Refitting the wheel cylinder is the reverse of the removal procedure. Bleed the hydraulic system as described in Section 4.

12 Rear brake shoes - removal and refitting

1 Chock the front wheels, jack up the rear of the car and support it with axle-stands. Remove the roadwheel.
2 Back-off the brake adjuster as described in Section 3.
3 Remove the brake drum. If the drum is difficult to remove screw two 8mm bolts into the drum and draw it off (photos) (Fig. 9.10).
4 Where brake shoe anti-rattle springs are fitted, use a pair of pliers and rotate the retainer through 90°. Lift away the retainer, spring , seat and pin.
5 Make a note of the locations of the shoe return springs and their fitted position. Free the shoes from the slots in the wheel cylinder and adjuster. Remove the shoes and return springs from the backplate.
6 Clean and inspect the shoes; if the linings are worn to less than the specified thickness, renew the shoes as a complete set.
7 Refitting is the reverse of the removal procedure.

13 Rear brake wheel cylinder (610 series) - removal, overhaul and refitting

1 Remove the brake drum and shoes as described in Section 12.
2 Wipe the top of the brake master cylinder reservoir and unscrew the cap. Place a piece of thick polythene over the top of the reservoir and refit the cap. This is to stop hydraulic fluid syphoning out; on models with a fluid level indicator it will be necessary to plug the open ends of the pipe to prevent loss of hydraulic fluid.
3 Wipe the union of the rear of the wheel cylinder and disconnect the metal pipe.
4 Straighten the ears and withdraw the split pin locking the handbrake cable yoke cotter pin to the lever at the rear of the wheel cylinder. Remove the cotter pin.
5 Ease off the rubber boot from the rear of the wheel cylinder.
6 Using a screwdriver carefully draw off the retaining plate, spring plate and shims from the rear of the wheel cylinder.
7 The wheel cylinder may now be lifted away from the brake backplate. Detach the handbrake lever from the wheel cylinder.
8 To dismantle the wheel cylinder first ease off the rubber retaining spring with a screwdriver, and the rubber dust cover itself.
9 Withdraw the piston from the wheel cylinder body and with the fingers remove the piston seal from the piston noting which way round it is fitted. (Do not use a metal screwdriver as this could scratch the piston).

12.3a Using bolts to draw off the drum   12.3b Rear brakes with drum removed

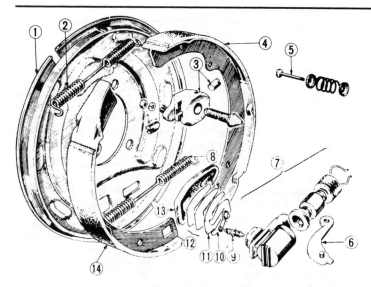

Fig. 9.10 Rear drum brake assembly (610 series) (Sec 12)

 1   Brake disc
 2   Return spring adjuster side
 3   Brake shoe adjuster
 4   Brake shoe assembly (leading)
 5   Anti-rattle pin
 6   Lever
 7   Rear wheel cylinder
 8   Return spring cylinder side
 9   Bleeder
10   Lock plate
11   Lock plate
12   Lock plate
13   Dust cover
14   Brake shoe assembly (trailing)

10 Inspect the inside of the cylinder for score marks caused by impurities in the hydraulic fluid. **NOTE**: *If the wheel cylinder requires renewal always ensure that the replacement is identical to the one removed.*

11 If the cylinder is sound, thoroughly clean it out with fresh hydraulic fluid.

12 The old rubber seal will probably be swollen and visibly worn, Smear a new rubber seal with hydraulic fluid and fit the correct way round to the piston.

13 Insert the piston into the bore taking care not to roll the lip of the seal and fit a new dust seal and retaining ring.

14 Using brake grease, smear the backplate where the wheel cylinder slides, and refit the handbrake lever on the wheel cylinder ensuring that it is the correct way round. The spindle of the lever must engage in the recess on the cylinder rims.

15 Slide the shims, and spring plate between the wheel cylinder and backplate. The retaining plate may now be inserted between the spring plate and wheel cylinder taking care the pips of the spring plate engage with the holes of the retaining plate.

16 Refit the rubber boot and reconnect the handbrake cable yoke to the handbrake lever. Insert the cotter pin head upwards and lock with a new split pin.

17 Reassembling the brake shoes and drum is the reverse sequence to removal. Finally bleed the hydraulic system as described in Section 4.

14 Rear brake wheel cylinder (810 series) - removal, overhaul and refitting

1   Remove the brake drum as described in Section 12
2   *Saloon and Hardtops (refer to Fig 9.12)*
    Apply the handbrake, Tap the stopper head, and remove the stopper and fastener as an assembly. Release the handbrake.
3   *Estate cars (refer to Fig. 9.13)*
    Apply the handbrake. Pull out the retaining pin and remove the stopper from the toggle lever.
4   Remove the brake shoes as described in Section 12.
5   On Saloon and Hardtop models disconnect the handbrake rear cable from the lever.
6   Disconnect the flexible brake hose, and plug the open end of the hose.
7   On Estate Cars remove the handbrake return spring, then the cross-rod cotter pin. Remove the dust cover and toggle lever with the adjuster assembly.
8   Unscrew the securing bolts and remove the wheel cylinder (photo).
9   On Saloon and Hardtop models prise the circlip off the brake shoe and remove the lever.
10 Remove the dust covers from the wheel cylinder and the parts can be dismantled. Note the order in which they are fitted. Clean and inspect the parts as described in Section 13.
11 Reassembly and refitting is the reverse of the removal procedure.

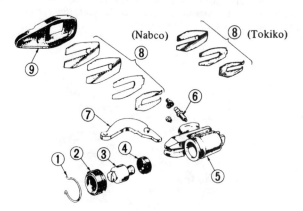

(Nabco)   (Tokiko)

Fig. 9.11 Exploded view of rear wheel cylinder (610 series) (Sec 13)

1	Circlip	6	Bleeder
2	Dust cover	7	Hand brake lever
3	Piston	8	Lock plates
4	Piston cup	9	Dust cover
5	Cylinder		

Apply brake grease to the points indicated in Fig 9.15 and 9.16. Ensure that the adjuster operates correctly.

12 After refitting, check and adjust the shoe-to-drum clearance by operating the handbrake several times. Bleed the hydraulic system as described in Section 4.

15 Brake master cylinder - removal and refitting

Models without servo unit

1   Straighten the split pin ears and withdraw it from the master cylinder pushrod yoke to pedal clevis pin.
2   Remove the clevis pin so disengaging the yoke from the pedal.
3   Wipe the top of each reservoir and unscrew the cap. Place some polythene over the reservoir neck and refit the cap. When a brake fluid level gauge is fitted into the cap it will be necessary to drain the reservoir by attaching a bleed tube to front and rear bleed nipples and pumping the pedal.
4   Wipe the hydraulic pipe unions and with an open ended spanner undo the unions and detach the pipe.
5   Undo and remove the two nuts and spring washers securing the master cylinder to the bulkhead. Carefully lift away ensuring that no hydraulic fluid drips on the paintwork as it acts as a solvent.
6   Refitting the master cylinder is the reverse sequence to removal. It will be necessary to bleed the hydraulic system as described in Section 4.

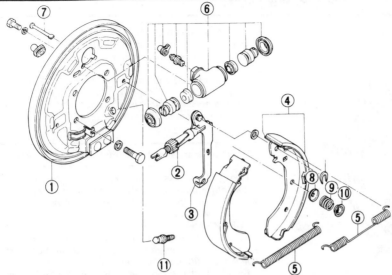

1 Brake disc
2 Adjuster
3 Lever
4 Brake shoe assembly
5 Return spring
6 Wheel cylinder
7 Anti-rattle pin
8 Spring seat
9 Anti-rattle spring
10 Retainer
11 Stopper assembly

Fig. 9.12 Exploded view of rear drum brake (810 Saloon and Hardtop) (Sec 14)

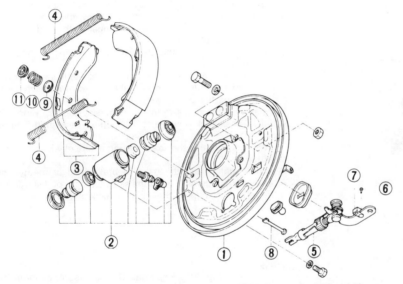

1 Brake disc
2 Wheel cylinder assembly
3 Brake shoe assembly
4 Return spring
5 Adjuster assembly
6 Stopper pin
7 Stopper
8 Anti-rattle pin
9 Spring seat
10 Anti-rattle spring
11 Retainer

Fig. 9.13 Exploded view of rear drum brake (810 Estate Car) (Sec 14)

14.8 Rear brake wheel cylinder

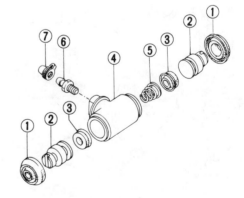

Fig. 9.14 Exploded view of rear wheel cylinder (810 series) (Sec 14)

1 Dust cover
2 Piston
3 Piston cup
4 Cylinder body
5 Spring
6 Bleeder
7 Bleeder cap

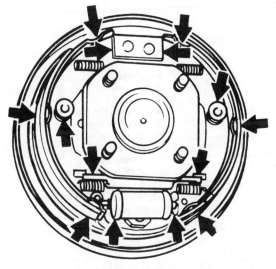

Fig. 9.15 Lubricating points of brake assembly (Sec 14)

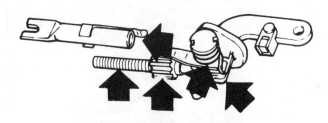

Fig. 9.16 Lubricating points of adjuster (Sec 14)

Models with servo unit

7   The sequence is almost identical to that described earlier in this Section with the exception that:

(a) *The brake pedal does not have to be detached from the pushrod.*
(b) *The master cylinder is attached to the forward end of the servo unit and not on the bulkhead.*

---

16 Brake master cylinder - dismantling and reassembly

Two types of master drum cylinder are fitted; one for disc brake and the other for drum brake models. They differ from each other in the reservoir capacity and check valve. A brake fluid level gauge is fitted on some models.

IMPORTANT: *Do not detach the reservoir from the master cylinder body. Should it be removed it must be discarded and a new one fitted. Do not attempt to remove or dismantle the brake fluid gauge if one is fitted to the reservoir.*

1   Remove both reservoir caps and drain out the hydraulic fluid.
2   Withdraw the pushrod from the end of the master cylinder and then remove the rubber dust cover. (Drum brake master cylinder only).
3   Using a pair of circlip pliers or screwdriver release the circlip (stopper ring) retaining the piston stopper in the end of the bore. Lift away the circlip and stopper.
4   Undo and remove the stopper screw from the underside of the cylinder body.
5   The primary and secondary piston assemblies may now be withdrawn from the cylinder bore. Make a special note of the assembly order as the parts are removed.
6   Unscrew the plugs from the underside of the cylinder body and withdraw the check valve parts. These must be kept in their respective sets.
7   Carefully remove the seals making a note of which way round they are fitted.
8   Thoroughly clean the parts in brake fluid or methylated spirits. After drying the items inspect the seals for signs of distortion, swelling, splitting or hardening although it is recommended new rubber parts

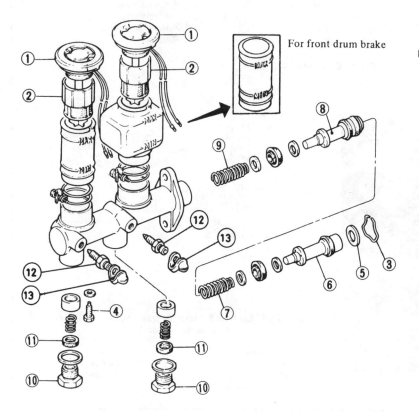

For front drum brake

Fig. 9.17 Exploded view of master cylinder (Sec 16)

1   Reservoir cap
2   Strainer
3   Stopper ring
4   Stopper screw
5   Stopper
6   Primary piston
7   Spring
8   Secondary piston
9   Spring
10 Plug
11 Check valve
12 Bleed screw
13 Dust cap

are always fitted after dismantling as a matter of course.

9 Inspect the bore and pistons for signs of deep scoring marks. Should there be any, fit a new cylinder. Make sure that the ports in the bore are clean by poking gently with a piece of wire.

10 As the parts are refitted to the cylinder bore make sure that they are thoroughly wetted with clean hydraulic fluid.

11 Fit new seals to the pistons making sure that they are the correct way round as noted during removal.

12 With the cylinder bore well lubricated insert the secondary return spring, secondary piston, primary return spring and primary piston into the bore. Take care not to roll the lips whilst inserting into the bore.

13 Refit the piston stop screw to the underside of the cylinder body.

14 Refit the piston stopper and retain with the circlip.

15 *Drum brake models only.* Pack the rubber dust cover with grease of the correct specification and place over the end of the master cylinder.

16 Insert the pushrod into the rubber dust cover.

17 Refit the check valves and retain with the plugs.

17 Vacuum servo unit - description

A vacuum servo unit is fitted into the brake system on some models either as standard fitment or an optional extra depending on the version or destined market. It is in series with the master cylinder to provide assistance to the driver when the brake pedal is depressed. This reduces the effort required by the driver to operate the brakes under all braking conditions.

The unit operates by vacuum obtained from the induction manifold and comprises basically a booster diaphragm and control valve assembly.

The servo unit and hydraulic master cylinder are connected together so that the servo unit piston rod (valve rod) acts as the master cylinder pushrod. The driver's braking effort is transmitted through another pushrod to the servo unit piston and its built in control system. The servo unit piston does not fit tightly into the cylinder, but has a strong diaphragm to keep its edges in constant contact with the cylinder wall, so ensuring an air tight seal between the two parts. The forward chamber is held under vacuum conditions created in the inlet manifold of the engine and, during periods when the brake pedal is not in use, the controls open a passage to the rear chamber so placing it under vacuum conditions as well. When the brake pedal is pressed the vacuum passage to the rear chamber is cut off and the chamber opened to atmospheric pressure. The consequent rush of air pushes the servo piston forward in the vacuum chamber and operates the main pushrod to the master cylinder.

The controls are designed so that assistance is given under all conditions and, when the brakes are not required, vacuum in the rear chamber is established when the brake pedal is released.

Under normal operating conditions the vacuum servo unit is very reliable and does not require overhaul except at very high mileage. In this case it is far better to obtain a service exchange unit, rather than repair the original. If overhaul is to be carried out make sure that the necessary kit is available.

18 Vacuum servo unit - removal and refitting

1 Slacken the clip securing the vacuum hose to the servo unit. Carefully draw the hose from its union.

2 Refer to Section 15 and remove the master cylinder.

3 Using a pair of pliers, extract the split pin in the end of the brake pedal to pushrod clevis pin. Withdraw the clevis pin. To assist this it may be necessary to release the pedal return spring.

4 Undo and remove the four nuts and spring washers that secure the unit to the bulkhead. Lift the unit away from the engine bulkhead.

5 Refitting the servo unit is the reverse sequence to removal. Check the brake pedal movement and adjust as necessary as described in Section 20.

19 Vacuum servo unit - dismantling, inspection and reassembly

Thoroughly clean the outside of the unit using a stiff brush and wipe with a non-fluffy rag. It cannot be too strongly emphasised that cleanliness is important when working on the servo unit. Before any attempt be made to dismantle it two items of equipment are required. Firstly, a baseplate must be made to enable the unit to be safely held in the vice. Secondly, a lever must be made similar to the one shown in Fig. 7.18. Without these items it is impossible to dismantle satisfactorily.

To dismantle the unit proceed as follows:

1 Using a file or scriber, mark a line across the two halves of the unit to act as a datum for alignment.

2 Fit the previously made base plate into a firm vice and attach the unit to the plate using the master cylinder studs.

3 Fit the lever to the four studs on the rear shell.

4 Use a piece of long rubber hose and connect one end to the adaptor on the engine inlet manifold and the other end to the servo unit. Start the engine and this will create a vacuum in the unit so drawing the two halves together.

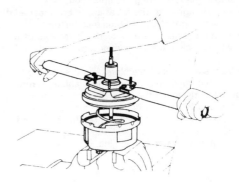

Fig. 9.18 Removing rear shell (Sec 19)

Fig. 9.19 Sectional view of servo unit (Sec 19)

1 Plate and seal	10 Air silencer filter
2 Push rod	11 Valve operating rod
3 Diaphragm	12 Valve return spring
4 Rear shell	13 Poppet return spring
5 Diaphragm plate	14 Exhaust valve
6 Seal	15 Valve plunger
7 Vacuum valve	16 Reaction drive
8 Poppet assembly	17 Diaphragm return spring
9 Valve body guard	18 Front shell

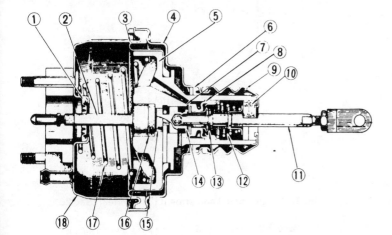

5   Rotate the lever in an anti-clockwise direction until the front shell indentations are in line with the recesses in the rim of the rear shell. Then press the lever assembly down firmly whilst an assistant stops the engine and quickly removes the vacuum pipe from the inlet manifold connector. Depress the operating rod so as to release the vacuum, whereupon the front and rear halves should part. If necessary, use a soft faced hammer and lightly tap the front half to break the bond.

6   Unscrew the locknut and yoke from the pushrod and then remove the valve body rubber gaiter. Separate the diaphragm assembly from the rear shell.

7   Using a screwdriver carefully prise out the retainer and then remove the bearing and seal from the shell. This operation should only be done if it is absolutely necessary to renew the seal or bearing.

8   Carefully detach the diaphragm from the diaphragm plate.

9   Using a screwdriver carefully and evenly remove the air silencer retainer from the diaphragm plate.

10 Withdraw the valve plunger stop key by lightly pushing on the valve operating rod and sliding from its location

11 Withdraw the silencer and plunger assembly.

12 Next remove the reaction disc.

13 Remove the two nuts and spring washers and withdraw the front seal assembly from the front cover. It is recommended that unless the seal is to be renewed it should be left in its housing.

14 Thoroughly clean all parts and wipe with a clean non-fluffy rag. Inspect for signs of damage, dirty or damaged threads, etc.,and obtain new parts as necessary. All seals must be renewed and for this a 'Major Repair Kit' should be purchased. This will also contain the special grease required during reassembly.

15 To reassemble first apply a little of the special grease to the sealing surface and lip of the seal. Fit the seal to the rear shell using a drift of suitable diameter.

16 Apply a little special grease to the sliding contact portions on the circumference of the plunger assembly.

17 Fit the plunger assembly and silencer into the diaphragm plate and retain in position with the stop key. As the plate is made of bakelite take care not to damage it during this operation.

18 Refit the diaphragm into the cover and then smear a little special grease on the diaphragm plate. Refit the reaction disc.

19 Smear a little special grease onto the inner wall of the seal and front shell with which the seal comes into contact. Refit the front assembly.

20 Fit the front shell to the base plate, and the lever to the rear shell. Reconect the vacuum hose. Position the diaphragm return spring in the front shell. Lightly smear the outer head of the diaphragm with the special grease and locate the diaphragm assembly in the rear shell. Position the rear shell assembly on the return spring and line up the previously made scriber marks.

21 An assistant should start the engine. Watching one's fingers very

carefully, press the two halves of the unit together and, using the lever tool, turn clockwise to lock the two halves together. Stop the engine and disconnect the hose.

22 Refit the servo unit to the vehicle as described in the previous Section. To test the servo unit for correct operation after overhaul, first start the engine and run for a minimum period of two minutes and then switch off. Wait for ten minutes and apply the footbrake very carefully, listening to hear the rush of air into the servo unit. This will indicate that vacuum was retained and, therefore, operating correctly.

20 Brake pedal - removal, refitting and adjustment

1   Note which way round the pedal return spring is fitted and remove the spring.

2   Withdraw the spring pin securing the brake pedal to pushrod yoke pushrod cotter pin. Remove the cotter pin and washer and then separate the pushrod from the pedal.

3   Undo and remove the nut securing the pedal fulcrum pin. Note that on RHD models the fulcrum pin nut must be unscrewed anti-clockwise whereas on LHD models it must be unscrewed clockwise.

4   Lift away the washer and withdraw the fulcrum pin. The pedal may now be lifted from its support bracket.

5   If the pedal split bushes have worn they may be removed by tapping out with a small drift.

6   Refitting is the reverse sequence to removal. Lubricate the bushes with a little lithium based grease.

7   Check the pedal height and fully depressed positions. Adjust as necessary at the pushrod yoke or switch to obtain the specified movements.

21 Handbrake - adjustment

Any excessive free movement of the handbrake will be automatically taken up when the rear brakes are adjusted. However in time the cable will stretch and it will be necessary to take up the free play by shortening the cable at the relay lever.

Never try to adjust the handbrake to compensate for wear on the rear brake linings. It is usually worn brake linings that lead to the excessive handbrake travel. If upon inspection the rear brake linings

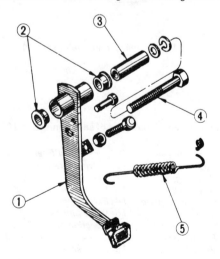

Fig. 9.20 Component parts of brake pedal assembly (Sec 20)

1   Brake pedal   4   Fulcrum pin
2   Pedal bush   5   Return spring
3   Pedal shaft sleeve

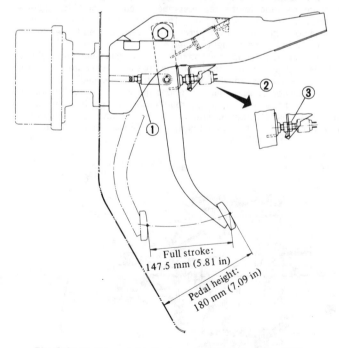

Full stroke:
147.5 mm (5.81 in)

Pedal height:
180 mm (7.09 in)

Fig. 9.21 Brake pedal adjustment (810 series) (Sec 20)

1   Push rod locknut   3   Brake lamp switch locknut
2   Brake lamp switch

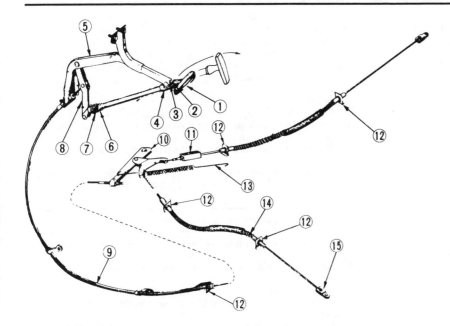

Fig. 9.22 Handbrake linkage (610 series) (Sec 21)

1   Control stem
2   Control ratchet spring
3   Control ratchet
4   Control guide
5   Control bracket
6   Control yoke
7   Lever spring
8   Control lever
9   Front cable
10   Centre lever
11   Rear cable adjuster
12   Cable lockplate
13   Return spring
14   Rear cable
15   Clevis

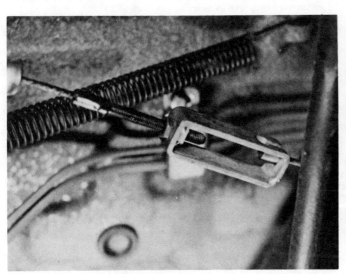

21.2 Adjusting the handbrake rear cable

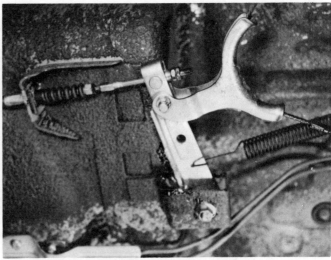

21.3 Adjusting the handbrake front cable

are in good condition, or they have been renewed recently and the handbrake reaches the end of its ratchet travel before the brakes operate the cables must be adjusted.

1   Refer to Section 3 and adjust the rear brakes.
2   Slacken the locknut and take up all the slack in the rear cable. Take care however, that there is no tension on the wheel cylinder lever when the slack has been removed (photo).
3   Adjust the front cable adjusting nut so that when the handbrake control lever is pulled with average driver effort the number of notches is as follows (photo):

    Rigid axle – centre-lever type: 5 to 6 notches
               – stick-type: 9 to 11 notches
    IRS   5 to 6 notches

4   Check that each wheel cylinder lever is returned to its original position when the handbrake control lever is in the fully off position and that the rear cables are not slack.

22 Handbrake front cable - removal and refitting

Stick-type control lever

1   Chock the front wheels, jack up the rear of the car and support on

firmly based stands.
2   Release the handbrake and remove the return spring.
3   Slacken the adjuster to locknut and separate the front cable from the control stem.
4   Undo and remove the nuts that secure the cable to the dash panel and remove the cable from the bulkhead side.
5   Refitting the front cable is the reverse sequence to removal. Apply a little lithium based grease to all moving parts and then adjust the cable as described in Section 21.

Centre-type control lever (Fig. 9.23)

6   Remove the console box as described in Chapter 12.
7   Disconnect the terminal from the handbrake warning light switch.
8   Remove the bolts securing the handbrake control lever to the floor. Remove the rubber grommet.
9   Remove the lockplate, adjusting nut and locknut.
10   Pull the cable into the car and remove it together with the control lever assembly.
11   Separate the front cable from the handbrake lever by breaking the securing pin and renew the front cable.
12   Refitting is the reverse of the removal sequence. Adjust the handbrake as described in Section 21.

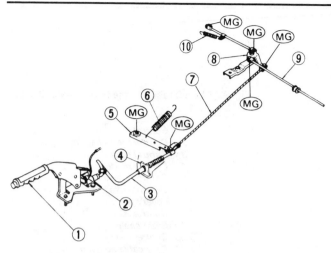

Fig. 9.23 Handbrake linkage – centre lever type (810 – rigid axle model) (Sec 22)

1	Control lever	6	Return spring
2	Brake warning switch	7	Rear cable
3	Front cable	8	Swing arm
4	Cable lockplate	9	Cross rod
5	Centre lever	10	Parking return spring

23 Handbrake rear cable - removal and refitting

IRS model (610 series)
1   Chock the front wheels, jack up the rear of the car and support on firmly based stands.
2   Working under the car disconnect the rear cable at the adjuster.
3   Detach the return spring from the centre lever.
4   Carefully pull out the lockplates and then withdraw the clevis pins which connect the rear cable to the rear wheel cylinder levers.

IRS model (810 series)
5   Unhook the return spring from the centre lever and disconnect the

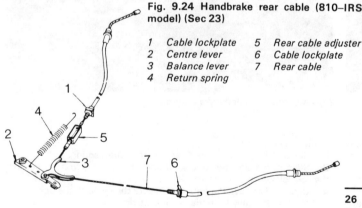

Fig. 9.24 Handbrake rear cable (810–IRS model) (Sec 23)

1	Cable lockplate	5	Rear cable adjuster
2	Centre lever	6	Cable lockplate
3	Balance lever	7	Rear cable
4	Return spring		

Fig. 9.26 Location of check valve (Sec 25)

rear cable at the adjuster.
6   Remove the cable lockplates from the rear suspension.
7   Remove the brake drum as described in Section 12.
8   Disconnect the rear cable from the adjuster lever and detach the spring. Disconnect the rear cable by lighly tapping the steel portion mating with the backplate.

Rigid axle model
9   Working under the car, detach the pull spring.
10   Remove the clevis pin on the balance lever side and on the wheel side and detach the crossrod.
11   Remove the nut which secures the crossrod balance lever from the rear axle housing.
12   Refitting the rear cable is the reverse sequence to removal. Lubricate all moving parts with a lithium based grease.

24 Handbrake control (stick type) - removal and refitting

1   Disconnect the terminal connector from the handbrake warning light switch.
2   Undo and remove the nuts securing the control bracket to the dash panel.
3   Withdraw the spring pin and cotter pin connecting the control guide with the control bracket. Lower the assembly and lift away from inside the car.
4   Refitting the control is the reverse sequence to removal. Lubricate all moving parts with a little lithium based grease. It may be necessary to adjust the handbrake as described in Section 21.

25 Check valve - removal and refitting

On models fitted with a vacuum servo unit a small check valve is fitted in the vacuum line and attached to the bulkhead. If its operation is suspect the car should be taken to the local dealer for a pressure test.
1   To remove the valve, undo and remove the securing bracket retaining screws and lift away the bracket. Slacken the two clips and detach the two hoses.
2   Refitting the check valve is the reverse sequence to removal.

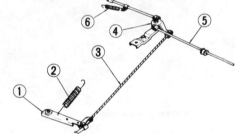

Fig. 9.25 Handbrake rear cable (rigid axle) (Sec 23)

1	Centre lever	4	Swing arm
2	Return spring	5	Cross rod
3	Rear cable	6	Parking return spring

26 Flexible brake hoses - inspection, removal and refitting

1   Periodically inspect the condition of the flexible brake hoses. If they appear swollen, chafed or when bent double with the fingers tiny cracks are visible, then they must be renewed (photo).
2   Always uncouple the rigid pipe from the flexible hose first, then release the end of the flexible hose from the support bracket. Now unscrew the flexible hose from the caliper or connector. If this method is followed, no kinking of the hose will occur.
3   When installing the hose, always use a new copper sealing washer.
4   When installation is complete, check that the flexible hose does not rub against the tyre or other adjacent components. Its attitude may be altered to overcome this by releasing its bracket support locknut and twisting the hose in the required direction by not more than one quarter turn.
5   Bleed the hydraulic system (Section 4).

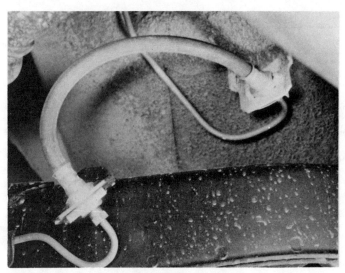
26.1 Inspect the condition of flexible brake hoses

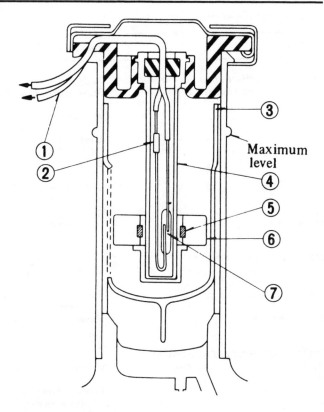

Fig. 9.27 Brake level fluid gauge (Sec 30)

Maximum level

1	Lead wire	5	Magnet
2	Resistor	6	Float
3	Filter	7	Lead switch
4	Case		

27 Rigid brake lines - inspection, removal and refitting

1   At regular intervals wipe the steel brake pipes clean and examine them for signs of rust or denting caused by flying stones.
2   Examine the fit of the pipes in their insulated securing clips and bend the tongues of the clips if necessary to ensure a positive fit.
3   Check that the pipes are not touching any adjacent components or rubbing against any part of the vehicle. Where this is observed, bend the pipe gently away to clear.
4   Any section of pipe which is rusty or chafed should be renewed. Brake pipes are available to the correct length and fitted with end unions from most Datsun dealers and can be made to pattern by many accessory suppliers. When installing the new pipes use the old pipes as a guide to bending and do not make any bends sharper than is necessary.
5   The system will of course have to be bled when the circuit has been reconnected.

28 Brake line pressure differential warning light switch

1   Models destined for certain markets have a warning light on the instrument panel to warn the driver when a pressure difference of 185 - 242 lbf/in^2 (13 - 17 kgf/cm^2) exists between the front and rear brake hydraulic systems.
2   A hydraulically operated warning light switch is mounted in the engine compartment and is connected to the front and rear brake systems.
3   When there is a pressure difference of 185 - 242 lbf/in^2 (13 - 17 kgf cm^2) between the two brake systems the internal valves will move towards the side with the lower pressure. The valve contacts the switch and the warning light circuit is completed.
4   Regularly check the valve unit for leaks which, if evident, must be corrected. Should the switch develop an internal fault it must be renewed as a complete unit.

29 NP (Nissan proportioning) valve - general

1   The NP valve completely separates the front and rear brake lines, allowing them to function independently, and preventing the rear

brakes from locking before the front brakes.
2   Damage, such as brake line leakage, in either the front or rear brake, will not affect the normal operation of the system.
3   It is recommended that every 24 000 miles (40 000 Km) valve operation be checked for correct operation. Remove all luggage and then drive the car to a dry concrete road. With the car travelling at 30 mph (50 kph) apply the brakes suddenly.
4   The valve is functioning normally when the rear wheels lock simultaneously with the front wheels or when the front wheels lock before the rear wheels.
5   Should the rear wheels lock before the front wheels then it is probable that the NP valve has developed an internal fault and it should be renewed.

30 Brake fluid level gauge

1   A brake fluid level gauge is fitted into the reservoir on some models and is designed to light the brake warning light on the instrument panel when the level of fluid falls below a certain level in the reservoir.
2   The float rides on the surface of the hydraulic fluid and when the level drops to the danger point, a magnet in the float operates a switch so completing the circuit.
3   To check the operation of the switch, with the ignition switched on, but the engine not running, slowly raise the cap and ascertain that the brake warning light is extinguished when the float is raised up to the cap.

See overleaf for 'Fault diagnosis – braking system'

31 Fault diagnosis – braking system

Symptom	Reason/s	Remedy
Pedal travels almost to floor before brakes operate		
Leaks and air bubbles in hydraulic system	Brake fluid level too low	Top up master cylinder reservoir. Check for leaks
	Wheel cylinder or caliper leaking	Dismantle wheel cylinder or caliper, clean, fit new rubbers and bleed brakes
	Master cylinder leaking (bubbles in master cylinder fluid)	Dismantle master cylinder, clean and fit new rubbers. Bleed brakes
	Brake flexible hose leaking	Examine and fit new hose if old hose leaking. Bleed brakes
	Brake line fractured	Replace with new brake pipe. Bleed brakes
	Brake system union loose	Check all unions in brake system and tighten as necessary. Bleed brakes
Normal wear	Linings over 75% worn	Fit new shoes and brake linings or pads
	Brakes badly out of adjustment	Jack up car and adjust brakes
Brake pedal feels springy		
Brake lining renewal	New linings not yet bedded-in	Use brakes gently until springy pedal feeling leaves
Excessive wear or damage	Brake drums or discs badly worn and weak or cracked	Fit new brake drums or discs
Lack of maintenance	Master cylinder securing nuts loose	Tighten master cylinder securing nuts. Ensure spring washers are fitted
Brake pedal feels spongy and soggy		
Leaks or bubbles in hydraulic system	Wheel cylinder or caliper leaking	Dismantle wheel cylinder or caliper, clean, fit new rubbers and bleed brakes
	Master cylinder leaking (bubbles in master cylinder reservoir)	Dismantle master cylinder, clean, and fit new rubbers and bleed brakes. Renew cylinder if internal walls scored
	Brake pipe or flexible hose leaking	Fit new pipe or hose
	Unlons in brake system loose	Examine for leaks, tighten as necessary
Excessive effort required to brake car		
Lining type of condition	Linings badly worn	Fit new brake shoes and linings or pads
	New linings recently fitted – not yet bedded-in	Use brakes gently until braking effort normal
	Harder linings fitted than standard causing increase in pedal pressure	Remove linings and replace with manufacturers recommended linings
Oil or grease leaks	Linings and brake drums or discs contaminated with oil, grease, or hydraulic fluid	Rectify source of leak, clean brake drums or discs, fit new linings
Brakes uneven and pulling to one side		
Oil or grease leaks	Linings and brake drums or discs contaminated with oil, grease or hydraulic fluid	Ascertain and rectify source of leak, clean brake drums or discs, fit new linings
Lack of maintenance	Tyre pressure unequal	Check and inflate as necessary
	Radial ply tyres fitted at one side of car only	Fit radial ply tyres of the same make to all four wheels
	Brake backplate loose	Tighten backplate securing nuts and bolts
	Brake shoes fitted incorrectly	Remove and fit shoes correct way round
	Different type of linings fitted at each wheel	Fit the linings specified by the manufacturers all round
	Anchorages for front or rear suspension loose	Tighten front and rear suspension pick-up points
	Brake drums or discs badly worn, cracked or distorted	Fit new brake drums or discs
Brakes tend to bind, drag, or lock on		
Incorrect adjustment	Brake shoes adjusted too tightly	Slacken off brake shoe adjusters
	Handbrake cable over-tightened	Slacken off handbrake cable adjustment
Wear or dirt in hydraulic system or incorrect fluid	Reservoir vent hole in cap blocked with dirt	Clean and blow through hole
	Master cylinder by-pass port restricted brakes seize in 'on' position	Dismantle, clean and overhaul master cylinder Bleed brakes
	Wheel cylinder or caliper seizes in 'on' position	Dismantle, clean and overhaul wheel cylinder or caliper. Bleed brakes
Mechanical wear	Brake shoe pull off springs broken, stretched or loose	Examine springs and replace if worn or loose
Incorrect brake assembly	Brake shoe pull off springs fitted wrong round, omitted, or wrong type used	Examine and rectify as appropriate
Neglect	Handbrake system rusted or seized in the 'on' position	Apply a freeing agent to free, clean and lubricate

Chapter 10 Electrical system

Contents

Specifications

Battery

Type	Lead acid
Voltage	12 volts
Polarity	Negative earth

Alternator

Make	Hitachi		
Type	LT130 - 41	LT150 - 05B	LT160 -19
Nominal rating	12V - 35A	12V - 50A	12V - 60A
Earth polarity	Negative	Negative	Negative
Output current	22 Amps	37.5 Amps	45 Amps
Pulley ratio	2.25 : 1	2.25 : 1	2.09 : 1

Voltage regulator

Model	TLIZ - 58
Regulating voltage	14.3 to 15.3 V at 20° C
Voltage coil resistance	10.5 ohms
Core gap	0.0236 - 0.0394 in (0.6 - 1.0 mm)
Point gap	0.0118 - 0.0157 in (0.3 - 0.4 mm)
Charge relay	
Release voltage	4.2 - 5.2 at 'N' terminal
Voltage coil resistance	37.8 ohms at 20° C (68° F)
Core gap	0.0315 - 0.0394 in (0.8 - 1.0 mm)
Point gap	0.0157 - 0.0236 in (0.4 - 0.6 mm)

Starter motor

Make		Hitachi	
Type		S114 - 103P (manual transmission)	S114 - 126M (automatic trnasmission)
Voltage		12V	12V
Output		1.0 kW	1.2 kW
Starting current		Less than 430A (6V)	Less than 540A (5V)
No load current		Less than 60A (12V)	Less than 60A (12V)
Shift type of pinion gear		Magnetic shift	Magnetic shift
Number of teeth on pinion		9	9
Number of teeth on ring gear		120	120
Brush length – new		0.7283 in (18.5 mm)	0.7283 in (18.5 mm)
Minimum brush length		0.4921 in (12.5 mm)	0.4921 in (12.5 mm)

Fusible link

Colour	Size, sq. in (mm²)	Continuous current	Max current (fuse melts in 5 secs)
Brown	0.0005 (0.3)	11A	Approx 60A
Red	0.0013 (0.85)	26A	Approx 250A

Bulb specification – 610 series

Bulb	General areas (Watts)	USA and Canada (Watts)
Headlamp	50/37.5	50/37.5
	37.5	37.5
Front combination lamp		
Turn signal/Parking lamp	-	27/8.3 (32/3)
Turn signal and Parking lamp	21 & 5	-
Side flasher lamp	5	-
Side marker lamp	-	8 (4)
Rear combination lamp		
Stop/Tail lamp	21/5	27/8.3 (32/3)
Turn signal lamp	21	27 (32)
Reverse lamp	21	27 (32)
Reverse lamp (Hardtop)	-	27 (32)
Number plate lamp	7.5	7.5 (6)
Number plate lamp (Europe)	5	-
Interior lamps		
Front	10	10 (-)
Rear	10	10 (-)
Boot	6	6 (-)

Bulb specifications – 810 series

Item	Capacity	Quantity
Headlamp (sealed beam)	12V-37.5/50W (High/Low)	4/2
Headlamp (semi-sealed)	12V-45/40W High/Low	4/2
Turn signal lamp	12V-21W	4
Side turn signal lamp	12V-5W	2
Clearance lamp	12V-5W	2
Stop and tail lamp	12V-21/5W	4 (2 for Station Wagon and Van)
Reverse lamp	12V-21W	2
Number plate lamp	12V-5W	2
Interior lamp	12V-10W	1
Meter illumination lamp	12V-3.4W	5 (6 for SSS model)
Key lamp	12V-1.4W	1
Main beam pilot lamp	12V-3.4W	1
Turn signal pilot lamp	12V-3.4W	2
Hazard warning lamp	12V-3.4W	1
Clock illumination lamp	12V-3.4W	1
Heater illumination lamp	12V-3.4W	1
Radio illumination lamp	12V-3.4W	1
Glove box lamp	12V-3.4W	1
Cigarette lighter illumination lamp	12V-3.4W	1
Ash tray lamp	12V-3.4W	1
Indicator lamp	12V-3.4W	1
Boot lamp (Saloon and Coupe)	12V-5W	1
Luggage boot lamp (Station Wagon)	12V-10W	1

Circuit colour code
Circuit system

Starting and ignition system
Charging system
Lighting system
Signal system
Instrument system
Others
Earth system

Standard colour	Supplementary colour	Supplementary colour to standard colour
B (Black)	W, Y	
W (White)	B, R, L	Y
R (Red)	W, B, G, Y, L	
G (Green)	W, B, R, Y, L	W, Br (Brown)
Y (Yellow)	W, B, G, R, L	
L (Blue)	W, R; Y	Y, Br, Lg (Light green)
B (Black)		

1 General description

The electrical system is 12 volt negative earth and the major components comprise a 12 volt battery, an alternator which is driven from the crankshaft pulley and a starter motor.

The battery supplies a steady current for the ignition, lighting, and other electrical circuits and provides a reserve of electricity when the current consumed by the electrical equipment exceeds that being produced by the alternator.

The alternator has a regulator which ensures a high output if the battery is in a low state of charge or the demand from the electrical equipment is high, and a low output if the battery is fully charged and there is little demand for the electrical equipment.

When fitting electrical accessories to cars with a negative earth system it is important, if they contain silicone diodes or transistors, that they are connected correctly, otherwise serious damage may result to the components concerned. Items such as radios, tape recorders, electric ignition systems, automatic headlight dipping etc., should all be checked for correct polarity.

It is important that the battery negative lead is always disconnected if the battery is to be boost-charged. Also if body repairs are to be carried out using electric arc welding equipment, the alternator must be disconnected otherwise serious damage can be caused to the more delicate instruments. Whenever the battery has to be disconnected it must always be reconnected with the negative terminal earthed.

2 Battery – removal and refitting

1 The battery should be removed once every three months for cleaning and testing. Disconnect the negative, then the positive, lead from the battery terminals by slackening the clamp bolts and lifting away the clamps (photo).

2 Undo and remove the nuts securing the clamps. Lift away the clamps. Carefully lift the battery from its carrier and hold it level to ensure that none of the electrolyte is spilled

3 Refitment is a direct reversal of the removal procedure. Fit the positive, then the negative, lead, and smear the terminals and clamps with vaseline to prevent corrosion. **NEVER use an ordinary grease.**

3 Battery – maintenance and inspection

1 Normal weekly battery maintenance consists of checking the electrolyte level of each cell to ensure that the separators are covered by $\frac{1}{4}$ inch of electrolyte. If the level has fallen top up the battery using distilled water only. Do not overfill. If a battery is overfilled or any electrolyte spilled, immediately wipe away and neutralize the excess as electrolyte attacks and corrodes very rapidly any metal it comes into contact with (photo).

2 As well as keeping the terminals clean and covered with petroleum jelly, the top of the battery, and especially the top of the cells, should be kept clean and dry. This helps to prevent corrosion and ensures that the battery does not become partially discharged by leakage through dampness and dirt.

3 Once every three months remove the battery and inspect the clamp nuts, clamps, tray and battery leads for corrosion (white fluffy deposits on the metal brittle to the touch). If any corrosion is found, clean off the deposits with ammonia and paint over the clean metal with an anti-rust/anti-acid paint.

4 At the same time inspect the battery case for cracks. If a crack is found, clean and plug it with one of the proprietary compounds marketed. If leakage through the crack has been excessive it will be necessary to refill the appropriate cell with fresh electrolyte as detailed later. Cracks are frequently caused to the top of a battery case by pouring in distilled water in the middle of winter *after,* instead of *before,* a run. This gives the water no chance to mix with the electrolyte and so the former freezes and splits the battery case.

5 If topping up the battery becomes excessive and the case has been inspected for cracks that could cause leakage, but none are found, the battery is being overcharged and the alternator control unit will have to be checked and reset.

6 With the battery on the bench, at the three monthly interval check, measure its specific gravity with a hydrometer to determine the state of the charge and condition of the electrolyte. There should be very little variation between the different cells and, if variation in excess of

2.1 The battery is located in the engine compartment

3.1 Checking the level of the electrolyte

0.025 is present, it will be due to either:-

(a) Loss of electrolyte from the battery caused by spillage or a leak resulting in a drop in the specific gravity of the electrolyte, when the deficiency was replaced with distilled water instead of fresh electrolyte.

(b) An internal short circuit caused by a buckled plate or a similar malady pointing to the likelihood of total battery failure in the near future

7   The specific gravity of the electrolyte from fully charged conditions at the electrolyte temperature indicated is listed in Table A. The specific gravity of a fully discharged battery at different temperatures of the electrolyte is given in Table B.

8   Specific gravity is measured by drawing up into the body of a hydrometer sufficient electrolyte to allow the indicator to float freely. The level at which the indicator floats show the specific gravity.

TABLE A

Specific gravity – battery fully charged

1.268 at 100°F or 38°C electrolyte temperature
1.272 at 90°F or 32°C electrolyte temperature
1.276 at 80°F or 27°C electrolyte temperature
1.280 at 70°F or 21°C electrolyte temperature
1.284 at 60°F or 16°C electrolyte temperature
1.288 at 50°F or 10°C electrolyte temperature
1.292 at 40°F or 4°C electrolyte temperature
1.296 at 30°F or -1.5°C electrolyte temperature

TABLE B

Specific gravity – battery fully discharged

1.098 at 100°F or 38°C electrolyte temperature
1.102 at 90°F or 32°C electrolyte temperature
1.106 at 80°F or 27°C electrolyte temperature
1.110 at 70°F or 21°C electrolyte temperature
1.114 at 60°F or 16°C electrolyte temperature
1.118 at 50°F or 10°C electrolyte temperature
1.122 at 40°F or 4°C electrolyte temperature
1.126 at 30°F or -1.5°C electrolyte temperature

4   Electrolyte – replenishment

1   If the battery is in a fully charged state and one of the cells maintains a specific gravity reading which is 0.025 or lower than the others and a check of each cell has been made with a voltmeter to check for short circuits (a four to seven second test should give a steady reading of between 1.2 and 1.8 volts), then it is likely that electrolyte has been lost from the cell with the low reading at some time.

2   Top up the cell with a solution of 1 part sulphuric acid to 2.5 parts of water. If the cell is already fully topped up draw some electrolyte out of it with the hydrometer. The total capacity of each cell is approximately $\frac{1}{3}$ pint.

3   When mixing the sulphuric acid and water *NEVER ADD WATER TO SULPHURIC ACID* - always pour the acid slowly onto the water in a glass container; stir continuously to keep the temperature down. *IF WATER IS ADDED TO SULPHURIC ACID IT WILL EXPLODE.*

5   Battery – charging

1   In winter time when a heavy demand is placed on the battery, such as when starting from cold, and much electrical equipment is continually in use, it is a good idea to occasionally have the battery fully charged from an external source at a rate of 3.5 to 4 amps.

2   Continue to charge the battery at this rate until no further rise in specific gravity is noted over a four hour period.

3   Alternatively, a trickle charger, charging at the rate of 1.5 amps can be safely used overnight.

4   Special rapid 'boost' charges which are claimed to restore the power of the battery in 1 to 2 hours are damaging unless they are thermostatically controlled as they can cause buckling resulting in the shedding of active material from the plates and the possibility of internal shorts.

6   Alternator – general description

The alternator is of the rotating field, ventilated design. It comprises principally, a laminated stator on which is wound a star connected 3 phase output; and an 8 pole rotor carrying the field windings.

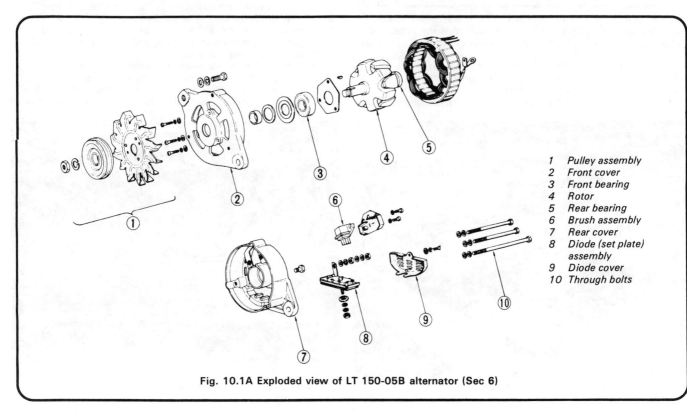

1   Pulley assembly
2   Front cover
3   Front bearing
4   Rotor
5   Rear bearing
6   Brush assembly
7   Rear cover
8   Diode (set plate) assembly
9   Diode cover
10   Through bolts

Fig. 10.1A Exploded view of LT 150-05B alternator (Sec 6)

The front and rear ends of thr shaft run in ball races each of which is lubricated for life and natural finish die cast end brackets incorporating the mounting lugs.

The rotor is belt driven from the engine through a pulley keyed to the rotor shaft and a pressed steel fan adjacent to the pulley draws cooling air through the machine. This fan forms an integral part of the alternator specifications., It has been designed to provide adequate air flow with minimum noise and to withstand the high stresses associated with maximum speed.

The brush gear of the field system is mounted in the slip ring end brackets. Two carbon brushes bear against a pair of concentric brass slip rings carried on a moulded disc attached to the end of the rotor. Also attached to the slip ring end bracket are six silicone diodes connected in a three phase bridge to rectify the generated alternating current for use in charging the battery and supplying power to the electrical system.

The alternator output is controlled by an electric voltage regulator unit and warning light control unit to indicate to the driver when all is not well.

7 Alternator – maintenance

1   The equipment has been designed for the minimum maintenance in service, the only items being subject to wear are the brushes and bearings.
2   Brushes should be examined after about 75 000 miles (120 000 km) and renewed if necessary. The bearings are pre-packed with grease for life and should not require further attention.
3   Check the V-belt regularly for correct adjustment as described in Chapter 2, Section 11.

8 Alternator – special procedures

Whenever the electrical system of the car is being attended to or an external means of starting the engine is used there are certain precautions that **MUST** be taken otherwise serious and expensive damage can result.
1   Always make sure that the negative terminal of the battery is earthed. If the terminal connections are accidently reversed or if the battery has been reverse charged the alternator will burn out.
2   The output terminal of the alternator must never be earthed but should always be connected directly to the positive terminal of the battery.
3   Whenever the alternator is to be removed, or when disconnecting, the terminals of the alternator circuit, always disconnect the battery first.
4   The alternator must never be operated without the battery to alternator cable connected.
5   If the battery is to be charged by external means always disconnect both battery cables before the external charge is connected.
6   Should it be necessary to use a booster charger or booster battery to start the engine always **DOUBLE** check that the negative cables are connected to negative terminals and positive cables to positive terminals.

9 Alternator – removal and refitting

1   Disconnect both battery leads, negative first.
2   Make a note of the terminal connections at the rear of the alternator and disconnect the cables and terminal connector.
3   Undo and remove the alternator adjustment arm bolt, slacken the alternator mounting bolts and remove the V-drive belt from the pulley.
4   Remove the remaining two mounting bolts and carefully lift the alternator away from the car.
5   Take care not to knock or drop the alternator; this can cause irreparable damage.
6   Refitting the alternator is the reverse sequence to removal.
7   Adjust the V-belt tension as described in Chapter 2, Section 11.

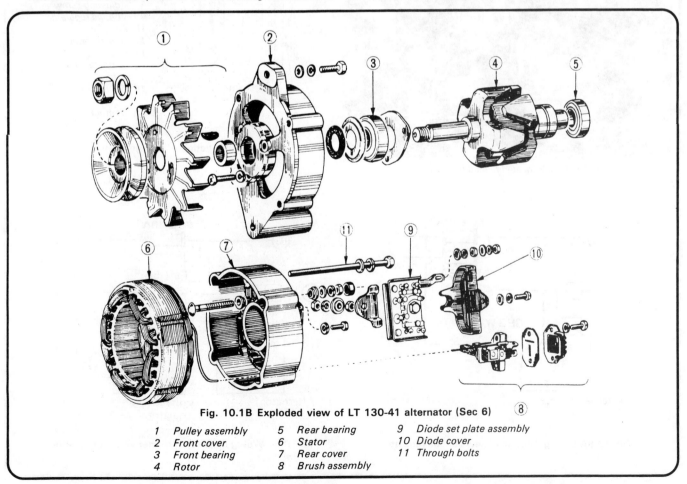

Fig. 10.1B Exploded view of LT 130-41 alternator (Sec 6)

1 Pulley assembly
2 Front cover
3 Front bearing
4 Rotor
5 Rear bearing
6 Stator
7 Rear cover
8 Brush assembly
9 Diode set plate assembly
10 Diode cover
11 Through bolts

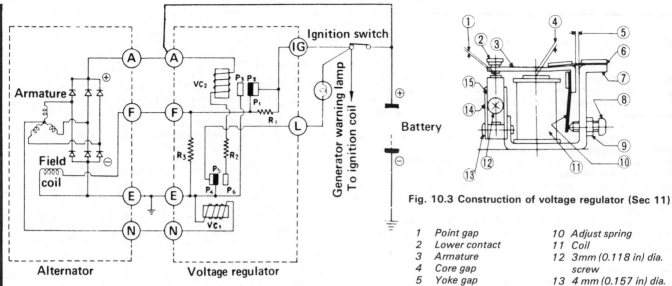

Fig. 10.2 Battery charging circuit (Sec 9)

Fig. 10.3 Construction of voltage regulator (Sec 11)

1	Point gap	10	Adjust spring
2	Lower contact	11	Coil
3	Armature	12	3mm (0.118 in) dia. screw
4	Core gap		
5	Yoke gap	13	4 mm (0.157 in) dia. screw
6	Connecting spring		
7	Yoke	14	Contact set
8	Adjusting screw	15	Upper contact
9	Locknut		

11.0 The voltage regulator is located behind the battery

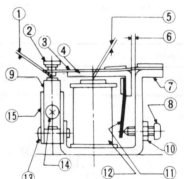

1	Point gap
2	Charge relay contact
3	Connecting spring
4	Armature
5	Core gap
6	Yoke gap
7	Yoke
8	Adjusting screw
9	Voltage regulator contact
10	Locknut
11	Adjust spring
12	Coil
13	3 mm (0.118 in) dia. screw
14	4 mm (0.157 in) dia. screw
15	Contact set

Fig. 10.4 Construction of charge relay (Sec 11)

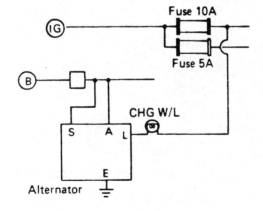

Fig. 10.5A Wiring diagram of new voltage regulator

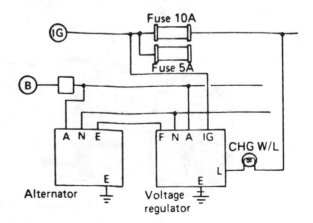

Fig. 10.5B Wiring diagram of former voltage regulator

10 Alternator – fault finding and repair

Due to the specialist knowledge and equipment required to test and service an alternator it is recommended that if the performance is suspect, the car be taken to an automobile electrician who will have the facilities for such work. Because of this recommendation no further detailed service information is given.

11 Voltage regulator – description

The regulator basically comprises a voltage regulator and a charge relay. The voltage regulator has two sets of contact points, lower and upper sets to control the alternator voltage. An armature plate placed between the two sets of contacts, moves upward, downward or vibrates. When closed the lower contacts complete the field circuit direct to earth, and the upper contacts when closed, complete the field circuit to earth through a field coil resistance and thereby produces the alternator output (photo).

The charge relay is basically similar to that of the voltage regulator. When the upper contacts are closed the ignition warning light extinguishes. The construction of the voltage regulator is basically identical to the charge relay. If the regulator performance is suspect refer to the recommendations given in Section 10.

On later models to improve performance an integrated circuit regulator has replaced the Tirrill voltage regulator. This regulator is built into the alternator. This can be interchanged with the old system as a set of alternator and main harness.

12 Starter motor – general description

The starter motor comprises a solenoid, a lever, starter drive gear and the motor. The solenoid is fitted to the top of the motor. The plunger inside the solenoid is connected to a centre pivoting lever the other end of which is in contact with the drive sleeve and drive gear.

When the ignition switch is operated, current from the battery flows through the series and shunt solenoid coils thereby magnetizing the solenoid. The plunger is drawn into the solenoid so that it operates the lever and moves the drive pinion into the starter ring gear. The solenoid switch contacts close after the drive pinion is partially engaged with the ring gear.

When the solenoid switch contacts are closed the starter motor rotates the engine while at the same time cutting current flow to the series coil in the solenoid. The shunt coils magnetic pull is now sufficient to hold the pinion in mesh with the ring gear.

When the engine is running and the driver releases the ignition switch so breaking the solenoid contact, a reverse current will flow through the series coil and a magnetic field will build up this time in the same direction in which the plunger moves back, out of the solenoid. When this happens the resultant force of the magnetic field is in the shunt coil and the series coil will be nil. A return spring then actuates ther lever causing it to draw the plunger out which will allow the solenoid switch contact to open. The starter motor stops.

An over-running clutch is fitted to give a more positive mesh engagement and disengagement of the pinion and ring gear. It uses a lever to slide the pinion along the armature shaft in or out of mesh with the ring gear. The over-run clutch is designed to transmit driving torque from the motor armature to the ring gear but also permits the pinion to over-run the armature after the engine has started.

13 Starter motor – testing on engine

1   If the starter motor fails to operate then check the condition of the battery by turning on the headlights. If they glow brightly for several seconds and then gradually dim, the battery is in an undercharged condition.

2   If the headlights continue to glow brightly and it is obvious that the battery is in good condition, then check the tightness of the earth lead from the battery terminal to its connection on the body frame. Also check the positive battery lead connections. Check the tightness of the connections at the rear of the solenoid. If available check the wiring with a voltmeter or test light for breaks or short circuits.

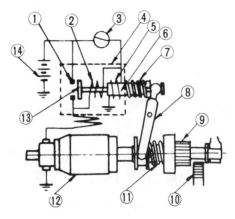

Fig. 10.6 Starter motor circuit (Sec 12)

1	Stationary contact	8	Shift lever
2	Series coil	9	Drive pinion
3	Ignition switch	10	Ring gear
4	Solenoid	11	Pinion sleeve spring
5	Shunt coil	12	Armature
6	Plunger	13	Movable contactor
7	Return spring	14	Battery

3   If the wiring is in order check the starter motor for continuity using a voltmeter.

4   If the battery is fully charged, the wiring is in order and the motor electrical circuit continuous and it still fails to operate, then it will have to be removed from the engine for examination. Before this is done, however, make sure that the pinion gear has not jammed in mesh with the ring gear due either to a broken solenoid spring or dirty pinion gear splines. To release the pinion, engage a low gear (not automatic) and with the ignition switched off, rock the car backwards and forwards which should release the pinion from mesh with the ring gear; if the pinion still remains jammed the starter motor must be removed.

14 Starter motor – removal and refitting

1   Disconnect the earth cable from the battery negative terminal.

2   Disconnect the black and yellow wire from the solenoid and the black cable from the battery terminal on the cover of the solenoid.

3   Remove the starter motor securing bolts, pull the starter forward, tilt it slightly to clear the motor shaft support from the flywheel ring gear and lift it away from the engine.

4   Refitting is the reversal of the removal sequence.

15 Starter motor – dismantling, servicing and reassembly

The starter motor fitted to cars with automatic transmission is of a heavy duty type but the information given in this Section applies to both types.

1   With the starter motor exterior clean place on the bench.

2   Slacken the nut securing the connecting plate to the solenoid 'M' terminal.

3   Undo and remove the three screws and spring washers that secure the solenoid to starter motor. Carefully lift away the solenoid.

4   Undo and remove the two long through bolts and spring washers retaining the brush cover. Lift away the brush cover.

5   Using a soft faced hammer carefully tap the side of the yoke at the pinion end and withdraw the yoke from over the armature.

6   Push the stop ring to the clutch side and carefully remove the circlip. Remove the stop ring and then the over-running clutch from the end of the armature shaft.

7   At this stage if the brushes are to be renewed, their flexible connectors must be unsoldered and the connectors of new brushes soldered in their place. Brushes should always be renewed when their length is less than the minimum specified.

8   Check that the brushes move freely in their holders. If they tend to stick then wash them with a petrol moistened cloth and, if necessary,

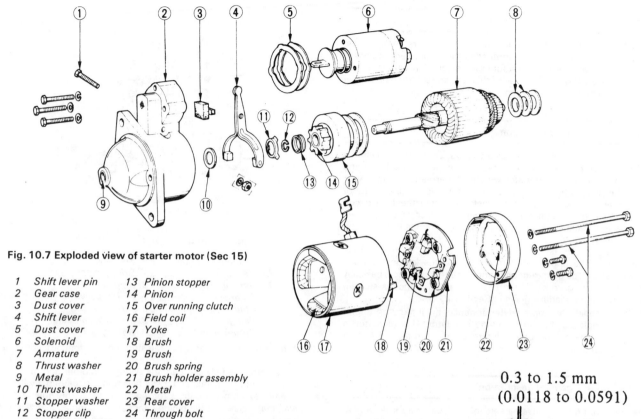

Fig. 10.7 Exploded view of starter motor (Sec 15)

1	Shift lever pin	13	Pinion stopper
2	Gear case	14	Pinion
3	Dust cover	15	Over running clutch
4	Shift lever	16	Field coil
5	Dust cover	17	Yoke
6	Solenoid	18	Brush
7	Armature	19	Brush
8	Thrust washer	20	Brush spring
9	Metal	21	Brush holder assembly
10	Thrust washer	22	Metal
11	Stopper washer	23	Rear cover
12	Stopper clip	24	Through bolt

lightly polish the sides of the brushes with a very fine file, until the brushes move quite freely in their holders.

9   Clean the commutator with a petrol moistened rag. If this fails to remove all the dark areas and spots, then wrap a piece of glasspaper round the commutator and rotate the armature.

10 If the commutator is very badly worn then it will have to be mounted in a lathe and with the lathe turning at high speed, skim the commutator and finish the surface by polishing with glass paper. If necessary, undercut the insulating mica so that the depth of it is from 0.0197 - 0.0315 inch (0.5 - 0.8 mm) using an old hacksaw blade ground to suit.

11 With the starter motor dismantled, test the four field coils for an open circuit. Connect a 12 volt battery with a 12 volt bulb in one of the leads between the field terminal post and the tapping points of the field coils to which the brushes are connected. An open circuit is proved by the bulb not lighting.

12 If the bulb lights, it does not necessarily mean that the field coils are in order, as there is a possibility that one of the coils will be earthed to the starter yoke or pole shoes. To check this, remove the lead from the brush connector and place it against a clean position on the starter yoke. If the bulb lights the field coils are earthing. Refitment of the field coils calls for the use of a wheel operated screwdriver, a soldering iron, caulking and riveting operations and is beyond the scope of the majority of owners. The starter yoke should be taken to a reputable electrical engineering works for new field coils to be fitted. Alternatively purchase an exchange starter motor.

13 If the armature is damaged this will be evident after visual inspection. Look for signs of burning, discolouration, and for conductors that have lifted away from the commutator.

14 Reassembly is the reverse sequence to removal. Locate a feeler gauge or vernier between the pinion front edge and the stopper. If the gap is not within the limits 0.012 - 0.059 inch (0.3 - 1.5 mm) new shim washers should be fitted.

16 Starter motor bushes – inspection and removal

1   With the starter motor stripped down check the condition of the bushes. They should be renewed when they are sufficiently worn to allow visible side movement of the armature shaft.

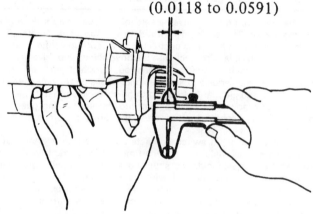

0.3 to 1.5 mm (0.0118 to 0.0591)

Fig. 10.8 Measuring the pinion front edge-to-stopper gap (Sec 15)

2   The old bushes are simply driven out with a suitable drift and new bushes inserted by the same method.

3   As the bushes are phosphor bronze it is essential that they are allowed to stand in SAE 30 engine oil for at least 24 hours before fitment.

17 Headlights – removal and refitting

1   To remove a headlight sealed beam unit first disconnect the battery.

2   Undo and remove the retaining screws securing either the radiator grille or the headlight finisher (photos).

3   Locate the headlight retaining ring screws and then loosen them. Do not disturb the beam alignment screws (photo).

4   The retaining ring may now be rotated clockwise and lifted away (photo).

5   Remove the headlight unit from the retaining ring and detach the terminal connector from the rear.

6   Refitting the sealed beam unit is the reverse sequence to removal. Ensure that the word 'top' on the lens is uppermost when fitted.

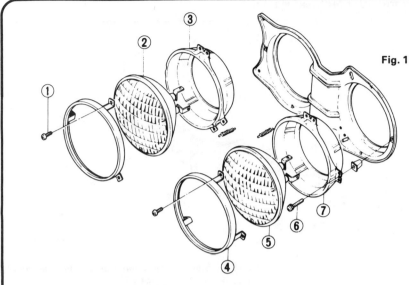

Fig. 10.9 Exploded view of headlamp assembly (Sec 17)

1 Screw
2 Headlamp beam
3 Headlamp mounting ring
4 Headlamp retaining ring
5 Headlamp beam
6 Aiming adjusting screw
7 Headlamp mounting ring

17.2a Removing headlight finisher securing screws

17.2b Headlight finisher removed

17.3 Loosening the headlight ring retaining screw

17.4 Removing the retaining ring

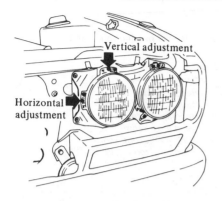

Fig. 10.10 Headlight beam aiming adjusting points (Sec 18)

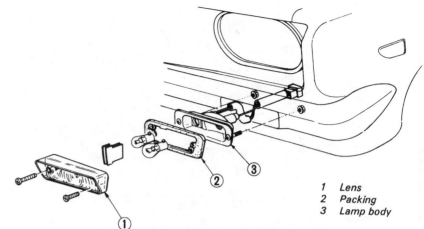

1   Lens
2   Packing
3   Lamp body

Fig. 10.11 Side and direction indicator light assembly (Sec 19)

18 Headlights – beam alignment

It is always advisable to have the beams reset by the local Datsun dealer who will have the necessary equipment to check and set the alignment correctly. Dual headlight units are difficult to set and without the special equipment can consume much time.

19 Side light and direction indicator bulbs – removal and refitting

1   Undo and remove the two screws securing the lens to the body. Lift away the lens taking care not to damage the seal (photo).
2   To detach the bulb press in and turn in an anti-clockwise direction to release the bayonet fixing. Lift away the bulb.
3   Refitting the bulb and lens is the reverse sequence to removal.
4   Should it be necessary to remove the complete light unit assembly, disconnect the cable connections to the light unit. On 810 models the unit is simply lifted away; on 610 models remove the flange nuts from the two mounting studs on the rear of the bumper and withdraw the unit.
5   Refitting the unit is the reverse of removal procedure. Ensure that the sealing gaskets are in good condition and correctly fitted.

19.1 Lifting away the lens

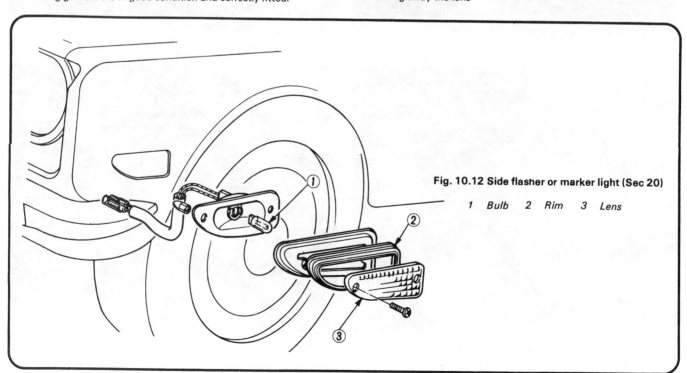

Fig. 10.12 Side flasher or marker light (Sec 20)

1   Bulb   2   Rim   3   Lens

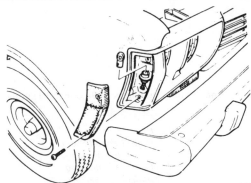

Fig. 10.13 Side marker lamp (later models) (Sec 20)

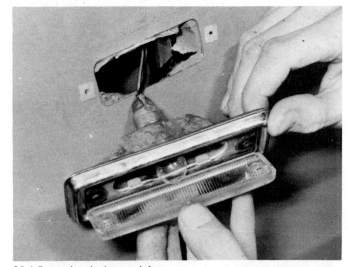

20.1 Removing the lens and rim

20 Side flasher or marker light

1 Undo and remove the two screws that secure the lens to the body. Lift away the lens and rim taking care not to damage the seal (photo).
2 To detach the bulb simply pull away from the socket.
3 Refitting the bulb, lens and rim is the reverse sequence to removal.
4 Should it be necessary to remove the complete light unit assembly first disconnect the battery.
5 Undo and remove the two screws that secure the lens to the body. Lift away the lens and rim taking care not to damage the seal.
6 Detach the cable connectors to the light unit and then draw it away from the front wing.
7 Refitting the unit is the reverse sequence to removal. Take care that the sealing gasket is in good condition and correctly fitted.

21 Rear direction indicator, stop and tail light bulb – removal and refitting

Saloon
1 Open the luggage compartment lid and, working at the rear of the unit, twist and pull out the socket and bulb assembly (Figs. 10.14/10.15).
2 To detach the bulb press in and turn in an anti-clockwise direction to release the bayonet fixing. Lift away the bulb.
3 Refitting the bulb and socket is the reverse sequence to removal.
4 Should it be necessary to remove the complete light unit assembly first disconnect the battery and then detach the cable connectors to the light unit.
5 Undo and remove the eight flange nuts at the rear of the unit.
6 Carefully draw the unit through the rear panel.
7 Refitting the unit is the reverse sequence to removal. Take care that sealing gaskets are in good condition and correctly fitted.

Estate Car
8 Undo and remove the three screws and washers and lift away the

lens taking care not to damage the sealing gasket (Figs. 10.16/10.17).
9 To detach, twist and pull the socket and bulb from the rear of the lens assembly.
10 To detach the bulb, press in and turn in an anti-clockwise direction to release the bayonet fixing. Lift away the bulb.
11 Refitting the bulb socket and lens assembly is the reverse sequence to removal.

22 Rear number plate light bulb – removal and refitting

Saloon models (single type)
1 Undo and remove the two lens cover securing screws and lift away the lens cover, lens and gasket. Take care not to damage the gasket (Figs. 10.18/10.19).
2 To detach the bulb, press in and turn in an anti-clockwise direction to release the bayonet fixing. Lift away the bulb.
3 Refitting the bulb and lens is the reverse sequence to removal.
4 Should it be necessary to remove the complete assembly, first disconnect the battery. Detach the cable connector to the light unit.
5 Undo and remove the three screws securing the light assembly to the bumper. Lift away the assembly.
6 Refitting the light assembly is the reverse sequence to removal.

Saloon models (double type)
7 Disconnect the battery earth cable.
8 Remove the two nuts securing the light assembly to the rear panel and disconnect the wiring at the connector.

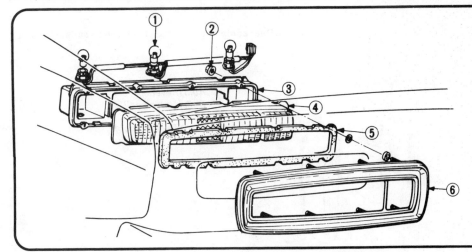

Fig. 10.14 Rear combination lamp – Saloon (610 series) (Sec 21)

1 Bulb
2 Flange nut
3 Lamp housing
4 Lens
5 Packing
6 Lens rim

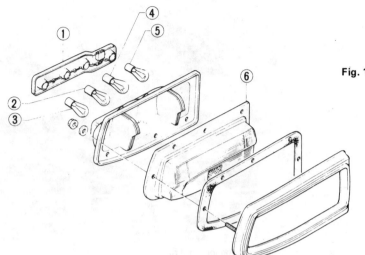

Fig. 10.15 Rear combination lamp – Saloon (810 series) (Sec 21)

1 Back cover
2 Bulb (Tail and Stop)
3 Bulb (Turn signal)
4 Bulb (Tail and Stop)
5 Bulb (Reverse)
6 Lens

9   Remove the light assembly.
10 Remove the socket from the assembly, push on the bulb, turn it anti-clockwise and remove it.
11 Refitting is the reverse of removal sequence.

Estate Car
12 Undo and remove the two screws securing the lens. Lift away the lens and gasket.
13 To detach the bulb, press in and turn in an anti-clockwise direction to release the bayonet fixing. Lift away the bulb.
14 Refitting the bulb and lens is the reverse sequence to removal.
15 Should it be necessary to remove the complete light unit assembly first disconnect the battery.
16 Remove the tailgate trim and then undo and remove the two tailgate handle securing nuts. Lift away the light assembly.
17 Refitting is a reversal of the removal procedure.

23 Reverse light unit – removal and refitting

1   Disconnect the battery earth cable and then detach the cable connectors to the light unit.
2   Refer to Section 21 and remove the left and right rear light assemblies.
3   Undo and remove the four flange nuts and draw the complete light assembly from the rear panel.
4   Refitting the light assembly is the reverse sequence to removal.

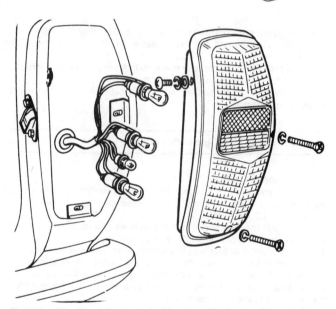

Fig. 10.16 Rear combination lamp – Estate (610 series) (Sec 21)

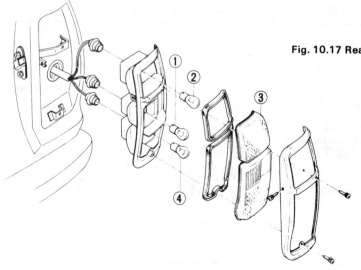

Fig. 10.17 Rear combination lamp – Estate (810 series) (Sec 21)

1 Bulb (Reverse)
2 Bulb (Turn signal)
3 Lens
4 Bulb (Tail and Stop)

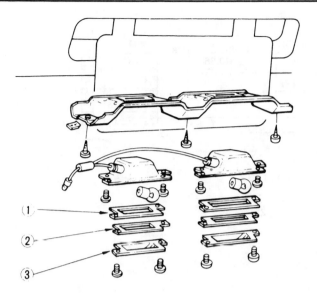

Fig. 10.18 Number plate lamp – Saloon (early 610 series)

1   Packing   2   Lens   3   Lens cover

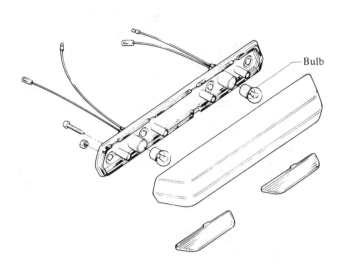

Fig. 10.19 Number plate lamp (single type) – Saloon (810 series)

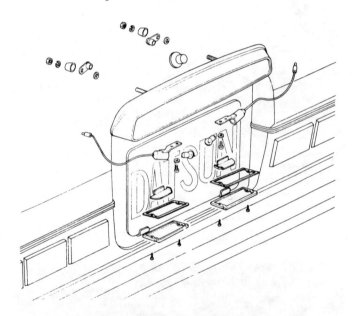

Fig. 10.20 Number plate lamp – Estate (610 series)

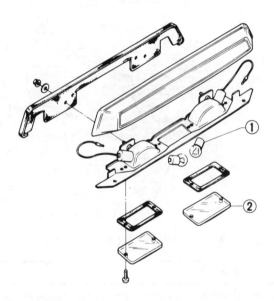

Fig. 10.21 Number plate lamp – Estate (810 series)

1   Bulb   2   Lens

8   Should it be necessary to remove the light unit first disconnect the battery for safety reasons.
9   Carefully detach the lens from the light body and then undo and remove the two retaining screws.
10 Draw the light body downward and disconnect the light leads from each connector.
11 Refitting the light assembly is the reverse sequence to removal.

---

25 Horn – fault tracing and rectification

1   If a horn works badly or fails completely first check the wiring leading to it for short circuit, blown fuse or loose connections. Also check that the horn is firmly secured and that there is nothing lying on the horn body (Fig. 10.22).
2   If a horn loses its adjustment it will not alter the pitch as the tone of a horn depends on the vibration of an air column. It will however give a softer or more harsh sound. Also excessive current will be required which is one cause for fuses to blow.
3   Further information on servicing is given in Section 26.

---

24 Interior light bulb – removal and refitting

Centre interior light

1   Carefully detach the lens from light body and unclip the festoon bulb.
2   Refitting the bulb and lens is the reverse sequence to removal.
3   Should it be necessary to remove the light unit first disconnect the battery.
4   Carefully pull on the light body and detach it from the roof panel. Disconnect the light leads at the connector.
5   Refitting the light assembly is the reverse sequence to removal. It will be observed that the assembly is held in position by spring pressure.

Rear interior light

6   Carefully detach the lens from the light body and unclip the festoon bulb.
7   Refitting the bulb and lens is the reverse sequence to removal.

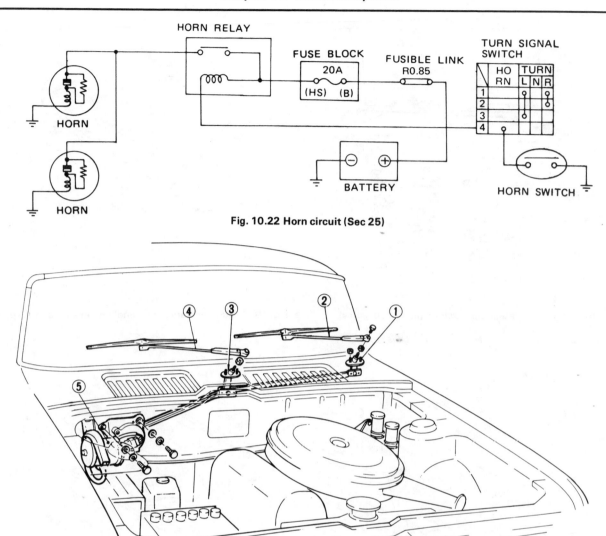

Fig. 10.22 Horn circuit (Sec 25)

Fig. 10.23 Windscreen wiper motor and linkage (Sec 27)

| 1 | Pivot (LH) | 2 | Wiper arm (LH) | 3 | Pivot (RH) | 4 | Wiper arm (RH) | 5 | Wiper motor |

26 Horn – adjustment

1   The horn should never be dismantled but it is possible to adjust it. This adjustment is to compensate for wear only and will not affect the tone. At the rear is a small adjustment screw on the broad rim nearly opposite to the terminal connector.
2   Slacken the locknut and turn the adjustment screw clockwise to increase the volume and to decrease the volume anti-clockwise. Tighten the locknut.

27 Windscreen wiper arm – removal and refitting

1   Before removing a wiper arm, turn the windscreen switch on and off to ensure the arms are in their normal parked position parallel with the bottom of the screen and the outer tips 0.787 in (20 mm) from the rubber.
2   To remove the arms, pivot the arm back, slacken the arm securing nut and detach the arm from the spindle (photo).
3   When refitting an arm, place it so it is in its correct relative parked position and tighten the arm securing nut.

28 Windscreen wiper motor – fault diagnosis and rectification

1   Should the windscreen wipers fail, or work very slowly then check

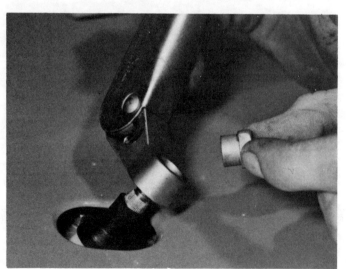

27.2 Removing windscreen wiper arm

the terminals for loose connections, and make sure the insulation of the external wiring is not broken or cracked. If this is in order then check the current the motor is taking by connecting a 1-20 volt ammeter in series in the circuit and turning on the wiper switch. Consumption should be between 2.3 - 3.1 amps.

2 If no current is flowing check that the fuse has not blown. The correct rating is 10 amps. If it has, check the wiring of the motor and other electrical circuits serviced by this fuse for short circuits. If the fuse is in good condition check the wiper switch.

3 Should the motor take a very low current ensure that the battery is fully charged. If the motor takes a high current then it is an indication that there is an internal fault or partially seized linkage.

4 It is possible for the motor to be stripped and overhauled but the availability of spare parts could present a problem. Either take a faulty unit to the local automobile electricians or obtain a new unit.

5 On later models the wiper is fitted with a three-speed control. *First position – intermittent wipe: second position – slow continuous wipe: third position – high speed continuous wipe.*

6 The intermittent wipe is controlled through an amplifier unit located below the bonnet lock release handle. In the event of failure in this particular motor setting, check all the electrical connections to the amplifier and if the fault still persists, renew the amplifier complete.

29 Windscreen wiper motor – removal and refitting

1 For safety reasons disconnect the battery earth cable.
2 Disconnect the wiper motor cable connector from the wiper motor.
3 Refer to Section 27 and remove the wiper arm and blade.
4 Release the six nylon clips and remove the cowl top grille.
5 Undo and remove the three bolts and spring washers securing the wiper motor to the body.
6 Undo and remove the nut that connects the motor shaft to the wiper linkage and then lift away the motor from the cowl top grille.
7 Refitting the windscreen wiper motor is the reverse sequence to removal. Reset the arms as described in Section 27.

30 Windscreen wiper linkage – removal and refitting

1 Refer to Section 29 and remove the windscreen wiper motor.
2 Undo and remove the two flange nuts securing the linkage pivot to the cowl top panel. The linkage may now be lifted out through the aperture.
3 Refitting the linkage is the reverse sequence to removal. Lubricate all moving parts with a little engine grade oil.

31 Windscreen washer – removal and refitting

1 Upon inspection it will be seen that the washer pump and reservoir are an integral assembly and is serviced as such (photo).
2 Before suspecting pump failure always check that all electrical connections are firm and clean and that there is also water in the

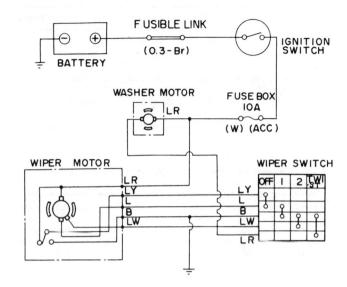

Fig. 10.24 Windscreen wiper/washer wiring diagram (Sec 28)

reservoir. Check that the jets are not blocked particularly if the car has just been polished.

3 To remove the assembly first remove the pipe located at the side of the windscreen wiper reservoir and lift away the reservoir.
4 Detach the electric pump cable connectors and then undo and remove the two pump securing bolts and spring washers. Lift away the pump.
5 To remove a jet undo and remove the jet bracket securing screw on the cowl top panel and lift away the jet. Detach from the plastic tube.
6 Reassembly is the reverse sequence to removal. If the piping is being renewed make sure that there are no sharp bends or kinks.
7 The nozzle should be adjusted to spray at the centre of each wiper blade arc.

32 Rear window wiper (Estate Car) – removal and refitting

1 Disconnect the earth cable from the battery.
2 Remove the wiper arm as described in Section 27.
3 Remove the tailgate trim and sealed screen. Disconnect the wiper motor cable connector from the wiper motor.
4 Undo the securing bolts and remove the wiper motor from the tailgate.
5 Refitting is the reverse of removal procedure. Fit the wiper arm at the correct angle to obtain the sweeping zone as shown in Fig. 10.26.

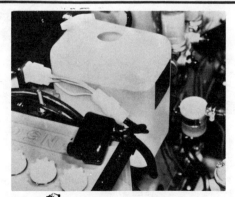

31.1 The windscreen washer reservoir

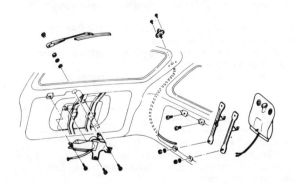

Fig. 10.25 Rear window (Estate Car) wiper mechanism (Sec 32)

33 Direction indicator and lighting switch – removal and refitting

1   Refer to Chapter 11 and remove the steering wheel.
2   Undo and remove the four cowling retaining screws and lift away
the upper and lower cowling halves.
3   For safety reasons disconnect the battery earth cable, and then
detach the switch leads at the connectors.
4   Remove the switch securing screws and lift away the switch
assembly.
5   Refitting the combination switch is the reverse sequence to
removal.

34 Flasher units – removal

1   The units are located on the foot pedal support bracket. The larger
one is the turn signal unit and the smaller one is the hazard warning
unit.
2   To renew either unit, simply pull it from its retaining clip and
disconnect the leads.

35 Lighting switch – removal and refitting

1   Undo and remove the four cowling retaining screws and lift away
the upper and lower cowling halves.
2   Disconnect the battery earth cable.
3   Undo and remove the two cluster cover securing screws and lift
away the cluster cover.
4   Undo and remove the five screws from the front of the cluster.
Also remove the one screw that secures the cluster to the instrument
panel at the rear. Lift the cluster away.
5   Remove the switch knob by depressing and turning anti-
clockwise.
6   The switch assembly may now be removed.
7   Refitting the lighting switch is the reverse sequence to removal.

36 Hazard warning switch – removal and refitting

1   Refer to Section 35 and follow the instructions given in
paragraphs 1 – 4 inclusive.
2   Detach the cable connector from the instrument panel harness.
3   The switch may now be removed from the cluster lid by releasing
the retaining spring tension and pushing out forwards.
4   Refitting the hazard warning switch is the reverse sequence to
removal.

37 Ignition switch – removal and refitting

1   Refer to Chapter 11 and remove the steering wheel. This is to give
better access but is not essential.
2   Undo and remove the four cowling retaining screws and lift away
the upper and lower cowling halves.
3   For safety reasons disconnect the battery earth cable, and then
detach the switch leads at the connectors.
4   Undo and remove the one screw and spring washer from the rear
of the switch. Lift away the switch.
5   Refitting the switch is the reverse sequence to removal.

38 Steering lock – removal and refitting

1   Refer to Section 37 and remove the ignition switch.
2   Using a drill of suitable diameter and an extractor, drill the centre
of the shear bolts and unscrew the shear bolts using the extractor.
3   Lift away the steering lock.
4   To refit the lock and ignition switch is the reverse sequence to
removal. Use two new shear bolts and tighten in a progressive manner
until the heads become detached.

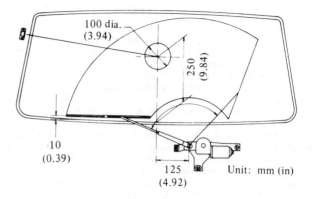

Fig. 10.26 Rear window wiper arm adjustment (Sec 32)

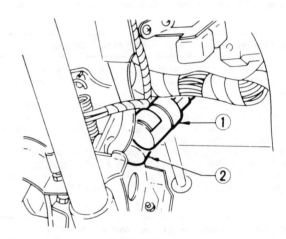

Fig. 10.27 Location of (1) turn signal flasher unit and (2) hazard
warning flasher unit (Sec 34)

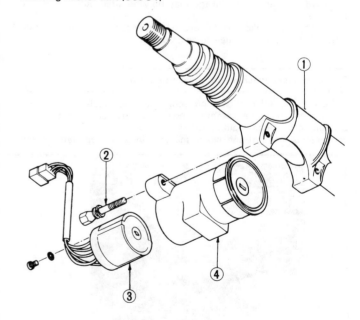

Fig. 10.28 Steering lock and ignition switch (early models)
(Sec 37)

1 *Steering lock clamp*	3 *Ignition switch*
2 *Self-shear type screw*	4 *Steering lock*

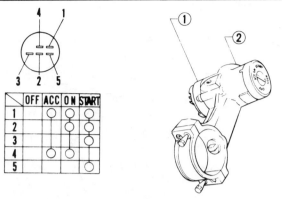

Fig. 10.29 Steering lock and ignition switch (later models)
(Sec 38)

1 *Ignition switch*
2 *Steering lock*

39 Theft protection system – description

1   The system comprises the ignition switch, door operated switch and a warning buzzer. The buzzer sounds when the driver's door is opened from inside the vehicle without the ignition key having been removed from the lock.

2   Apart from checking the security of the electrical wiring, any malfunction will necessitate renewal of the door switch, the buzzer or both. It should be noted that the door switch also serves to actuate the interior courtesy light.

40 Starter interlock system – general description

1   This system is installed in some vehicles destined for operation in North America (not Canada) and in certain other territories.

2   The system ensures that the engine will start and the warning buzzer and lamp will remain inoperative only when the following condition has been complied with:

   Front seat belts are fastened *after* driver or passenger seated.

3   For the purpose of vehicle maintenance, the engine can be started if neither front seat is occupied (belts remain unfastened).

4   The warning buzzer and lamp come on immediately should the driver or front passenger not have fastened his belt and the gearshift lever is in any position except neutral and the ignition key is turned ON. The starter interlock relay operates if the key is turned to the START position under these conditions.

5   In an emergency, the engine can be started by turning the ignition key to ON and then pressing the button on the emergency switch under the bonnet and then turning the ignition switch to START.

41 Starter interlock system – component testing and renewal

1   *The seat switch* is located beneath the driver's and passenger's seats.

2   To remove a switch, the seat must be unbolted from the floor (4 bolts) and turned upside down.

3   *The interlock unit* is mounted under the passenger seat. To remove it, disconnect the leads at the two connectors and then unbolt the passenger seat (4 bolts). The unit is secured by two screws.

4   To check the switch, use a test lamp between connector 'E' and each connector pin in turn. When the top cover of the switch is depressed, continuity should exist but when released, the circuit should be open.

5   *The belt switch* is integral with the seat belt fastener and in the event of a fault, both components must be renewed as an assembly. Remove the switch after unbolting the seat.

6   Test for continuity between two leads from the seat belt switch using a test lamp. When the seat belt is fastened there should not be continuity but when released, continuity should exist.

7   *The interlock relay* is located within the engine compartment together with the *neutral relay*. Either unit may be removed after disconnecting the connector plug.

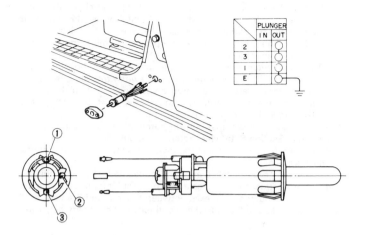

Fig. 10.30 Theft protection door switch (Sec 39)

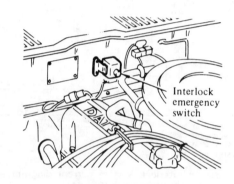

Fig. 10.31 Starter interlock system emergency switch (Sec 40)

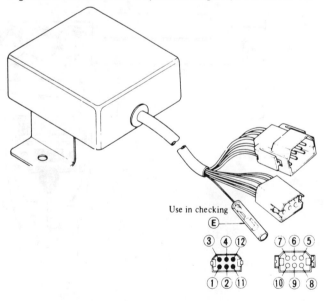

Fig. 10.32 Starter interlock unit (Sec 41)

1 *From driver's seat switch*	7 *From interlock relay*
2 *For driver's belt switch*	8 *For battery*
3 *From passenger's seat switch*	9 *From driver's seat switch*
4 *For passenger seat switch*	10 *From passenger's seat switch*
5 *From battery*	11 *For neutral switch or relay*
6 *From ignition switch*	12 *For oil pressure switch*

8   To test the interlock relay, use a test lamp and check that continuity exists only between 1 and 3 and 4 and 5. When 12 volts dc is applied to 4 and 5, continuity must exist between 1 and 2 instead of 1 and 3. During this last test, the battery positive terminal must be connected to connector pin 1.

9   *A neutral switch* is installed on the rear extension housing of the manual gearbox. The serviceability of the switch may be checked by using a test lamp between the two switch leads. When the switch plunger is depressed, continuity should now exist but when it is extended, continuity should be established.

10 *The inhibitor switch* installed on automatic transmission units is described in Section 6, to which reference should be made. The switch performs the function of a neutral switch as required by the starter interlock system.

11 *The neutral relay* installed adjacent to the interlock relay within the engine compartment can be tested with a test lamp. In a serviceable condition, continuity should exist between 5 and 6 and 2 and 4. If 12 volts dc is applied to 5 and 6, then continuity will exist between 1 and

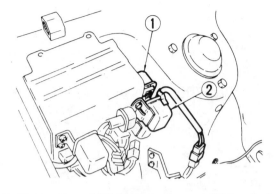

Fig. 10.33 Location of (1) neutral relay and (2) interlock relay (Sec 41)

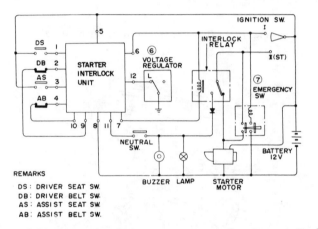

Fig. 10.34 Starter interlock system current diagram – manual transmission (Sec 41)

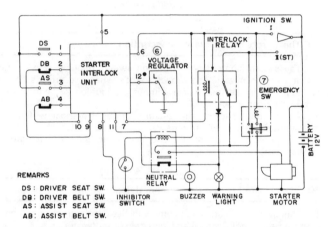

Fig. 10.35 Starter interlock system circuit diagram – automatic transmission (Sec 41)

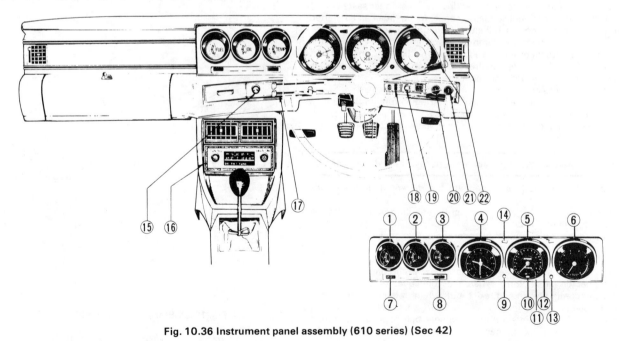

Fig. 10.36 Instrument panel assembly (610 series) (Sec 42)

1 Fuel meter
2 Oil pressure meter
3 Water temperature meter
4 Clock
5 Speedometer
6 Tachometer
7 Handbrake warning lamp
8 Generator warning lamp
9 Clock control
10 Main beam pilot lamp
11 Odometer
12 Trip meter
13 Trip meter re-set control
14 Turn signal pilot lamp
15 Cigar lighter
16 Radio
17 Heater control
18 Rear window defroster
19 Hazard switch
20 Lighting switch
21 Wiper/washer switch
22 Turn signal/lighting switch

3 instead of between 2 and 4.

12 *The interlock emergency switch* can be tested in the following manner. When the switch button is depressed, continuity should exist between 2 and 4 and 3 and 1. When 12 volts dc is applied to 3 and 1 and the button depressed, continuity will be maintained between 2 and 4 even after the button is released.

42 Instrument panel and cover – removal and refitting

1 Disconnect the battery earth cable.

2 Undo and remove the four cowling retaining screws and lift away the upper and lower cowling halves.

3 Undo and remove the two instrument panel cover retaining screws and lift away the cover.

4 Undo and remove the two crosshead screws located above the steering column. Also undo and remove the two crosshead screws one located in each outer instrument aperture at the top.

5 Carefully pull the instrument panel forward as far as possible.

6 Working behind the instrument panel disconnect the multi pin connector from the rear of the printed circuit housing.

7 Disconnect the speedometer cable from the rear of the speedometer head.

8 Make a careful note of any additional cable connections to the terminals on the printed circuit housing and detach these.

9 The instrument cluster assembly may now be removed from the instrument panel.

43 Speedometer head – removal and refitting

1 Refer to Section 42 and remove the instrument cluster lid.

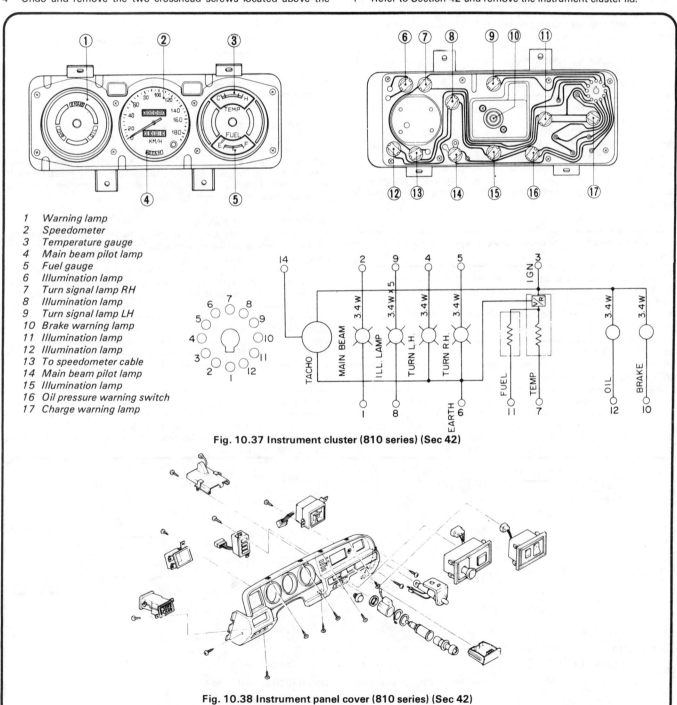

1 Warning lamp
2 Speedometer
3 Temperature gauge
4 Main beam pilot lamp
5 Fuel gauge
6 Illumination lamp
7 Turn signal lamp RH
8 Illumination lamp
9 Turn signal lamp LH
10 Brake warning lamp
11 Illumination lamp
12 Illumination lamp
13 To speedometer cable
14 Main beam pilot lamp
15 Illumination lamp
16 Oil pressure warning switch
17 Charge warning lamp

Fig. 10.37 Instrument cluster (810 series) (Sec 42)

Fig. 10.38 Instrument panel cover (810 series) (Sec 42)

2   If an odometer is fitted remove the trip control knob.
3   Undo and remove the six screws and lift away the printed circuit housing together with the speedometer head, water temperature gauge and fuel gauge.
4   Undo and remove the two screws securing the speedometer head to the printed circuit housing. Lift away the speedometer head.
5   Refitting the speedometer head is the reverse sequence to removal.

44 Fuel gauge and water temperature gauge – description

1   The fuel gauge circuit comprises a tank sender unit located in the fuel tank (Chapter 3) and the fuel gauge. The sender unit has a float attached and this rides on the surface of the petrol in the tank. At the end of the float arm is a contact and rheostat which control current flowing to the fuel gauge.
2   The water temperature gauge circuit comprises a meter and thermal transmitter which is screwed into the side of the engine cylinder block. This is fitted with a thermistor element which signals any cooling system water temperature variation as a change in resistance. This therefore controls the current flowing to the meter.
3   The fuel gauge and water temperature gauge are provided with a bi-metal arm and heater coil. When the ignition is switched on, current flows so heating the coil. With this heat the bi-metal arm is distorted and therefore moves the pointer.
4   Because a slight tolerance may occur on the fuel or water temperature gauge due to a fluctuation in voltage, a voltage regulator is used to supply a constant voltage resulting in more consistent readings. The output voltage to the meter circuits is 8 volts.
5   If it is found that both the fuel gauge and water temperature gauges operate inaccurately then the voltage regulator should be suspect.

45 Fuel gauge and water temperature gauge – removal and refitting

1   Refer to Section 42 and remove the instrument cluster lid.
2   Undo and remove the screws securing the meter to the printed circuit housing. Lift away the meter.
3   Refitting the meter is the reverse sequence to removal.

46 Warning lights – general

Oil pressure warning light

A switch is fitted to the engine lubrication system so that with the ignition switched on, a warning lamp will light when the engine is either stationary or the oil pressure has fallen below 5.7 - 8.5 lbf/in^2 (0.4 - 0.6 kgf/cm^2) when the engine is running normally and the oil pressure passes the minimum pressure mark so the pressure switch opens the circuit and the light is extinguished.

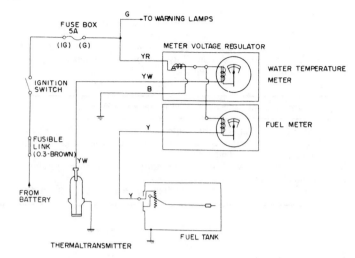

Fig. 10.39 Circuit diagram – fuel gauge, temperature gauge and voltage regulator (610 series) (Sec 44)

Handbrake warning light

Whenever the handbrake is applied and the ignition switched on, the warning lamp will light. When the handbrake is released so the light is extinguished. On some models, this light is also used as a warning light to indicate when the brake fluid in the master cylinder reservoir falls below a predetermined level. For further information on the switch refer to Chapter 9, Section 30.

Alternator warning light

The alternator warning lamp lights when the ignition is switched on but the engine stationary and stays on when the alternator fails to charge with the engine running.

With the ignition switched on the warning light circuit is closed and current flows from the ignition switch to the warning light, through the regulator and to earth. When the engine is started and the alternator commences operation the output current from the N terminal opposes the current flowing from the warning light. As the current from the N terminal increases the solenoid is energised and the warning light relay contacts are opened so breaking the warning light earth circuit. The light will then extinguish. Further information on the regulator will be found in Section 11.

47 Tachometer – fitting

1   Refer to Section 42 and remove the cluster lid.
2   Carefully remove the tachometer aperture mask and fit the instrument to the aperture.

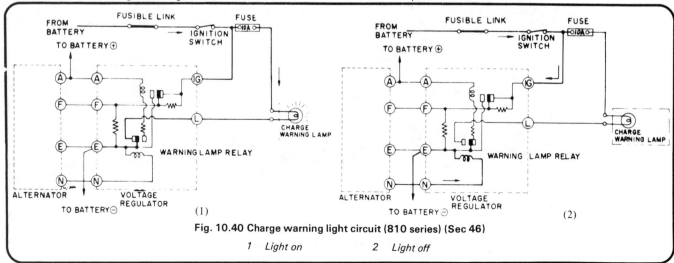

Fig. 10.40 Charge warning light circuit (810 series) (Sec 46)

1 Light on   2 Light off

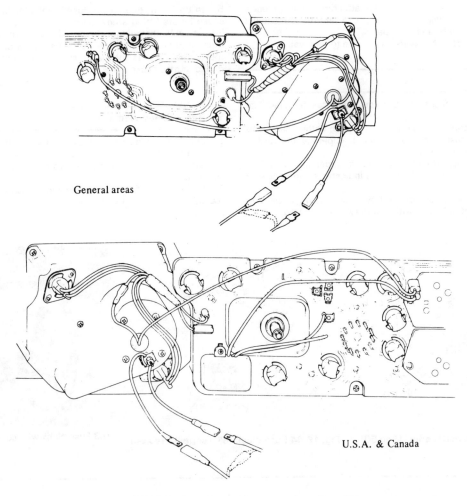

General areas

U.S.A. & Canada

Fig. 10.41 Tachometer cable connections (Sec 47)

3   Disconnect the black/white and black/green wires at the connector plug. These cables are located along the lower portion of the instrument panel.
4   Connect the tachometer cables to the disconnected plug ends in series.
5   Connect the remaining leads of the tachometer to the combination meter printed circuit terminals.
6   Refit the cluster lid.

48 Electric clock – fitting

1   Refer to Section 42 and remove the cluster lid and instrument panel.
2   Carefully remove the clock aperture mask and fit the clock to the aperture.
3   Connect the lead from the clock to the blue/white cable which is located along the lower portion of the instrument panel.
4   Connect the remaining leads of the clock to the terminals on the combination meter printed circuit.
5   Refit the cluster lid.

49 Radio – removal and refitting

1   Refer to Section 42 and remove the cluster lid and instrument panel.
2   Detach the aerial plug from the connector located at the rear of the instrument panel aperture.
3   Make a note of the electrical connections and detach from the terminal connectors located behind the radio set.
4   Disconnect the speaker cables from the radio set.

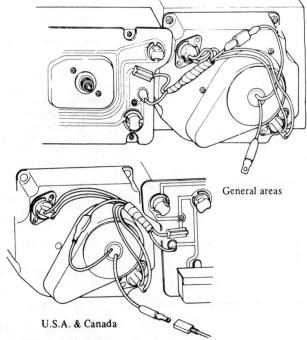

General areas

U.S.A. & Canada

Fig. 10.42 Electric clock cable connections (Sec 48)

5   The radio may be removed once the attachments have been released. Their location will depend on the type of set fitted but usually requires removal of the knobs and front panel.
6   Refitting the radio set is the reverse sequence to removal.

50 Fusible link and fuses – general

1   The fusible link and fuses are protective devices for electrical circuits.
2   The fusible link is connected alongside the main battery cable and when the current increases beyond the rated amperage the fusible metal melts and the circuit is broken.
3   The fuse block is located on the side panel under the dash. The circuits protected by the individual fuses are indicated on the cover of the fuse block (photo).
4   A melted fusible link can be detected by either a visual inspection or by carrying out a continuity test with a battery and test lamp.

5   In the event of a fuse or fusible link blowing, always establish the cause before fitting a new one. This is most likely to be due to faulty insulation in the wiring circuit. Always carry a spare fuse for each rating and never be tempted to substitute a piece of wire or a nail for the correct fuse as this can result in the electrical component being ruined or may cause a fire.

51 Rear window demister

1   The filament is of printed circuit type on the interior surface of the rear window. Normal care should be exercised when cleaning the glass so that any rings which may be worn do not scratch or damage the filament.
2   In the event of the filament being broken it can be repaired using special conductive silver composition but this is a job for your Datsun dealer.

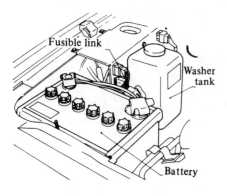

Fig. 10.43 Fusible link (810 series) (Sec 50)

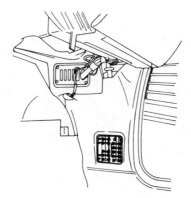

Fig. 10.44 Fuse block (810 series) (Sec 50)

50.3 Fuse block with cover removed

52 Fault diagnosis

Symptom	Reason/s	Remedy
Starter motor fails to turn engine	Battery discharged	Charge battery
	Battery defective internally	Fit new battery
	Battery terminal leads loose or earth lead not securely attached to body	Check and tighten lead
	Loose or broken connections in starter motor circuit	Check all connections and tighten any that are loose
	Starter motor switch or solenoid faulty	Test and replace faulty components with new
	Starter motor pinion jammed in mesh with flywheel gear ring	Disengage pinion by engaging gear and rocking car back and forward
	Starter brushes badly worn, sticking, or brush wires loose	Examine brushes, renew as necessary, tighten down brush wires
	Commutator dirty, worn or burnt	Clean commutator, recut if badly burnt
	Starter motor armature faulty	Overhaul starter motor, fit new armature
	Field coils earthed	Overhaul starter motor
Starter motor turns engine very slowly	Battery in discharged condition	Charge battery
	Starter brushes badly worn, sticking or brush wires loose	Examine brushes, renew as necessary, tighten down brush wires
	Loose wires in starter motor circuit	Check wiring and tighten as necessary
Starter motor operates without turning engine	Starter motor pinion sticking on the screwed sleeve	Remove starter motor, clean starter motor drive
	Pinion or flywheel gear teeth broken or worn	Fit new ring gear to flywheel, and new pinion to starter motor drive
Starter motor noisy or excessively rough	Pinion or flywheel gear teeth broken or worn	Fit new ring gear to flywheel, or new pinion to starter motor drive
	Starter drive main spring broken	Dismantle and fit new main spring
	Starter motor retaining bolts loose	Tighten starter motor securing bolts. Fit new spring washer if necessary

Symptom	Reason/s	Remedy
Battery will not hold charge for more than a few days	Battery defective internally	Remove and fit new battery
	Electrolyte level too low or electrolyte too weak due to leakage	Top up electrolyte level to just above plates
	Plate separators no longer fully effective	Remove and fit new battery
	Battery plates severely suplhated	Remove and fit new battery
	Battery terminal connections loose or corroded	Check terminals for tightness, and remove all corrosion
	Short in lighting circuit causing continual battery drain	Trace and rectify
	Regulator unit not working correctly	Take car to specialist
Ignition light fails to go out, battery runs flat in a few days	Fan belt loose and slipping or broken	Check, renew and tighten as necessary
	Alternator faulty	Take car to specialist

Failure of individual electrical equipment to function correctly is dealt with alphabetically, item by item, as follows:

Symptom	Reason/s	Remedy
Fuel gauge gives no reading	Fuel tank empty	Fill fuel tank
	Electric cable between tank sender unit and gauge earthed or loose	Check cable for earthing and joints for tightness
	Fuel gauge case not earthed	Ensure case is well earthed
	Fuel gauge supply cable interrupted	Check and renew cable if necessary
	Fuel gauge unit broken	Renew fuel gauge
Fuel gauge registers full all the time	Electric cable between tank unit and gauge broken or disconnected	Check over cable and repair as necessary
Horn operates all the time	Horn push either earthed or stuck down	Disconnect battery earth. Check and rectify source of trouble
	Horn cable to horn push earthed	Disconnect battery earth. Check and rectify source of trouble
Horn fails to operate	Blown fuse	Check and renew if blown. Ascertain cause
	Cable or cable connection loose, broken or disconnected	Check all connections for tightness and cables for breaks
	Horn has an internal fault	Renew horn
Horn emits intermittent or unsatisfactory noise	Cable connections loose	Check and tighten all connections
	Horn incorrectly adjusted	Adjust horn until best note obtained
Lights do not come on	If engine not running, battery discharged	Push-start car, charge battery
	Light bulb filament burnt out or bulbs broken	Test bulbs in live bulb holder
	Wire connections loose, disconnected or broken	Check all connections for tightness and wire cable for breaks
	Light switch shorting or otherwise faulty	By-pass light switch to ascertain if fault is in switch and fit new switch as appropriate
Lights come on but fade out	If engine not running battery discharged	Push-start car and charge battery (not automatics)
Lights give very poor illumination	Lamp glasses dirty	Clean glasses
	Reflector tarnished or dirty	Fit new reflectors
	Lamps badly out of adjustment	Adjust lamps correctly
	Incorrect bulb with too low wattage fitted	Remove bulb and renew with correct grade
	Existing bulbs old and badly discoloured	Renew bulb units
	Electrical wiring too thin not allowing full current to pass	Re-wire lighting system
Lights work erratically – flashing on and off, especially over bumps	Battery terminals or earth connections loose	Tighten battery terminals and earth connection
	Lights not earthing properly	Examine and rectify
	Contacts in light switch faulty	By-pass light switch to ascertain if fault is in switch and fit new switch as appropriate
Wiper motor fails to work	Blown fuse	Check and renew fuse if necessary
	Wire connections loose, disconnected or broken	Check wiper wiring. Tighten loose connections
	Internal defect	Renew wiper motor
Wiper motor works very slowly and takes excessive current	Drive to wheelboxes too bent or unlubricated	Examine drive and straighten out severe curvature. Lubricate
	Wheelbox spindle binding or damaged	Remove, overhaul or renew
Wiper motor works but wiper blades remain static	Driving cable rack disengaged or faulty	Examine and if faulty, renew
	Wheel box gear and spindle damaged or worn	Examine and if faulty, renew

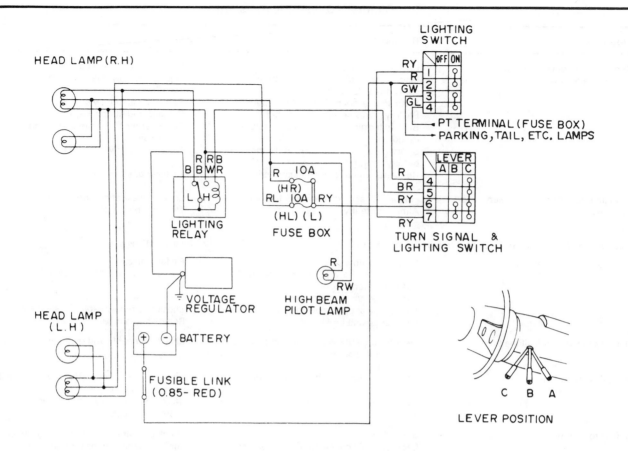

Fig. 10.45 Circuit diagram – lighting system (LHD-610 series)

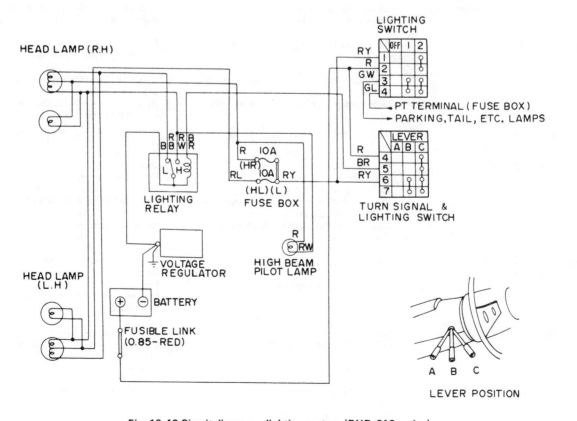

Fig. 10.46 Circuit diagram – lighting system (RHD-610 series)

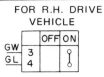
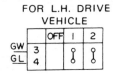

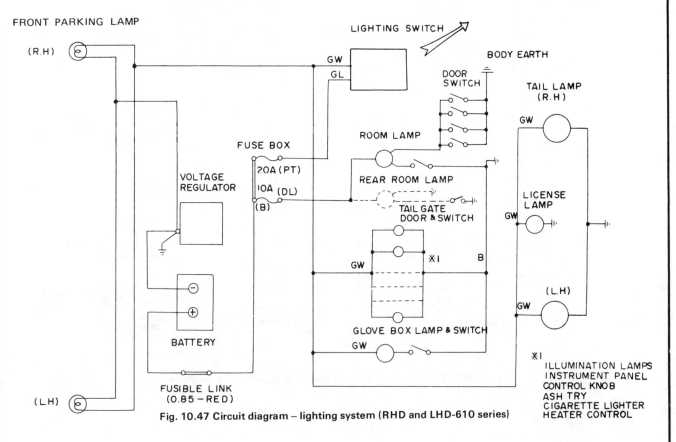

Fig. 10.47 Circuit diagram – lighting system (RHD and LHD-610 series)

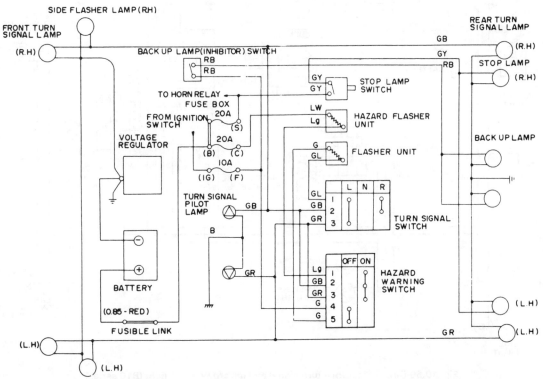

Fig. 10.48 Circuit diagram – back-up lamp, turn signal lamp (hazard warning lamp) and stop lamp (610 series)

178

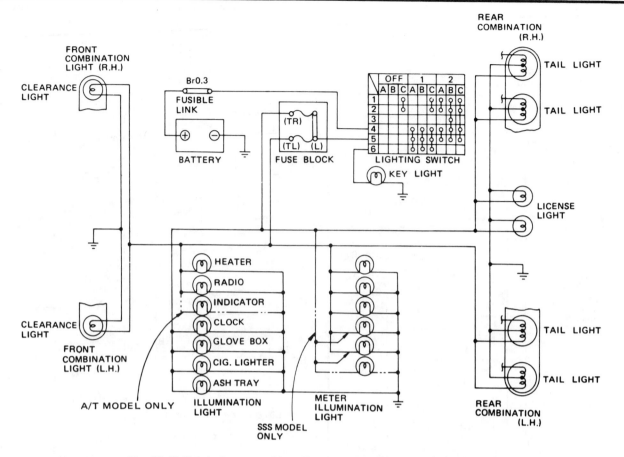

Fig. 10.49 Circuit diagram – side, tail and number plate lamp (810 series)

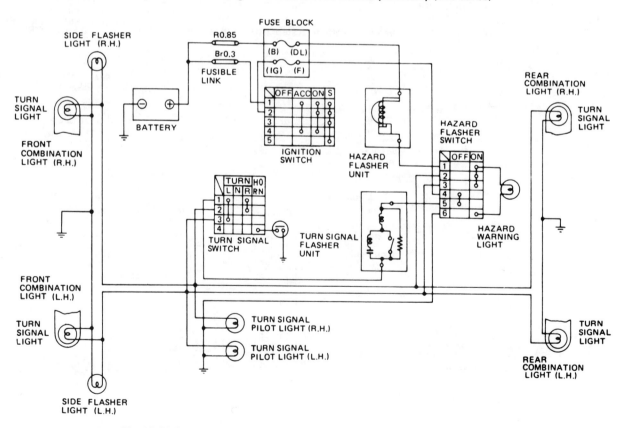

Fig. 10.50 Circuit diagram – turn signal and hazard warning light (810 series)

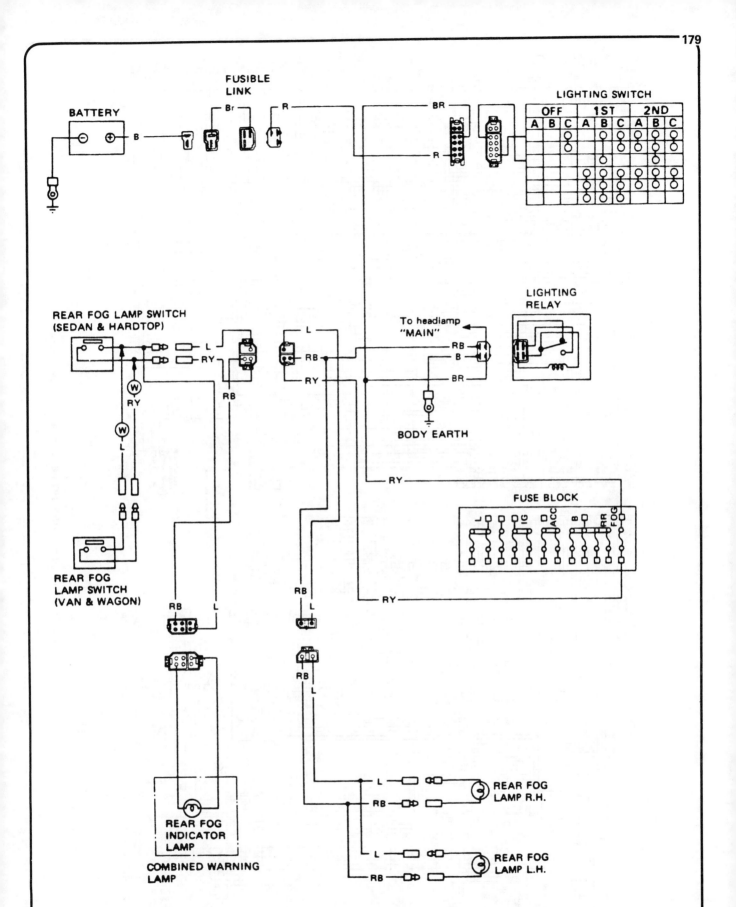

Fig. 10.51 Circuit diagram – fog lamps (810 series)

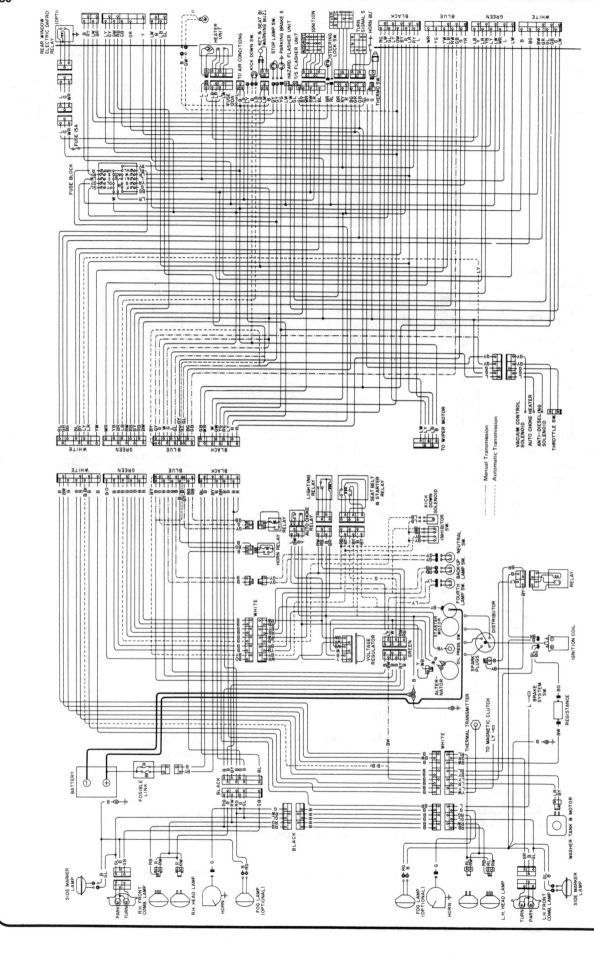

Fig. 10.52 Wiring diagram — USA 1973 610 series (continued below)

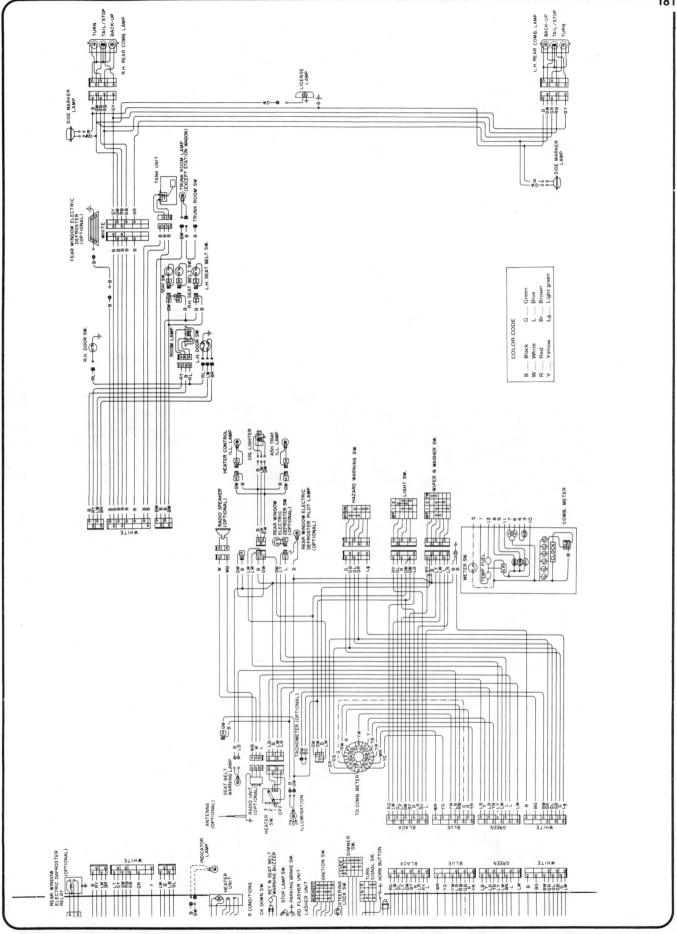

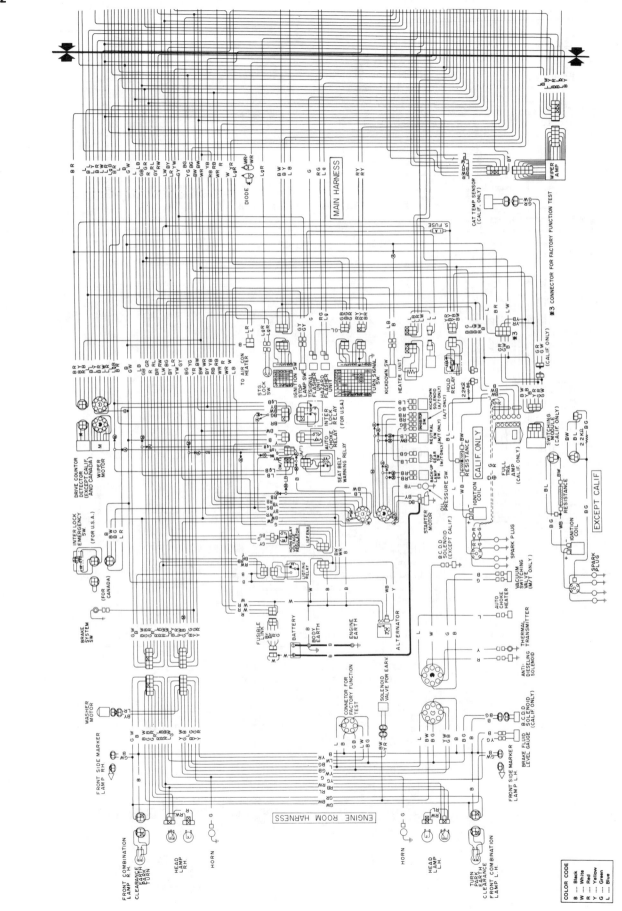

Fig. 10.53 Wiring diagram – USA 1975 610 series *(continued below)*

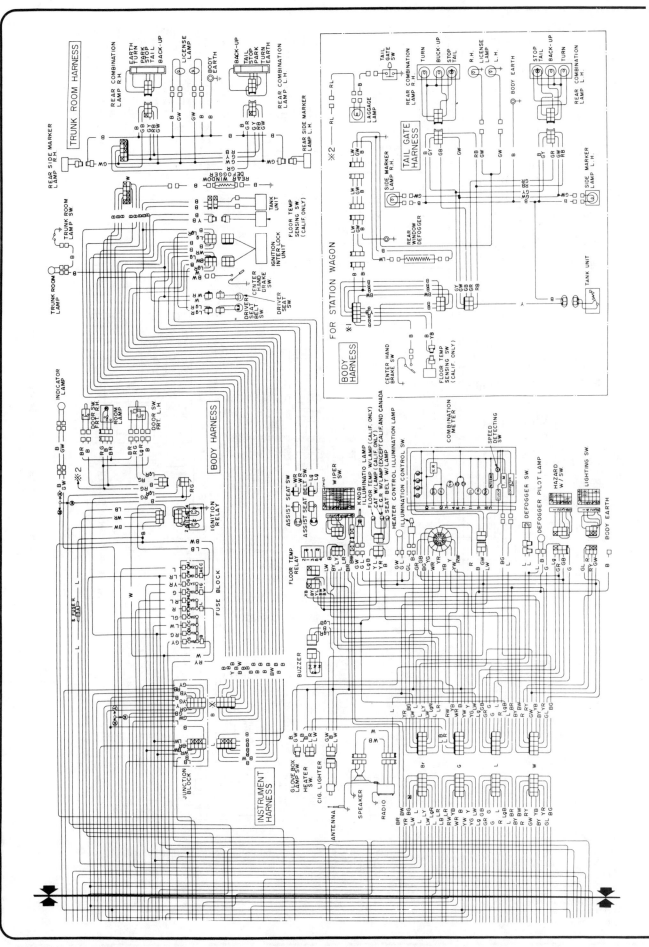

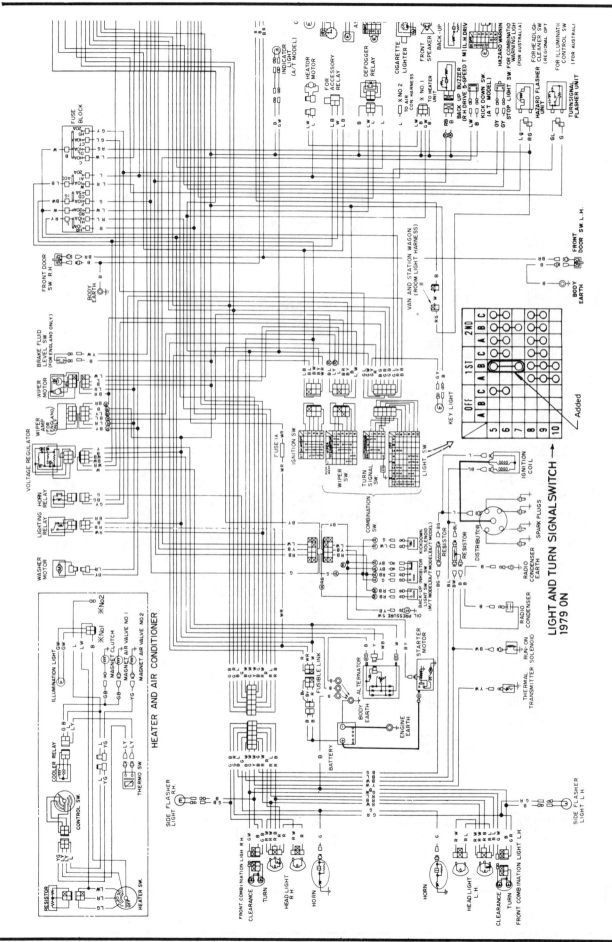

Fig. 10.54 Wiring diagram — Europe 1977-on 810 Series *(continued below)*

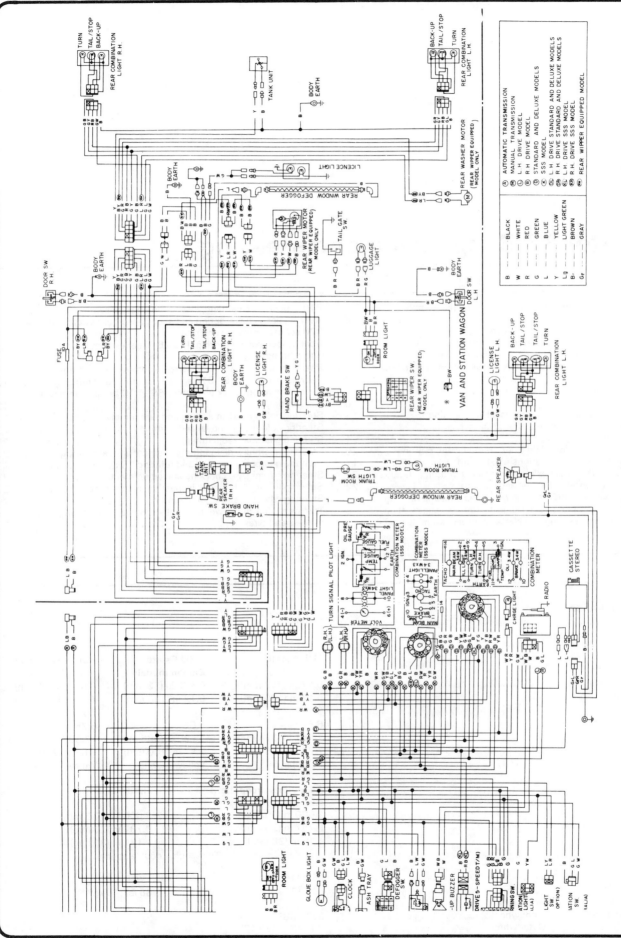

Chapter 11 Suspension and steering

Contents

Specifications

Front suspension

Type . . . . Independent strut

Suspension details - 610 series

Coil spring:

	LHD Estate	RHD Estate Saloon models	Hard suspension
Wire diameter	0.472 in (12 mm)	0.472 in (12 mm)	0.512 in (13 mm)
Coil diameter	5.12 in (130 mm)	5.12 in (130 mm)	5.12 in (130 mm)
No. of coils	8	8	7.75
No. of effective coils	6.5	6.5	6.25
Free length	14.61 in (371 mm)	15.20 in (386 mm)	12.99 in (330 mm)
Fitted height	7.28 in (185 mm)	7.87 in (200 mm)	7.87 in (200 mm)
Colour mark	Red/orange	Yellow/orange	Yellow/yellow

Strut assembly:

	All models except hard suspension	Hard suspension
Outer diameter	2.000 in (50.8 mm)	2.000 in (50.8 mm)
Piston rod diameter	0.787 in (20 mm)	0.787 in (20 mm)
Piston diameter	1.18 in (38 mm)	1.181 in (30 mm)
Shock absorber type	Telescopic - double acting	

Damping force:

Expansion	88 lbf (40 kgf)	176 lbf (80 kgf)
Contraction	5 lbf (25 kgf)	88 lbf (40 kgf)

Suspension angles:- (unladen condition)

Toe-out on turns - Inner wheel . . . . 37° - 38°

- Outer wheel . . . . 30° 42' - 32° 42'

Suspension details - 810 series

	RHD (Soft suspension)	RHD (Hard suspension)	LHD
Coil spring			
Free length:			
RH spring	16.61 in (422 mm)	14.41 in (366 mm)	14.41 in (366 mm)
LH spring	15.53 in (394.5 mm)	13.82 in (351 mm)	14.41 in (366 mm)
Colour mark:			
RH spring	White/pink	Blue/white	Blue/white
LH spring	Red/green	White/green	Blue/white

Strut assembly:
Outer diameter .... 2.000 in (50.8 mm)
Piston rod diameter .... 0.87 in (22 mm)
Piston diameter .... 1.26 in (32 mm)
Shock absorber type .... Telescopic, double-acting

Damping force:	Soft suspension	Hard suspension
Expansion	88 lbf (40 kgf)	176 lbf (80 kgf)
Contraction	55 lbf (25 kgf)	99 lbf (45 kgf)

Steering angle:
Inner wheel .... 38°
Outer wheel .... 31° 30'

Wheel alignment (unladen) – 610 series

Model		Camber	Castor	Kingpin inclination	Toe-in in (mm)
RH drive Saloon	Standard Suspension	1° 05' to 2° 35'	50' to 2° 20'	6° 15' to 7° 45'	0.276 to 0.394 (7 to 10)
	Hard *2 Suspension	1° 00' to 2° 30'	55' to 2° 25'	6° 20' to 7° 50'	0.236 to 0.354 (6 to 9)
LH drive Saloon	Standard Suspension	1° 05' to 2° 35'	40' to 2° 10'	6° 15' to 7° 45'	0.276 to 0.394 (7 to 10)
	Hard *2 Suspension	1° 00' to 2° 30'	45' to 2° 25'	6° 20' to 7° 50'	0.236 to 0.354 (6 to 9)
LH drive Saloon *1	Standard Suspension	1° 00' to 2° 30'	40' to 2° 10'	6° 20' to 7° 50'	0.236 to 0.354 (6 to 9)
	Hard *2 Suspension	55' to 1° 25'	45' to 2° 15'	6° 25' to 7° 55'	0.197 to 0.315 (5 to 8)
RH drive Estate car	Standard Suspension	1° 00' to 2° 30'	45' to 2° 15'	6° 20' to 7° 50'	0.236 to 0.354 (6 to 9)
	Hard *2 Suspension	1° 05' to 2° 35'	45' to 2° 15'	6° 15' to 7° 45'	0.276 to 0.394 (7 to 10)
LH drive Estate car	Standard Suspension	1° 10' to 2° 40'	55' to 2° 25'	6° 10' to 7° 40'	0.315 to 0.433 (8 to 11)
	Hard *2 Suspension	1° 05' to 2° 35'	45' to 2° 15'	6° 15' to 7° 45'	0.276 to 0.394 (7 to 10)

*1   for USA & Canada
*2   Optional parts

Wheel alignment (unladen) - 810 series

Wheel size	Camber	Castor	Kingpin inclination	Toe-in in (mm)
14 in	10' to 1° 40'	1° 5' to 2° 35'	7° to 8° 30'	0 to 0.08 (0 to 2)
13 in	10' to 1° 40'	1° 5' to 2° 35'	7° to 8° 30'	0.08 to 0.16 (2 to 4)

Rear suspension

Type:
Saloon models .... Independent coil spring, semi-trailing arm with double-acting shock absorber
Estate Cars .... Semi-elliptic leaf spring with double-acting shock absorber

610 series - Saloon models

Coil spring:
Wire diameter .... 0.571 in (14.5 mm)
Coil diameter .... 3.54 in (90 mm)
Coil turns: -   Standard suspension 9.25
              -   Hard suspension 9.5
Free length:
Standard suspension
RH drive - RH .... 12.6 in (321 mm)
RH drive - LH .... 12.1 in (307 mm)
LH drive .... 12.6 in (321 mm)

Hard suspension
  RH drive - RH .... 12.0 in (306 mm)
  RH drive - LH .... 11.8 in (299 mm)
  LH drive .... 12.0 in (306 mm)
Fitted height:
  Standard suspension
    RH drive - RH .... 9.02 in (229 mm)
    RH drive - LH .... 8.46 in (215 mm)
    LH drive .... 9.02 in (229 mm)
  Hard suspension
    RH drive - RH .... 9.02 in (229 mm)
    RH drive - LH .... 8.74 in (222 mm)
    LH drive .... 9.02 in (229 mm)
Suspension angles:

Application	All models except hard suspension				Hard suspension			
	RHD		LHD		RHD		LHD	
	Unladen	Laden *	Unladen	Laden *	Unladen	Laden *	Unladen	Laden *
Toe-in - in (mm)	0.1181 to 0.3150 (3 to 8)	-0.2362 to 0.157 (-6 to 4)	0.1969 to 0.5906 (5 to 15)	-0.1969 to 0.1969 (-5 to 5)	0.0787 to 0.4724 (2 to 12)	-0.1969 to 0.1969 (-5 to 5)	0.1181 to 0.5118 (3 to 13)	-0.1969 to 0.1969 (-5 to 5)
Camber	1° 40'	-1° 35'	2° 00'	-1° 10'	1° 10'	-1° 25'	1° 35'	-1° 00'

  *Load - 4 persons average weight 150 lb (68 kg) each.

Rear shock absorber
Stroke .... 8.6 in (220 mm)
Max. length .... 23.4 in (595 mm)
Damping force:
  Standard suspension
    Expansion .... 75 - 123 lbf (34 - 56 kgf)
    Contraction .... 46 - 86 lbf (21 - 39 kgf)
  Hard suspension
    Expansion .... 121 - 170 lbf (55 - 77 kgf)
    Contraction .... 73 - 112 lbf (33 - 51 kgf)
Driveshaft and journal:
  Sliding resistance .... Less than 44 lbf (20 kgf)
  Radial play of ball spline .... Less than 0.0394 in (1 mm)
  Axial play of spider journal .... Less than 0.0008 in (0.02 mm)
  Journal swinging torque .... Less than 8.7 lbf in (10 kgf cm)

Rear axleshaft
Turning torque .... Less than 3.9 lbf in (4.5 kgf cm)
  - at hub bolt .... Less than 1.8 lbf (0.8 kgf)
End play .... Less than 0.0059 in (0.15 mm)

810 series – Saloon models

	Soft suspension	Hard suspension
Coil spring:		
Free length	15.28 in (388 mm)	14.53 in (369 mm)
Colour mark	Yellow/pink	Pink/blue
Shock absorber:		
Maximum length	21.10 in (536 mm)	
Stroke	6.89 in (175 mm)	
Damping force:		
Expansion	99 lbf (45 kgf)	132 lbf (60 kgf)
Contraction	62 lbf (28 kgf)	73 lbf (33 kgf)
Wheel alignment		
Toe-in	0.157 - 0.551 in (4 - 14 mm)	
Camber	50' - 2° - 20'	
Driveshaft and journal		
Sliding resistance	11 - 44 lbf (5 - 20 kgf)	
Radial play of ball spline	Less than 0.04 in (1 mm)	
Axial play of spider journal	Less than 0.0008 in (0.02 mm)	
Journal swinging torque	Less than 8.7 lbf in (10 kgf cm)	
Rear axleshaft		
Turning torque	Less than 6.1 lbf in (7.0 kgf cm)	
at hub bolt	Less than 2lbf (1.2 kgf)	
End play	Less than 0.012 in (0.3 mm)	

Estate car
610 series
Leaf spring

Standard suspension	Leaf 1	Leaf 2	Leaf 3	Leaf 4	Leaf 5
Length	57.3 in (1456 mm)	40.8 in (1036 mm)	30.7 in (780 mm)	20.6 in (524 mm)	9.0 in (228 mm)
Width	2.362 in (60 mm)	2.362 in (60 mm)	2.362 in (60 mm)	2.362 in (60 mm)	1.969 in (50 mm)

Thickness	0.1575 in (4 mm)	0.1575 in (4 mm)	0.1575 in (4 mm)	0.1575 in (4 mm)	0.1969 in (5 mm)

Hard suspension

	Leaf 1	Leaf 2	Leaf 3	Leaf 4	
Length	57.5 in (1461 mm)	42.3 in (1074 mm)	34.1 in (865 mm)	26.6 in (675 mm)	
Width	2.362 in (60 mm)	2.362 in (60 mm)	2.362 in (60 mm)	2.362 in (60 mm)	
Thickness	0.2756 in (7 mm)	0.2756 in (7 mm)	0.2362 in (6 mm)	0.4724 in (12 mm)	

Camber (Laden)
Standard suspension .... 0.592 in (15 mm) per 584 lbf (265 kgf)
Hard suspension .... 0.592 in (15 mm) per 705 lbf (320 kgf)
Rear axle end play .... 0.0039 - 0.0177 in (0.1 - 0.45 mm)
Thickness of rear axle case end shim .... 0.0030 in (0.075 mm)

810 series
Leaf spring

	Hard suspension	Soft suspension
Dimensions - length x width x thickness-number of leaves in (mm)	47.24 x 2.36 x 0.28 - 2 47.24 x 2.36 x 0.24 - 1 47.24 x 2.36 x 0.51 - 1 (1200 x 60 x 7 - 2) (1200 x 60 x 6 - 1) (1200 x 60 x 13 - 1)	47.24 x 2.36 x 0.24 - 5 (1200 x 60 x 6 - 5)

Camber (unladen)
Soft suspension .... 5.91 in (150 mm)
Hard suspension .... 4.72 in (120 mm)

Steering
Type .... Recirculating ball, nut and worm

610 series
Ratio .... 15 : 1
Turns - lock to lock 3.3
Ball stud:
Axial play .... 0.0039 - 0.0197 in (0.1 - 0.5 mm)
Swing torque .... Less than 3.62 lbf ft (0.5 kgf m)
Steering wheel play .... Less than 1.378 in (35 mm) at outer circumference of steering wheel

Worm bearing starting torque:
New bearing .... 55.60 - 83.40 inf oz (4.0 - 6.0 kgf cm)
Re-adjusting bearing .... 27.80 - 55.60 inf oz (2.0 - 4.0 kgf cm)
Worm bearing shim:
Standard total thickness .... 0.0591 in (1.5 mm)
Adjustment shim   1 .... 0.0300 in (0.762 mm)
                      2 .... 0.0100 in (0.254 mm)
                      3 .... 0.0050 in (0.127 mm)
                      4 .... 0.0020 in (0.050 mm)
End play between sector shaft and adjustment screw .... 0.0004 - 0.0012 in (0.01 - 0.03 mm)
Adjustment shim   1 .... 0.0618 in (1.575 mm)
                      2 .... 0.0610 in (1.550 mm)
                      3 .... 0.0598 in (1.525 mm)
                      4 .... 0.0591 in (1.500 mm)
Gear backlash at pitman arm top end .... Less than 0.0039 in (0.1 mm)

810 series
Ratio .... 16.48 : 1
Turns-lock to lock 3.4
Steering wheel play .... Less than 1.4 in (35 mm) at outer circumference
Oil capacity .... 0.5 Imp pt (0.28 litre, 0.625 US pt)
Wormshaft turning torque .... 69 - 174 inf oz (5.0 - 12.5 kgf cm)
Worm bearing preload .... 56 - 111 inf oz (4.0 - 8.0 kgf cm)
Worm bearing shim:
Standard total thickness .... 0.0591 in (1.5 mm)
Adjusting shim thickness .... 0.0300 in (0.762 mm)
                                                        0.0099 in (0.254 mm)
                                                        0.0050 in (0.127 mm)
                                                        0.0020 in (0.050 mm)
Endplay between sector shaft and adjusting screw .... 0.0004 - 0.0012 in (0.01 - 0.03 mm)
Adjusting shim thickness .... 0.0620 - 0.0630 in (1.575 - 1.600 mm)
                                                        0.0610 - 0.0620 in (1.550 - 1.575 mm)
                                                        0.0600 - 0.0610 in (1.525 - 1.550 mm)
                                                        0.0591 - 0.0600 in (1.500 - 1.525 mm)
                                                        0.0581 - 0.0591 in (1.475 - 1.500 mm)
                                                        0.0571 - 0.0581 in (1.450 - 1.475 mm)

Backlash at gear arm top end . . . .   Less than 0.0039 in (0.1 mm)
Tie rod length:
    Steering gear arm side . . . .   14.25 in (362 mm)
    Idler arm assembly side . . . .   14.41 in (366 mm)

Wheels and tyres

For information about tyre sizes and pressures consult your dealer

Torque wrench settings

	lbf ft	kgf m
Front suspension		
Stabilizer bar connecting rod nut	8.7 - 12	1.2 - 1.7
Stabilizer bar fixing bracket bolt	10 - 13	1.4 - 1.8
Tension rod fixing nut	33 - 40	4.5 - 5.5
Tension rod-to-transverse link	35 - 46	4.9 - 6.3
Tension rod bracket fixing bolt	37 - 50	5.1 - 6.9
Transverse link-to-body frame	65 - 72	9 - 10
Balljoint-to-transverse link	14 - 18	1.9 - 2.5
Balljoint-to-knuckle arm	40 - 55	5.5 - 7.6
Strut assembly-to-knuckle arm	53 - 72	7.3 - 9.9
Strut assembly-to-body frame	18 - 25	2.5 - 3.5
Piston rod self locking nut	43 - 54	6.0 - 7.5
Gland packing	51 - 94	7.0 - 13
Rear suspension (IRS) - all models		
Rear wheel bearing locknut	181 - 239	25 - 33
Brake disc backplate fixing bolt	20 - 27	2.7 - 3.7
Driveshaft flange bolt	36 - 43	5 - 6
Rear suspension member mounting nut	51 - 72	7 - 10
Differential mounting member locknut	51 - 72	7 - 10
Suspension arm pin nut	51 - 72	7 - 10
Differential-to-mounting member nut	43 - 58	6 - 8
Propeller shaft flange nut	14 - 20	2.0 -2.7
Differential-to-suspension member nut	36 - 51	6 - 8
Wheel nut	58 - 65	8 - 9
610 series		
Shock absorber upper end locknut	12 - 16	1.6 - 2.2
Shock absorber lower end bolt	12 - 16	1.6 - 2.2
Bump rubber fixing nut	12 - 16	1.6 - 2.2
Rear suspension mounting bolt (front)	80 - 108	11 - 15
Rear suspension mounting bolt (rear)	145 - 217	20 - 30
810 series		
Shock absorber mounting insulator-to-body nuts	19 - 29	2.6 - 4.0
Shock absorber lower end bolt	43 - 58	6 - 8
Rear stabilizer mounting bracket nut	23 - 30	3.2 - 4.2
Driveshaft side yoke bolt	23 - 30	3.2 - 4.2
Rear suspension (leaf spring)		
Shock absorber upper bracket bolt	6.5 - 8.7	0.9 - 1.2
Shock absorber lower end nut	26 - 35	3.6 - 4.8
Rear spring U-bolt (clip)	43 - 47	6.0 - 6.5
Spring shackle	43 - 47	6.0 - 6.5
Spring front pin	43 - 47	6.0 - 6.5
Spring front bracket fixing bolt	43 - 47	6.0 - 6.5
Brake disc backplate securing nut	16 - 20	2.2 - 2.7
Differential gear carrier to axle case nut	14 - 18	2.0 - 2.5
Propeller shaft flange bolt	14 - 20	2.0 - 2.7
Bump rubber fixing nut	6.5 - 8.7	0.9 - 1.2
Torque arrester fixing nut	6.5 - 8.7	0.9 - 1.2
Wheel nut	58 - 65	8 - 9
Drain and filler plug	30 - 50	4.2 - 6.9
Steering		
Pitman arm nut	94 - 108	13 - 15
Rear cover bolts	11 - 18.	1.5 - 2.5
Sector shaft cover bolts	11 - 18.	1.5 - 2.5
Sector shaft adjusting screw locknut	14.5 - 18.	2.0 - 2.5
Steering gear housing to body bolts	43.4 - 57.8	6.0 - 8.0
Idler arm to frame bolts	31.8 - 44.1	4.4 - 6.1
Ball stud nuts	39.8 - 55.0	5.5 - 7.6
Tie-rod locknuts (610 series)	31.8 - 44.1	4.4 - 6.1
Steering wheel nuts	28.9 - 36.2	4.0 - 5.0
Column clamp bolts	9.40 - 13.0	1.3 - 1.8
Rubber coupling-to-worm shaft bolt	28.9 - 36.2	4.0 - 5.0
Rubber coupling securing bolts	10.8 - 15.9	1.5 - 2.2
Tie-rod adjusting tube clamp nut (810 series)	8 - 12	1.1 - 1.7

1 General description

The front suspension system comprises a single strut with the shock absorber forming the spindle around which the front wheels are able to pivot. It is surrounded at its upper end by a coil spring, the top mounting of which is the upper mounting and is secured to the underside of the front wheel housing.

The shock absorber piston rod is secured to the upper centre of the spring upper mounting by a thrust bearing assembly which is mounted in rubber.

At the lower end of the suspension unit strut is attached the suspension foot which also carries the wheel hub stub axle. Also attached to the lower end, is bolted the steering arm bracket which turns in a sealed balljoint on a transverse arm hinged to the front suspension crossmember.

Two tension rods which are secured to the ends of the link arms at one end and to the crossmember rubber mounting at the other, control lateral movement of the suspension unit.

A stabiliser bar is attached to the body sub-frame forward of the suspension and connected between the outer end of each suspension unit control arm by a rubber bush. This ensures parallel vertical movement between the two arms and restricts forward movement of the body, relative to the suspension.

The balljoints at the foot of the struts are sealed for life and the upper parts of the shock absorber are protected by a collapsible rubber boot located within the coil spring.

Any excessive vertical movement is prevented by bump rubbers and rebound stoppers in each shock absorber.

Steering geometry angles – caster, camber and king pin inclination – are set during production and cannot be adjusted in service. Should a deviation from these settings exist it is an indication of worn parts or accident damage.

The front wheels are mounted on the stub axles and run on ball bearings packed with grease and sealed for a life of 30 000 miles (48 000 km).

The rear suspension will be one of two types. With Saloon models a main crossmember which is mounted on, but insulated from, the body and acts as a support for the two independently sprung suspension arms which carry the rear wheel bearings.

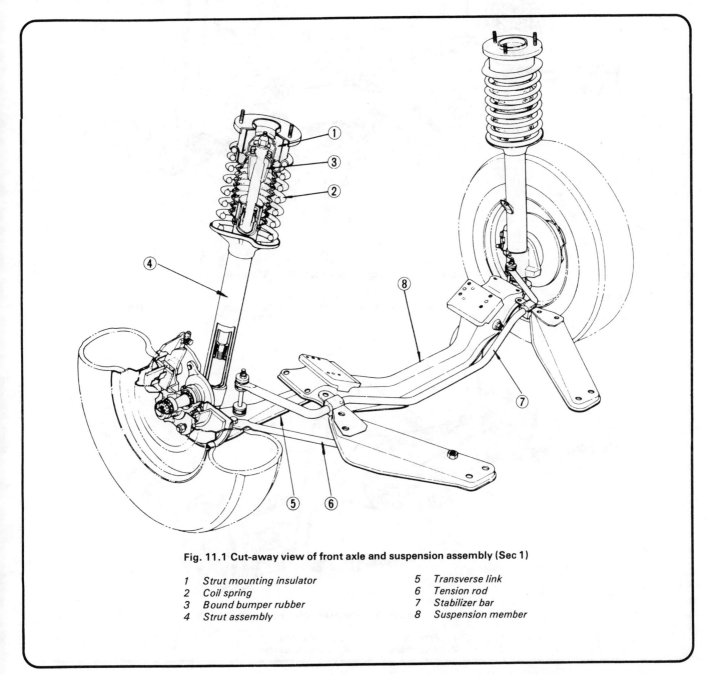

Fig. 11.1 Cut-away view of front axle and suspension assembly (Sec 1)

1   Strut mounting insulator
2   Coil spring
3   Bound bumper rubber
4   Strut assembly

5   Transverse link
6   Tension rod
7   Stabilizer bar
8   Suspension member

On 610 series, the coil springs are mounted between the suspension arms forward of the shock absorbers; on 810 series, the coil springs are mounted on the same shaft as the shock absorbers.

The final drive unit is mounted between the centre of the crossmember and a separate mounting at the rear. Drive to the rear wheel is via telescopic driveshafts with a Hooke's type universal joint at the outer ends.

On Estate cars the rear suspension comprises semi-elliptic leaf springs with double acting tubular shock absorbers mounted forward of the rear axle housing and attached to the spring mounting plate at the lower end. The upper mountings are secured to the underside of the body. The shock absorbers are mounted in rubber bushes.

The forward end of the leaf spring is retained and mounted by a nut and bolt, and rubber bush. The rear mounting is of rubber bushes and bolts.

A bump rubber is secured to the underside of the body directly above the centre of the axle casing to absorb excessive spring deflection.

A spring centre bolt is located in a hole in the axle housing bracket and the spring is attached to the assembly with two U-bolts, mounting

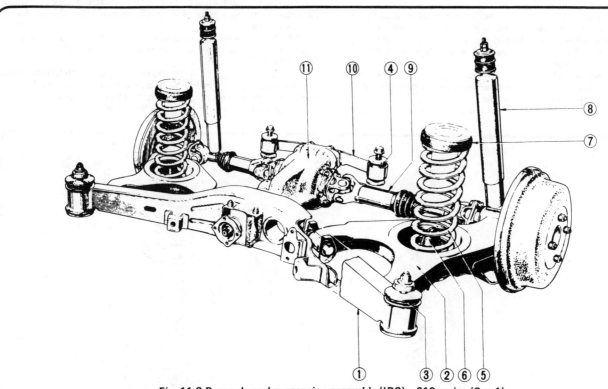

Fig. 11.2 Rear axle and suspension assembly (IRS) – 610 series (Sec 1)

1	Suspension member		insulator	5	Coil spring	8	Shock absorber		member
2	Suspension arm	4	Differential mounting	6	Bumper rubber	9	Drive shaft	11	Differential carrier
3	Member mounting		insulator	7	Spring seat	10	Differential mounting		

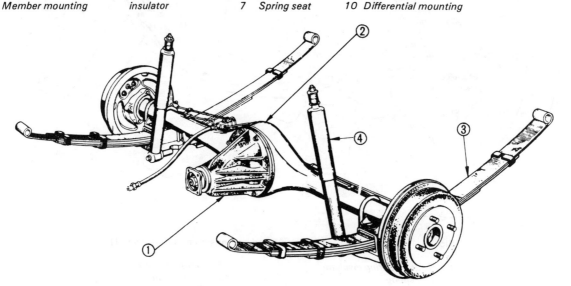

Fig. 11.3 Rear axle and suspension assembly – rigid axle (Sec 1)

| 1 | Final drive | 3 | Leaf spring |
| 2 | Axle casing | 4 | Shock absorber |

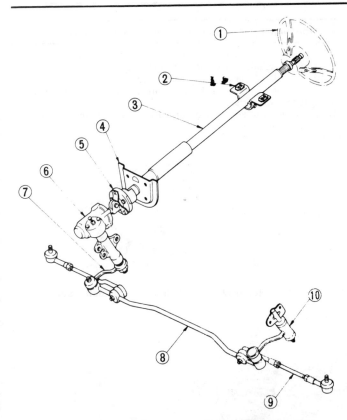

Fig. 11.4 Steering system – component parts (Sec 1)

1	Steering wheel	6	Steering gear
2	Column clamp	7	Gear arm
3	Steering column	8	Cross rod
4	Jacket tube flange	9	Side rod
5	Rubber coupling	10	Idler arm

plate and self locking nuts. To reduce inter-leaf friction and prolong life, plastic inserts are fitted to the ends of the lower spring leaves.

The steering gear is of the worm and nut pattern with re-circulating ball bearings as the link between the nut and worm on the end of the steering shaft within the steering column.

The steering shaft at the worm end rotates in two ball type thrust bearings and at the steering wheel end in a nylon bush. The selector shaft moves in bronze bushes and has an oil seal at its lower end. The upper end of the sector shaft engages a rack which is integral with the ball nut.

Steering shaft bearing adjustment is controlled by shims between the steering box and the steering column flange. Sector shaft end thrust is controlled by an adjusting screw and locknut of the steering box top cover.

The steering gear linkage consists of a steering connecting rod, located by a ball joint at one end to the steering gear pitman arm, and at the other end to the idler arm. The idler arm pivots on a bracket to the bodyframe.

On either end of the steering linkage is an adjustable tie-rod which is attached by ball joints to the steering arms on the front suspension units. These tie-rods provide a means of setting front wheel toe-in.

2 Front wheel hub (drum brakes) – removal and refitting

1 Apply the handbrake, chock the rear wheels, jack up the front of the car and support on firmly based axle-stands. Remove the road wheel.

2 Refer to Chapter 9 and remove the brake drum. For this it may be necessary to release the brake adjustment.

3 Using a screwdriver carefully prise off the dust cover from the centre of the hub.

4 Straighten the ears of the split pin and withdraw the split pin.

5 Undo and remove the hub nut and washer Lift away the outer

bearing cone.

6 The hub may now be drawn off the stub axle.

7 To dismantle the hub place the assembly in a vice and with a suitable drift, remove the grease seal.

8 Lift away the inner bearing cone and then using a drift remove the inner and outer tracks from the interior of the hub assembly. Note which way round the tapers face.

9 Wash the bearings, cups and hub assembly in paraffin and wipe dry with a non-fluffy rag.

10 Inspect the bearing outer tracks and cones for signs of overheating, scoring, corrosion or damage. Assemble each race and check for roughness of movement. If any of these signs are evident new races must be fitted.

11 To reassemble the front hub first fit the bearing outer tracks making sure that the tapers face outwards. Use a suitable diameter tubular drift and drive fully home.

12 Pack the two bearing cone assemblies with a recommended grease.

13 Insert the inner bearing cone assembly and then refit the seal, lip innermost, using the tubular drift. Take care that it is not distorted as it is being driven home.

Fig. 11.5 Removal of hub nut (drum brake) (Sec 2)

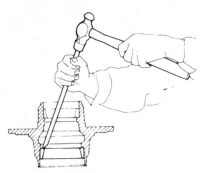

Fig. 11.6 Driving out the wheel bearing outer race (Sec 2)

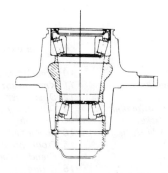

Fig. 11.7 Correct packing of grease in hub (shaded area) (Sec 2)

14 Smear a little grease on the seal lip to provide initial lubrication.
15 Pack the hub with grease and refit to the stub axle.
16 Insert the outer bearing cone assembly and refit the washer and nut. Tighten the nut to a torque wrench setting of 21·7 – 25·3 lbf ft (3·0 – 3·5 kgf m) and then turn the hub assembly several times to seat the bearing.
17 Recheck the stub axle nut torque wrench setting (upper limit) and then back off the nut one quarter of a turn until there is no end play between the nut and bearing.
18 Line up the holes in the castellated nut and stub axle and lock with a new split pin. Refit the dust cover.
19 Refit the brake drum, adjust the brakes and refit the road wheel.

3 Front wheel hub (disc brakes) – removal and refitting

1 Apply the handbrake, chock the rear wheels, jack up the front of the car and support on firmly based axle-stands. Remove the road wheel.
2 Refer to Chapter 9 and disconnect the hydraulic brake hose at the chassis end.
3 Undo and remove the bolts that secure the caliper assembly to the stub axle flange and lift away the caliper assembly.
4 Follow the instructions given in Section 2 paragraphs 4 to 18 inclusive.
5 Refit the caliper and bleed the brake hydraulic system as described in Chapter 9. Refit the roadwheel.

4 Front brake disc – removal, inspection and refitting

1 Refer to Section 3 and remove the hub and disc assembly.
2 Mark the relative positions of the hub and disc so that they may be refitted in their original positions unless new parts are to be fitted.
3 Undo and remove the bolts securing the disc to the hub and separate the two parts.
4 Clean the disc and inspect for signs of deep scoring, chipping or cracking. If evident, a new disc should be obtained.

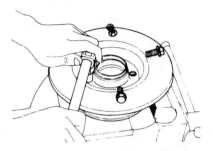

Fig. 11.8 Removal of disc to hub securing bolts (Sec 4)

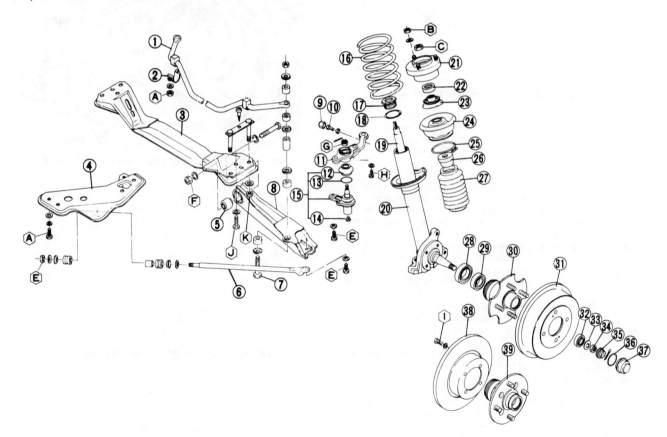

Fig. 11.9 Exploded view of axle and suspension assembly (Sec 5)

1 Stabilizer bar	10 Steering stopper bolt	20 Strut sub-assembly	30 Wheel hub for drum brake
2 Stabilizer mounting bracket	11 Knuckle arm	21 Strut mounting insulator	31 Brake drum
3 Suspension crossmember	12 Dust cover	22 Strut mounting bearing	32 Outer wheel bearing
4 Tension rod bracket	13 Dust cover clamp	23 Dust seal	33 Wheel bearing washer
5 Transverse link bushing	14 Filler plug	24 Spring upper seat	34 Wheel bearing nut
6 Tension rod	15 Lower ball joint assembly	25 Snap ring	35 Adjusting washer
7 Connecting rod	16 Front spring	26 Bound bumper	36 O-ring
8 Transverse link	17 Gland packing	27 Dust cover	37 Hub cap
9 Cap	18 O-ring	28 Grease seal	38 Disc brake rotor
	19 Shock absorber	29 Inner wheel bearing	39 Wheel hub for disc brake

5   To refit the disc check that the two mating faces are really clean and assemble the two parts. Refit the securing bolts and tighten to a final torque wrench setting of 38 lbf ft (5·3 kgf m).
6   Reassemble the hub to the stub axle as described in Section 3.
7   If a dial indicator gauge is available check for disc run-out which should not exceed 0·0024 in (0·06 mm) at the outer circumference. Should this figure be exceeded check that the mating faces are clean and refit to the hub 180° from its first position. If the run-out is still excessive a new disc and/or hub will be necessary.

5 Front axle and suspension assembly – removal and refitting

1   Chock the rear wheels, apply the handbrake, jack up the front of the car and support on firmly based axle-stands. Remove the roadwheels.
2   Undo and remove the self tapping screws securing the splash board to the front area of the engine compartment. Lift away the splash board.
3   Undo and remove the nut securing the brake pipe to the bodyframe. Withdraw the brake hose lock spring and then the brake hose. Plug the open end of the hose and pipe to stop dirt ingress.
4   Straighten the ears and remove the split pin from the side rod socket ball joint securing nut.
5   Undo and remove the castellated nut and separate the side rod socket from the knuckle arm.
6   Undo and remove the one nut which holds the tension rod to the body mounted bracket. Also remove the two nuts that secure the tension rod to the transverse link.
7   The tension rod may now be lifted away.
8   Undo and remove the four bolts and spring washers that secure the tension rod bracket to the underside of the body. Lift away the tension rod bracket.
9   Undo and remove the stabiliser bracket securing nut and bolt from each chassis side member. Lift away the stabiliser bar from the underside of the car.
10 Using an overhead hoist and chains threaded through the engine mounted lifting brackets, support the weight of the engine.
11 Undo and remove the engine mounting securing bolts and release the mountings by lifting the engine slightly. Take care not to damage the radiator hoses.
12 Using a jack located under the centre of the suspension cross-member raise the front of the car until the suspension members are in the fully extended position if this condition has not already been achieved in paragraph 1.
13 Undo and remove the bolts securing the crossmember to the chassis members and support the weight of the crossmember.
14 Working under the bonnet undo and remove the nuts that secure the top of the struts to the inner wing panels.
15 Check that all suspension attachments have been released and then with the help of an assistant manipulate the complete assembly from the front of the car.
16 Refitting the front axle and suspension assembly is the reverse sequence to removal but the following additional points should be noted:

(a) Carefully inspect the tension rod and stabiliser for signs of distortion or accident damage.
(b) Check all rubber parts including the stabiliser and tension rod mountings for signs of oil contamination or deterioration. Should there be any such evidence the item(s) must be renewed.
(c) Tighten the attachments to the torque settings given in the specifications.

6 Front suspension spring and strut assembly – removal and refitting

1   Chock the rear wheels, apply the handbrake, jack up the front of the car and support on firmly based axle-stands. Remove the roadwheels.
2   Undo and remove the nut securing the brake pipe to the body frame. Withdraw the brake hose lock spring and then the brake hose. Plug the open end of the hose and pipe to stop dirt ingress.

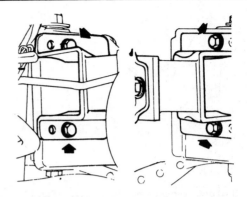
Fig. 11.10 Location of engine mounting bolts (Sec 5)

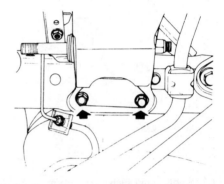
Fig. 11.11 Suspension crossmember attachments (Sec 5)

3   Undo and remove the nut securing the brake hose to the strut mounted bracket. Detach the brake hose from the bracket.
4   *Disc brake models only.* Undo and remove the bolts that secure the caliper to the strut assembly. Lift away the caliper assembly.
5   Undo and remove the bolts holding the strut to the knuckle arm.
6   Using a long metal bar, carefully force the transverse link down until the knuckle arm has been detached from the bottom of the strut.
7   Place a jack or suitable packing under the strut to support its weight during the next operation.
8   Working under the bonnet undo and remove the three nuts fastening the top of the strut to the inner wing panel (Fig. 11.14).
9   Carefully lower the jack or remove the packing and lift away the suspension strut assembly (photo).
10 Refitting the suspension strut assembly is the reverse sequence to removal, but the following additional points should be noted:

(a) Make sure that the brake hose is secure and not twisted or kinked.
(b) When fitting the steering knuckle arm to the bottom of the strut assembly, apply a liquid sealer to the area shown in Fig. 11.15 to prevent rusting of the ball stud.
(c) Tighten the strut to body nut to a torque wrench setting of 18 – 26 lbf ft (2.5 – 3.5 kgf m) and the steering knuckle arm to strut bolt to a torque wrench setting of 53 – 72 lbf ft (7.3 – 9.9 kgf m).

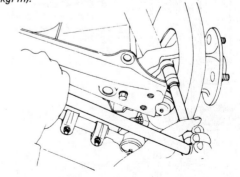
Fig. 11.12 Removing the knuckle arm bolts (Sec 6)

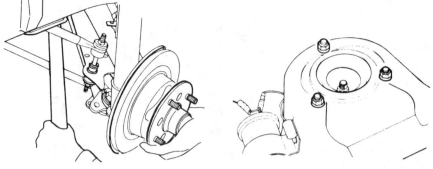

Fig. 11.13 Using a metal bar to detach knuckle arm (Sec 6)

Fig. 11.14 Strut upper securing nuts (Sec 6)

6.9 Front suspension spring and strut

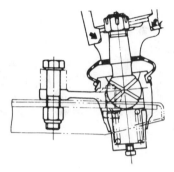

Fig. 11.15 Apply liquid sealer to points arrowed (Sec 6)

Fig. 11.16 Sectional view of strut assembly (Sec 7)

1   Gland packing assembly
2   Oil seal
3   O-ring
4   Piston rod guide assembly
5   Cylinder
6   Rebound stopper
7   Strut-outer casing
8   Piston rod
9   Check valve spring retainer
10 Check valve spring
11 Check valve plate
12 Piston ring
13 Valve plate
14 Piston body
15 Nut
16 Bolt
17 Distance collar
18 Spring retainer
19 Check valve spring
20 Bottom valve body
21 Check valve plate
22 Valve plate
23 Nut
24 Bottom plate

7 Front suspension spring and strut assembly – dismantling, inspection and reassembly

It is recommended that, if the strut assembly is in need of overhaul or it is necessary for new coil springs to be fitted, this job be left to the local Datsun garage. The reason for this is that special tools are necessary to compress the spring, keep the spring in a compressed state and to dismantle the strut assembly.

The following instructions are given for those who wish to attempt the job. Before removing the strut assembly from the car it is necessary to fit clips to the coil spring to keep it in the compressed condition. These should be either borrowed from the local Datsun garage or made up using some high tensile steel rod at least 0.5 inch (12.70 mm) in diameter with the ends bent over. The length should accommodate as many coils as possible. Refer to Section 6 and follow the instructions given in paragraph 1. Then place a jack under the strut and compress the road spring by raising the jack. Fit the spring clips and tie firmly in place with strong wire or cord. Now follow the instructions given in paragraph 2 to 9 inclusive.

To overhaul the strut assembly proceed as follows.

1   Thoroughly clean the unit by working in paraffin and then wiping dry with a clean non-fluffy rag.

2   Fit the coil spring compressor to the suspension unit, make sure that it is correctly positioned and then compress the spring. This is not applicable if the spring clips are in position.

3   Carefully prise the circlip from the dust cover.

4   Undo and remove the self-locking nut. A new one will be necessary on reassembly.

5   Lift off the strut insulator, strut bearing, oil seal, upper spring seat and rubber bump stop.

6   Remove the coil spring still in the compressed state.

7   Push the piston rod down until it reaches its fully retracted position.

8   It is now necessary for the gland packing to be removed. Ideally a special tool should be used but it may be improvised using a wrench.

9   Remove the O-ring from the top of the piston rod guide.

10 Lift out the piston rod together with the cylinder. **IMPORTANT.** *The piston and piston rod guide must never be removed from the cylinder as these are set relative to each other.*

11 Tilt the inner cylinder and allow the hydraulic fluid to drain out into a container. Also drain out any fluid inside the outer casing. Fresh fluid will be required during reassembly.

12 Wash all parts in petrol and wipe dry. Make quite sure no dirt is allowed to contact any internal parts.

13 Always renew the gland packing, and O-ring when the strut has been dismantled.

14 Inspect the outer casing for signs of distortion, cracking or accident damage and obtain new if any such condition is apparent.

15 Inspect the spindle for hair line cracks on the base or damaged threads. If evident the complete strut assembly should be renewed.

16 Inspect the rubber and metal joint for signs of damage or deterioration. Obtain new parts if evident.

17 If noise originated from the strut when driving over rough road surfaces the cause is probably due to the strut mounting bearing having worn. Obtain a new bearing assembly.

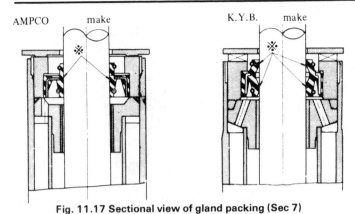

Fig. 11.17 Sectional view of gland packing (Sec 7)

Apply grease at these points

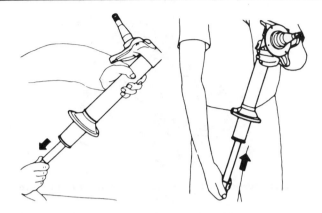

Fig. 11.18 Bleeding the shock absorber (Sec 7)

18 Before reassembly commences make sure that every part is really clean and free from dust.

19 Fit the piston rod and cylinder into position in the outer casing.

20 Fill the assembly with the recommended grade of hydraulic fluid. For AMPCO (ATSUGI) units use 325 cc or KYB (KAYABA) units use 322 cc. Do not deviate from the quoted amounts otherwise the operating efficiency of the unit will be altered.

21 Place the rod guide on the top of the piston rod guide and refit the gland packing.

22 Lubricate the sealing lips with a little multi-purpose grease and tighten the gland packing to a torque wrench setting of 51 – 94 lbf ft (7 – 13 kgf m). This will have to be estimated if the special tool is not available. **Note.** *When tightening the gland packing the piston rod must be extended approximately 4.724 in (120 mm) from the end of the outer casing to expel most of the air out of the strut.*

23 It is now necessary to bleed the shock absorber system by holding the strut with the spindle end down and pulling the piston rod out completely.

24 Now invert the strut so that the spindle end is uppermost and push the piston rod inward as far as it will go.

25 Repeat the procedure described in paragraph 23 several times until an equal pressure is felt during both strokes.

26 Pull the piston rod out fully and fit the rebound rubber, to prevent the piston rod falling by its own weight.

27 Locate the spring on the lower spring seat with the end fitted into the recess and compress the spring with the special tool if spring clips are not fitted.

28 Refit the dust cover, upper spring seat, mounting bearing and insulator.

29 Lubricate the arrowed parts shown in Fig. 11.19 with a little multi-purpose grease.

30 Refit the piston rod self locking nut and tighten to a torque wrench setting of 43 – 54 lbf ft (6 – 7·5 kgf m).

31 With the spring correctly located release the spring compressor. If clips have been used leave in position until the strut has been reassembled to the car.

32 Raise the rebound rubber until it is seated under the upper spring seat.

33 The strut assembly is now ready for refitting to the car.

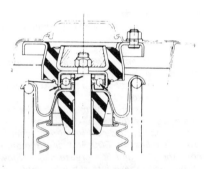

Fig. 11.19 Section through top of strut assembly showing grease points (arrowed) (Sec 7)

8 Transmission and lower balljoint – removal and refitting

1 Chock the rear wheels, apply the handbrake, jack up the front of the car and support on firmly based axle-stands. Remove the relevant roadwheel.

2 Undo and remove the bolts which secure the knuckle arm in position.

3 Straighten the ears and withdraw the split pin from the side rod socket balljoint castellated nut. Undo and remove the nut and separate the side rod socket from the knuckle arm.

4 The tension rod and stabiliser should now be detached from the transverse link.

5 Using a pry bar increase the space between the steering linkage and transverse link to remove the transverse link.

6 Undo and remove the transverse link securing nuts and lift the link

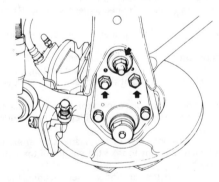

Fig. 11.20 Location of transverse link securing nuts (arrowed) (Sec 8)

away from the suspension member.

7 Undo and remove the balljoint securing nut and lift the balljoint from the transverse link.

8 Wash all parts and wipe dry. Carefully inspect the transverse link for signs of cracks, distortion or accident damage. Should the rubber and inner tube joints be sticky or show signs of cracking the transverse link should be renewed as a complete assembled unit.

9 Inspect the balljoint for end play and damage. Check the dust cover for cracks and deterioration. Should there be end play or damage to the balljoint a new one must be fitted. Generally a new balljoint

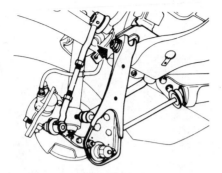

Fig. 11.21 Location of transverse link inner attachments (arrowed) (Sec 8)

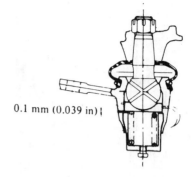

0.1 mm (0.039 in)

Fig. 11.22 Lower ball joint free movement (Sec 8)

assembly is supplied complete with a dust cover. It is not possible to dismantle and overhaul the balljoint assembly.

10 Inspect the transverse link bushing and if it is worn or the rubber contaminated it must be renewed. The old bush may be drifted out and a new one fitted. Take care to ensure that the bush is fitted the correct way round.

11 Refitting the transverse link and lower balljoint is the reverse sequence to removal, but the following additional points should be noted:

(a) *Do not fully tighten the transverse link mounting bolts until the car has been lowered to the ground*

(b) *Tighten the balljoint bolt to a torque wrench setting of 14 – 18 lbf ft (1.9 – 2.5 kgf m).*

(c) *Tighten the transverse link mounting bolts to a torque wrench setting of 35 – 46 lbf ft (4.9 – 6.3 kgf m)*

(d) *A new balljoint should now be lubricated and then at intervals of 30 000 miles (50 000 km) or 48 months. To lubricate, remove the plug and fit a grease nipple. Slowly pump a little multi-purpose grease into the joint until the old grease has been forced out. Remove the grease nipple and refit the plug.*

9 Rear suspension (IRS – 610 series) – removal and refitting

1 Chock the front wheels, jack up the rear of the car and support on firmly based axle-stands positioned under the body. Remove the road wheel.

2 Release the handbrake and then disconnect the handbrake at the equaliser.

3 Refer to Chapter 7 and remove the propeller shaft.

4 Slacken the clips and disconnect the exhaust pipe at the joint next to the drive pinion flange and at the rear silencer. Remove the silencer and pipe.

5 Refer to Chapter 9 and disconnect the two rear brake flexible pipes at the unions on the suspension arms. Plug the open ends to stop dirt ingress.

6 Position a jack under one of the suspension arms and raise the arm by a sufficient amount to take the weight of the coil spring from the shock absorbers.

7 Undo and remove the nut and washer securing the lower shock absorber mounting. Detach the shock absorber and recover the rubber bushes.

8 Carefully lower the suspension arm so as to release the coil spring.

9 Carry out operations 6, 7 and 8 for the second side of the suspension assembly.

10 Support the weight of the complete suspension assembly with a trolley jack under the final drive assembly.

11 Undo and remove the four self locking nuts and washers. These are located at each suspension member mounting and final drive housing member mounting.

12 Carefully lower the jack so that the flexible mountings are clear of the mounting bolts and then pull the assembly rearward and away from the car.

13 Recover the spring seats from the upper end of the springs. Lift each spring from its lower seat in the suspension arm. Unless the springs are to be renewed, do not get them mixed up.

14 Refitting the rear suspension assembly is the reverse sequence to removal. The following additional points should however, be noted:

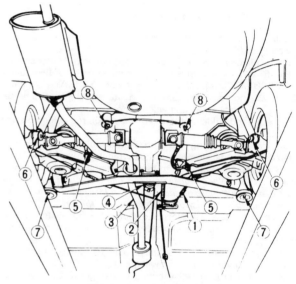

Fig. 11.23. Rear suspension attachment points (Sec 9)

1	Handbrake cable	5	Brake hose
2	Return spring	6	Brake hose
3	Exhaust pipe	7	Cross member mounting
4	Propeller shaft	8	Differential mounting

Fig. 11.24 Removing rear axle and suspension assembly (Sec 9)

(a) *Check the clearance between the outer lip of the rubber insulator and the face of the washer and if it exceeds 0·197 inch (5 mm) new insulator rubbers should be fitted. Use a bolt, nut, washers and tube to remove and fit the new bushes*

(b) *If the insulator rubbers have not been renewed make sure that they are a good fit and in alignment*

(c) *All attaching bolts should be checked for damage to the threads. If suspect fit new bolts*

10 Rear suspension (IRS – 810 series) – removal and refitting

1   Refer to Section 9 and carry out operations 1 to 5 inclusive.
2   Support under the centre of the suspension member and differential gear carrier with a jack.
3   Disconnect the shock absorbers at the lower mountings.
4   Remove the two nuts at each end of the suspension member mounting and differential mounting.
5   Carefully lower the jack, support the suspension assembly so that it does not fall off the jack, and pull the assembly rearward from under the car.

6   Refitting the suspension assembly is the reverse of the removal procedure, noting the following points:

(a) Ensure that the suspension member and differential mounting member are correctly lined-up.
(b) The rubber insulators should be aligned as shown in Fig. 11.26 and inserted from the underside.
(c) The tightening torque must be as specified.
(d) Don't forget to bleed the brakes as described in Chapter 9, Section 4.

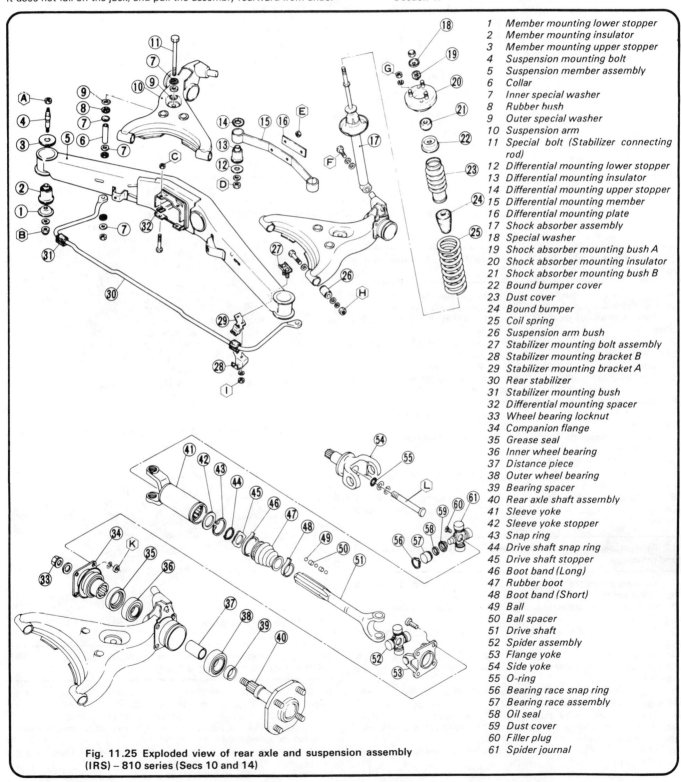

1   Member mounting lower stopper
2   Member mounting insulator
3   Member mounting upper stopper
4   Suspension mounting bolt
5   Suspension member assembly
6   Collar
7   Inner special washer
8   Rubber bush
9   Outer special washer
10 Suspension arm
11 Special bolt (Stabilizer connecting rod)
12 Differential mounting lower stopper
13 Differential mounting insulator
14 Differential mounting upper stopper
15 Differential mounting member
16 Differential mounting plate
17 Shock absorber assembly
18 Special washer
19 Shock absorber mounting bush A
20 Shock absorber mounting insulator
21 Shock absorber mounting bush B
22 Bound bumper cover
23 Dust cover
24 Bound bumper
25 Coil spring
26 Suspension arm bush
27 Stabilizer mounting bolt assembly
28 Stabilizer mounting bracket B
29 Stabilizer mounting bracket A
30 Rear stabilizer
31 Stabilizer mounting bush
32 Differential mounting spacer
33 Wheel bearing locknut
34 Companion flange
35 Grease seal
36 Inner wheel bearing
37 Distance piece
38 Outer wheel bearing
39 Bearing spacer
40 Rear axle shaft assembly
41 Sleeve yoke
42 Sleeve yoke stopper
43 Snap ring
44 Drive shaft snap ring
45 Drive shaft stopper
46 Boot band (Long)
47 Rubber boot
48 Boot band (Short)
49 Ball
50 Ball spacer
51 Drive shaft
52 Spider assembly
53 Flange yoke
54 Side yoke
55 O-ring
56 Bearing race snap ring
57 Bearing race assembly
58 Oil seal
59 Dust cover
60 Filler plug
61 Spider journal

Fig. 11.25 Exploded view of rear axle and suspension assembly (IRS) – 810 series (Secs 10 and 14)

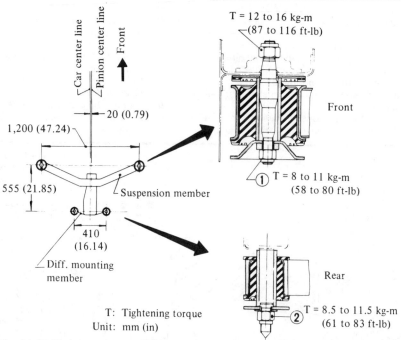

Fig. 11.26 Fitting rear suspension mounting insulators – (IRS) 810 series (Sec 10)

11 Rear suspension coil spring (IRS – 610 series) – removal and refitting

1   Chock the front wheels, jack up the rear of the car and support the body on firmly supported stands. Remove the roadwheel.
2   Undo and remove the drive-flange nuts located next to the backing plate.
3   Straighten the ears and withdraw the split pin retaining the hand-brake cable clevis pin. Remove the clevis pin.
4   Undo and remove the rebound rubber securing nut.
5   Position a jack under the suspension arm and lift sufficiently to relieve spring pressure on the shock absorber.
6   Undo and remove the shock absorber lower mounting support securing nut. Detach the shock absorber from the lower support mounting.
7   Carefully lower the jack and lift away the coil spring, rebound rubber and spring seat.
8   Inspect the coil spring for signs of excessive rusting, coil failure or distortion. If evident a pair of new springs should be fitted to ensure the car stands evenly on the road.
9   Refitting the coil spring is the reverse sequence to removal. Always check the spring seat rubbers for deterioration and renew if evident.

12 Rear suspension shock absorber (IRS – 610 series) – removal and refitting

1   Working inside the luggage compartment undo and remove the two nuts from the upper end of the shock absorber.
2   Undo and remove the retaining nut from the lower support mounting.
3   The shock absorber may now be contracted and lifted away from the car.
4   Inspect the shock absorber for signs of hydraulic fluid leaks. Should there be any evidence of this, a new shock absorber must be obtained.
5   Clean the exterior and wipe with a non-fluffy rag. Inspect the shaft for signs of corrosion or distortion, and the body for damage.
6   Check the action by expanding and contracting to ascertain if equal resistance is felt on both strokes. If the resistance is very uneven the unit must be renewed.
7   Check the rubber bushes and washers for deterioration and obtain new if evident.
8   Refitting is the reverse sequence to removal.

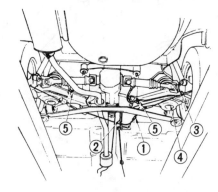

Fig. 11.27 Suspension coil spring removal points – (IRS) 610 series (Sec 11)

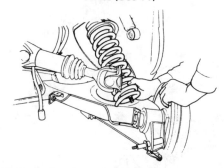

Fig. 11.28 Removing the coil spring – (IRS) 610 series (Sec 11)

13 Rear suspension coil spring and shock absorber assembly (IRS – 810 series) – removal and refitting

1   Chock the front wheels, jack up the rear of the car and support the body with axle-stands. Remove the road wheel.
2   Position a jack under the suspension arm to support it.
3   Working inside the boot, remove the three nuts securing the shock absorber mounting insulator to the body.
4   Disconnect the lower end of the shock absorber by removing the bolt securing it to the suspension arm.
5   Lift out the coil spring and shock absorber assembly (photo).

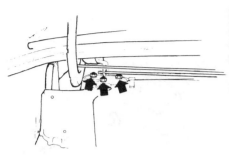

Fig. 11.29 Shock absorber upper mounting nuts (IRS) 810 series (Sec 13)

13.5 Rear suspension coil spring and shock absorber (810 series)

Fig. 11.30 Compressing the coil spring (Sec 14)

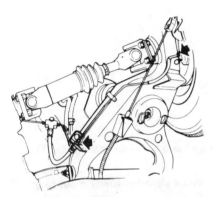

Fig. 11.31 Detachment points of brake hose and pipe (Sec 15)

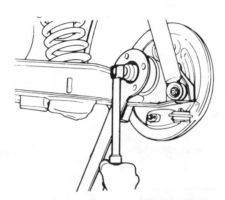

Fig. 11.32 Removing the wheel bearing lock nut (Sec 15)

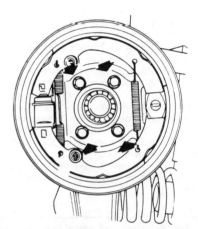

Fig. 11.33 Backplate securing bolts (Sec 15)

6   Refitting is the reverse of the removal procedure. Fit the top end of the assembly first. Tighten the mounting insulator-to-body nuts to 19 – 29 lbf ft (2·6 – 4·0 kgf m) and the shock absorber lower end bolt to 43 – 58 lbf ft (6 – 8 kgf m).

Note: *On later models a new one-piece shock absorber mounting has been used. This is interchangeable, as a set, with the previous two-piece version.*

14 Rear suspension coil spring and shock absorber assembly (IRS – 810 series) – dismantling, inspection and reassembly

1   Dismantling of the coil spring and shock absorber assembly require the use of a suitable spring compressor. The Datsun tool is shown in Fig. 11.30.
2   Wrap rag round the shock absorber, fit clamps and mount in a vice. Take care not to damage the body of the shock absorber.
3   Mark the position of the shock absorber mounting insulator and lower end pin so that they can be reassembled in the same position.
4   Using a spring compressor tool, compress the spring far enough to allow the mounting insulator to be turned by hand.
5   Remove the piston rod self-locking nut and washer. Release the compression on the spring and remove the spring compressor.
6   Take out the shock absorber mounting bush A (refer to Fig. 11.25), insulator, bush B, bumper cover, dust cover, and bumper. Lift off the coil spring.
7   Check the shock absorber for oil leakage and cracks, and the piston rod for straightness. Renew any rubber parts that show signs of wear, damage or deterioration. Check the spring to the Specifications at the beginning of this Chapter.
8   Reassembly is the reverse of the dismantling sequence. Ensure that the coil spring is located in the lower seat and the flat face of the spring is at the top. Fit the mounting insulator and lower end pin of the

shock absorber in the positions marked at dismantling. Always fit a new self-locking nut.

15 Rear suspension arm (IRS – 610 series) – removal and refitting

1   Chock the front wheels, jack up the rear of the car and support the body on firmly based axle-stands. Remove the roadwheel.
2   Refer to Chapter 9 and remove the brake drum.
3   Undo and remove the four bolts and detach the drive shaft from the axle flange. Tie back out of the way with string or wire.
4   Refer to Chapter 9 and detach the handbrake cable from the wheel cylinder lever and from the equaliser lever. Also detach the brake flexible hose from the main line pipe. Plug the ends to stop dirt ingress.
5   Undo and remove the wheel bearing locknut and remove the axle shaft and wheel bearing assembly. Further information will be found in Section 17.
6   Undo and remove the four backplate securing bolts and lift away the complete backplate assembly.
7   Refer to Section 12 and remove the shock absorber.
8   Slowly lower the jack used when removing the shock absorber and lift away the coil spring, spring seat and rebound rubber.
9   Undo and remove the self locking nuts from the two bolts which connect the suspension arm to the suspension member. Lift away the suspension arm (Fig 11.34).
10 Inspect the suspension arm bushes and if worn use a bolt, nut, washers and tubing to draw out the old bushes and fit new ones.
11 Refitting the rear suspension arm is the reverse sequence to removal. The following additional points should be noted:

  (a) *Always use new self locking nuts.*
  (b) *Finally tighten all suspension attachments when the car is resting on the ground.*
  (c) *It will be necessary to bleed the brake hydraulic system as described in Chapter 9.*

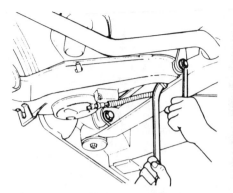

Fig. 11.34 Removing suspension arm securing nuts (Sec 15)

16.3 Disconnect the shock absorber

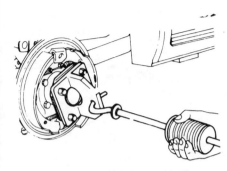

Fig. 11.35 Using a slide hammer to remove rear axle shaft (Sec 17)

16 Rear suspension arm (IRS – 810 series) – removal and refitting

1   Refer to Section 15 and carry out the operations described in paragraphs 1 to 5 inclusive.
2   Remove the stabiliser bar (if fitted) from the suspension arm.
3   Disconnect the lower end of the shock absorber by removing the bolt securing it to the suspension arm (photo).
4   Remove the suspension arm pins which attach the suspension arm to the suspension member and withdraw the suspension arm.
5   Inspect the suspension arm rubber bushes; if worn or deformed use a bolt, nut, washers and a piece of tubing to draw out the old bushes and fit new ones.
6   Refitting the rear suspension arm is the reverse of the removal sequence. Refer to Section 15 paragraph 11 for additional points to be noted.

17 Rear axleshaft and wheel bearings (IRS) – removal and refitting

1   Chock the front wheels, jack up the rear of the car and support the body on firmly based axle-stands. Remove the roadwheel.
2   Refer to Chapter 9 and remove the brake drum.
3   Undo and remove the four bolts and detach the drive shaft from the axle flange. Tie back out of the way with string or wire.
4   Hold the companion flange with a large wrench and then undo and remove the axle shaft and wheel bearing lock nut.
5   Using a soft faced hammer drive the axle shaft outward through the suspension arm boss. Recover the companion flange. If very tight a slide hammer will be required.
6   Undo and remove the four bolts retaining the grease shield to the axle flange. Lift away the grease catcher.
7   The inner bearing and seal may now be removed using a suitable metal drift.
8   Again using a metal drift drive out the outer bearing. The bearings once removed cannot be reused as they will probably be damaged so they must only be removed for renewal.
9   Thoroughly wash all components and wipe dry with a non-fluffy rag.
10   Inspect the machined surfaces of the companion flange for damage and renew if necessary.
11   Check the axleshaft for signs of damage, distortion or wear. Obtain a new shaft if any such evidence exists.
12   Inspect the bearing spacer for signs of wear or damage.
13   To reassemble first repack the bearings with the recommended grease. Lubricate the inside of the bearing hub.
14   Using a tube of suitable diameter carefully drift the inner bearing into the housing. As the race is of the semi-sealed type, the sealed face must face toward the companion flange.
15   If it has been found necessary to fit a new suspension arm make sure that the correct coding bearing spacer is used. If the suspension arm hub is marked with a letter A, then the bearing spacer to be used must also be marked with a letter A. This is very important otherwise a clearance between the spacer and bearing of 0·002 inch (0·05 mm) will not be maintained. On 610 series the markings are A, B or C and on 810 series the hub and spacer are marked N, M or P.

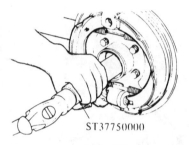

Fig. 11.36 Removing oil seal and inner bearing (Sec 17)

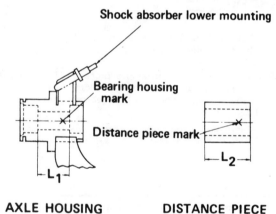

Fig. 11.37 Matching marks on axle housing and distance piece (Sec 17)

16   Fit the bearing spacer into the housing and then drift the new outer bearing into the housing using a suitable diameter tubular drift.
17   As the race is of the semi-sealed type the sealed face must face towards the outside.
18   Smear a little grease onto the seal lips and then fit the inner and outer seals to the housing.
19   Refit the grease shield and secure with the four bolts.
20   Insert the axleshaft into the housing and position the companion flange over the end of the axle.
21   Hold the companion flange with a wrench, fit a new wheel bearing locknut and tighten to a torque of 181 – 239 lbf ft (25 – 33 kgf m).
22   Using a dial test indicator, check that there is an axleshaft endplay of 0 – 0·006 in (0·015 mm) for 610 series and less than 0·012 in (0·3 mm) for 810 series.
23   If the specified endplay cannot be obtained, fit a different spacer. After checking the endplay stake the wheel bearing locknut.
24   Fit the driveshaft to the companion flange and tighten the four securing bolts.
25   Refitting is now the reverse of the removal procedure.

18 Driveshaft (IRS) – removal and refitting

1 Chock the front wheels, jack up the rear of the car and support on firmly based axle-stands. Remove the roadwheel.
2 With a scriber or file, mark the driveshaft and output flanges and the driveshaft and stub axle companion flanges to ensure that they are reconnected in their original positions.
3 Undo and remove the four securing bolts (and nuts) at each end of the driveshaft and detach the driveshaft (photo).
4 On later models disconnect the driveshaft from the differential by removing the side yoke securing bolt and remove the side yoke together with the driveshaft (photo).
5 Refitting is the reverse of the removal procedure.

19 Driveshaft (IRS) – dismantling, inspection and reassembly

1 There are two reasons for dismantling the driveshaft. Firstly for lubrication purposes at 30 000 miles (50 000 km) intervals and secondly for overhaul due to wear. If the latter is applicable, always ensure that there are spare parts available.
2 Using a pair of circlip pliers, remove the circlip located at the end of the needle bearing cups at the sleeved end of the shaft.
3 If the assembly is being dismantled for lubrication only, it is only necessary to disconnect the trunnion and cups at the sleeve yoke.
4 Using a soft metal drift carefully tap in one of the bearing cups so as to push the other bearing through the yoke.
5 Lift the bearing out carefully using the fingers only so as not to dislodge the needle rollers.
6 Using the soft metal drift again, tap the end of the trunnion of the bearing previously removed, so as to push the second bearing through the yoke. As previously described, carefully remove the bearing.
7 Manipulate the yoke over the ends of the trunnion so as to remove the flange and trunnion from the sleeve yokes.
8 Where renewal of the needle bearing and trunnion assembly is necessary, follow the instructions already given to remove the needle bearing and trunnion from the flange yoke. Should it be necessary, treat the driveshaft assembly in a similar manner.
9 Using a pair of circlip pliers, remove the circlip and then withdraw the plug and O-ring from the yoke end of the sleeve.
10 To make removal of the circlip and stop plate on the end of the

18.3 Remove the flange securing bolts

18.4 Remove the side yoke securing bolt

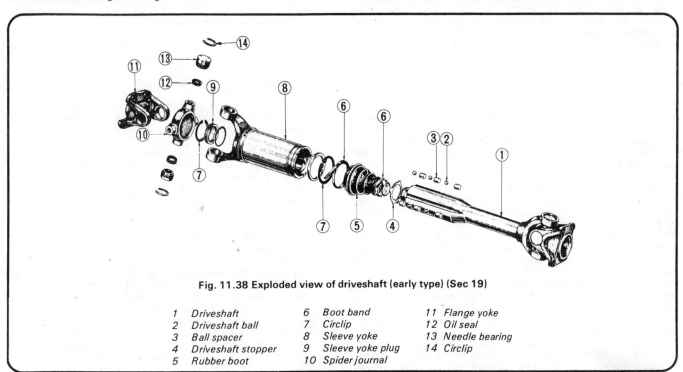
Fig. 11.38 Exploded view of driveshaft (early type) (Sec 19)

1 Driveshaft	6 Boot band	11 Flange yoke
2 Driveshaft ball	7 Circlip	12 Oil seal
3 Ball spacer	8 Sleeve yoke	13 Needle bearing
4 Driveshaft stopper	9 Sleeve yoke plug	14 Circlip
5 Rubber boot	10 Spider journal	

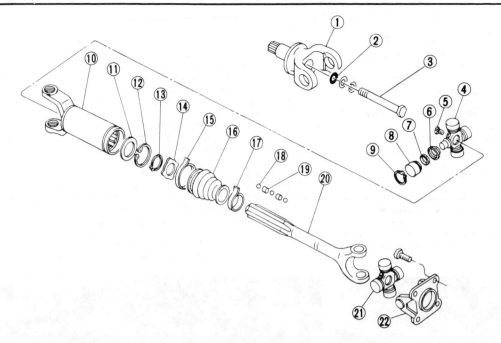

1   Side yoke
2   O-ring
3   Side yoke bolt
4   Spider journal
5   Filler plug
6   Dust cover
7   Oil seal
8   Bearing race assembly
9   Bearing race snap ring
10   Sleeve yoke
11   Sleeve yoke stopper
12   Circlip
13   Driveshaft snap ring
14   Driveshaft stopper
15   Boot band (long)
16   Rubber boot
17   Boot band (short)
18   Ball
19   Ball spacer
20   Driveshaft
21   Spider assembly
22   Flange yoke

Fig. 11.39 Exploded view of driveshaft (later type) (Sec 19)

shaft easy, push the sleeve down the shaft.
11 Slacken the clip that holds the rubber boot to the sleeve and slide the boot from the sleeve.
12 Remove the circlip and ring from the end of the sleeve.
13 Using a scriber or file, mark the shaft and sleeve to ensure correct refitting in their original positions.
14 Slide the shaft out from the sleeve taking great care not to lose any of the spacers or ball bearings.
15 Slacken the second clip holding the rubber boot to the shaft and remove the boot from the shaft.
16 Before inspection, clean all parts and wipe dry with a non-fluffy rag.
17 Inspect the driveshaft for signs of wear or damage. Also check to see that it is not distorted. Check the sleeve in a similar manner.
18 Check the steel spacers and ball bearings for wear or damage.
Note: *Sleeve yoke, balls, spacers and driveshafts are not available as spares. If any of these parts are defective, the ....shaft must be renewed as an assembly.*
19 Inspect the yoke plug O-ring and rubber boot for signs of deterioration or splitting, and obtain new, if evident.
20 Inspect the yoke eyes in the sleeve, shaft and flanges for signs of wear between the needle roller bearings and trunnion. If evident it will be necessary to fit new needle roller bearings and trunnion assemblies.
21 If a dial indicator gauge is available push the driveshaft into the sleeve as far as possible and determine the amount of play between the shaft and sleeve. This must not be in excess of 0·004 in (0·1 mm).
22 Finally check for radial play between the shaft and sleeve.
23 To reassemble, first fit a new rubber boot onto the driveshaft and secure with the clip.
24 Smear some grease onto the shaft splines and place the steel balls and spacers in their grooves. Pack a little grease between them.
25 Slide the driveshaft into the sleeve, aligning the previously made marks. Take care not to dislodge any of the ball bearings or spacers.
26 Fit the ring and circlip into the end of the sleeve.
27 Gently push the shaft up the sleeve and fit the stop plate and circlip to the end of the shaft. Now pull the shaft out as far as possible.
28 Inject 1·25 ounces (35 gms.) of grease into the sleeve from the yoke end.
29 Fit a new O-ring onto the yoke plug and refit the plug and circlip.
30 Place the rubber boot over the sleeve and secure the end of the boot with the clips.
31 Manipulate the trunnion into position in the yoke and lubricate the needle roller bearings with grease.
32 Refit the needle bearing cups and seals into position in the yoke.
33 Finally fit a circlip to each of the needle bearing cups. To control axial play of the joint, circlips in four different thicknesses are available

to set the axial play to not more than 0·0008 inch (0·02 mm).
34 The driveshaft assembly is now ready for refitting to the car.

20 Rear axle and suspension (rigid axle) – removal and refitting

1   Chock the front wheels, jack up the rear of the car and support the body on firmly based axle stands. Remove the roadwheels.
2   Using a jack, preferably of the trolley type, support the weight of the rear axle.
3   Refer to Chapter 9 and detach the handbrake cable from the equaliser lever.
4   Refer to Chapter 7 and remove the propeller shaft.
5   Refer to Chapter 9 and disconnect the brake hydraulic hose from the three way connector on the axle casing. Plug the open ends to stop dirt ingress.
6   Undo and remove each shock absorber's lower mounting securing nuts and detach the shock absorbers from the spring seats.
7   Undo and remove the bolts securing the rear end of the springs from the shackle. Detach the springs from the rear shackles.
8   Unbolt and remove the bolts holding the spring to the front brakes.
9   Lower the jack and draw the complete rear suspension assembly rearward from the car.
10   Refitting the rear suspension unit is the reverse sequence to removal. Check the tightness of all attachments with the weight of the car on the ground.

21 Rear shock absorber (rigid axle) – removal and refitting

1   Chock the front wheels, jack up the front of the car and support on firmly based stands. Remove the road wheel.
2   Undo and remove the bolts that secure the upper end of the shock absorber to the body.
3   Undo and remove the nut and washer fixing the shock absorber to the spring plate attachment. Detach the shock absorber and lift away from the car.
4   Inspect the shock absorber for signs of hydraulic fluid leaks, should there be such evidence, it must be discarded and a new one obtained.
5   Clean the exterior and wipe with a non-fluffy rag. Inspect the shaft for signs of corrosion or distortion and the body for damage.
6   Check the action by expanding and contracting to ascertain if equal resistance is felt on both strokes. If the resistance is very uneven the unit must be renewed. It may be found that resistance is greater on the upward stroke than on the downward stroke and this is permissible.

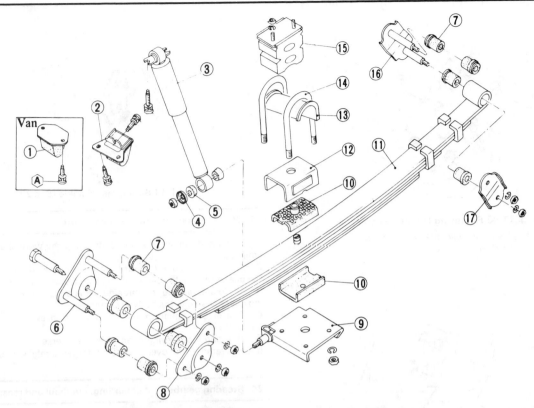

Fig. 11.40 Exploded view of rear suspension – Estate Car (Sec 20)

1 Torque arrester (For Van)	6 Front pin assembly	10 Spring seating pad	14 U-bolt (Spring clip)
2 Torque arrester (For Estate)	7 Spring bush	11 Rear spring assembly	15 Rear axle bumper
3 Shock absorber assembly	8 Front pin outer plate	12 Location plate	16 Shackle pin assembly
4 Special washer	9 Lower spring seat	13 Rear axle plate	17 Shackle
5 Shock absorber bush			

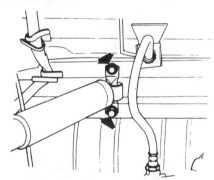

Fig. 11.41 Shock absorber upper mounting (Sec 21)

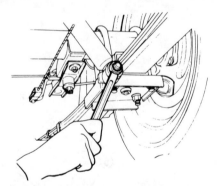

Fig. 11.42 Disconnecting the shock absorber from lower mounting (Sec 21)

7   Check the rubber bushes and washers for deterioration and obtain new if evident.
8   Refitting is the reverse sequence to removal.

22 Rear spring (rigid axle) – removal and refitting

1   Chock the front wheels, jack up the rear of the car and support on firmly based stands. Remove the road wheel.
2   Place the jack under the centre of the rear axle casing and raise until the strain is taken from the shock absorbers.
3   Undo and remove the nut and washer that secures the shock absorber to the spring plate attachment. Detach the shock absorber and contract until it is clear of the axle housing.
4   Lower the jack until the weight of the axle has been taken from the spring.
5   Undo and remove the U-bolt nuts and lift away the mounting

plate. If tight tap with a hammer but take care not to damage the U-bolt threads (Fig. 11.43).
6   Undo and remove the rear shackle nuts and washers.
7   Lift away the shackle plates noting the correct positioning of the shackle pins. The bottom nut must be fitted towards the centre of the car (Fig. 11.44).
8   Rest the axle on wood blocks and lower the rear of the spring to the ground. Recover the two rubber bushes from the body spring shackle hanger.
9   Undo and remove the nut from the front hanger bolt and tap out the bolt with a soft faced hammer.
10 The spring may now be removed from the car.
11 If any of the shackles or rubber bushes are worn they must be renewed together with the pins if they show signs of wear.
12 Refitment is a straightforward reversal of the dismantling process. Do not fully tighten the attachments until the car has been lowered to the ground and the spring is in its normal position. If this is not done the rubber bushes will require frequent renewal.

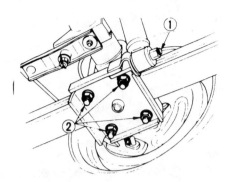

Fig. 11.43 Removing U-bolts (Sec 22)

  1 *Shock absorber lower attachment*
  2 *U-bolt securing nuts*

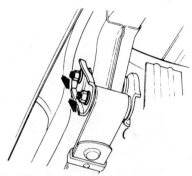

Fig. 11.44 Spring rear shackle (Sec 22)

23 Steering gearbox – removal and refitting

1   Undo and remove the bolt connecting the wormshaft and rubber coupling.
2   Undo and remove the nut from the sector shaft and then separate the gear arm from the sector shaft using a universal puller.
3   Undo and remove the three nuts and bolts which secure the steering gear housing to the body side member.
4   The steering gearbox may now be lifted away from the engine compartment.
5   Refitting the steering gearbox is the reverse sequence to removal. If it was removed for overhaul, do not forget to refill with oil.

24 Steering gearbox – dismantling, overhaul and reassembly

1   Wash the exterior of the steering gearbox and wipe dry with a non-fluffy rag.
2   Undo and remove the filler plug, invert the gearbox and drain the oil.
3   Undo and remove the nut securing the pitman arm to the sector shaft. Lift away the spring washer.

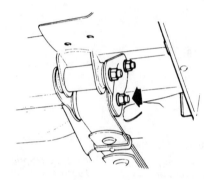

Fig. 11.45 Spring front shackle (Sec 22)

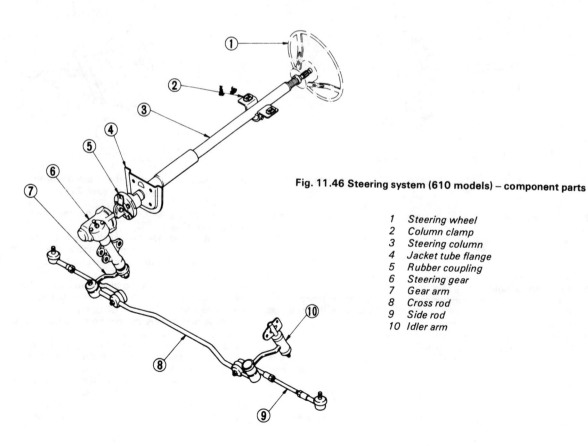

Fig. 11.46 Steering system (610 models) – component parts

  1   *Steering wheel*
  2   *Column clamp*
  3   *Steering column*
  4   *Jacket tube flange*
  5   *Rubber coupling*
  6   *Steering gear*
  7   *Gear arm*
  8   *Cross rod*
  9   *Side rod*
  10   *Idler arm*

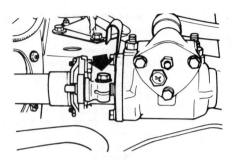

Fig. 11.47 Removing rubber coupling securing bolt (Sec 23)

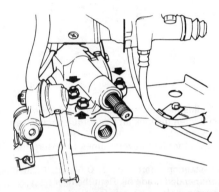

Fig. 11.48 Steering gearbox mounting bolts (Sec 23)

4 Using a universal puller draw the arm from the splines on the selector shaft.

5 Slacken the locknut and back off the sector shaft adjustment screw in a clockwise direction.

6 Undo and remove the sector shaft cover securing bolts and then lift away the cover. Carefully withdraw the sector shaft.

7 Undo and remove the three rear cover securing bolts and lift away the cover.

8 The bearing adjustment shims and steering worm assembly may now be lifted away.

9 Using a suitable diameter drift remove the oil seal.

10 Do not attempt to remove the sector shaft needle bearings from the steering gear housing. If these are worn or damaged the complete housing assembly must be renewed.

11 Do not attempt to dismantle the ball nut and wormshaft assembly. If necessary a new wormshaft assembly must be obtained.

12 Wash all parts and wipe dry with a non-fluffy rag. Lay the parts out ready for inspection.

13 Inspect the sector shaft gear tooth surfaces for pitting, burrs, cracks or any other damage. Inspect the shaft splines for signs of wear or distortion. If evident new parts should be obtained.

14 Inspect the steering worm ball nut gear tooth surfaces for signs of pitting, burrs, wear or other damage. The ball nut must rotate smoothly on the worm gear.

15 Move the ball nut to either end of the worm gear and gradually tilt until the ball nut moves down on the worm gear under its own weight. Any signs of binding indicates wear and a new assembly should be obtained.

16 Inspect the wormshaft bearings for signs of pitting or corrosion. Should the sector shaft needle bearings show signs of wear or damage a complete new housing should be obtained.

17 Whenever the steering gearbox is dismantled new oil seals should be fitted.

18 To reassemble first apply a little multi-purpose grease to the oil seal lip and carefully press or drift the new seal into the rear cover.

19 Fit the O-ring, wormshaft assembly and worm bearing shims to the gear housing. The thicker shims must be fitted to the gear housing side.

20 Refit the rear cover and tighten the securing bolts to a torque wrench setting of 11 – 18 lbf ft (1·5 – 2·5 kgf m).

21 The worm bearing pre-load should be adjusted by selecting suitable thickness bearing shims until an initial turning torque of 56 – 83 inf oz (4·0 – 6·0 kgf cm) is obtained. The standard shim thickness is 0·0591 inch (1·5 mm) but a range of 4 additional shims are available (see Specifications).

22 Fit the adjustment screw into the T-shaped groove in the sector shaft head. Adjust the endplay between the shaft and adjustment screw until it is 0·0004 – 0·0012 in. (0·01 – 0·03 mm) by selecting suitable adjustment shims. A range of shims is available (see Specifications) (Fig. 11.51).

23 Turn the sector shaft by hand until the ball nut is in the centre of its travel range. Fit the sector shaft together with the adjustment screw into the gear housing. Make sure that the centre gear of the sector shaft engages with the centre gear of the ball nut.

24 Apply a little non-hardening sealer to the sector shaft cover mating face of the gear housing. Fit the gasket and smear some more sealer

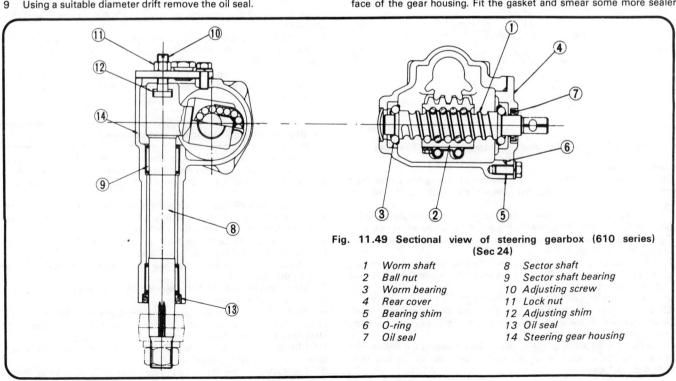

Fig. 11.49 Sectional view of steering gearbox (610 series) (Sec 24)

1	Worm shaft	8	Sector shaft
2	Ball nut	9	Sector shaft bearing
3	Worm bearing	10	Adjusting screw
4	Rear cover	11	Lock nut
5	Bearing shim	12	Adjusting shim
6	O-ring	13	Oil seal
7	Oil seal	14	Steering gear housing

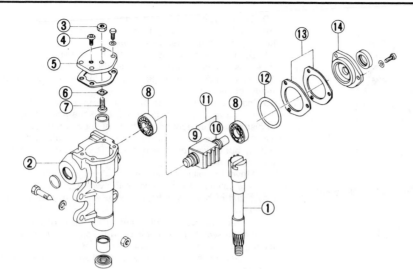

Fig. 11.50 Exploded view of steering gearbox (810 series) (Sec 24)

1   Sector shaft
2   Steering gear housing
3   Lock nut
4   Filler plug
5   Sector shaft cover
6   Sector shaft adjusting shim
7   Sector shaft adjusting screw
8   Worm bearing
9   Ball nut
10 Worm shaft
11 Steering worm assembly
12 O-ring
13 Worm bearing shim
14 Rear cover

Fig. 11.51 Measuring the endplay between sector shaft and adjustment screw (Sec 24)

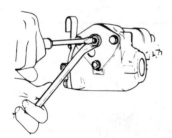

Fig. 11.52 Final adjustment of steering gearbox (Sec 24)

onto the gasket.
25 Turn the adjustment screw clockwise so drawing the sector shaft cover onto the gear housing. Refit the securing bolts but do not fully tighten yet.
26 Pull the sector shaft towards the cover by approximately 0·08 – 0·12 in. (2 – 3 mm) by screwing the adjusting screw anti-clockwise. Tighten the sector shaft cover securing bolts to a torque wrench setting of 11 – 18 lbf ft (1·5 – 2·5 kgf m).
27 Now push the sector shaft against the ball nut gear by gradually turning the adjustment screw until the sector shaft gear lightly meshes with the ball nut gear.
28 Tighten the adjustment screw locknut.
29 Fit the gear arm to the sector shaft and move the sector shaft several times from the side of the gear arm and make sure that it turns smoothly without signs of binding.
30 Adjust the backlash at the neutral point by turning the adjustment screw until the movement of the pitman arm top end is less than 0·004 in. (0·1 mm).

31 Turn the adjustment screw clockwise approximately $\frac{1}{8}$ – $\frac{1}{6}$th rotation and then tighten the locknut to a torque wrench setting of 11 – 18 lbf ft (1.5 – 2.5 kgf m).
32 Move the sector shaft several times to ensure freedom of movement.
33 Refill the steering gearbox with 0·5 pint (0·28 litre, 0·625 US pints) of recommended grade oil. Refit the filler plug.
34 The steering gear is now ready for refitting to the car.
35 Recheck the steering gearbox adjustment as described in Section 25.
36 Finally check the alignment of the steering wheel.

25 Steering gearbox – adjustment

1   Jack up the front of the car until the weight of the car is just off the tyre treads.
2   Turn the steering wheel until the wheels are in the straight-ahead position.
3   Lower the jack and check the amount of free travel on the circumference of the steering wheel. This should be less than 1·4 in (35 mm).
4   If this is exceeded slacken the locknut and turn the adjustment nut until the correct degree of steering wheel free movement is obtained. Tighten the locknut.
5   Raise the jack and turn the steering wheel from lock to lock to check for tight spots. If evident it is possible that the steering gearbox requires overhaul.

26 Steering linkage – removal, inspection and refitting

1   Chock the rear wheels, apply the handbrake, jack up the front of the car and support on firmly based stands. Remove the roadwheels.
2   Withdraw the split pins and then undo and remove the castellated nuts.
3   Detach the balljoints from the steering arms with a universal balljoint separator. Do not shock with a hammer as this can cause premature failure if the parts are to be refitted.
4   Next detach the balljoints from the pitman and idler in the same manner as described in paragraphs 2 and 3.
5   The connecting rod and tie-rods may now be removed from the front of the car.
6   Undo and remove the bolts and spring washers securing the idler assembly to the body member.
7   Clean all parts in paraffin and wipe dry. Carefully examine the connecting rod and tie-rods for signs of bending. Do not attempt to straighten but renew if these parts have been damaged.
8   Check the rubber bushing fitted to the idler arm. If it has deteriorated it must be renewed.
9   Carefully examine the balljoints for excessive play or wear. If they

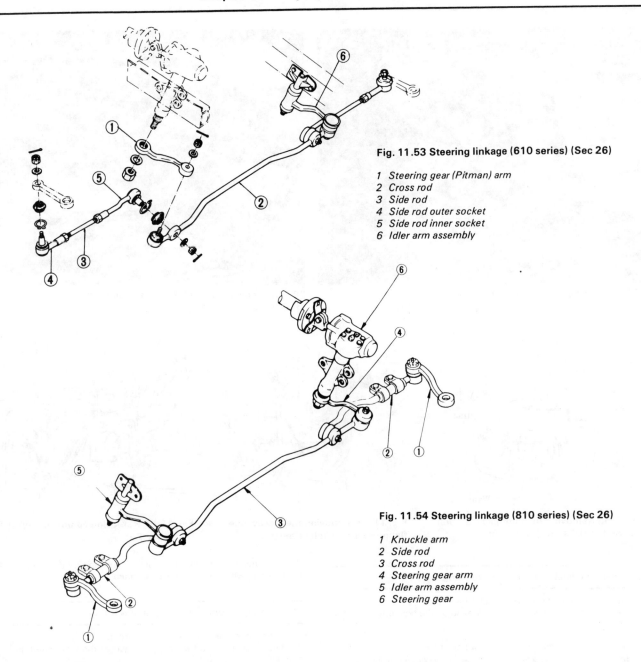

Fig. 11.53 Steering linkage (610 series) (Sec 26)

1 Steering gear (Pitman) arm
2 Cross rod
3 Side rod
4 Side rod outer socket
5 Side rod inner socket
6 Idler arm assembly

Fig. 11.54 Steering linkage (810 series) (Sec 26)

1 Knuckle arm
2 Side rod
3 Cross rod
4 Steering gear arm
5 Idler arm assembly
6 Steering gear

are worn they must be renewed as a complete assembly.

10 Refitting the assembly is the reverse sequence to removal. The following additional points should however be noted.

   (a) *Reassembly of the idler arm will be eased if a little soapy water is placed on the outer surface of the bush and then pressed into the idler arm until the bush protrudes equally at each end. On some models nylon bushes may be found.*

   (b) *Measure and then set the length of the tie-rods between the ball stud centres. The correct measurement should be:*

     610 series – 12.331 in (313.2 mm)
     810 series – 14.25 in (362 mm), steering gear arm side
                  14.41 in (366 mm), idler arm assembly side.

     Adjust as necessary before refitting. On 810 series make sure that the adjusting tube is screwed into the socket 1.38 in (35 mm) Lock the tie-rod adjusting tube clamp so that the balljoint on the knuckle arm side is at 90° to the connecting rod balljoint (photo).

   (c) *The front wheel alignment will have to be checked after the linkage is refitted; refer to Section 27.*

27 Steering geometry – checking and adjustment

1 Unless the front suspension has been damaged the castor angle, camber angle and king pin inclination angles will not alter, provided, of course, that the suspension balljoints are not worn in any way.

2 The toe-in of the front wheels is a measurement which may vary more frequently and could pass unnoticed, if, for example, a steering tie-rod was bent. When fitting new tie-rods balljoints, for example, it will always be necessary to reset the toe-in.

3 Indications of incorrect wheel alignment (toe-in) are uneven tyre wear on the front wheels and erratic steering particularly when turning. To check toe-in accurately needs optical alignment equipment, so this is one job that must be left to the local Datsun garage. Ensure that they examine the linkage to ascertain the cause of any deviation from the original setting

26.10 Tie rod adjusting tube (810 series)

28.2 Steering wheel with horn pad removed
(810 series)

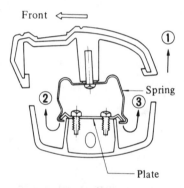

Fig. 11.55 Removing the horn pad – Saloon
and Estate (810 series) (Sec 28)

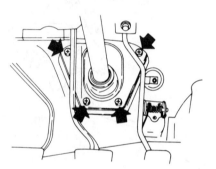

Fig. 11.56 Removing the jacket tube
flange securing bolts (Sec 29)

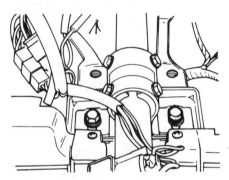

Fig. 11.57 Removing column clamp securing
bolts (Sec 29)

28 Steering wheel – removal and refitting

1   Disconnect the battery positive terminal.
2   Remove the horn pad. This will depend on the type fitted (photo).

   (a) Two spoke type. Simply pull out horn pad.
   (b) Three spoke type with stamp ⊕. Simply pull out horn pad.
   (c) Three spoke type less stamp. Depress the horn ring and then turn in an anti-clockwise direction.
   (d) 810 – Hardtop models, remove the bolts from the rear of the steering wheel; lift the horn pad and disconnect the horn lead.
   (e) 810 – Saloon and Estate models; pull the horn pad out until the spring touches the plate. Slide the horn pad in direction 'Front', see Fig. 11.55, and disengage, first the top (1), then the bottom of the spring from the plate (2) and (3).

3   Using a suitable size box spanner or socket undo and remove the nut securing the steering wheel to the shaft.
4   With a pencil or scriber mark the relative positions of the steering wheel hub and shaft to assist refitment.
5   Using the palms of the hand on the rear of the steering wheel spokes thump the steering wheel so releasing it from the splines on the shaft. If it is very tight a puller will have to be used.
6   Refitting the steering wheel is the reverse sequence to removal. Should new parts be fitted or the initial alignment marks lost, jack up the front of the car and turn the wheels to the straight-ahead position. Lower the car again. Fit the steering wheel so .that the spokes are parallel with the ground.

7   Refit the securing nut and horn pushes and road test to check that the steering wheel is correctly positioned.

29 Steering column – removal and refitting

1   Disconnect the battery positive terminal.
2   Undo and remove the bolt that secures the wormshaft and rubber coupling.
3   If a remote control linkage is fitted this should next be removed.
4   Refer to Section 28 and remove the steering wheel.
5   Undo and remove the four screws securing the upper and lower steering column shell covers. Part the two shell halves and lift away.
6   Undo and remove the two screws securing the direction indicator switch to the column. Detach the multi-pin connector from the halves and lift away the switch assembly.
7   Refer to Chapter 12 and remove the parcel shelf.
8   Undo and remove the four bolts that secure the outer column flange to the dash panel.
9   Undo and remove the two bolts securing the column clamp.
10   The steering column may now be lifted away from inside the car. Take care not to touch the headlining or upholstery.
11   Refitting the steering column assembly is the reverse sequence but the following additional points should be noted making reference to Fig. 11.58.

   (a) Make sure the front wheels are in the straight-ahead position.
   (b) Insert the column end through the dash panel and connect with the wormshaft serrations. The punch mark at the top end of the column shaft should face uppermost. Secure with the bolt (A).

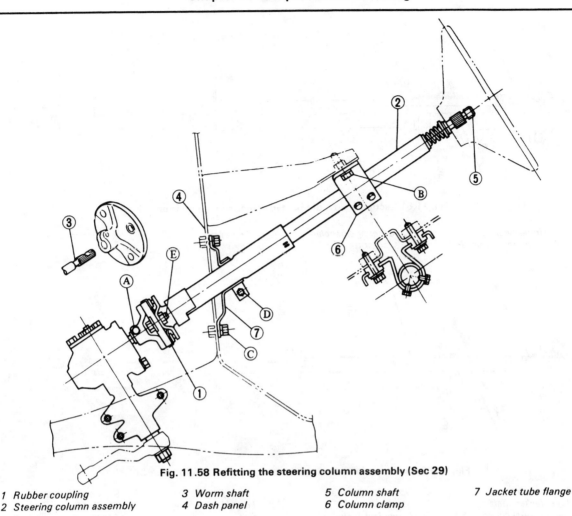

Fig. 11.58 Refitting the steering column assembly (Sec 29)

1 Rubber coupling
2 Steering column assembly
3 Worm shaft
4 Dash panel
5 Column shaft
6 Column clamp
7 Jacket tube flange

(c) Secure the upper column assembly to the dash with the four bolts (B).
(d) Slacken the bolt (D) and tighten the bolts (C). Retighten bolt (D).
(e) Road test to check that there are no tight spots between the two locks.

30 Steering column – dismantling and reassembly

Before attempting to dismantle the column assembly the following points should be noted:

(a) If the car has been in a front end accident and a collapsible column is fitted no attempt should be made to dismantle it, but it should be renewed as a complete assembly.
(b) With a conventional rigid column be prepared to purchase a complete assembly due to difficulty in obtaining individual spare parts.

Should the steering wheel prove difficult to rotate smoothly and there is nothing amiss with the remainder of the steering or suspension systems then proceed as follows.

1 Using a pair of circlip pliers remove the circlip at the top end of the steering column shaft. Remove the washers and spring.
2 Carefully draw the column shaft from the column tube ensuring the upper and lower bearings are not damaged.
3 Inspect the column bearings for signs of damage, excessive wear or looseness. If evident remove the old bearings and fit new (if available) or obtain a new column tube assembly.
4 Carefully inspect the column tube for signs of damage, in the form of buckling or bending. Do not attempt to straighten but obtain a new

assembly.
5 Check the column spring and obtain new if damaged or shows obvious signs of weakening.
6 Collapsible steering column. Measure the dimension 'A' in Figs. 11.59 and 11.60 as applicable. The original new dimension should be 7·237 in (183·8 mm) for 610 series and 16·27 in (413·5 mm) on 810 series. If the dimension 'A' is less than specified it is an indication that the jacket tube has been collapsed. Do not attempt to expand it.

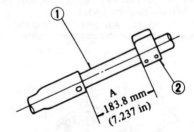

Fig. 11.59 Measuring dimension A – 610 models (Sec 30)

1 Jacket tube
2 Column clamp

Fig. 11.60 Measuring dimension A – 810 models (Sec 30)

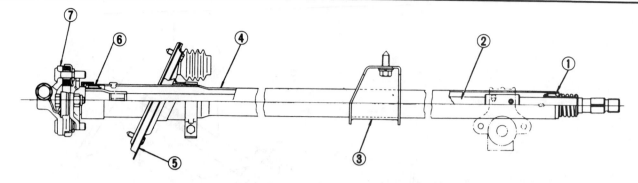

Fig. 11.61 Sectional view of rigid type steering column (Sec 30)

1 Upper bearing	3 Steering post clamp	5 Jacket tube flange	7 Rubber coupling
2 Steering column shaft	4 Jacket tube	6 Lower bearing	

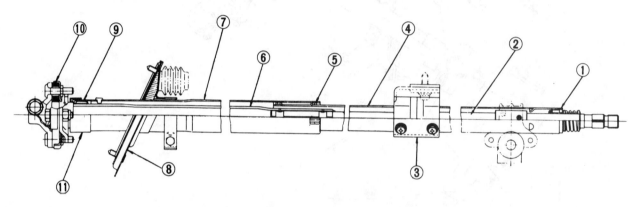

Fig. 11.62 Sectional view of collapsible type steering column (Sec 30)

1 Upper bearing	4 Upper jacket tube	7 Lower jacket tube	9 Lower bearing
2 Upper jacket shaft	5 Steel ball	8 Lower jacket tube	10 Rubber coupling
3 Steering post clamp	6 Lower jacket shaft	flange	11 Column dust cover

Measure dimension 'B' as shown in Fig. 11.63. The standard dimension is 0 in (0 mm) and if the jacket tube is crushed the distance 'B' becomes larger. Check the steering wheel for axial play because if the jacket tube has collapsed this play will increase.

7   If the car has been in an accident it is possible that the splines on the sector shaft have distorted so this must be checked.

8   Reassembly of the steering column is the reverse of the dismantling procedure. The following additional points should be noted:

(a) *Lubricate the column bearings, spring, dust seal and sliding parts with multi-purpose grease*

(b) *Take care not to apply any undue stress to the steering column in an axial direction as this could well cause the jacket tube to collapse.*

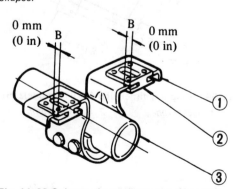

Fig. 11.63 Column clamp dimension (Sec 30)

1 Column clamp	3 Jacket tube
2 Block	

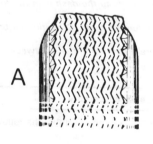

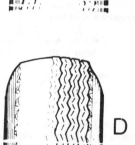

Fig. 11.64 Tyre wear patterns (Sec 31)

A   'Feathering' due to incorrect toe-in
B   Over-inflation
C   Under-inflation
D   Wear due to incorrect camber, worn wheel bearings and fast cornering

31 Wheels and tyres

1 The roadwheels are of pressed steel type.
2 Periodically remove the wheels, clean dirt and mud from the inside and outside surfaces and examine for signs of rusting or rim damage and rectify as necessary.
3 Apply a smear of light grease to the wheel studs before screwing on the nuts and finally tighten them to the specified torque.
4 The tyres fitted may be of crossply, bias belt or radial construction according to territory and specification. Never mix tyres of different construction and always check and maintain the pressures regularly.
5 If the wheels have been balanced on the vehicle then it is important that the wheels are not moved round the vehicle in an effort to equalise tread wear. If a wheel is removed, then the relationship of the wheel studs to the holes in the wheel should be marked to ensure exact refitment, otherwise the balance of wheel, hub and tyre will be upset.
6 Where the wheels have been balanced off the vehicle, then they may be moved round to equalise wear. Include the spare wheel in any rotational pattern. If radial tyres are fitted, do not move the wheels from side to side but only interchange the front and rear wheels on the same side.
7 Balancing of the wheels is an essential factor in good steering and road holding. When the tyres have been in use for about half their useful life the wheels should be rebalanced to compensate for the lost tread rubber due to wear.
8 Inspect the tyre walls and treads regularly for cuts and damage and where evident, have them professionally repaired.

32 Fault diagnosis – suspension and steering

Before diagnosing faults from the following chart check the irregularities are not caused by:
1 *Binding brakes*
2 *Incorrect 'mix' of radial and cross-ply tyres*
3 *Incorrect type pressures*
4 *Misalignment of the body frame*

Symptoms	Reason/s	Remedy
Steering wheel can be moved considerably before any sign of movement is apparent at the road wheels	Wear in steering linkage, gear and column coupling	Check all joints and gears. Renew as necessary
Vehicle difficult to steer in a straight line - 'Wanders'	As above Wheel alignment incorrect (shown by uneven front tyre wear) Front wheel bearings loose Worn suspension unit swivel joints	As above Check wheel alignment Adjust or renew Renew as necessary
Steering stiff and heavy	Incorrect wheel alignment (uneven or excessive tyre wear) Wear or seizure in steering linkage joints Wear or seizure in suspension linkage joints Excessive wear in steering gear unit	Check and adjust Grease or renew Grease or renew Adjust or renew
Wheel wobble and vibration	Road wheels out of balance Road wheels buckled Wheel alignment incorrect Wear in steering and suspension linkages Broken front spring	Balance wheels Check for damage Check Check or renew Renew
Excessive pitching and rolling on corners and during braking	Defective shock absorber and/or broken spring	Renew

Chapter 12 Bodywork and fittings

Contents

1 General description

The body used in 610 series models is of the combined body and underframe integral construction type where all panels are welded. The only exception is the front wings which are bolted in position. This makes a very strong and torsionally rigid shell whilst acting as a positive location for attachment of the major units.

Three body types are used on models covered by this manual, Saloon (Sedan), Hardtop (Coupe) and Estate Car (Station Wagon), and many body parts are interchangeable between the models.

The body style for the Saloon models is of a long front compartment and shorter luggage compartment. The engine compartment is sufficiently wide to give good access to the power unit. The luggage compartment has a larger capacity than first impressions give because the spare wheel compartment is below the floor level.

The body on the Hardtop model has the front pillar, door support, roof rail and rear quarter specially reinforced because of the under door aperture.

All major units are insulated from the main body so as to minimise road and power unit noise throughout the speed range of the car. The underside and inside of the floor are coated with a special sealer/sound deadening medium and the inside is, in addition, padded with asphalt panels.

For safety reasons the front and rear ends are designed to absorb impact under crash and collision conditions.

The body on the 810 series is basically of the same construction but with different styling. The body has a lower waistline and larger windows, and the Hardtop model has small opera windows fitted. The body is 1.7 in (43.2 mm) longer and 1.2 in (30.5 mm) wider. The wheelbase is the same as the 610 series.

2 Maintenance – bodywork and underframe

The general condition of a vehicle's bodywork is the one thing that significantly affects its value. Maintenance is easy but needs to be regular. Neglect, particularly after minor damage, can lead quickly to further deterioration and costly repair bills. It is important also to keep watch on those parts of the vehicle not immediately visible, for instance the underside, inside all the wheel arches and the lower part of the engine compartment.

The basic maintenance routine for the bodywork is washing – preferably with a lot of water, from a hose. This will remove all the loose solids which may have stuck to the vehicle. It is important to flush these off in such a way as to prevent grit from scratching the finish. The wheel arches and underframe need washing in the same way to remove any accumulated mud which will retain moisture and tend to encourage rust. Paradoxically enough, the best time to clean the underframe and wheel arches is in wet weather when the mud is thoroughly wet and soft. In very wet weather the underframe is usually cleaned of large accumulations automatically and this is a good time for inspection.

Periodically, except on vehicles with a wax-based underbody protective coat, it is a good idea to have the whole of the underframe of the vehicle steam cleaned, engine compartment included, so that a thorough inspection can be carried out to see what minor repairs and renovations are necessary. Steam cleaning is available at many garages and is necessary for removal of the accumulation of oily grime which sometimes is allowed to become thick in certain areas. If steam cleaning facilities are not available, there are one or two excellent grease solvents available which can be brush applied. The dirt can then be simply hosed off. Note that these methods should not be used on vehicles with wax-based underbody protective coating or the coating will be removed. Such vehicles should be inspected annually, preferably just prior to winter, when the underbody should be washed down and any damage to the wax coating repaired. Ideally, a completely fresh coat should be applied. It would also be worth considering the use of such wax-based protection for injection into door panels, sills, box sections etc, as an additional safeguard against rust damage.

After washing paintwork, wipe off with a chamois leather to give an unspotted clear finish. A coat of clear protective wax polish will give added protection against chemical pollutants in the air. If the paintwork sheen has dulled or oxidised, use a cleaner/polisher combination to restore the brilliance of the shine. This requires a little effort, but such dulling is usually caused because regular washing has been neglected. Care needs to be taken with metallic paintwork, as special non-abrasive cleaner/polisher is required to avoid damage to the finish. Always check that the door and ventilator opening drain holes and pipes are completely clear so that water can be drained out. Bright work should be treated in the same way as paintwork. Windscreens and windows can be kept clear of the smeary film which often appears by the use of a proprietary glass cleaner. Never use any form of wax or other body or chromium polish on glass.

3 Maintenance – upholstery and carpets

Mats and carpets should be brushed or vacuum cleaned regularly to keep them free of grit. If they are badly stained remove them from the vehicle for scrubbing or sponging and make quite sure they are dry before refitting. Seats and interior trim panels can be kept clean by wiping with a damp cloth. If they do become stained (which can be more apparent on light coloured upholstery) use a little liquid detergent and a soft nail brush to scour the grime out of the grain of the material. Do not forget to keep the headlining clean in the same way as the upholstery. When using liquid cleaners inside the vehicle do not over-wet the surfaces being cleaned. Excessive damp could get into the seams and padded interior causing stains, offensive odours or even rot. If the inside of the vehicle gets wet accidentally it is worthwhile taking some trouble to dry it out properly, particularly where carpets are involved. *Do not leave oil or electric heaters inside the vehicle for this purpose.*

4 Minor body damage – repair

The photographic sequences on pages 222 and 223 illustrate the operations detailed in the following sub-sections.

Repair of minor scratches in bodywork

If the scratch is very superficial, and does not penetrate to the metal of the bodywork, repair is very simple. Lightly rub the area of the scratch with a paintwork renovator, or a very fine cutting paste, to remove loose paint from the scratch and to clear the surrounding bodywork of wax polish. Rinse the area with clean water.

Apply touch-up paint to the scratch using a fine paint brush; continue to apply fine layers of paint until the surface of the paint in the scratch is level with the surrounding paintwork. Allow the new paint at least two weeks to harden: then blend it into the surrounding paintwork by rubbing the scratch area with a paintwork renovator or a very fine cutting paste. Finally, apply wax polish.

Where the scratch has penetrated right through to the metal of the bodywork, causing the metal to rust, a different repair technique is required. Remove any loose rust from the bottom of the scratch with a penknife, then apply rust inhibiting paint to prevent the formation of rust in the future. Using a rubber or nylon applicator fill the scratch with bodystopper paste. If required, this paste can be mixed with cellulose thinners to provide a very thin paste which is ideal for filling narrow scratches. Before the stopper-paste in the scratch hardens, wrap a piece of smooth cotton rag around the top of a finger. Dip the finger in cellulose thinners and then quickly sweep it across the surface of the stopper-paste in the scratch; this will ensure that the surface of the stopper-paste is slightly hollowed. The scratch can now be painted over as described earlier in this Section.

Repair of dents in bodywork

When deep denting of the vehicle's bodywork has taken place, the first task is to pull the dent out, until the affected bodywork almost attains its original shape. There is little point in trying to restore the original shape completely, as the metal in the damaged area will have stretched on impact and cannot be reshaped fully to its original contour. It is better to bring the level of the dent up to a point which is about $\frac{1}{8}$ in (3 mm) below the level of the surrounding bodywork. In cases where the dent is very shallow anyway, it is not worth trying to pull it out at all. If the underside of the dent is accessible, it can be hammered out gently from behind, using a mallet with a wooden or plastic head. Whilst doing this, hold a suitable block of wood firmly against the outside of the panel to absorb the impact from the hammer blows and thus prevent a large area of the bodywork from being 'belled-out'.

Should the dent be in a section of the bodywork which has a double skin or some other factor making it inaccessible from behind, a different technique is called for. Drill several small holes through the metal inside the area – particularly in the deeper section. Then screw long self-tapping screws into the holes just sufficiently for them to gain a good purchase in the metal. Now the dent can be pulled out by pulling on the protruding heads of the screws with a pair of pliers.

The next stage of the repair is the removal of the paint from the damaged area, and from an inch or so of the surrounding 'sound' bodywork. This is accomplished most easily by using a wire brush or abrasive pad on a power drill, although it can be done just as effectively by hand using sheets of abrasive paper. To complete the preparation for filling, score the surface of the bare metal with a screwdriver or the tang of a file, or alternatively, drill small holes in the affected area. This will provide a really good 'key' for the filler paste.

To complete the repair see the Section on filling and re-spraying.

Repair of rust holes or gashes in bodywork

Remove all paint from the affected area and from an inch or so of the surrounding 'sound' bodywork, using an abrasive pad or a wire brush on a power drill. If these are not available a few sheets of abrasive paper will do the job just as effectively. With the paint removed you will be able to gauge the severity of the corrosion and therefore decide whether to renew the whole panel (if this is possible) or to repair the affected area. New body panels are not as expensive as most people think and it is often quicker and more satisfactory to fit a new panel than to attempt to repair large areas of corrosion.

Remove all fittings from the affected area except those which will act as a guide to the original shape of the damaged bodywork (eg headlamp shells etc). Then, using tin snips or a hacksaw blade, remove all loose metal and any other metal badly affected by corrosion. Hammer the edges of the hole inwards in order to create a slight depression for the filler paste.

Wire brush the affected area to remove the powdery rust from the surface of the remaining metal. Paint the affected area with rust inhibiting paint; if the back of the rusted area is accessible treat this also.

Before filling can take place it will be necessary to block the hole in some way. This can be achieved by the use of aluminium or plastic mesh, or aluminium tape.

Aluminium or plastic mesh is probably the best material to use for a large hole. Cut a piece to the approximate size and shape of the hole to be filled, then position it in the hole so that its edges are below the level of the surrounding bodywork. It can be retained in position by several blobs of filler paste around its periphery.

Aluminium tape should be used for small or very narrow holes. Pull a piece off the roll and trim it to the approximate size and shape required, then pull off the backing paper (if used) and stick the tape over the hole; it can be overlapped if the thickness of one piece is insufficient. Burnish down the edges of the tape with the handle of a screwdriver or similar, to ensure that the tape is securely attached to the metal underneath.

Bodywork repairs – filling and re-spraying

Before using this Section, see the Sections on dent, deep scratch, rust holes and gash repairs.

Many types of bodyfiller are available, but generally speaking those proprietary kits which contain a tin of filler paste and a tube of resin hardener are best for this type of repair. A wide, flexible plastic or nylon applicator will be found invaluable for imparting a smooth and well contoured finish to the surface of the filler.

Mix up a little filler on a clean piece of card or board – measure the hardener carefully (follow the maker's instructions on the pack) otherwise the filler will set too rapidly or too slowly.

Using the applicator apply the filler paste to the prepared area; draw the applicator across the surface of the filler to achieve the correct contour and to level the filler surface. As soon as a contour that approximates to the correct one is achieved, stop working the paste – if you carry on too long the paste will become sticky and begin to 'pick up' on the applicator. Continue to add thin layers of filler paste at twenty-minute intervals until the level of the filler is just proud of the surrounding bodywork.

Once the filler has hardened, excess can be removed using a metal plane or file. From then on, progressively finer grades of abrasive paper should be used, starting with a 40 grade production paper and finishing with 400 grade wet-and-dry paper. Always wrap the abrasive paper around a flat rubber, cork, or wooden block – otherwise the surface of the filler will not be completely flat. During the smoothing of the filler surface the wet-and-dry paper should be periodically rinsed in water. This will ensure that a very smooth finish is imparted to the filler at the final stage.

At this stage the 'dent' should be surrounded by a ring of bare metal, which in turn should be encircled by the finely 'feathered' edge of the good paintwork. Rinse the repair area with clean water, until all of the dust produced by the rubbing-down operation has gone.

Spray the whole repair area with a light coat of primer – this will show up any imperfections in the surface of the filler. Repair these imperfections with fresh filler paste or bodystopper, and once more smooth the surface with abrasive paper. If bodystopper is used, it can be mixed with cellulose thinners to form a really thin paste which is ideal for filling small holes. Repeat this spray and repair procedure until you are satisfied that the surface of the filler, and the feathered edge of the paintwork are perfect. Clean the repair area with clean water and allow to dry fully.

The repair area is now ready for final spraying. Paint spraying must be carried out in a warm, dry, windless and dust free atmosphere. This condition can be created artificially if you have access to a large indoor working area, but if you are forced to work in the open, you will have to pick your day very carefully. If you are working indoors, dousing the floor in the work area with water will help to settle the dust which would otherwise be in the atmosphere. If the repair area is confined to one body panel, mask off the surrounding panels; this will help to minimise the effects of a slight mis-match in paint colours. Bodywork fittings (eg chrome strips, door handles etc) will also need to be masked off. Use genuine masking tape and several thicknesses of newspaper for the masking operations.

Before commencing to spray, agitate the aerosol can thoroughly, then spray a test area (an old tin, or similar) until the technique is mastered. Cover the repair area with a thick coat of primer; the thickness should be built up using several thin layers of paint rather than one thick one. Using 400 grade wet-and-dry paper, rub down the

surface of the primer until it is really smooth. While doing this, the work area should be thoroughly doused with water, and the wet-and-dry paper periodically rinsed in water. Allow to dry before spraying on more paint.

Spray on the top coat, again building up the thickness by using several thin layers of paint. Start spraying in the centre of the repair area and then, using a circular motion, work outwards until the whole repair area and about 2 inches of the surrounding original paintwork is covered. Remove all masking material 10 to 15 minutes after spraying on the final coat of paint.

Allow the new paint at least two weeks to harden, then, using a paintwork renovator or a very fine cutting paste, blend the edges of the paint into the existing paintwork. Finally, apply wax polish.

5 Major body repairs

Where serious damage has occurred or large areas need renewal due to neglect, it means certainly that completely new sections or panels will need welding in and this is best left to professionals. If the damage is due to impact it will also be necessary to completely check the alignment of the underframe structure. Due to the principle of construction the strength and shape of the whole can be affected by damage to a part. In such instances the services of a Datsun agent with specialist checking jigs are essential. If a frame is left misaligned it is first of all dangerous as the vehicle will not handle properly and secondly ueven stresses will be imposed on the steering, engine and transmission, causing abnormal wear or complete failure. Tyre wear may also be excessive.

6 Bumpers – removal and refitting

Front bumpers
1   For safety reasons disconnect the battery positive terminal.
2   Disconnect the front direction indicator light cable connectors.

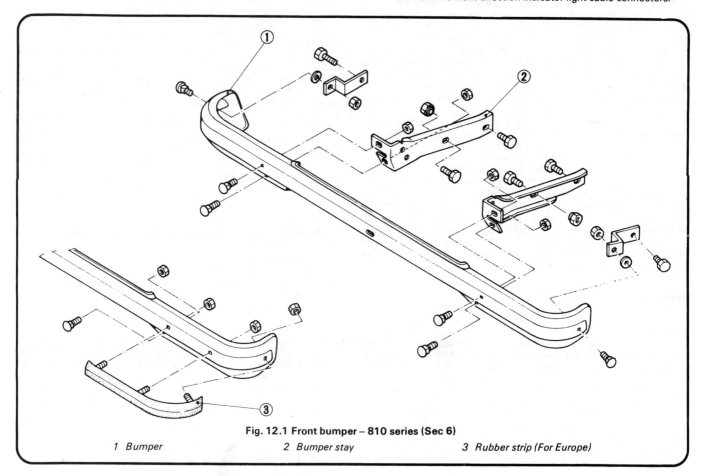

Fig. 12.1 Front bumper – 810 series (Sec 6)

1 Bumper   *2 Bumper stay*   *3 Rubber strip (For Europe)*

3 Undo and remove the bolts and washers securing the front bumper side bracket to the lower side of the front wing.
4 Undo and remove the bolts that secure the front bumper stay to body side member and draw the front bumper forward from the body. Take care not to scratch the paintwork.
5 Refitting the front bumper is the reverse sequence to removal.

Rear bumpers
6 *Saloon models only:* Disconnect the battery positive terminal. Disconnect the cable connectors to the rear number plate light.
7 Undo and remove the bolts that secure the rear bumper stay to the

body side member.
8 Carefully draw the rear bumper rearward from the body.
9 Refitting the rear bumper is the reverse sequence to removal.

Impact absorbing bumpers
10 Models destined for North America incorporate gas filled shock absorbers to absorb impact at speeds below 5 mph (8 km/h).
11 Removal and refitting is straightforward but on no account must any attempt be made to dismantle, puncture or apply heat to a shock absorber.

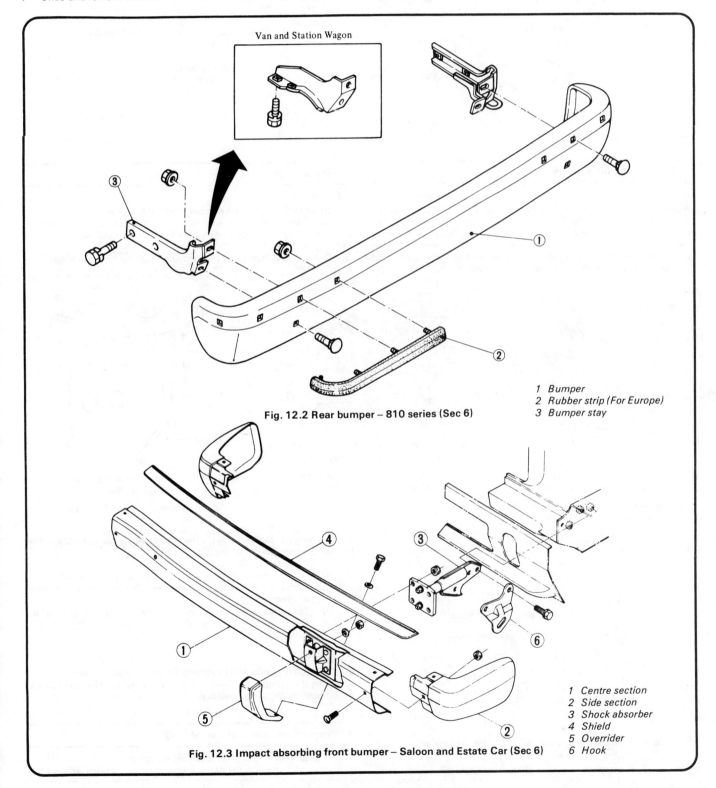

Van and Station Wagon

1 Bumper
2 Rubber strip (For Europe)
3 Bumper stay

Fig. 12.2 Rear bumper – 810 series (Sec 6)

1 Centre section
2 Side section
3 Shock absorber
4 Shield
5 Overrider
6 Hook

Fig. 12.3 Impact absorbing front bumper – Saloon and Estate Car (Sec 6)

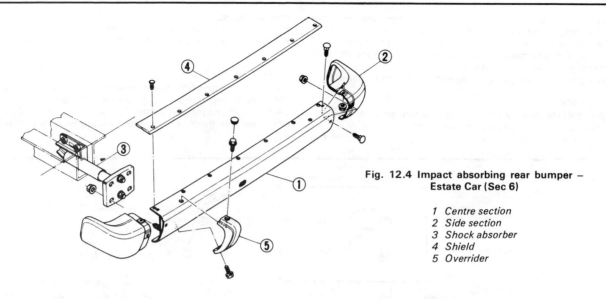

**Fig. 12.4 Impact absorbing rear bumper –
Estate Car (Sec 6)**

1 Centre section
2 Side section
3 Shock absorber
4 Shield
5 Overrider

7 Windscreen and rear window – renewal

If you are unfortunate enough to have a windscreen or rear window shatter fitting a replacement is one of the few jobs that the average owner is advised to leave to a body repair specialist. The reason for this is that the glass is not located in the body in the normal manner but uses a special sealer and clips. Body specialists are familiar with the special procedures involved and have the equipment necessary, so in this case leave it to the specialist.

8 Radiator grille – removal and refitting

610 series
1   Refer to Section 6 and remove the front bumper.
2   Undo and remove the six screws securing the top of the grille to the front body crossmember and the five screws securing the bottom of the grille to the body.
3   Draw the radiator grille forward and lift away from the front of the car.

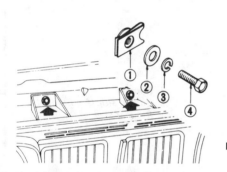

**Fig. 12.5 Radiator grille upper securing
screw and nut assembly (Sec 8)**

1 Spring nut   3 Spring washer
2 Plain washer   4 Screw

**Fig. 12.6 Radiator grille lower securing
screw and nut assembly (Sec 8)**

1 Spring nut   3 Plain washer
2 Vinyl washer   4 Screw

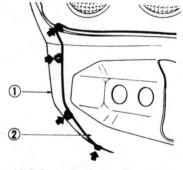

**Fig. 12.7 Front apron-to-wing attachment –
610 series (Sec 9)**

1 Front wing   2 Front apron

4   Refitting the radiator grille is the reverse sequence to removal. The following additional points should be noted:

   (a) Fit the lower centre securing screw first and then the remainder in a diagonal manner. This will ensure correct alignnment.
   (b) Take great care not to spill any brake fluid or engine oil on the grille as chemical fluids can cause damage to the moulding.

810 series
5   The radiator grille and headlamp finisher can be removed without removing the bumper on Saloon and Estate Cars. On Hardtop models the bumper must be removed first.

**Fig. 12.8 Screws securing front apron to bonnet lock stay – 610
series (Sec 9)**

1 Front apron   2 Bonnet lock stay

9 Front apron – removal and refitting

1   Refer to Section 8 and remove the radiator grille.
2   Undo and remove the front apron securing screws around the

outer edges and centre of the panel.
3   Lift away the front apron panel.
4   Refitting the front apron is the reverse sequence to removal.

10 Front wing – removal and refitting

1   Disconnect the battery
2   Refer to Section 6 and remove the front bumper.
3   Refer to Section 8 and remove the radiator grille.
4   Refer to Section 9 and remove the front apron.
5   Refer to Section 11 and remove the cowl top grille.
6   Undo and remove the screws that secure the sill moulding. Lift away the moulding.
7   Disconnect the side marker/flasher cable from the main harness.
8   Undo and remove the two wing securing screws at the bottom of panel adjacent to the sill.
9   Undo and remove the one screw at the upper rear end near to the wiper spindle.
10   Undo and remove the four screws securing the upper edge to the inner wing panel.
11   Undo and remove the three screws securing the leading edge of

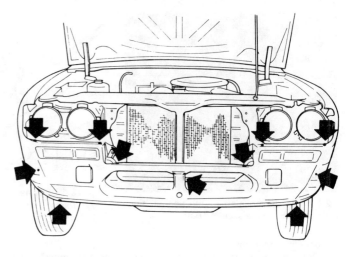

Fig. 12.9 Front apron attaching points – 810 series (Sec 9)

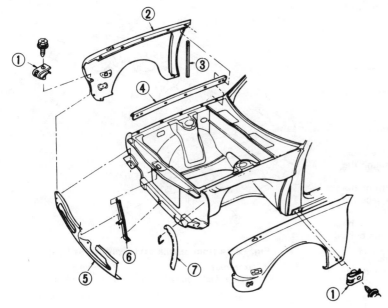

Fig. 12.10 Exploded view of front wings and apron – 610 series (Sec 10)

1   Spring nut
2   Front wing
3   Baffle filler
4   Rubber insert
5   Front apron
6   Bonnet lock stay
7   Sealing rubber

the wing to the body.
12   Check that no other attachments have been left in position and lift away the wing panel.
13   Refitting the front wing is the reverse sequence to removal.
14   For location of attaching screws on 810 series refer to Fig. 12.11.

11 Cowl top grille – removal and refitting

1   Refer to Chapter 10 and remove the windscreen wiper arms and blades.
2   Open the bonnet and then using a screwdriver carefully ease up the inner and outer fasteners which secure the front end of the cowl top grille to the body.
3   Draw the cowl top grille forward and lift away from the body.
4   Refitting the cowl top grille is the reverse sequence to removal.

12 Bonnet – removal and refitting

1   Open the bonnet and, to act as a datum for refitting, mark the position of the hinges on the bonnet using a soft pencil (photo).
2   With the assistance of a second person hold the bonnet in the open position, undo and remove the bolts, spring and plain washers that hold each hinge to the bonnet. Lift away the bonnet taking care not to scratch the top of the wing.
3   Whilst the bonnet is being lifted away take care when detaching

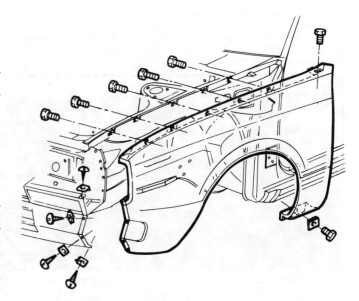

Fig. 12.11 Front wing attaching points – 810 series (Sec 10)

12.1 Mark the position of the bonnet hinge before removing the securing bolts

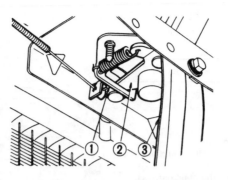

Fig. 12.12 Bonnet lock assembly (Sec 13)
1 Stopper   3 Bonnet lock stay
2 Bonnet lock

Fig. 12.13 Bonnet lock adjustment (Sec 13)
1 Locknut   3 Safety catch
2 Lock plunger

the bonnet support rod.

4   Refitting the bonnet is the reverse sequence to removal. Any adjustment necessary may be made at the hinge, catch or rubber bump pads on the front panel. Lubricate the hinge pivots and lock with a little engine oil.

13 Bonnet lock and control cable – removal and refitting

1   Refer to Section 8 and remove the radiator grille.
2   Undo and remove the two bolts and spring washers securing the lock to the front panel.
3   Disconnect the cable from the lock arm.
4   Undo and remove the two bolts and washers securing the lock to the dashboard side trim.
5   Release the outer cable from the support clips and pull the cable into the passenger compartment. Take care as it passes through the bulkhead grommet.
6   The lock plunger and safety catch may be removed from the underside of the bonnet by undoing and removing the two securing bolts, spring and plain washers.
7   Refitting the lock is the reverse sequence to removal. It may be necessary to adjust the lock. Before tightening the lock securing bolts line it up with the plunger. Do not lock the bonnet at this stage as it could be difficult to open again! Tighten the lock securing bolts.
8   To adjust the plunger slacken the locknut and using a screwdriver in the end of the plunger turn in the required direction. Lock by tightening the locknut.
9   Lubricate the lock and plunger with a little grease or engine oil.

14 Boot lid (Saloon) – removal and refitting

1   Open the boot lid and, using a soft pencil, mark the outline of the hinges on the lid to act as a datum for refitting.

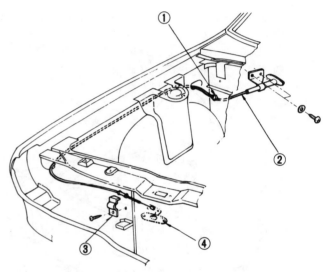

Fig. 12.14 Bonnet lock cable control (Sec 13)
1 Grommet   3 Cable clamp
2 Bonnet lock control cable   4 Bonnet lock

2   With the assistance of a second person hold the boot lid in the open position and then remove the two bolts, spring and plain washers to each hinge (photo).
3   Lift away the boot lid.
4   Refitting the boot lid is the reverse sequence to removal. If necessary adjust the position of the hinges relative to the lid until the

14.2 Boot lid securing bolts

14.5 Boot lid lock mechanism

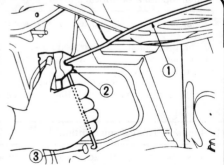

Fig. 12.15 Detaching torsion bar end – Saloon (Sec 15)
1 RH torsion bar
2 Torsion bar bracket
3 Hole for torsion bar end

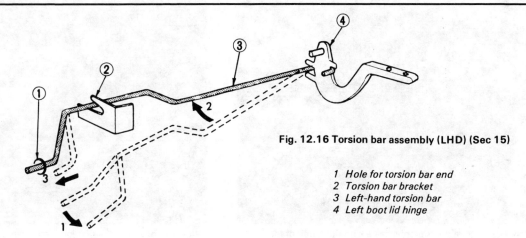

Fig. 12.16 Torsion bar assembly (LHD) (Sec 15)

1 Hole for torsion bar end
2 Torsion bar bracket
3 Left-hand torsion bar
4 Left boot lid hinge

Fig. 12.17 Exploded view of tailgate lock and striker (Sec 16)

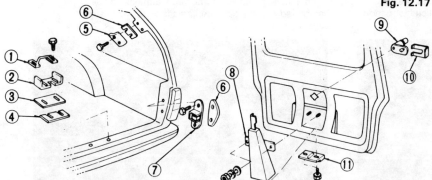

1   Striker
2   Tailgate striker
3   Friction plate
4   Shim
5   Bump rubber
6   Shim
7   Down position stopper
8   Tailgate lock
9   Lock cylinder
10 Clip
11 Tailgate striker catch

lid is centralised in the aperture.
5   To obtain a watertight fit between the boot lid and weather-strip move the striker up and down or side to side as necessary (photo).

15 Boot lid torsion bar (Saloon) – removal and refitting

1   Open the boot lid and then remove the luggage compartment finisher panel securing screws. Lift away the finisher panel.
2   Support the boot lid with a piece of wood and carefully draw the end of the left torsion bar out of the hole drilled in the side panel – Watch your fingers!
3   Detach the torsion bar from the bracket and hinge.
4   The right-hand torsion bar is now removed in a similar manner to the left-hand torsion bar.
5   To refit the assembly first position the end of the right-hand torsion bar onto the right boot lid hinge.
6   Twist the torsion bar rearward and engage the bar in the torsion bar bracket.
7   Fit the left-hand torsion bar in a similar manner to the right.

16 Tailgate (Estate car) – removal and refitting

1   Open the tailgate and support it in the open position with a piece of wood. The assistance of a second person is required to hold the tailgate as it is detached from the hinge.
2   Using a soft pencil, mark the outline of the hinge on the tailgate to act as a datum for refitting.
3   Undo and remove the three bolts and washers securing each hinge to the tailgate and carefully lift away the tailgate.
4   Refitting the tailgate is the reverse sequence to removal.
5   Should it be necessary to adjust the position of the tailgate in the aperture, it may be moved up or down and side to side at the tailgate to hinge securing bolts. The fore and aft movement adjustment is obtained by slackening the bolts securing the tailgate hinge to the body.

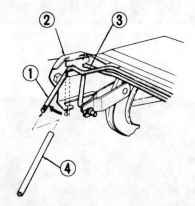

Fig. 12.18 Removing tailgate torsion bar (Sec 17)

1 Left torsion bar   3 Right torsion bar
2 Tailgate hinge   4 Pipe lever

17 Tailgate torsion bar (Estate Car) – removal and refitting

1   Open the tailgate and support it in the open position with a piece of wood.
2   Undo and remove the fixing that secures the tailgate hinge cover to body, lift away the cover.
3   Undo and remove the screws fixing the head-lining rear end to the tailgate aperture rail panel (clean hands). Detach the head-lining.
4   Using a suitable piece of pipe, detach the right and left torsion bars in that order. The bars are painted yellow at the points to accommodate the pipe.
5   Refitting the torsion bars is the reverse of the removal sequence.

This sequence of photographs deals with the repair of the dent and paintwork damage shown in this photo. The procedure will be similar for the repair of a hole. It should be noted that the procedures given here are simplified — more explicit instructions will be found in the text

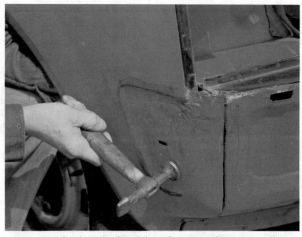

In the case of a dent the first job — after removing surrounding trim — is to hammer out the dent where access is possible. This will minimise filling. Here, the large dent having been hammered out, the damaged area is being made slightly concave

Now all paint must be removed from the damaged area, by rubbing with coarse abrasive paper. Alternatively, a wire brush or abrasive pad can be used in a power drill. Where the repair area meets good paintwork, the edge of the paintwork should be 'feathered', using a finer grade of abrasive paper

In the case of a hole caused by rusting, all damaged sheet-metal should be cut away before proceeding to this stage. Here, the damaged area is being treated with rust remover and inhibitor before being filled

Mix the body filler according to its manufacturer's instructions. In the case of corrosion damage, it will be necessary to block off any large holes before filling — this can be done with aluminium or plastic mesh, or aluminium tape. Make sure the area is absolutely clean before ...

... applying the filler. Filler should be applied with a flexible applicator, as shown, for best results; the wooden spatula being used for confined areas. Apply thin layers of filler at 20-minute intervals, until the surface of the filler is slightly proud of the surrounding bodywork

Initial shaping can be done with a Surform plane or Dreadnought file. Then, using progressively finer grades of wet-and-dry paper, wrapped around a sanding block, and copious amounts of clean water, rub down the filler until really smooth and flat. Again, feather the edges of adjoining paintwork

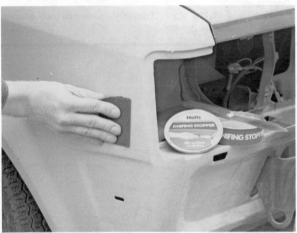

Again, using plenty of water, rub down the primer with a fine grade wet-and-dry paper (400 grade is probably best) until it is really smooth and well blended into the surrounding paintwork. Any remaining imperfections can now be filled by carefully applied knifing stopper paste

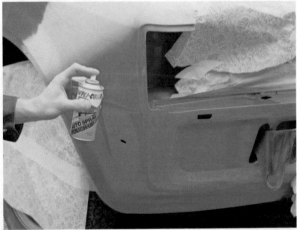

The top coat can now be applied. When working out of doors, pick a dry, warm and wind-free day. Ensure surrounding areas are protected from over-spray. Agitate the aerosol thoroughly, then spray the centre of the repair area, working outwards with a circular motion. Apply the paint as several thin coats

The whole repair area can now be sprayed or brush-painted with primer. If spraying, ensure adjoining areas are protected from over-spray. Note that at least one inch of the surrounding sound paintwork should be coated with primer. Primer has a 'thick' consistency, so will find small imperfections

When the stopper has hardened, rub down the repair area again before applying the final coat of primer. Before rubbing down this last coat of primer, ensure the repair area is blemish-free — use more stopper if necessary. To ensure that the surface of the primer is really smooth use some finishing compound

After a period of about two weeks, which the paint needs to harden fully, the surface of the repaired area can be 'cut' with a mild cutting compound prior to wax polishing. When carrying out bodywork repairs, remember that the quality of the finished job is proportional to the time and effort expended

18 Front and rear door – removal and refitting

610 series
Front door

1 Refer to the relevant sections and remove the front bumper, radiator grille, front apron, windscreen wiper blades and cowl top panel.
2 Undo and remove the screws that secure the sill moulding. Lift away the moulding.
3 Open the front door and place a support under the door to take its weight. The help of an assistant should also be enlisted to hold the door.
4 Remove the bolts securing the door hinge to the body. There are three bolts to each hinge.
5 Lift away the front door from the side of the car.
6 Refitting the front door is the reverse sequence to removal.

Rear door

7 Open the front door and retain in the open position.
8 Open the rear door and place a support under the door to take its weight. The help of an assistant should also be enlisted to hold the door.
9 Remove the bolts securing the door hinge to the body. There are three bolts to each hinge.
10 Lift away the rear door from the side of the car.

11 Refitting the rear door is the reverse sequence to removal.

Adjustment

12 Correct door alignment may be obtained by adjusting the position of the door hinge and lock striker.
13 The door hinge and striker may be moved up and down as well as fore and aft by slackening the securing bolts and moving the hinge in the required direction. It will be found necessary to use a cranked spanner when adjusting the front door hinges.

810 series
Front door

14 Open the door fully and place a support under the door to take its weight.
15 Remove the bolts securing the door to the hinges and lift away the door (photo).
16 Refitting the door is the reverse of the removal procedure.

Rear door

17 The rear door is removed and refitted in the same 2£fl as the front door.

Adjustment

18 Adjustment of the door alignment is carried out as described above for 610 models (photo).

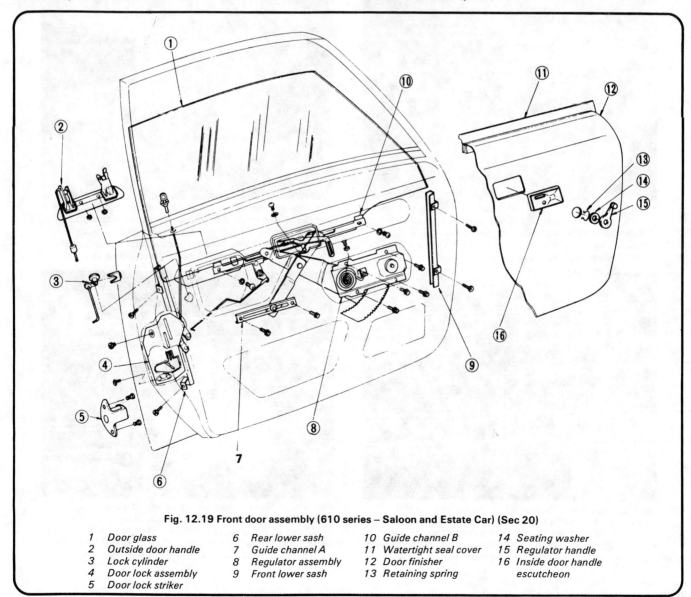

Fig. 12.19 Front door assembly (610 series – Saloon and Estate Car) (Sec 20)

1 Door glass	6 Rear lower sash	10 Guide channel B	14 Seating washer
2 Outside door handle	7 Guide channel A	11 Watertight seal cover	15 Regulator handle
3 Lock cylinder	8 Regulator assembly	12 Door finisher	16 Inside door handle
4 Door lock assembly	9 Front lower sash	13 Retaining spring	escutcheon
5 Door lock striker			

19 Door trim and interior handles – removal and refitting

1   Open the door and, using a metal hook, withdraw the window regulator handle retaining spring clip (photo).
2   This photo shows the retaining spring in position.
3   Undo the self tapping screw securing the lock handle finisher. Lift away the finisher (photos).
4   Undo and remove the two screws securing the arm rest to the door inner panel. Lift away the arm rest (photo). On Hardtop models the covers must be levered off to provide access to the securing screws.
5   Ease back the door handle finishers then undo and remove the two securing screws. Lift away the door handle.
6   The door trim inner panel may now be detached from the door inner panel. Using a knife or hacksaw blade (with the teeth ground down) inserted between the door trim panel and door inner panel, carefully ease each clip from its hole in the door inner panel.
7   When all clips are free lift away the door trim panel (photo).

8   Inspect the dust and splash shields to ensure that they are correctly fitted and also not damaged.
9   Inspect the trim panel retaining clips and inserts for excessive corrosion or damage. Obtain new ones as necessary.
10   Refitting the door trim panel is the reverse sequence to removal. With the door glass up the regulator handle should be pointing upwards 45° to the front on 610 series and 60° for 810 series.

20 Door lock and striker (610 series) – removal and refitting

1   Refer to Section 19 and remove the door trim.
2   Pull back the dust and splash shield (photo).
3   Undo and remove the two screws that secure the interior door handle assembly to the inner panel. Remove the interior door handle.
4   Undo and remove the screws securing the remote control and lock knob and remove the assembly.
5   Undo and remove the two nuts and washers securing the exterior door handle to the door outer panel. Lift away the exterior handle.

18.15 Front door hinge securing bolts

18.18 Adjust the position of the door striker as required

19.1 Removing regulator handle

19.2 Spring clip located in regulator handle

19.3a Removal of lock handle finisher screw (610 series)

19.3b Removal of lock handle finisher screw (810 series)

19.4 Removing the arm rest securing screws

19.7 Door trim ready for lifting away

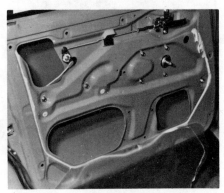
20.2 Dust and splash shield pulled back

6   Detach the remote control rod from the door lock cylinder.
7   Undo and remove the screws that secure the lock to the door panel. Lift away the lock assembly.
8   Undo and remove the two screws fixing the door lock striker to the door pillar. Lift away the striker.
9   Refitting the door lock assembly is the reverse sequence to removal. Lubricate all moving parts with engine oil.
10   Should adjustment be necessary this must be carried out before the trim panel is refitted. The correct clearance between the door lock lever and adjustment nut must be less than 0·039 in (1·0 mm).
11   To adjust the interior door handle free play move the interior door handle assembly fore and aft in the elongated holes until there is a free play of 0·039 in (1·0 mm). Do not attempt to bend the door lock lever connecting the control rod.
12   The door lock striker can be moved both vertically and horizontally to align with the door lock latch.

21 Door lock cylinder (610 series) – removal and refitting

1   Refer to Section 19 and remove the door trim.
2   Pull back the dust and splash shield.
3   Disconnect the control rod from the door lock cylinder.
4   Remove the lock spring that secures the doorlock cylinder to the outside door panel and then withdraw the door lock cylinder from the door.
5   Refitting the door lock cylinder is the reverse sequence to removal.

22 Door lock and control (810 series) – removal and refitting

1   Remove the door window glass as described in Section 25.
2   Remove the interior door handle attaching screw.
3   Disconnect the rod connecting the interior handle to the door lock,

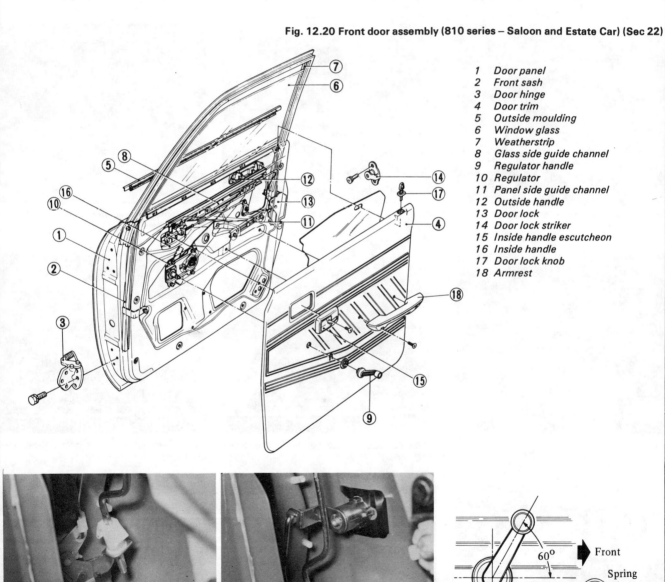

Fig. 12.20 Front door assembly (810 series – Saloon and Estate Car) (Sec 22)

1   Door panel
2   Front sash
3   Door hinge
4   Door trim
5   Outside moulding
6   Window glass
7   Weatherstrip
8   Glass side guide channel
9   Regulator handle
10 Regulator
11 Panel side guide channel
12 Outside handle
13 Door lock
14 Door lock striker
15 Inside handle escutcheon
16 Inside handle
17 Door lock knob
18 Armrest

22.3 Disconnecting door lock control rod   22.5 Rod connecting key cylinder to door lock   Fig. 12.21 Fitting the regulator handle
                                                                                                         (810 series) (Secs 22 and 25)

60°

Front

Spring

at the lock (photo).
4   Remove the bellcrank attaching screw.
5   Disconnect the rod connecting the key cylinder to the door lock at the lock (photo).
6   Detach the rod connecting the outside handle to the door lock at the outside handle lever.
7   Remove the door lock assembly and the outside handle.
8   Refitting is the reverse of the removal sequence. When fitting the outside handle, adjust the clearance between the adjusting nut and the lever from the door lock to 0 – 0·04 in (1 mm), see Fig. 12.22.

23 Front door window glass and regulator (610 series) – removal and refitting

This Section is applicable to Saloon and Estate car models, but not Hardtop models. See Section 24 for this information.
1   Lower the door glass and then referring to Section 19 remove the door trim.
2   Remove the door exterior weatherstrip and door lock knob.
3   Undo and remove the screws that secure the front lower sash and remove the front lower sash from the door glass. It is not necessary to draw the front lower sash out of the door before removing the door glass.
4   Support the weight of the door glass with a piece of wood and then undo and remove the screws that secure the front guide channel to the glass backplate.
5   Carefully lift the door glass upward and lift it away from the door.
6   Undo and remove the screws holding the guide channel and regulator base. Remove the regulator assembly by drawing it through the lower opening of the door inner panel.
7   Undo and remove the screws fixing the rear lower sash and lift this away from the door.
8   Finally remove the front lower sash.
9   Refitting the door glass and regulator is the reverse sequence to removal. It will however be necessary to adjust the door glass alignment by adjusting the front and rear lower sashes and guide channel. To do this proceed as described in the following paragraphs.
10 With the door trim removed, temporarily tighten the front and rear lower sashes.
11 Raise the glass and adjust the rear lower sash from side to side so as to align the glass and front lower sash. Check that the glass moves up and down freely.
12 With the glass in the raised position, adjust the glass until it is parallel with the top rail of the door sash by moving the guide channel up or down. The sideward free play of glass can be adjusted by moving the front lower sash fore and aft.

24 Front door window glass and regulator (610 series – Hardtop model) – removal and refitting

1   With the door trim removed as described in Section 19 lower the door glass (Fig. 12.23).
2   Remove the door outside moulding.
3   Carefully drive out the inner pin of the clip securing the outside finisher and then remove the retaining clip and outside finisher and weatherstrip from the door.
4   Raise the door glass until the upper stops appear in the upper apertures of the interior door panel. Remove the glass upper stoppers.
5   Lower the door glass and support its weight with a piece of wood. Undo and remove the screws that secure the backplate to the guide channel.
6   Lift the door glass upwards and remove through the glass aperture.
7   Remove the bolts holding the front and rear guide rails. Lift away the guide from the door.
8   Undo and remove the screws that secure the guide channel, regulator arm base and regulator.
9   Remove the guide channel, regulator arm base and regulator from the aperture in the inner door panel.
10 Refitting the door window glass and regulator is the reverse sequence to removal but it will be necessary to adjust the glass position and regulator assembly as described in the following paragraphs.
11 With the door trim removed, raise the glass and temporarily tighten the upper and lower bolts securing the guide rail. As these

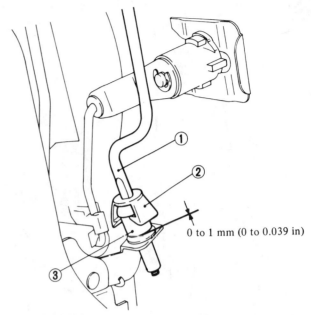

Fig. 12.22 Adjusting door lock control (810 series) (Sec 22)

1 Outside handle rod   2 Clip   3 Adjusting nut

0 to 1 mm (0 to 0.039 in)

locate in elongated holes position the guide rail in its middle position. For the lower adjustment bolt fully tighten it and then back off nine turns. Secure in this position with the locknut.
12 Adjust the guide rail upper adjustment bolts so that the clearance between the door exterior panel and glass outside face is 0·346 – 0·4134 in (8·5 – 10·5 mm).
13 Refit the door outside finisher ensuring the door outside weatherstrip contacts the door glass correctly when the door glass is raised or lowered.
14 Raise the door glass to its fully up position and align the door glass with the body weatherstrip. This will ensure a watertight seal.
15 Correct alignment can be obtained by adjusting the guide rails and guide channel.
16 Raise the glass to its fully up position and adjust the upper glass stops so that the clearance between the top of the glass and body side weatherstrip is 0·000 – 0·0394 in (0 – 1·0 mm).
17 With the glass still raised move the top edge of the glass to body side weatherstrip so as to obtain a tight seal by adjusting the guide rail lower bolts evenly.
18 Now turn the lower adjustment bolts clockwise to release the top edge of the glass from the body side weatherstrip and anti-clockwise to tighten.
19 Ensure that all top edges of the glass give an even and tight fit. Also ensure that the clearance between the top of the glass and the end of the glass guide is 0·000 – 0·0197 in (0 – 0·5 mm) just before contacting the door glass with the door side weatherstrip.
20 Check the operation of the complete system for freedom of movement and then lubricate all moving parts with engine oil.

25 Front door window glass and regulator (810 series – Saloon and Estate Car models) – removal and refitting

1   Refer to Section 19 and remove the door trim.
2   Remove the door exterior moulding.
3   Loosen the front and rear sash attaching screws.
4   Back-off the nuts securing the glass guide to the glass side guide channel in the opening of the door panel.
5   Lift out the door window glass.
6   Remove the bolts securing the regulator base plate and guide channel to the door panel and withdraw the regulator through the opening in the inside door panel.
7   Refitting is the reverse of the removal procedure. Set the regulator handle as shown in Fig. 12.21 with the window fully closed. If the glass is tilted forward, correct by lowering the guide channel as necessary. If it is tilted backwards, raise the guide channel as required.

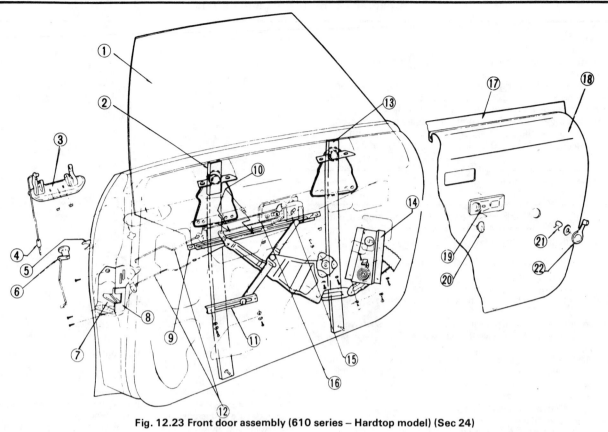

Fig. 12.23 Front door assembly (610 series – Hardtop model) (Sec 24)

1	Door glass	7	Door lock assembly	13	Front guide rail	19	Inside door handle
2	Rear guide rail	8	Spacer	14	Regulator assembly		escutcheon
3	Outside door handle	9	Guide channel B	15	Inside door handle	20	Door lock dial
4	Adjusting nut	10	Rod holder	16	Dust cover	21	Retaining spring
5	Lock spring	11	Guide channel A	17	Watertight seal cover	22	Regulator handle
6	Lock cylinder	12	Door lock rod	18	Door finisher		

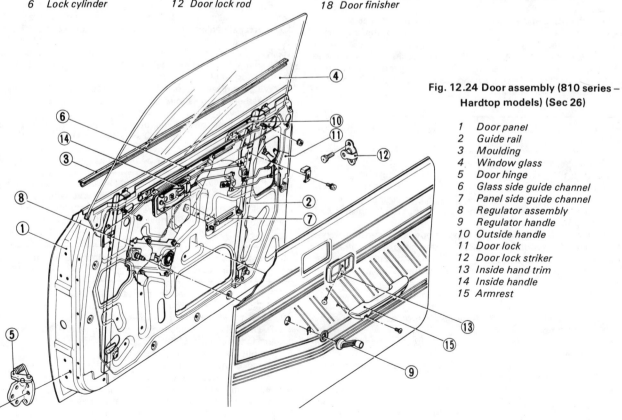

Fig. 12.24 Door assembly (810 series – Hardtop models) (Sec 26)

1 Door panel
2 Guide rail
3 Moulding
4 Window glass
5 Door hinge
6 Glass side guide channel
7 Panel side guide channel
8 Regulator assembly
9 Regulator handle
10 Outside handle
11 Door lock
12 Door lock striker
13 Inside hand trim
14 Inside handle
15 Armrest

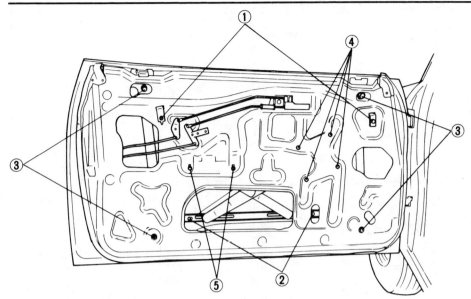

Fig. 12.25 Removing door regulator and glass (810 series – Hardtop) (Sec 26)

1 Upper stopper attaching bolts
2 Glass-to-glass side guide channel bolts
3 Guide rail attaching bolts
4 Regulator plate attaching bolts
5 Panel side guide channel attaching bolts

26 Front door window glass and regulator (810 series – Hardtop model) – removal and refitting

1 Remove the door trim as described in Section 19 and lower the glass completely.
2 Remove the outside moulding.
3 Remove the upper stoppers, see Fig. 12.25.
4 Detach the glass from the glass side guide channel.
5 Remove the bolts securing the guide rail, and remove the glass and guide rail as an assembly.
6 Remove the bolts attaching the regulator plate and guide channel to the door inner panel and remove the regulator through the opening in the door panel.
7 Refitting is the reverse of the removal procedure. When fitting the guide rail and roller, apply grease to the sliding surfaces.
8 After refitting the window it will be necessary to adjust the glass position as described in the following paragraphs.
9 Roughly locate the lower adjusting screws of the guide rail in their proper positions, adjust the clearance between glass and upper side of the outer door panel to 0·47 in (12 mm) at any point with the upper adjusting screws, see Fig. 12.26.
10 Adjust the lower adjusting screws of the guide rail so that its upper end is 0.039 – 0.059 in (1·0 – 1·5 mm) beyond the lower side of the weatherstrip.
11 Adjust the glass height so that the distance between the upper face of the glass and the outer lip of the weatherstrip is 0·020 – 0·039 in (0·5 – 1·0 mm) and tighten the upper stoppers. Be sure to secure the panel side guide channel in place with its forward portion slightly lowered, see Fig. 12.27.
12 Open and close the window a few times, checking for correct operation and freedom of movement.

27 Rear door window glass and regulator (610 series) – removal and refitting

1 Refer to Section 19 and remove the door trim inner panel.
2 Lower the door glass and then remove the door lock knob and grommet (Fig. 12.28).
3 Remove the door outside weatherstrip and rear sash.
4 Undo and remove the screws that secure the guide channel to the glass backplate and carefully ease the glass out of the door glass aperture.
5 Remove the rear sash and front lower sash from the door.
6 Undo and remove the screws that secure the guide channel and regulator to the door inner panel.
7 The regulator assembly may now be lifted away through the lower opening of the door inner panel.
8 Refitting the regulator and glass assemblies is the reverse sequence to removal. It will however be necessary to align the glass in

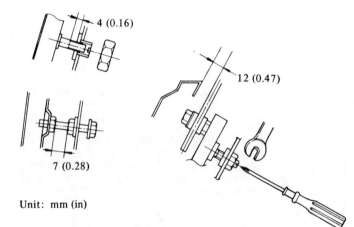

Unit: mm (in)

Fig. 12.26 Adjusting clearance between glass and outer door panel (810 Hardtop) (Sec 26)

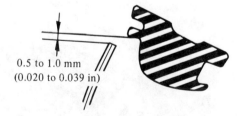

0.5 to 1.0 mm
(0.020 to 0.039 in)

Fig. 12.27 Glass height adjustment (810 series – Hardtop) (Sec 26)

the aperture. The front lower sash may be adjusted until it is parallel with the rear sash and can be moved from side to side. To adjust the sideways free play of the door glass slacken the lower securing screw and move the rear sash in the necessary direction. The tilt adjustment of the glass can be achieved by moving the guide channel up and down. Finally lubricate all moving parts with engine grade oil.

28 Rear door window glass and regulator (810 series) – removal and refitting

1 Refer to Section 27 and carry out operations 1–3 inclusive.
2 Remove the rear partition sash and rear door sash attaching screws.
3 Remove the bolts securing the glass backplate to the guide

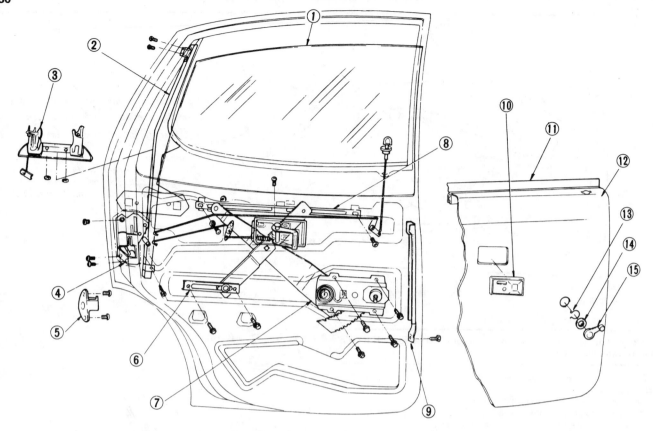

Fig. 12.28 Rear door assembly (610 series – Saloon and Estate Car) (Sec 27)

1	Door glass	5	Door lock striker	9	Front lower sash	13	Retaining spring
2	Rear sash	6	Guide channel A	10	Inside handle escutcheon	14	Seating washer
3	Outside door handle	7	Regulator assembly	11	Watertight seal cover	15	Regulator handle
4	Door lock assembly	8	Guide channel B	12	Door finisher		

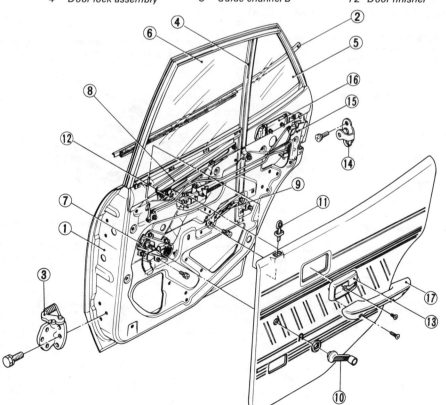

Fig. 12.29 Rear door assembly (810 series – Saloon and Estate Car) (Sec 28)

1 Door panel
2 Outside moulding
3 Door hinge
4 Rear partition sash
5 Rear partition window glass
6 Glass
7 Regulator
8 Glass side guide channel
9 Panel side guide channel
10 Regulator handle
11 Door lock knob
12 Inside handle
13 Inside handle escutcheon
14 Door lock striker
15 Door lock
16 Outside handle
17 Armrest

channel and draw the door glass out of the door.

4   Remove the screws securing the guide channel and regulator base, and withdraw the regulator assembly through the lower opening of the door inside panel.

5   Refitting is the reverse of the removal procedure. Lubricate all friction surfaces. Fore and aft adjustment is made by loosening the glass securing bolts, and adjustment to correct tilt is by moving the panel side guide channel up or down as required.

29 Rear side window glass (Hardtop) – removal and refitting

1   Remove the rear seat cushion and backrest from the interior of the car.

2   Remove the seat belt anchorage and kicking plate.

3   Now lower the side window glass and remove the arm next and regulator handle. The handle is retained by a spring clip and may be drawn out of position using a suitable metal hook.

4   Remove the rear side finisher and watertight seal cover.

5   Next remove the draught finisher and if a seat belt anchorage is located on the rear quarter panel this should also be detached.

6   Release the clips holding the rear corner finisher to the body with a screwdriver and lift away the corner finisher.

7   Remove the inner seal and bracket and then raise the glass until the regulator arm bracket appears in the upper opening of the inside panel. Support the glass with a wood block and then remove the nuts that secure the regulator arm bracket to the side window backplate.

8   Back off the guide plate upper and lower adjustment bolt locknuts and then unscrew the adjustment bolts from the backplate.

9   Raise the window glass and guide panel and remove them towards the interior.

10   Undo and remove the regulator securing bolts from the inner panel and lift the regulator assembly out through the lower opening in the inner panel.

11   Refitting the window glass and regulator assembly is the reverse sequence to removal. It will however be necessary to adjust the position of the glass as described in the following paragraphs before the trim panels are refitted.

12   With the window glass in the lowest position temporarily tighten the guide plate adjustment bolts in the centre of the elongated holes. Tighten the bolts fully and then back off eight turns and lock in position with the locknut.

13   Adjust the guide plate upper adjusting bolts so as to obtain a clearance of $0.3346 - 0.4134$ in ($8.5 - 10.5$ mm) between the rear wing panel and window glass outside face.

14   Fit the rear wing finisher and make sure that the window glass is carefully aligned with the weatherstrip when the window glass moves up and down.

15   Close the front door and raise the door glass and side window glass.

16   Align the side window glass with the door glass and body side weatherstrip by setting the guide plate adjustment bolts until, with the glass up there is a clearance between the glass and side weatherstrip

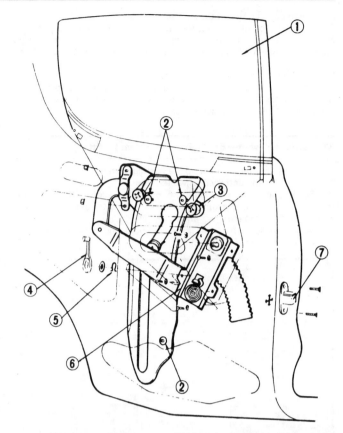

Fig. 12.30 Rear side assembly (610 series – Hardtop) (Sec 29)

1	Side window glass	5	Retaining spring
2	Guide plate adjusting bolts	6	Regulator assembly
3	Guide roller	7	Door lock striker
4	Regulator handle		

of $0.1181 - 0.1969$ in ($3.0 - 5.0$ mm) on 610 series and 0.24 in (6 mm) on 810 series.

17   Before fitting the trim panels apply grease to all friction surfaces.

30 Centre console – removal and refitting

1   Remove the gear change lever knob.

2   Undo and remove the self-tapping screws securing the rear console to the floor panel. Carefully lift away the rear console.

3   Undo and remove the self-tapping screws holding the front

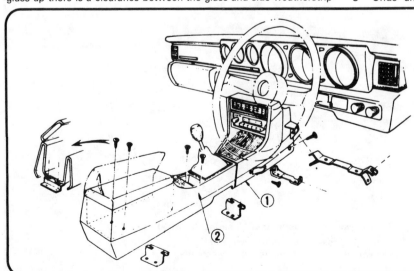

Fig. 12.31 Centre console assembly (610 series) (Sec 30)

1   Front console
2   Rear console

console to parcel tray and the side securing screws.

4   If a radio or other electrical accessories are fitted to the front console, disconnect the battery positive terminal and then detach the electrical connections to the console. Make a note of these connections.

5   The front console may now be lifted away.

6   Refitting the centre console is the reverse sequence to removal. Do not tighten the screws until all have been started. Use a small screwdriver to line up the screw holes.

31 Heater and ventilation unit – removal and refitting

1   Refer to Chapter 2 and drain the cooling system.

2   Disconnect the battery positive terminal.

3   Slacken the hose clips and disconnect the inlet and outlet hoses from the heater. Place cloth under these unions to absorb any water that could drip from the open ends.

4   Move the seats back as far as possible and remove the centre console as described in Section 30.

5   Next remove the centre ventilator and detach the large diameter heater duct hose.

6   Detach the demister hose from each side of the heater unit.

7   Detach the cable securing clips from the air mixture door, mode door and defrost compartment door. Disconnect the cables from the door control levers.

8   Disconnect the heater motor cables from the two terminal connectors.

9   Remove the three bolts holding the heater unit in position. There are two bolts on the side unit and one on the top of the heater unit.

10 Carefully lift away the heater unit ensuring that no water is allowed to drain out of the heater matrix.

11 Refitting the heater unit is the reverse sequence to removal. It will be necessary to adjust the controls as described later in this Chapter.

32 Heater control assembly – removal and refitting

1   Refer to Section 31 and remove the heater unit.

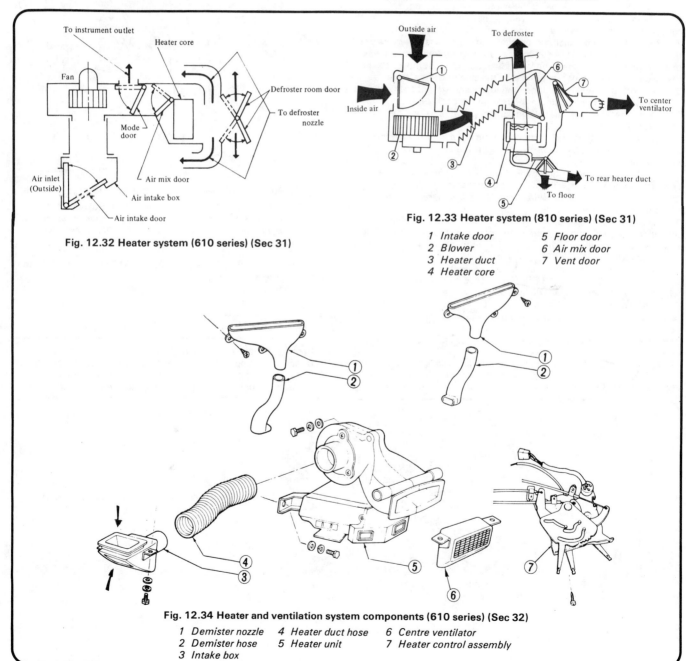

Fig. 12.32 Heater system (610 series) (Sec 31)

Fig. 12.33 Heater system (810 series) (Sec 31)

1 Intake door   5 Floor door
2 Blower   6 Air mix door
3 Heater duct   7 Vent door
4 Heater core

Fig. 12.34 Heater and ventilation system components (610 series) (Sec 32)

1 Demister nozzle   4 Heater duct hose   6 Centre ventilator
2 Demister hose   5 Heater unit   7 Heater control assembly
3 Intake box

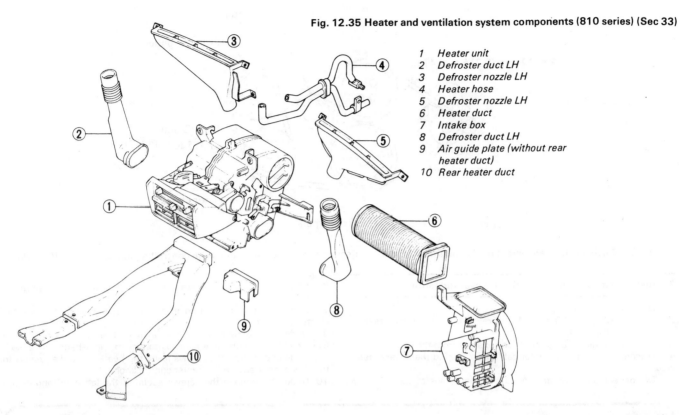

Fig. 12.35 Heater and ventilation system components (810 series) (Sec 33)

1 Heater unit
2 Defroster duct LH
3 Defroster nozzle LH
4 Heater hose
5 Defroster nozzle LH
6 Heater duct
7 Intake box
8 Defroster duct LH
9 Air guide plate (without rear heater duct)
10 Rear heater duct

2 Carefully draw the finisher forward. It is retained in position with clips.
3 Undo and remove the control securing screws and lift away the assembly.
4 To refit the control assembly is the reverse sequence to removal.

33 Heater air intake box – removal and refitting

1 Detach the heater duct hose and then disconnect the control cable from the air intake door.
2 Undo and remove the screw that secures the air intake box in position and lift away the unit.
3 Refitting the air intake box is the reverse sequence to removal.

34 Heater matrix – removal and refitting

1 Refer to Chapter 2 and drain the engine cooling system.
2 Slacken the hose clips and disconnect the heater inlet and outlet hoses from the heater unit. Place cloth underneath to absorb any coolant.
3 Release the clips and remove the heater box grille.
4 The heater matrix may now be pulled out of the heater unit. Take care that water does not spill out.
5 Check the matrix for blockage by flushing out with water. Repair any leaks with a proprietary sealer.
6 Refitting the heater matrix is the reverse sequence to removal.

35 Heater motor – removal and refitting

1 Before removing the motor for suspected failure, it is worthwhile testing the circuit and motor first. Inspect the fuse and fusible link for signs of failure and all cable connections for cleanliness and security.
2 Disconnect the leads at the connector, move the ignition switch to the ACC position and connect a test light lead to the blue/white terminal connector plug in the instrument harness side and a second lead

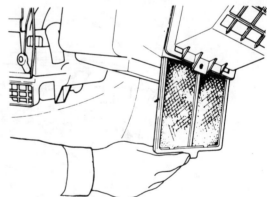

Fig. 12.36 Location of air filter (air conditioning system) (Sec 36)

to earth. The lamp should light.
3 If the motor operation is sluggish, test by connecting directly to a fully charged battery. If unsatisfactory operation is still experienced remove the motor and take it to a local automobile electrician for inspection.
4 To remove the motor first remove the heater unit as detailed in Section 31.
5 Undo and remove the three motor securing screws and lift away the heater motor.
6 Refitting the heater motor is the reverse sequence to removal.

36 Air conditioning – general

Should an air conditioning unit be fitted and its performance is unsatisfactory or it has to be removed to give access to other parts it is recommended that this be left to the local Datsun garage. This is because the unit is of a complex nature and specialist knowledge and equipment is required to service the unit. This is definitely a case of 'If all is well leave well alone' (Figs. 12.36 and 12.37).

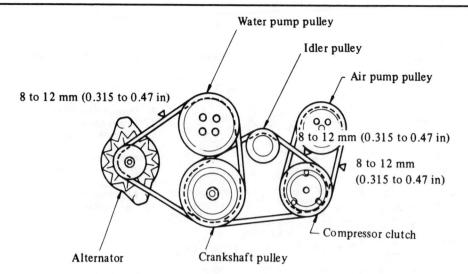

Fig. 12.37 Drive belt arrangement on air conditioning and air injection system (exhaust emission control) equipped vehicles (Sec 36)

37 Instrument panel (610 series) – removal and refitting

1 Disconnect the battery.
2 Refer to Chapters 10 and 11 and remove the horn bar, steering wheel and shell assembly.
3 Disconnect the heater control cable clamps from the heater unit.
4 Disconnect the speedometer cable from behind the speedometer lead.
5 Disconnect the body and instrument harnesses at the multi-pin plug.
6 Carefully remove the instrument garnishes from the instrument panel.
7 Remove the cluster lid cover securing screws and lift away the cluster lid cover.
8 Undo and remove the five screws that secure the right-hand cluster lid to the instrument panel. Lift away the right-hand cluster lid.
9 Undo and remove the screws fixing the heater control assembly to the cluster lid. Remove the heater control knobs.
10 Undo and remove the screws securing the left-hand and centre

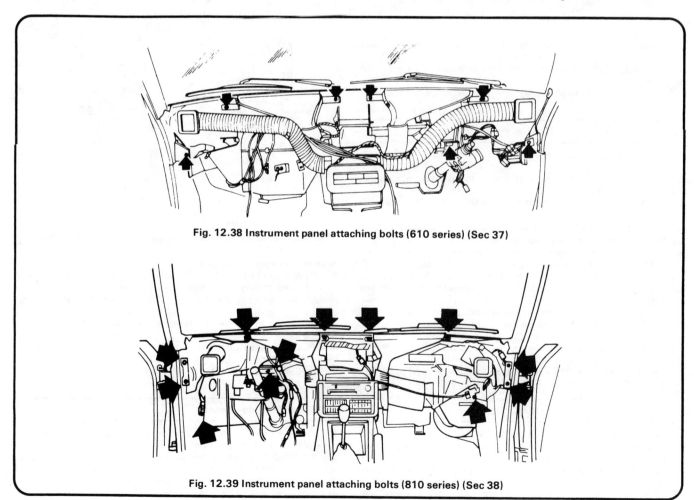

Fig. 12.38 Instrument panel attaching bolts (610 series) (Sec 37)

Fig. 12.39 Instrument panel attaching bolts (810 series) (Sec 38)

cluster lids to the instrument panel. Lift away the left-hand and centre cluster lids.
11 Undo and remove the seven bolts securing the instrument panel to the body and carefully lift away the instrument panel.
12 Refitting the instrument panel and cluster lids is the reverse sequence to removal.

38 Instrument panel (810 series) – removal and refitting

1   Disconnect the battery earth cable.
2   Remove the bolts securing the instrument panel to the upper dash panel.
3   Refer to Chapter 11 and remove the steering wheel and shelf covers.
4   Remove the bolts securing the steering post to the pedal bracket and the bolt securing the instrument panel to the pedal bracket.
5   Remove the bolt attaching the parcel shelf to the instrument panel.
6   Disconnect the speedometer cable from behind the specdometer.
7   Remove the manual choke cable knob.
8   Remove the bolts attaching the instrument panel to the dash side brackets.
9   Disconnect the connectors from the instrument harness at both ends and lift away the instrument panel.
10 Refitting is the reverse of the removal procedure (photo).

38.10 Instrument panel and controls (810 series)

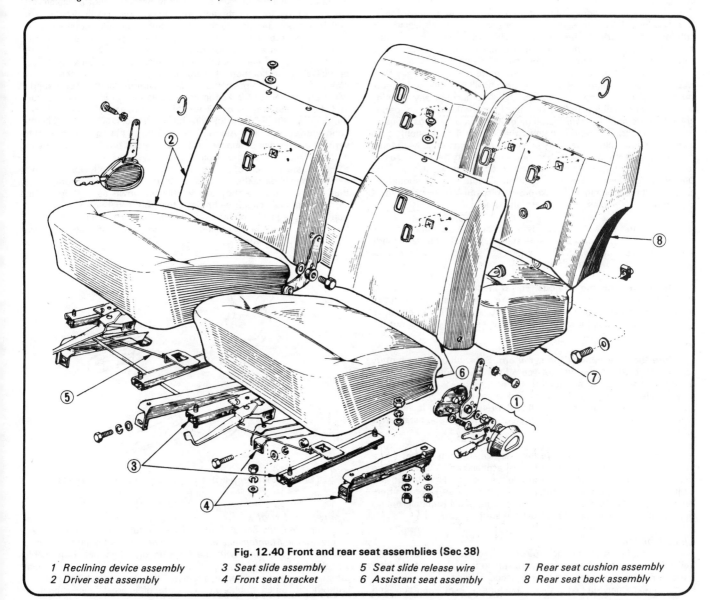

Fig. 12.40 Front and rear seat assemblies (Sec 38)

1 Reclining device assembly	3 Seat slide assembly	5 Seat slide release wire	7 Rear seat cushion assembly
2 Driver seat assembly	4 Front seat bracket	6 Assistant seat assembly	8 Rear seat back assembly

Fault diagnosis

Introduction

The vehicle owner who does his or her own maintenance according to the recommended schedules should not have to use this section of the manual very often. Modern component reliability is such that, provided those items subject to wear or deterioration are inspected or renewed at the specified intervals, sudden failure is comparatively rare. Faults do not usually just happen as a result of sudden failure, but develop over a period of time. Major mechanical failures in particular are usually preceded by characteristic symptoms over hundreds or even thousands of miles. Those components which do occasionally fail without warning are often small and easily carried in the vehicle.

With any fault finding, the first step is to decide where to begin investigations. Sometimes this is obvious, but on other occasions a little detective work will be necessary. The owner who makes half a dozen haphazard adjustments or replacements may be successful in curing a fault (or its symptoms), but he will be none the wiser if the fault recurs and he may well have spent more time and money than was necessary. A calm and logical approach will be found to be more satisfactory in the long run. Always take into account any warning signs or abnormalities that may have been noticed in the period preceding the fault – power loss, high or low gauge readings, unusual noises or smells, etc – and remember that failure of components such as fuses or spark plugs may only be pointers to some underlying fault.

The pages which follow here are intended to help in cases of failure to start or breakdown on the road. There is also a Fault Diagnosis Section at the end of each Chapter which should be consulted if the preliminary checks prove unfruitful. Whatever the fault, certain basic principles apply. These are as follows:

Verify the fault. This is simply a matter of being sure that you know what the symptoms are before starting work. This is particularly important if you are investigating a fault for someone else who may not have described it very accurately.

Don't overlook the obvious. For example, if the vehicle won't start, is there petrol in the tank? (Don't take anyone else's word on this particular point, and don't trust the fuel gauge either!) If an electrical fault is indicated, look for loose or broken wires before digging out the test gear.

Cure the disease, not the symptom. Substituting a flat battery with a fully charged one will get you off the hard shoulder, but if the underlying cause is not attended to, the new battery will go the same way. Similarly, changing oil-fouled spark plugs for a new set will get you moving again, but remember that the reason for the fouling (if it wasn't simply an incorrect grade of plug) will have to be established and corrected.

Don't take anything for granted. Particularly, don't forget that a 'new' component may itself be defective (especially if it's been rattling round in the boot for months), and don't leave components out of a fault diagnosis sequence just because they are new or recently fitted. When you do finally diagnose a difficult fault, you'll probably realise that all the evidence was there from the start.

Electrical faults

Electrical faults can be more puzzling than straightforward mechanical failures, but they are no less susceptible to logical analysis if the basic principles of operation are understood. Vehicle electrical wiring exists in extremely unfavourable conditions – heat, vibration and chemical attack – and the first things to look for are loose or corroded connections and broken or chafed wires, especially where the wires pass through holes in the bodywork or are subject to vibration.

All metal-bodied vehicles in current production have one pole of the battery 'earthed', ie connected to the vehicle bodywork, and in nearly all modern vehicles it is the negative (–) terminal. The various electrical components – motors, bulb holders etc – are also connected to earth, either by means of a lead or directly by their mountings. Electric current flows through the component and then back to the battery via the bodywork. If the component mounting is loose or corroded, or if a good path back to the battery is not available, the circuit will be incomplete and malfunction will result. The engine and/or gearbox are also earthed by means of flexible metal straps to the body or subframe; if these straps are loose or missing, starter motor, generator and ignition trouble may result.

Assuming the earth return to be satisfactory, electrical faults will be due either to component malfunction or to defects in the current supply. Individual components are dealt with in Chapter 10. If supply wires are broken or cracked internally this results in an open-circuit, and the easiest way to check for this is to bypass the suspect wire temporarily with a length of wire having a crocodile clip or suitable connector at each end. Alternatively, a 12V test lamp can be used to verify the presence of supply voltage at various points along the wire and the break can be thus isolated.

If a bare portion of a live wire touches the bodywork or other earthed metal part, the electricity will take the low-resistance path thus formed back to the battery: this is known as a short-circuit. Hopefully a short-circuit will blow a fuse, but otherwise it may cause burning of the insulation (and possibly further short-circuits) or even a fire. This is why it is inadvisable to bypass persistently blowing fuses with silver foil or wire.

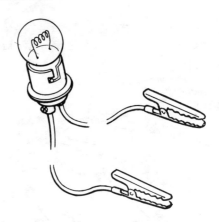

Simple test lamp is useful for tracing electrical faults

Spares and tool kit

Most vehicles are supplied only with sufficient tools for wheel changing; the *Maintenance and minor repair* tool kit detailed in *Tools and working facilities*, with the addition of a hammer, is probably sufficient for those repairs that most motorists would consider attempting at the roadside. In addition a few items which can be fitted without too much trouble in the event of a breakdown should be carried. Experience and available space will modify the list below, but the following may save having to call on professional assistance:

Spark plugs, clean and correctly gapped
HT lead and plug cap — long enough to reach the plug furthest from the distributor
Distributor rotor, condenser and contact breaker points
Drivebelt(s) — emergency type may suffice
Spare fuses
Set of principal light bulbs
Tin of radiator sealer and hose bandage
Exhaust bandage
Roll of insulating tape
Length of soft iron wire
Length of electrical flex
Torch or inspection lamp (can double as test lamp)
Battery jump leads
Tow-rope
Ignition waterproofing aerosol
Litre of engine oil
Sealed can of hydraulic fluid
Emergency windscreen
Worm drive clips
Tube of filler paste

If spare fuel is carried, a can designed for the purpose should be used to minimise risks of leakage and collision damage. A first aid kit and a warning triangle, whilst not at present compulsory in the UK, are obviously sensible items to carry in addition to the above.

When touring abroad it may be advisable to carry additional spares which, even if you cannot fit them yourself, could save having to wait while parts are obtained. The items below may be worth considering:

Throttle cable
Cylinder head gasket
Alternator brushes
Fuel pump repair kit
Tyre valve core

One of the motoring organisations will be able to advise on availability of fuel etc in foreign countries.

Engine will not start

Engine fails to turn when starter operated
Flat battery (recharge, use jump leads, or push start)
Battery terminals loose or corroded
Battery earth to body defective

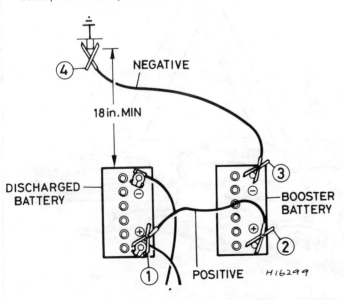

Jump start lead connections for negative earth vehicles — connect leads in order shown

Engine earth strap loose or broken
Starter motor (or solenoid) wiring loose or broken
Automatic transmission selector in wrong position, or inhibitor switch faulty
Ignition/starter switch faulty
Major mechanical failure (seizure)
Starter or solenoid internal fault (see Chapter 10)

Starter motor turns engine slowly
Partially discharged battery (recharge, use jump leads, or push start)
Battery terminals loose or corroded
Battery earth to body defective
Engine earth strap loose
Starter motor (or solenoid) wiring loose
Starter motor internal fault (see Chapter 10)

Starter motor spins without turning engine
Flat battery
Starter motor pinion sticking on sleeve
Flywheel gear teeth damaged or worn
Starter motor mounting bolts loose

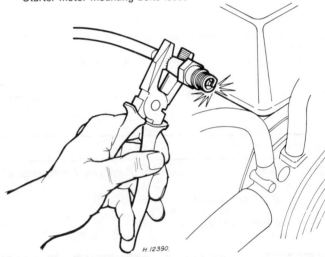

Crank engine and check for spark. Note use of insulated tool to hold spark plug

Engine turns normally but fails to start
Damp or dirty HT leads and distributor cap (crank engine and check for spark)
Dirty or incorrectly gapped distributor points (if applicable)
No fuel in tank (check for delivery at carburettor)
Excessive choke (hot engine) or insufficient choke (cold engine)
Fouled or incorrectly gapped spark plugs (remove, clean and regap)
Other ignition system fault (see Chapter 4)
Other fuel system fault (see Chapter 3)
Poor compression
Major mechanical failure (eg camshaft drive)

Engine fires but will not run
Insufficient choke (cold engine)
Air leaks at carburettor or inlet manifold
Fuel starvation (see Chapter 3)
Ballast resistor defective, or other ignition fault (see Chapter 4)

Engine cuts out and will not restart

Engine cuts out suddenly — ignition fault
Loose or disconnected LT wires
Wet HT leads or distributor cap (after traversing water splash)
Coil or condenser failure (check for spark)
Other ignition fault (see Chapter 4)

Engine misfires before cutting out – fuel fault
  Fuel tank empty
  Fuel pump defective or filter blocked (check for delivery)
  Fuel tank filler vent blocked (suction will be evident on releasing
  cap)
  Carburettor needle valve sticking
  Carburettor jets blocked (fuel contaminated)
  Other fuel system fault (see Chapter 3)

Engine cuts out – other causes
  Serious overheating
  Major mechanical failure (eg camshaft drive)

Engine overheats

Ignition (no-charge) warning light illuminated
  Slack or broken drivebelt – retension or renew (Chapter 2)

Ignition warning light not illuminated
  Coolant loss due to internal or external leakage (see Chapter 2)
  Thermostat defective
  Low oil level
  Brakes binding
  Radiator clogged externally or internally
  Engine waterways clogged
  Ignition timing incorrect or automatic advance malfunctioning
  Mixture too weak

Note: *Do not add cold water to an overheated engine or damage may
result*

Low engine oil pressure

*Gauge reads low or warning light illuminated with engine
running*
  Oil level low or incorrect grade
  Defective gauge or sender unit
  Wire to sender unit earthed
  Engine overheating

Oil filter clogged or bypass valve defective
Oil pressure relief valve defective
Oil pick-up strainer clogged
Oil pump worn or mountings loose
Worn main or big-end bearings

Note: *Low oil pressure in a high-mileage engine at tickover is not
necessarily a cause for concern. Sudden pressure loss at speed is far
more significant. In any event, check the gauge or warning light sender
before condemning the engine.*

Engine noises

Pre-ignition (pinking) on acceleration
  Incorrect grade of fuel
  Ignition timing incorrect
  Distributor faulty or worn
  Worn or maladjusted carburettor
  Excessive carbon build-up in engine

Whistling or wheezing noises
  Leaking vacuum hose
  Leaking carburettor or manifold gasket
  Blowing head gasket

Tapping or rattling
  Incorrect valve clearances
  Worn valve gear
  Worn timing chain
  Broken piston ring (ticking noise)

Knocking or thumping
  Unintentional mechanical contact (eg fan blades)
  Worn fanbelt
  Peripheral component fault (generator, water pump etc)
  Worn big-end bearings (regular heavy knocking, perhaps less
  under load)
  Worn main bearings (rumbling and knocking, perhaps worsening
  under load)
  Piston slap (most noticeable when cold)

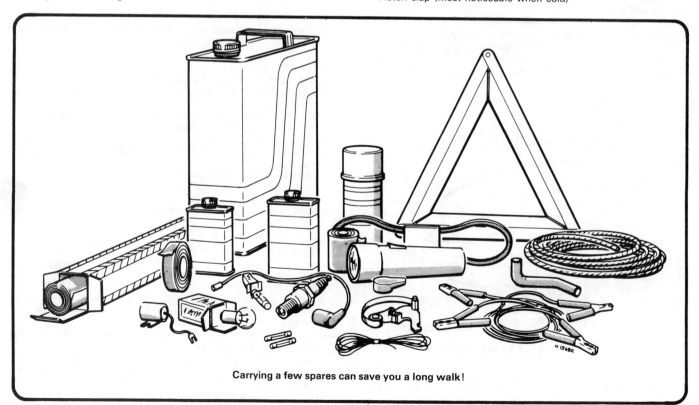

Carrying a few spares can save you a long walk!

General repair procedures

Whenever servicing, repair or overhaul work is carried out on the car or its components, it is necessary to observe the following procedures and instructions. This will assist in carrying out the operation efficiently and to a professional standard of workmanship.

Joint mating faces and gaskets

Where a gasket is used between the mating faces of two components, ensure that it is renewed on reassembly, and fit it dry unless otherwise stated in the repair procedure. Make sure that the mating faces are clean and dry with all traces of old gasket removed. When cleaning a joint face, use a tool which is not likely to score or damage the face, and remove any burrs or nicks with an oilstone or fine file.

Make sure that tapped holes are cleaned with a pipe cleaner, and keep them free of jointing compound if this is being used unless specifically instructed otherwise.

Ensure that all orifices, channels or pipes are clear and blow through them, preferably using compressed air.

Oil seals

Whenever an oil seal is removed from its working location, either individually or as part of an assembly, it should be renewed.

The very fine sealing lip of the seal is easily damaged and will not seal if the surface it contacts is not completely clean and free from scratches, nicks or grooves. If the original sealing surface of the component cannot be restored, the component should be renewed.

Protect the lips of the seal from any surface which may damage them in the course of fitting. Use tape or a conical sleeve where possible. Lubricate the seal lips with oil before fitting and, on dual lipped seals, fill the space between the lips with grease.

Unless otherwise stated, oil seals must be fitted with their sealing lips toward the lubricant to be sealed.

Use a tubular drift or block of wood of the appropriate size to install the seal and, if the seal housing is shouldered, drive the seal down to the shoulder. If the seal housing is unshouldered, the seal should be fitted with its face flush with the housing top face.

Screw threads and fastenings

Always ensure that a blind tapped hole is completely free from oil, grease, water or other fluid before installing the bolt or stud. Failure to do this could cause the housing to crack due to the hydraulic action of the bolt or stud as it is screwed in.

When tightening a castellated nut to accept a split pin, tighten the nut to the specified torque, where applicable, and then tighten further to the next split pin hole. Never slacken the nut to align a split pin hole unless stated in the repair procedure.

When checking or retightening a nut or bolt to a specified torque setting, slacken the nut or bolt by a quarter of a turn, and then retighten to the specified setting.

Locknuts, locktabs and washers

Any fastening which will rotate against a component or housing in the course of tightening should always have a washer between it and the relevant component or housing.

Spring or split washers should always be renewed when they are used to lock a critical component such as a big-end bearing retaining nut or bolt.

Locktabs which are folded over to retain a nut or bolt should always be renewed.

Self-locking nuts can be reused in non-critical areas, providing resistance can be felt when the locking portion passes over the bolt or stud thread.

Split pins must always be replaced with new ones of the correct size for the hole.

Special tools

Some repair procedures in this manual entail the use of special tools such as a press, two or three-legged pullers, spring compressors etc. Wherever possible, suitable readily available alternatives to the manufacturer's special tools are described, and are shown in use. In some instances, where no alternative is possible, it has been necessary to resort to the use of a manufacturer's tool and this has been done for reasons of safety as well as the efficient completion of the repair operation. Unless you are highly skilled and have a thorough understanding of the procedure described, never attempt to bypass the use of any special tool when the procedure described specifies its use. Not only is there a very great risk of personal injury, but expensive damage could be caused to the components involved.

Safety first!

Professional motor mechanics are trained in safe working procedures. However enthusiastic you may be about getting on with the job in hand, do take the time to ensure that your safety is not put at risk. A moment's lack of attention can result in an accident, as can failure to observe certain elementary precautions.

There will always be new ways of having accidents, and the following points do not pretend to be a comprehensive list of all dangers; they are intended rather to make you aware of the risks and to encourage a safety-conscious approach to all work you carry out on your vehicle.

Essential DOs and DON'Ts

DON'T rely on a single jack when working underneath the vehicle. Always use reliable additional means of support, such as axle stands, securely placed under a part of the vehicle that you know will not give way.

DON'T attempt to loosen or tighten high-torque nuts (e.g. wheel hub nuts) while the vehicle is on a jack; it may be pulled off.

DON'T start the engine without first ascertaining that the transmission is in neutral (or 'Park' where applicable) and the parking brake applied.

DON'T suddenly remove the filler cap from a hot cooling system – cover it with a cloth and release the pressure gradually first, or you may get scalded by escaping coolant.

DON'T attempt to drain oil until you are sure it has cooled sufficiently to avoid scalding you.

DON'T grasp any part of the engine, exhaust or catalytic converter without first ascertaining that it is sufficiently cool to avoid burning you.

DON'T allow brake fluid or antifreeze to contact vehicle paintwork.

DON'T syphon toxic liquids such as fuel, brake fluid or antifreeze by mouth, or allow them to remain on your skin.

DON'T inhale dust – it may be injurious to health (see *Asbestos* below).

DON'T allow any spilt oil or grease to remain on the floor – wipe it up straight away, before someone slips on it.

DON'T use ill-fitting spanners or other tools which may slip and cause injury.

DON'T attempt to lift a heavy component which may be beyond your capability – get assistance.

DON'T rush to finish a job, or take unverified short cuts.

DON'T allow children or animals in or around an unattended vehicle.

DO wear eye protection when using power tools such as drill, sander, bench grinder etc, and when working under the vehicle.

DO use a barrier cream on your hands prior to undertaking dirty jobs – it will protect your skin from infection as well as making the dirt easier to remove afterwards; but make sure your hands aren't left slippery. Note that long-term contact with used engine oil can be a health hazard.

DO keep loose clothing (cuffs, tie etc) and long hair well out of the way of moving mechanical parts.

DO remove rings, wristwatch etc, before working on the vehicle – especially the electrical system.

DO ensure that any lifting tackle used has a safe working load rating adequate for the job.

DO keep your work area tidy – it is only too easy to fall over articles left lying around.

DO get someone to check periodically that all is well, when working alone on the vehicle.

DO carry out work in a logical sequence and check that everything is correctly assembled and tightened afterwards.

DO remember that your vehicle's safety affects that of yourself and others. If in doubt on any point, get specialist advice.

IF, in spite of following these precautions, you are unfortunate enough to injure yourself, seek medical attention as soon as possible.

Asbestos

Certain friction, insulating, sealing, and other products – such as brake linings, brake bands, clutch linings, torque converters, gaskets, etc – contain asbestos. *Extreme care must be taken to avoid inhalation of dust from such products since it is hazardous to health.* If in doubt, assume that they *do* contain asbestos.

Fire

Remember at all times that petrol (gasoline) is highly flammable. Never smoke, or have any kind of naked flame around, when working on the vehicle. But the risk does not end there – a spark caused by an electrical short-circuit, by two metal surfaces contacting each other, by careless use of tools, or even by static electricity built up in your body under certain conditions, can ignite petrol vapour, which in a confined space is highly explosive.

Always disconnect the battery earth (ground) terminal before working on any part of the fuel or electrical system, and never risk spilling fuel on to a hot engine or exhaust.

It is recommended that a fire extinguisher of a type suitable for fuel and electrical fires is kept handy in the garage or workplace at all times. Never try to extinguish a fuel or electrical fire with water.

Fumes

Certain fumes are highly toxic and can quickly cause unconsciousness and even death if inhaled to any extent. Petrol (gasoline) vapour comes into this category, as do the vapours from certain solvents such as trichloroethylene. Any draining or pouring of such volatile fluids should be done in a well ventilated area.

When using cleaning fluids and solvents, read the instructions carefully. Never use materials from unmarked containers – they may give off poisonous vapours.

Never run the engine of a motor vehicle in an enclosed space such as a garage. Exhaust fumes contain carbon monoxide which is extremely poisonous; if you need to run the engine, always do so in the open air or at least have the rear of the vehicle outside the workplace.

If you are fortunate enough to have the use of an inspection pit, never drain or pour petrol, and never run the engine, while the vehicle is standing over it; the fumes, being heavier than air, will concentrate in the pit with possibly lethal results.

The battery

Never cause a spark, or allow a naked light, near the vehicle's battery. It will normally be giving off a certain amount of hydrogen gas, which is highly explosive.

Always disconnect the battery earth (ground) terminal before working on the fuel or electrical systems.

If possible, loosen the filler plugs or cover when charging the battery from an external source. Do not charge at an excessive rate or the battery may burst.

Take care when topping up and when carrying the battery. The acid electrolyte, even when diluted, is very corrosive and should not be allowed to contact the eyes or skin.

If you ever need to prepare electrolyte yourself, always add the acid slowly to the water, and never the other way round. Protect against splashes by wearing rubber gloves and goggles.

When jump starting a car using a booster battery, for negative earth (ground) vehicles, connect the jump leads in the following sequence: First connect one jump lead between the positive (+) terminals of the two batteries. Then connect the other jump lead first to the negative (–) terminal of the booster battery, and then to a good earthing (ground) point on the vehicle to be started, at least 18 in (45 cm) from the battery if possible. Ensure that hands and jump leads are clear of any moving parts, and that the two vehicles do not touch. Disconnect the leads in the reverse order.

Mains electricity

When using an electric power tool, inspection light etc, which works from the mains, always ensure that the appliance is correctly connected to its plug and that, where necessary, it is properly earthed (grounded). Do not use such appliances in damp conditions and, again, beware of creating a spark or applying excessive heat in the vicinity of fuel or fuel vapour.

Ignition HT voltage

A severe electric shock can result from touching certain parts of the ignition system, such as the HT leads, when the engine is running or being cranked, particularly if components are damp or the insulation is defective. Where an electronic ignition system is fitted, the HT voltage is much higher and could prove fatal.

Conversion factors

Length (distance)
Inches (in)	X	25.4	= Millimetres (mm)	X 0.0394	= Inches (in)
Feet (ft)	X	0.305	= Metres (m)	X 3.281	= Feet (ft)
Miles	X	1.609	= Kilometres (km)	X 0.621	= Miles

Volume (capacity)
Cubic inches (cu in; in^3)	X	16.387	= Cubic centimetres (cc; cm^3)	X 0.061	= Cubic inches (cu in; in^3)
Imperial pints (Imp pt)	X	0.568	= Litres (l)	X 1.76	= Imperial pints (Imp pt)
Imperial quarts (Imp qt)	X	1.137	= Litres (l)	X 0.88	= Imperial quarts (Imp qt)
Imperial quarts (Imp qt)	X	1.201	= US quarts (US qt)	X 0.833	= Imperial quarts (Imp qt)
US quarts (US qt)	X	0.946	= Litres (l)	X 1.057	= US quarts (US qt)
Imperial gallons (Imp gal)	X	4.546	= Litres (l)	X 0.22	= Imperial gallons (Imp gal)
Imperial gallons (Imp gal)	X	1.201	= US gallons (US gal)	X 0.833	= Imperial gallons (Imp gal)
US gallons (US gal)	X	3.785	= Litres (l)	X 0.264	= US gallons (US gal)

Mass (weight)
Ounces (oz)	X	28.35	= Grams (g)	X 0.035	= Ounces (oz)
Pounds (lb)	X	0.454	= Kilograms (kg)	X 2.205	= Pounds (lb)

Force
Ounces-force (ozf; oz)	X	0.278	= Newtons (N)	X 3.6	= Ounces-force (ozf; oz)
Pounds-force (lbf; lb)	X	4.448	= Newtons (N)	X 0.225	= Pounds-force (lbf; lb)
Newtons (N)	X	0.1	= Kilograms-force (kgf; kg)	X 9.81	= Newtons (N)

Pressure
Pounds-force per square inch (psi; lbf/in^2; lb/in^2)	X	0.070	= Kilograms-force per square centimetre (kgf/cm^2; kg/cm^2)	X 14.223	= Pounds-force per square inch (psi; lbf/in^2; lb/in^2)
Pounds-force per square inch (psi; lbf/in^2; lb/in^2)	X	0.068	= Atmospheres (atm)	X 14.696	= Pounds-force per square inch (psi; lbf/in^2; lb/in^2)
Pounds-force per square inch (psi; lbf/in^2; lb/in^2)	X	0.069	= Bars	X 14.5	= Pounds-force per square inch (psi; lbf/in^2; lb/in^2)
Pounds-force per square inch (psi; lbf/in^2; lb/in^2)	X	6.895	= Kilopascals (kPa)	X 0.145	= Pounds-force per square inch (psi; lbf/in^2; lb/in^2)
Kilopascals (kPa)	X	0.01	= Kilograms-force per square centimetre (kgf/cm^2; kg/cm^2)	X 98.1	= Kilopascals (kPa)

Torque (moment of force)
Pounds-force inches (lbf in; lb in)	X	1.152	= Kilograms-force centimetre (kgf cm; kg cm)	X 0.868	= Pounds-force inches (lbf in; lb in)
Pounds-force inches (lbf in; lb in)	X	0.113	= Newton metres (Nm)	X 8.85	= Pounds-force inches (lbf in; lb in)
Pounds-force inches (lbf in; lb in)	X	0.083	= Pounds-force feet (lbf ft; lb ft)	X 12	= Pounds-force inches (lbf in; lb in)
Pounds-force feet (lbf ft; lb ft)	X	0.138	= Kilograms-force metres (kgf m; kg m)	X 7.233	= Pounds-force feet (lbf ft; lb ft)
Pounds-force feet (lbf ft; lb ft)	X	1.356	= Newton metres (Nm)	X 0.738	= Pounds-force feet (lbf ft; lb ft)
Newton metres (Nm)	X	0.102	= Kilograms-force metres (kgf m; kg m)	X 9.804	= Newton metres (Nm)

Power
Horsepower (hp)	X	745.7	= Watts (W)	X 0.0013	= Horsepower (hp)

Velocity (speed)
Miles per hour (miles/hr; mph)	X	1.609	= Kilometres per hour (km/hr; kph)	X 0.621	= Miles per hour (miles/hr; mph)

Fuel consumption*
Miles per gallon, Imperial (mpg)	X	0.354	= Kilometres per litre (km/l)	X 2.825	= Miles per gallon, Imperial (mpg)
Miles per gallon, US (mpg)	X	0.425	= Kilometres per litre (km/l)	X 2.352	= Miles per gallon, US (mpg)

Temperature
Degrees Fahrenheit = (°C x 1.8) + 32

Degrees Celsius (Degrees Centigrade; °C) = (°F - 32) x 0.56

*It is common practice to convert from miles per gallon (mpg) to litres/100 kilometres (l/100km), where mpg (Imperial) x l/100 km = 282 and mpg (US) x l/100 km = 235

Index

Printed by
J H Haynes & Co Ltd
Sparkford Nr Yeovil
Somerset BA22 7JJ England